WRITING IN POLITICAL SCIENCE

A Practical Guide

Second Edition

by

Diane E. Schmidt
California State University, Chico

LONGMAN

An Imprint of Addison Wesley Longman, Inc.

New York • Reading, Massachusetts • Menlo Park, California • Harlow, England
Don Mills, Ontario • Sydney • Mexico City • Madrid • Amsterdam

Editor-in-Chief: Priscilla McGeehon
Acquisitions Editor: Eric Stano
Marketing Manager: Megan Galvin-Fak
Development Editor: Mark Toews
Cover Design: Teresa Ward

Writing in Political Science: A Practical Guide, Second Edition
Diane E. Schmidt

Please visit our website at http://www.awlonline.com

ISBN: 0-321-06998-6

12345678910-VG-01040000

PREFACE

As political scientists, we are rarely directly involved in politics; instead, we write about it the same way sports commentators report on baseball games. We theorize and conjecture but rarely play the game. Some of us keep statistics about our players, some of us just provide the color commentary while the players are in the arena, and some of us analyze the actions of the players to see how the winners won and the losers lost. Mostly, we study and learn by observing and providing a reasoned perspective about political activities.

What political scientists do best is write. Part of what this book is about is writing in political science. It is not a formal book of style nor is it a tome on what it means to think critically about politics or to be a political scientist. It is a practical, sometimes irreverent, and usually serious guide to becoming a color commentator, armchair quarterback, or an expert on politics. It is about becoming a professional in political science and communicating with a community of students and scholars of government and policy. In other words, this book is a guide to communicating about political events, about political ideas, about political passions, and about political agendas. It is not just about writing; it is about <u>thinking</u> about politics, <u>reading</u> about politics, and <u>arguing</u> about politics.

There are many reasons why I wrote this book. I noticed early in my teaching career that students in my courses, regardless of their major or class standing or grade point average, exhibited a general confusion about what and how to communicate in political science assignments. My first response was to condemn the public high school system and the English department for not training students to write coherently. But that was too easy. Upon investigation, I found that there was a different approach to writing among political science, English composition, and the hard sciences. Approximately at the same time I discovered the Writing Across the Curriculum approach, I received the best, most instructive assessment of the problem from a retiring English composition professor. She said, "I'm not surprised that your students are having problems. We teach them to write for us. If you want them to write well in political science, teach them to write for political science." That, in a nutshell, is what Writing Across the Curriculum promotes. That, in a nutshell, is what this book is intended to accomplish.

I wrote this book for political science majors and for students who are passing through the discipline as an elected activity. But this guide is more than an abridged writer's guide with explicit references to political science writing assignments. In addition to outlining the standard form for student assignments, the guide provides practical information and advice about criteria used to evaluate student assignments. It provides and uses the vocabulary of the political science discourse community while keeping the directions and formats simple enough to understand and execute without guidance from an instructor. Anyone who can follow a recipe in a cookbook, read an auto repair manual, or use an automatic teller machine at a bank, can follow the instructions in this book and turn out a professional level, high quality manuscript concerning politics.

Unfortunately, this book is not a jump-start for writing and the directions must be followed closely. The advice in this book cannot compensate for poor effort or preparation. Although many parts of this guide mirror sections of general stylebooks and English composition textbooks, it is not a substitute for a comprehensive style guide or a course in composition. This guide stresses the application of general principles of expository writing to common projects and assignments given to students in political science classes. The style and composition sections are designed to enhance and refresh skills already acquired through introductory composition coursework. These sections build on standard writing forms while applying them to the kind of study and investigation conducted in the discipline of political science.

In many ways, this guide is an extended information sheet, not unlike those given to students by their professors. In addition to stating criteria for assignments, it includes gentle reminders about critical thinking, research habits, and general formatting of manuscripts. The guide provides the instruction and examples of political science writing assignments that help students begin and end in the right direction for meeting the instructor's expectations.

More importantly, the guide provides examples, yes, examples of actual student manuscripts written for the sole purpose of getting a grade. None of the student papers were (was) written expressly for the book. Some were written before I ever conceived the idea of writing the book. With a few exceptions, the papers were written by students in my courses and reflect some of the best examples of papers produced by following the format and structure directions for the particular type of writing assignment required in those courses.

In fact, the examples in this guide are some of its most distinguishing and beneficial aspects. Unlike standard guides for writing research papers or even guides to writing in political science, this guide provides, in exhaustive detail, an explanation about the difference between writing an analysis of legislation or an analysis of a public policy and how to write them both. Because it is important for students to see, not just told, that different courses and different subfields in political science have different forms and expectations for written research, there is an example for every exercise and every assignment listed in the book.

Because the book includes both the directions concerning form and examples that exhibit an application of such forms, students will, with or without an instructor's help, be able to choose and narrow a topic, formulate a research agenda, execute a study, write about the findings, and learn something about politics at the same time. The examples in this guide, though very good, are not necessarily the most spectacular work performed concerning the topic or assignment requirements. Those standards are difficult and almost impossible for most people to achieve. No, the examples reflect the efforts of good, hard-working, conscientious students who followed directions, researched their topics earnestly, and produced fine manuscripts which encompass a reasoned perspective on their topics. With the instructor's help, students can use the advice and examples as templates for classroom work. Without the instructor, students may reasonably assume that some approximation of an example related to the course focus will be a good approach.

There is one aspect of this book that may not seem obvious at first that I should explain. The examples in this guide are particularly skewed toward American government, public policy, public law, and public administration. There are several reasons for this. Although I am cross-trained in all these areas, I teach American government and public policy. The examples come from my students because I know their potential. I set the goals, structured the incentives for achieving them, and measured how closely they were achieved. The examples are testimony to the utility of providing the students a clear statement of goals, of expectations, and of standards for assignments. I know these techniques work because they have worked for me at every course level from introductory to graduate classes.

Because the techniques used in this guide are based on a Writing Across the Curriculum perspective, they have also worked for colleagues and students in several subfields, several disciplines, and several institutions who adopted this book in draft form. My book was used to help train Lithuanian masters students in a Masters in Public Administration program, in Lithuania! From freshman to graduate level, from history to anthropology, this guide has been helpful for instructors and students alike. Just like a recipe for cheesecake or barbecue, the application of these techniques varies between users. Instructors put in their own personal touches, accents, and emphasis. In contrast, my students sent copies to friends and siblings and taken the guide along to law or graduate school because of its versatility and straightforward, understandable advice.

Nonetheless, the principles and advice in the guide can be applied to political theory, comparative government, and international relations. Wherever possible and appropriate, I have provided instruction and advice about using the materials in these fields. The topic section has examples of choosing subfield specific topics for all subfields. The section on enhancing comprehension and synthesis as well as the section on handling and processing class materials are standard. The section on conventional papers includes a short discussion of how such papers are used in other subfields. The advice concerning assignments requiring special analytical techniques and assignments in applied political science can be utilized for any institutional level regardless of the country on which or in which it was performed. Finally, the section on managing and preserving achievements for career development is not subfield specific.

Thus, what the guide lacks in discipline breadth, it makes up for in depth and comprehensiveness related to instructing on the discourse, the professional standards, and the method of discovery in political science as a profession. The examples were taken from a cross-section of student writing styles and issues of interest to many students. While each paper exhibits a unique perspective, the thread that ties them together is the salient and controversial nature of each topic. As with any work, some gross errors were made by students and thus corrected. Some typographical errors are my fault. I have never been a good copy editor for my own work. For the most part, the papers clearly reflect the students' efforts. Small mistakes in logic as well as some usage errors were preserved to maintain the personality and spirit of the writers. As teaching tools, they are instructive. As statements on political events, they are interesting and well reasoned. As examples, they set standards that are attainable. This combination makes these student papers assets to the guide and makes the goals of the guide attainable.

For the second edition, I added sections on Internet research, Internet source evaluation, reading tables and graphs, creating tables and graphs, writing editorials, writing case studies, and referencing. The section on Internet research was co-authored by one of my students. Unlike other Internet guides that are written by technicians or scholars in the field, this new section provides practical techniques *actually used by students* for student research. So much of the advice is written for users who actually enjoy "surfing" the net. I have found that my students prefer direct practical advice for locating information fast. This section provides the minimum information on Internet terminology while focusing the student's attention on efficient Internet use.

I also added an expanded section on research methods and statistical research. Because the Internet provides a dearth of data, and because spreadsheet technology is so user-friendly, I added a section to locating and using data. I included a section on primary research for conducting interviews, creating surveys, and analyzing surveys. Included in this new section is advice on reading and constructing tables, graphs, and figures. I also included a section on finding secondary sources and data on the Internet. I provided Web site addresses and advice for using Web based information.

I also expanded and improved the referencing section. I added a formats for Internet citations both in the text as well as in the bibliography. I also provided comparative formats for *MLA, Chicago Manual of Style*, and *APA styles*. For each type of source, I provided an example from each of the three styles.

Finally, I added new material on case study approaches and editorial writing. Editorial writing is a skill that helps students participate in the process after leaving their educational institutions. Further, unlike concept or position papers, the case study approach to the study of politics provides opportunities for students to apply what they learned in class to a specific agency or entity. I included two types of case studies. The first type is an academic case study approach where students learn to evaluate an analysis problems in organizations. The second type is a problem solving case study where the student chooses a particular problem, researches it, and provides an a recommendation for resolving the problem.

In sum, this is not just another writing guide. It is a complete guide for being or becoming a professional in political science. It can be used from freshman to graduate level coursework, from entering a student career to graduating and pursuing a professional career after graduation. It is a style guide, a class handout, a writing manual, an organizing guide, and a resume guide. It is everything students need to begin their research, their writing, and their careers. Enjoy!

****
ACKNOWLEDGEMENTS

      I wish to express my appreciation to the many people who encouraged me and helped me in the preparation of first or second edition of this book, including Bruce Appleby, Bob Lorinskas, Terry Plain, Sari Ramsey, Jerry Hostetler, Amy Andrews, Leila Niehuser, Cecilia Lause, Mark Toews, and Beth McMillin. I am also indebted to my students especially Mary Andrews, Annette Allison, Susan Toomire, and Judith Ferrer, who have been complementary and supportive of my efforts in this second edition to help them develop professionally.

      Finally, I am indebted to friends for their unconditional support of this project including Kay Heidbreder, Marji Morgan, Suzy Parker, Teresa Murphy, Cindy McKinney, Cindy McGee, Jim Mallien, Joan Brown, and Bonnie Hallman for their supporting friendship. They have been friends when I needed them. I also want to thank my family, especially my mother Margie Brown for her support and pride in my accomplishments. Last, but not least, I wish to thank sons Casey and Jonathan for being patient during my never ending string of projects and my husband, Alan, for his contributions to the text and his support and understanding when I was too involved in this project to worry about less pressing matters. These people have stayed close to me as I recuperate from life's trauma. These are the people I cherish most and have been my greatest inspiration. Thank you.

Diane E. Schmidt
Chico, CA
January 2, 2000

DEDICATION

TO ALAN, CASEY, JONATHAN, AND MARGIE
AND
IN MEMORY OF MARGARET AND AUSBY

TABLE OF CONTENTS

SECTION ONE

POLITICAL INQUIRY

INTRODUCTION

This writing guide is designed to help students sharpen, reinforce, and develop good writing and research habits in political science. Writing is a process through which we learn to communicate with others. No one expects students to be perfect writers. We all learn and help each other learn. Through organization, writing and re-writing drafts, and logical presentation of our ideas, we engage in an intellectual process which helps us grow and be a part of the discourse community of political science.

What the guide is supposed to do:

1.   Sharpen writing skills particular to political science.

2.   Provide information to students about standards and expectations concerning political science writing.

3.   Help students differentiate between writing for political science and other disciplines.

What the guide cannot do:

1.   This material does not teach primary writing skills.

2.   This material is not intended to be a substitute for a formal class in writing.

3.   This material will not teach grammar, spelling, or punctuation.

4.   This material cannot substitute for poor preparation.

THE POLITICAL SCIENCE WRITER'S BOOKSHELF

Students are encouraged to purchase at least one general stylebook and one writing supplement. Students should have a variety of writing aids on their bookshelves regardless of their level of writing proficiency. While this book is a complete guide to writing political science manuscripts, it is not a substitute for a reference text in basic writing techniques. This book offers practical advice and techniques for effective, efficient, and professional level research and writing in political science. It is structured to introduce students to the discipline and discourse of standard political science writing styles and formats. The books listed below cover non-standard formats or routine general style problems more directly. The selection of these texts is based on the author's library of writing aids. Although the books listed below are quality aids, there are substitutes available for many of these in the campus or local community bookstores.

Standard English Writing Style Books and Supplements

Aaron, Jane E. 2000. *The Little, Brown Essential Handbook for Writers*. 3rd ed. NY: Addison Wesley.

American Heritage Dictionary. 1994. NY: Dell Pub., Co.

Brittain, Robert. 1990. *A Pocket Guide to Correct Punctuation*. Revised by Benjamin Griffith. 3rd ed. Hauppague, NY: Barron's Educational Series, Inc.

Chicago Manual of Style. 1993. 14th ed. Chicago: University of Chicago Press.

Ellsworth, Blanche and John A. Higgins. 1997. *English Simplified*. 8th ed. NY: Addison Wesley.

Fogiel, M. 1998. *Handbook of English*. Piscataway, NY: Research and Education Association.

Follett, Wilson. 1998. *Modern American Usage*. NY: Hill and Wang.

Hacker, Diana. 1997. *A Pocket Style Manual*. 2nd ed. NY: Bedford/St. Martin's Press.

Hopper, Vincent, et al. 1997. *A Pocket Guide to Correct Grammar*. 3rd ed. Hauppague, NY: Barron's Educational Series, Inc.

Lester, James. 1990. *Writing Research Papers*. NY: Addison Wesley.

Obrecht, Fred. 1999. *Minimum Essentials of English*. 2nd ed. Hauppague, NY: Barron's Educational Series, Inc.

Silverman, Jan. 1999. et al. *Rules of Thumb: A Guide for Writers*. 4th ed. NY: McGraw-Hill.

Strunk, William Jr. and E.B. White. 2000. *The Elements of Style*. Boston, MA: Allyn and Bacon.

Yates, Jean. 1996. *Master the Basics—English*. Hauppague, NY: Barron's Educational Series, Inc.

Methods and Statistical Guides

Cleveland, William S. 1994. *The Elements of Graphing Data*. Monterey, CA.: CRC Press

Cole, Richard L. 1996. *Introduction to Political Science and Policy Research*. NY: St. Martin's Press.

Creswell, John W. 1994. *Research Design: Qualitative and Quantitative Approaches*. Thousand Oaks, CA: Sage Publications.

Cuzzort, R. P. and James S. Vrettos. 1996. *The Elementary Forms of Statistical Reason*. NY: St. Martin's Press.

Fowler Jr., Floyd J. 1993. *Survey Research Methods*. Newbury Park, CA: Sage Publications, Inc.

Jones, Laurence F. and Edward Olson. 1996. *Political Science Research: A Handbook of Scope and Method*. NY: HarperCollins.

Melone, Albert P. 1990. *Researching Constitutional Law*, IL: Scott, Foresman and Co..

Stokey, Edith and Richard Zeckhauser. 1978. *A Primer For Policy Analysis*. NY.: W.W. Norton & Co.

Weisberg, Herbert F. 1996. *An Introduction to Survey Research, Polling, and Data Analysis*. NY: Sage Publications.

Internet Guides

Ackerman, Ernest and Karen Hartman. 1998. *Searching and Researching on the Internet and the World Wide Web*. Wisonville, OR: Frankin, Beedle, & Associates, Inc.

Harnack, Andrew and Eugene Kleppinger. 1998. *Online!: A Reference Guide to Using Internet Sources*. NY: St. Martin's Press.

Stull, Andrew T. 2000. *Political Science on the Internet*. Adapted for Political Science by James A. Puetz. Upper Saddle River, NJ: Prentice Hall.

Wedding, Ken and Doug Gotthoffer. 1999. *Quick Guide to the Internet For Political Science*. Boston, MA: Allyn and Bacon.

Political Dictionaries and Encyclopedias

Bealey, Frank. 1999. *The Blackwell Dictionary of Political Science*. NY: Basil Blackwell.

Miller, David Janet Coleman, William Connolly and Alan Ryan. Editors. *1991   The Blackwell Encyclopaedia of Political Thought*. NY: Basil Blackwell.

THE ART OF POLITICAL INQUIRY DEFINED

Many students are unaware that writing assignments for political science classes requires different skills from those required for English composition, creative writing, and journalism courses. Although the basic skills are the same, political scientists, as members of a discipline:

1.   ask different questions and seek different answers to questions than those of the humanities and physical sciences.

2.   are interested in more than a description of what happened, where something happened, or when something happened.
3.   are interested in the political process or the causal connections between political events.

An event or a phenomenon must be politically relevant for it to be of interest to political science scholars. Of course, the standard definition of what is politically relevant is often in the eye of the beholder!

A general rule for writing in political science classes is to always ask yourself, before you write anything: What are the politics or power relationships existing in a political event?

Professional Level Research

Professional research in political science is based on the acquisition of scientific knowledge. Locating scientific knowledge requires developing or applying theories either through induction (based on observations) or deduction (based on prior expectations). According to Jones and Olson (1996) such theories include

1. **Systems theory**: this theory explains political activities as part of a process or system. Researchers using this theory explain political phenomena by examining elements in the political environment (citizen activism, parties, interests groups, etc.)

2. **Power theory**: this theory explains political activities by examining the power relationship between individuals or groups.

3. **Goals theory**: this theory explains political activities by examining the purpose or goals of political phenomena

Professional Methods of Investigation:

There are a variety of approaches to examining political phenomena.

1. **Philosophical Method**: those using this approach examine the scope, purpose, and values of government activity. Often, those using this method ask how *should* government act.

2. **Historical Method**: those using this approach examine what conditions contributed to the occurrence of government activity.

3. **Comparative Method**: those using this approach compare and contrast experiences of governments, states, and other political entities.

4. **Juridical Method**: those using this approach examine the legal basis for government activities.

5. **Behavioral Method**: those using this approach study the behavior of political actors by examining data collected on actual political occurrences.

6. **Post-behavioral Method**: those using this approach examine, usually with mathematical models, not only observed behavior but values associated with the behavior.

For more information on political inquiry in political science, see Laurence F. Jones and Edwards C. Olson. 1996. *Political Science Research: A Handbook of Scope and Method.* NY: HarperCollins.

TYPES OF STUDENT WRITING

Although professional level research is rarely expected of students, political science assignments often immolates professional research. Below is a list of common types of writing assignments required in political science classes.

Analysis: these assignments usually ask students to examine the relationships between the parts of a political document or some political events. Typically, these assignments require the student to provide a perspective or reasoned opinion about the significance of an event or a document. For example, students may be required to assert and defend an opinion about the most important features in the Bill of Rights.

Argument: these assignments often require the student to prove or debate a point. Typically, these assignments ask for normative assertions supported by evidence and examples. For instance, instructors may ask students to provide an argument supporting (or not) automatic voter registration, random drug testing, or a constitutional amendment protecting the flag.

Cause and effect: these assignments typically require the student to speculate about the reasons some political event has occurred. For example, students may be asked why people vote, why do members of Congress worry about their images, what caused the civil war, or why some people are disillusioned with government.

Classify: these assignments usually ask the student to identify the pattern or system of classifying objects such as types of voters, types of political systems, or types of committees in congress.

Compare or contrast: these assignments usually ask the student to identify the differences and similarities between political roles, political systems, or political events.

Definition: these assignments usually ask the student to define a political concept, term, or phrase such as democracy, socialism, or capitalism. Students must provide examples of distinguishing features and differentiate the topic from others in its functional class.

Process: these assignments usually ask the student to describe how some political phenomena relate functionally to other political phenomena. For example, students may be asked to describe how media influence voting behavior or how decisions are made in committees.

THE PROCESS OF POLITICAL INQUIRY:

Professional political scientists, as part of a discourse community, engage in a process of political inquiry that involves using research techniques, critical thinking skills, and theory building. In general, political inquiry involves posing a question (a hypothesis), collecting data, analyzing the data, and drawing conclusions about whether the data supports the hypothesis.

Understanding the nature of evidence and uses of data to support an assertion or hypothesis is critical to the inquiry process. The process functionally relates questions to evidence to conclusions to knowledge.

HYPOTHESIS

EVIDENCE

CONCLUSIONS

KNOWLEDGE

A **hypothesis** is a generalization that can be tested. Hypotheses state **expected** relationships between the *dependant variable* (the event being explained) and the *independent variables* (occurrences that caused or are associated with causing the event). Most importantly, hypotheses assert precisely how a change in the independent variable(s) change(s) the dependent variable.

Data are **evidence**. There are two kinds of data:

> **Quantitative evidence**: objective or numerical data usually from surveys, polls, tests, or experiments.
>
>> **Nominal data**: numbers assigned to categories of events   (1=Democrat, 2=Rebublican). Each occurrence may belong to only on category.
>>
>> **Ordinal data** numbers are assigned to categories of events and are rank ordered from more to less (more conservative to less conservative).
>>
>> **Interval data**: numbers are associated with the exact and constant values of the event (such as age or income)
>
> **Qualitative evidence**: subjective or authoritative data usually from interviews, firsthand observations, inference, or expert opinions.

Conclusions are assertions made by the author concerning the relationship between the hypothesis and the evidence.

Knowledge is what we have learned from political inquiry. The goal of all political inquiry is to contribute to a universal body of knowledge. As scholars, we are obliged to learn and contribute to this body of knowledge.

THE AUTHOR'S ARGUMENT:
THE NATURE OF ASSERTIONS

Sometimes, in conversation with friends and colleagues, we take for granted that assertions or statements are true or are reasonably close to being correct. Sometimes we even switch from opinions to beliefs to facts as though they were of the same class of statements. These terms, however, have specific meanings and, as critical thinkers, we need to distinguish clearly between statements of fact, of opinion, of belief, and of prejudice.

> **Beliefs** are convictions based on personal faith, values, perceptions of morality, and cultural experiences. They are not based on fact or evidence. Like facts, they cannot be disproved and are not subject to argument.

Facts are verifiable information. They do not make good assertions because the truth of a fact is not debatable.

Opinions are judgements based on facts. A thesis sentence of an argument is an opinion. Opinions are testable and arguable because they are viewpoints arrived at through the examination of facts and evidence. Opinions are not arguments--arguments with supporting evidence are used to support opinions.

Prejudices are opinions that have been formed on insufficient or unexamined evidence. They are often thoughtless oversimplifications and typically reflect a narrow-minded view of the world. They are testable and easily refutable by the presentation of facts and evidence.

THE AUTHOR'S EVIDENCE:
SUPPORTING AN ARGUMENT WITH DATA

The strength of an argument rises and falls based on the evidence or data presented by the writer to support an assertion. Specificity and breadth are the main characteristics of good supporting evidence. To convince readers of the correctness of an assertion, writers must provide readers with evidence that is accurate and relevant (relating directly to the point).

Data and evidence are essentially the same thing. We typically use the word 'data' to refer to numerical evidence. This, however, need not be the case. Whatever we use to support our arguments can be seen as data. We use our own observations or those of others to back up our assertions. Evidence varies in strength based on its individual properties and the contexts of its use. Whether these data are facts, expert opinions, examples, or statistics, we use them, in combination, to support our arguments.

Examples are specific references or instances of the point being made and are typically referred to as anecdotal evidence. The strength of anecdotal evidence is found in its generalizability and representativeness.

Expert opinions are judgements made by authorities based on their experience with evidence and assessment of the facts. When facts are unavailable, expert opinions are the next strongest evidence a writer can supply to support an argument. Expert opinions are some of the strongest kinds of evidence a writer can use.

Facts are statements that can be verified. They are the strongest proof or evidence a writer can supply to support an assertion. They are also the most difficult kind of evidence to obtain.

Statistics are often called probabilistic evidence because they are based on probabilities of correctness and depend on strict adherence to representative sampling technique. Statistics are not facts: they are the next best things to facts when facts are unavailable. Unfortunately, statistics alone provide weak support for an argument. Together with expert opinion and examples, statistics can provide powerful support for arguments.

A WORD ON STATISTICAL METHODS AND EVIDENCE

In more advanced political science courses, instructors may give students the opportunity to include quantitative evidence that has been produced through data analysis. Whether students have collected the data themselves or used a data bank produced by someone else, it is likely that the data are in "raw" form. This means that the data are in the form of lists of numbers or items. To make these lists of numbers meaningful, it is often necessary to summarize the data by using statistics.

The best way to approach data analysis is through a social science statistics course. To refresh your memory or learn how to do a statistical technique or write about one, obtain a copy of Harvey J. Brightman's, *Statistics in Plain English*, Belmont, CA: Duxbury Press, 1986. This book has just about everything a student needs to know about data analysis. It is written without jargon in a casual, readable, simple, and unintimidating way. Without burdening the reader with details, the authors describe and provide examples of simple elementary statistical analysis as well as techniques that are more sophisticated. It is a handy reference guide for looking up statistical terms and explanations of significance tests that are frequently used in scholarly political science materials as evidence of a theory's validity.

Another way to learn about statistical techniques for data analysis is to view a Public Broadcasting Service series entitled *Against All Odds: Inside Statistics*. This is available on VHS videocassettes. There are twenty-six individual half-hour programs which de-mystify statistical methods by providing living examples of using mathematical formulas to measure social phenomena. The series appeared on PBS television stations in fall 1989 and was produced for a mass audience. Check the college or university tape and film library to see if it contains a copy of this series. If not, obtain a copy through an inter-library loan. The programs examine everything from a definition of statistics to time series analysis to conducting a case study.

Finally, another way to learn about statistical methods for social science is to browse through or study the many books produced by Sage Publications, Inc. The Quantitative Applications in the Social Sciences Series and the Applied Social Research Methods Series together contain over seventy books on methodology in social science. Write for a list of books in the series to Sage Publications, Inc. or ask the reference librarian or the campus bookstore for a list of publications by Sage Publications.

Tips for Using Raw Data

Raw data can be used in a number of ways. Raw data can be converted to statistics, into tables, figures, and graphs.

Statistics: We use elementary statistics every day. Means, modes, percentages, frequencies, and ratios are used in mass media, advertisements, political speeches, and informal conversation to summarize data.

Means: A mean is an average. It is found by first adding all the numerical values in one category together to find the sum. Divide the sum by the number of items in the category. Round the number off to the nearest value.

Grades for student A was 75, student B was 75, student C was 64, and student D was 56.

Add: $80 + 75 + 64 + 56 = 275$ Divide: $275 / 4 = 68.75$

Rounded to 69. This is the average grade.

Percentages: Divide the number of a specific type of thing by the total number of all items in a category and multiply by 100.

Number of students voting in elections: 2000

Number of students enrolled in school: 10,000

Percentage voting: $2000/10000 = .2$ $.2 \times 100 = 20\%$

Mode: is the category with the greatest number of cases. Find this by looking for repeated values.

Grades for student A was 75, student B was 75, student C was 64, and student D was 56.

The mode is 75 because two students received this score and only one student each received 64 and 56.

Frequency: is how many different items are in a group or category. Find this by counting the number of each item in a category.

In a group of 125 people, there are 60 Democrats, 45 Republicans, and 20 Independents.

The frequency of Democrats is the number of them, 60, of Republicans is 45, and of Independents is 20.

Ratios: a proportion. It is used to compare the proportion of one number to another for relative value. Find this by creating a fraction out of the two numbers. Reduce the fraction until it cannot be reduced any further. The ratio is the larger number compared to the smaller number in the fraction.

In a group of 4500 women and men public administrators, there are 3000 men and 1500 women. To find ratio of men to women, create a fraction. 3000/1500.

Create a now reduce it 30/15 = 2/1.

The ratio of men to women is 2 to 1.

Rates: these compare the number of occurrences of an event in a jurisdiction to the total population of that jurisdiction. This is done by dividing the frequency of the occurrence by the total population of the jurisdiction. Because the denominator (total population) is so much larger than the numerator (the frequency of occurrence), it is necessary to multiply them by a base number (such as 100 or 1,000 or 10,000) to convert the small decimal number into a whole number. (Events/Population)*(Base number)

A county of 15, 600 people had 32 accidents last year. Now, do the following: 32/15600=.00202

Now multiply .00202 by a base of 1000. (.00202) * 1000=2.02

The rate is 2.02 per 1,000 of population

Percentage Change: this measures the change in the frequency of an event over time. It is calculated by examining the amount of change in two frequencies of the came occurrence from one period to the next. To calculate this, the subtract the frequency of the earlier event from the frequency of the later event and divide by the frequency of the earlier event and then transform the result into a percentage by multiplying by 100. [(Event in time 2) – (Event in time 1)/(Event in time 1)] * 100.

A county had 2800 people in 1988 and 3500 people in 1998.

Now calculate (3500-2800)/2800=.25

Now change the figure into a percentage   .25 * 100=25% increase in population

Frequently Used Statistical Terms.

There are a number of common statistical terms used for simple statistics.

Variables: these are things, usually measured by numbers that vary in the frequency or level in which they occur. Employment rates or the percentage of people voting in an election will differ from one time to the next. They are variables because neither occurs at a constant rate.

Causal Relationship: the term describes the relationship between variables where one or some variables (independent) causes another variable (dependent) to move in either a positive (increases or decreases) or a negative (opposite) direction when it increases or decreases. A statistical method to approximate this is called regression analysis.

Correlation: the term describes how characteristics vary in the same direction (positive) or in opposite directions (negative). Correlation suggests only that variable moves in these directions, not that one variable causes another's movement.

Standard Deviation: one of the most often used measures of variation. It is the degree to which an individual frequency differs from the mean, as compared to other frequencies. Most computer applications will calculate this for you.

Significance: a term used to suggest that a measure is valid. There are tests of significance of the relationship between variables. Often authors will refer to a measure as significant at a probability level of .05 or .01. These are probabilities that the authors are wrong about the nature of the relationship between variables or items. This means the measure is probably valid.

Tables:

Tables can be composed of either raw data or data that has been transformed into statistics. According to Cuzzort and Vrettos (1996), the format and information in a table should be self-supporting and presented simply.

Format for Constructing a Table: A good table should, by itself, contain all the relevant information need to read and interpret the data.

> **Title:** The title should tell the reader what the data refer to, where the data were collected, when the data were collected, what kind of data is listed, source of the data, and categories in the table. The information can be listed in the title or footnoted at the bottom of the table.

> **Amount of Data**: The data listed in the columns and rows should not exceed 12 for most tables. Of course, the number of rows (horizontal) and columns (vertical) depends on what data are being presented. Obviously listing grades for a class of thirty violates this rule of thumb; the point is to keep the presentation simple.

> **Labels:** Each row and each column must be labeled. In general, whatever is being explained is usually listed on the left-hand side and whatever is being used to explain it is listed across the top of the table.

> **Data Presented:** their raw form (absolute values) should accompany percentages (relative values).

> **Legible Spacing**: Each row and column should be spaced so that the table is easy to read. Vertical lines and bold horizontal lines can be used to separate important divisions in tables.

> **Cells Complete:** Each space (cell) in the table should include information. If no data are available for that cell, it should tell the reader by indicating *not available* or *N/A*. Even data that are zero or near zero should be displayed. Data that are near zero should be displayed in decimals (i.e. .003).

Advice for Reading a Table:

> **Take a little bit at a time!** Identify the items that are interesting and relevant to your paper.

> **Identify the outliers (extreme values).** Look for values that are much higher or lower than the most common values. Are they reasonable and fit with reality? If not, there might be an error in the data set.

> **Examine the context**: Identify information that challenges theories or contradicts what is generally known and assumed.

> **Be conservative**: Do not overstate the importance of the data results.

In Table 1, the author exhibits the association between party dominance in each chamber in Congress and confirmation of presidential appointees. At first glance, the table appears as just a set of numbers. Now, notice the outliers. The extreme values in Kennedy numbers of withdrawn and Clinton's first administration are different than those of the rest of the presidents. Why? They both faced a democratic Congress so why did they withdraw so many more than other presidents? Does this contradict or confirm what is known or assumed? How important are these results? Why did Carter, Bush, and Clinton have so many nominees left unconfirmed? What does this say about their presidencies or their abilities to work with Congress?

EXAMPLE OF A TABLE

TABLE 1[a]: PRESIDENTIAL NOMINATIONS AND SENATE ACTION BY CONGRESS AND POLITICAL DIVISION SINCE 1960

Congress	President	Senate Democrats	Senate Republicans	Confirmed	Withdrawn	Rejected	Unconfirmed
87th	Kennedy	64	36	100741	1279	0	829
88th	Johnson	67	33	120201	0	6	1953
89th	Johnson	68	32	120865	0	173	1981
90th	Johnson	64	36	118231	0	4	1966
91st	Nixon	58	42#	133797	2	487	178
92nd	Nixon	54	44#	114909	11	0	2133
93rd	Nixon	56	42#	131254	15	0	3069
94th	Ford	61	37	131378	6	0	3801
95th	Carter	61	38	124730	66	0	12713
96th	Carter	58	41	154665	18	0	1458
97th	Reagan	46	53*	184844	55	7	1346
98th	Reagan	46	54*	97262	4	0	610
99th	Reagan	47	53*	95811	16	0	3787
100th	Reagan	55	45#	88721	23	1	5933
101st	Bush	55	45#	88078	48	1	7951
102nd	Bush	56	44#	75349	24	0	756
103rd	Clinton	57	43#	76122	1080	0	2741
104rd	Clinton	48	52*	73711	22	0	8472

[a] Data taken from History of Congressional Elections
(http://clerweb.house.gov/histrecs.../elections/political/divisions.html); Kurian 1994; Mackenzie 1996; Stanley and Niemi 1998. Table created by Diane Schmidt and Shelly Tall (1999).
[b] * indicates Republican dominance.
[c] # indicates close Republican margin

Graphic Displays

Graphic displays, often referred to as graphs, figures, diagrams, and charts, are dramatic visual illustrations of data. Like tables, graphic displays may be used with raw or statistically transformed data.

Types of Graphic Displays:

Bar Graph: This displays ordinal or nominal data either horizontally or vertically by category. The height or length of the bar represents the frequency of occurrences for each category.

Histogram: This displays interval data using bars. The height and width of the bars relate to the size of the interval. The area of the bar represents the frequency of the occurrences.

Pie Charts: This displays the proportion of each part of a nominal or ordinal category. The circle represents the entire category (for example, voters) and the divisions show the different parts to the category (for example, the proportion of Democrats, Republicans, and Independents).

Pictograms: These are another way of presenting pie charts. The only difference is that an icon or picture is used to represent the proportion of each category.

Line Diagram: This displays interval data by connecting all the cases with a continuous line. These graphs show how the data change over time.

Format of Graphic Displays

Title: The title should tell the reader what the data refer to, where the data were collected, when the data were collected, what kind of data is listed, source of the data, and categories in the graphical display. The information can be listed in the title or footnoted at the bottom of the illustration.

Amount of Data: The data listed in illustrations should be presented simply. All data presented should exhaust the category—that is, include all parts of the category.

Labels: Each part of the illustration must be labeled. For line graphs, whatever is being explained is usually listed on the left-hand side and whatever is being used to explain it is listed across the bottom of the graph. For figures, charts, and pictures, each division must be labeled clearly. Distinctions are generally made by color coding, creating a legend, or using shading.

Cells Complete: Each space (cell) in the illustration should include information. The illustration should make complex data and ideas simpler to understand.

Advice for Reading Graphic Displays:

A good graphical display should communicate concepts and ideas with precision and efficiency. The illustration should show the reader visually the nature of the relationship between two or more events or political phenomena.

Size Matters!: Notice the size of the bars, proportions, or "peaks and valleys" in the illustration. Identify the events that are interesting and relevant to your paper.

Identify the dramatic shifts in values. Look for values that are much higher or lower than the other values. What does this say about the relationship between the events?

Examine the relative proportions: Identify relative relationships that challenges theories or contradicts what is generally known and assumed.

EXAMPLE OF TWO TYPES OF GRAPHS

Look at the two illustrations below. Both use data from Table 1, however, the data presented are only from one category and one part of the data. Which one is easier to read? Which one best illustrates the relationship between presidential administration and number of nominees left unconfirmed?

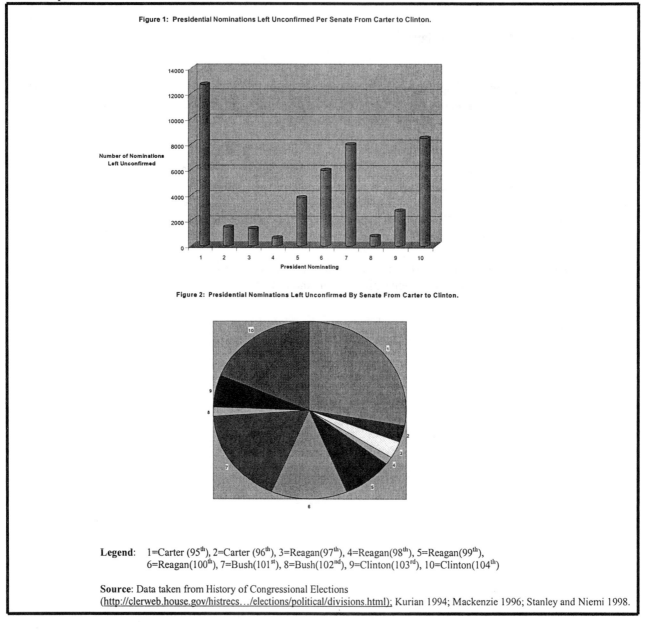

Figure 1: Presidential Nominations Left Unconfirmed Per Senate From Carter to Clinton.

Figure 2: Presidential Nominations Left Unconfirmed By Senate From Carter to Clinton.

Legend: 1=Carter (95th), 2=Carter (96th), 3=Reagan(97th), 4=Reagan(98th), 5=Reagan(99th),
6=Reagan(100th), 7=Bush(101st), 8=Bush(102nd), 9=Clinton(103rd), 10=Clinton(104th)

Source: Data taken from History of Congressional Elections
(http://clerweb.house.gov/histrecs.../elections/political/divisions.html); Kurian 1994; Mackenzie 1996; Stanley and Niemi 1998.

SECTION TWO

CRITICAL THINKING ABOUT POLITICS

CRITICAL THINKING: THE CORNERSTONE OF POLITICAL INQUIRY

If we as political scholars are obliged to contribute to a body of knowledge, then we must learn to ask questions that are politically interesting. Critical thinking skills separate students who are information sponges from those who are information filters (*Critical Thinking*...).

- **Sponges** indiscriminately, unquestioningly absorb information.

- **Filters** sort information and ask questions not only about the information provided but also about the validity of the evidence and assumptions used to produce the information.

- **Filters** sort the politically relevant from the irrelevant. Not all information is worth analyzing.

CRITICAL THINKERS

- Define problems, examine evidence, and analyze the assumptions leading to a conclusion.

- Question arguments, causal theories, evidence, broad generalizations, and simple correlation.

- Are open to both sides of an argument.

- Are prepared to examine and poke holes in all arguments, even their own.

CRITICAL THINKING DEFINED

When listening to a speaker or reading a document, essay, article, or book, students must first identify the structure of the author's argument. A good argument usually identifies an issue, provides reasons, and concludes something. Second, the student must examine the structure of the author's conclusion. Within each structure, we can ask questions about the validity of the evidence and assumptions.

HOW TO THINK CRITICALLY

The first step in obtaining critical thinking skills is understanding and identifying what to look for in a written work (Schmidt, et al.*; Critical Thinking*...; Fowler and Aaron, pp. 128-158).

First: Identify the author's argument or hypothesis.

- ♦ Ask yourself, what is the author's point?

- ♦ Look for the thesis statement.

- ♦ Know what an argument is and is not.

  - An argument is not a fact, a definition, an example, or descriptive information.

  - An argument or a hypothesis poses a testable question.

Second: Identify what the author uses as evidence.

- Find out how the author supports the point made in the work.

- Look for data.

- Identify what kind of data or types of evidence are used.
    - Is it qualitative or quantitative?
    - If it is statistical data, examine the method used to collect it.
    - If it is qualitative data, examine the context in which it is being used.
- Know what is evidence and what is not.

    - Evidence is facts, survey results, and examples, authoritative opinion.
    - Evidence is not hearsay, the author's personal opinion, speculation, or values espoused by the author.

Third: Identify the author's conclusion.

- What does the author say about the relationship between the hypothesis and the evidence?

- Know what a conclusion is and is not.

    - A conclusion is not a fact, a definition, an example, or descriptive information.
    - A conclusion asserts that the question posed is either supported or not by the evidence.
- Look for identifying or indicator words to locate the conclusion:

    - Words such as, *thus, therefore, in fact, it follows that, as a result, the point is,* and *it has been shown* indicate a concluding statement.

CRITICAL THINKING AND REASONING

Learning to think and write critically means commanding a sense of what properties a good well reasoned argument should possess. Reasoning is essential to the writing process. In fact, sound reasoning is more important in political science writing than creativity and eloquence. Political science writing depends heavily on arguments about the structure of political or power relationships. Because of this, communicating a point about an issue is dependent on a clear, well-reasoned exposition of the evidence.

Much of the work of political scientists is based on a scientific method of inquiry. The scientific method is based on inductive and deductive reasoning as well as inference and generalization. Here are some brief definitions of these terms (Fowler and Aaron, pp. 132-137).

> **Inductive reasoning**: generalizing from observations or attributing a cause to a set of observed circumstances.

> **Deductive reasoning**: applying generalizations or conclusions that are accepted as true to slightly different but similar situations or issues.

> **Inference**: a conclusion based on evidence. This is based on inductive reasoning.

> **Generalization**: a characterization based on the assumption that what applies in one set of circumstances also applies in similar circumstances.

POLITICAL INQUIRY AND INDUCTIVE REASONING

Inductive reasoning involves a process of collecting enough data or evidence to make a confident assertion about political or power relationships. We can infer a conclusion after examining and collecting information about what an author thinks about an issue.

> Inference and inductive reasoning are important steps in the process used by political scientists to identify the causal relationships between political phenomena.

> Inference and inductive reasoning provide the mechanism by which political scientists use data to increase the body of political knowledge.

> Inference and inductive reasoning promote sound conclusions based on sound evidence.

Most of what we know or think we know about politics and political behavior is based on inductive reasoning. Conclusions in voting studies, for example, are primarily based on inductive reasoning from empirical evidence. If we want to know what factors influence the voting turnout of the elderly, we would need to observe some behavior:

Observation: After conducting a survey based on a representative random sample of the elderly, we observe that most of the elderly say that they vote only when social security is in jeopardy.

Observation: We find that exit polls show that when social security is an issue a large number of the elderly vote.

Conclusion: Based on these two pieces of evidence, we can reasonably conclude, through inductive reasoning, that most of the elderly are motivated to vote when their interests are threatened.

POLITICAL INQUIRY AND DEDUCTIVE REASONING:

Political scientists also use deductive reasoning but it is less obvious than the use of inductive reasoning. Deductive reasoning underlies many of the arguments used in political science writing. Through deductive reasoning, we can use the generalizations we asserted through inference to make an argument about specific cases.

Deductive reasoning is composed of at least two factual statements (premises) and a conclusion. This constitutes a syllogism. A syllogism is simply two premises stating facts or judgements that together lead to a conclusion. The conclusion must derive from the premises.

EXAMPLE OF DEDUCTIVE REASONING

Premise: Most elderly citizens vote when their interests are threatened.
Premise: Many of the elderly are worried about the stability of the social security system.
Conclusion: Many of the elderly will vote in the next election.

Unfortunately, not all deductive arguments are presented clearly. Some deductive arguments will rely on either unstated (implied) premises or will overstate a premise.

EXAMPLE OF IMPLIED PREMISE

"Many of the elderly are worried about the stability of the social security system, so they will vote in the next election."

The premise, that the elderly vote when their interests are threatened, is left unstated.

EXAMPLE OF OVERSTATED PREMISE

"The elderly always vote when their interests are threatened. Many of the elderly are worried about the stability of the social security system, so they will vote in the next election."

The first premise overstates the generalization because it would be hard to apply it to all circumstances. Absolute words such as all, no one, never, or always force the generalization to apply strictly to every case and circumstance. Premises that cannot be applied to every case use limiting words such as some, many, and often.

COMMON PROBLEMS IN CRITICAL THINKING:

Once an argument is offered, the author is obligated to address the argument directly with evidence, and then reach a reasonable conclusion. There are, however, common problems in logical exposition of an argument, which influence the reasonableness and validity of an author's point (Fowler and Aaron, pp. 137-143).

Examine the lists of common problems in critical thinking located below. After the definition of each problem is an example. These examples were taken from student answers to an essay question concerning the desirability of requiring poor women with small children to work in order to receive public aid.

BEGGING THE QUESTION

An argument begs the question when the author treats a debatable opinion as a proven fact.

Example: Welfare mothers should have to work for their money because they only have children to collect free money.

Problem: This author assumes that receiving money without working for it causes women to have babies which is a highly questionable generalization at best.

IGNORING THE QUESTION

An argument ignores the question when the author appeals to the reader with reasons that have nothing to do with the issues raised. The most common occurrence of these errors is found in political campaign slogans and commercial advertising. Authors ignore or evade the question when they engage in one or more of the following:

Emotional appeals--appeals to the reader's sense of decency, fear, or pity.

> **Example**: "Any self-respecting woman would not take money she did not earn, even from the government."

> **Problem**: The author suggests that poor women are not good, decent people but provides no proof of that assertion. The author is appealing to the reader's sense of decency.

Snob appeal--appealing to the reader's desire to be like someone they admire.

> **Example**: "Pioneer women were able to raise families without government aid while their husbands were off on cattle drives or fighting wars."

> **Problem**: The author is appealing to a glorified image of rugged women settlers. The author is suggesting that women who are able to take care of their families alone are like pioneer women and those who cannot take care of their families are not living up to their potential. While the assertion itself is debatable, the example of pioneer women is inappropriate because it is based on a stereotypical image, not reality.

Bandwagon approach--appealing to the reader's desire to be like everyone else.

> **Example**: "Every hard working American resents giving money to people who do not work for it."

> **Problem**: The author creates an impossible situation for the reader. Because many people like to think of themselves as hard workers, to be part of this group the reader must adopt the same attitude toward cash assistance for poor women. The assertion is debatable and presents an inappropriate reason for being against cash assistance.

Flattery--projecting qualities on the reader.

> **Example**: "As an intelligent and hard working person, you should resent giving people money for doing nothing."

> **Problem:** The author is projecting the qualities of being intelligent and hard working onto the reader. The statement implies that disagreeing with the author is tantamount to admitting that the reader does not exhibit these qualities.

Ad hominem--personalizing the issue by concentrating on the real or imagined negative characteristics of those who hold different or opposing views.

> **Example:** "Because most people work hard for their money, the only people who continue to support free money to lazy women are old, drugged out hippies and know-it-all liberal scholars."

Problem: The author projects the negative, currently and socially unacceptable images of old hippies and overbearing liberals on to the supporters of cash assistance to poor women. The author is counting on the reader to reject cash assistance for poor women based on its association with those unpopular stereotypical images.

FAULTY REASONING

Fallacies or errors in reasoning are problems because they weaken the author's argument.

Hasty generalizations--a generalization that is based on very little evidence or which overstates.

> **Example**: "Welfare mothers are just lazy. I know of two welfare mothers who do nothing but watch television all day."

> **Problem**: The author is generalizing about all poor women receiving public assistance on the basis of two such women he or she has observed. A selection of two observations is much too small a sample to make a generalization about an entire class of people.

Oversimplification--stating that one event caused another when there is either no relationship or where other causes exist.

> **Example**: "Providing free money to mothers may actually cause more harm than good for their children. Children of welfare mothers rarely excel in school."

> **Problem**: The author suggests that cash assistance to mothers discourages their children from achieving in school. There is no reason to believe that cash assistance causes poor scholastic achievement. There are a host of other causes, however, which contribute low achievement of children in general. Cash poor schools, overcrowding, malnutrition, and poor health care are but just a few alternative causal variables in poor scholastic achievement regardless of the source of the child's family income.

Post hoc fallacy--jumping to the conclusion that event A caused event B just because event A occurred earlier.

> **Example**: "The availability of free money to poor families causes these families to break up. Fathers leave so that their families can collect welfare."

> **Problem**: The author suggests that the only reason fathers leave their families is the availability of cash assistance. Application for public aid is a response to families in trouble; it does not necessarily follow that public aid causes families to break up. Fathers leaving their families is not a necessary or sufficient condition for receiving public aid.

False dilemma--stating that a complex question has only two answers that are both good, both bad, or one good and one bad.

>**Example**: "By continuing to provide free money to poor mothers, we can expect only a continuation of poverty or an erosion of the American work ethic."

>**Problem**: The author suggests that continuing public aid to poor mothers can only result in two undesirable conditions. The author neglects to identify other possible resulting conditions that are desirable, such as a reduction in the number of children who are malnourished, from continuing public aid.

Non sequitur--when two ideas are presented with no logical connection.

>**Example**: "Providing free money has done nothing to improve the quality of life among the poor. Wealthy and middle class citizens continue to take tax deductions for charitable contributions."

>**Problem:** The author is suggesting that because people still make contributions to charity, no change in the situation of the poor has resulted from public assistance to poor mothers. There is no logical connection between public assistance and tax deductions for charity. The contribution need not be for the poor to be deductible.

False analogy--assuming that things that are alike in one respect are alike in other respects.

>**Example**: "In general, welfare mothers are characterized by poor work skills and little work experience. Few will take the initiative to acquire new skills or work at low skilled jobs without a coercive incentive such as working for their welfare checks."

>**Problem:** While the author's assertion about the skills and experience of welfare mothers may be valid, there is no logical reason to accept that all welfare mothers will resist acquiring training unless coerced. If given the opportunity to acquire job skills and experience, some may do so and some may not. We cannot predict, based on receiving public aid, whether or not a person will seek to improve his or her marketability.

TIPS FOR CRITICAL THINKING

Below is a summary checklist followed by a detailed set of questions that students should ask themselves as they read a book, an article, or an essay. There are two classes of questions. One set examines the author's argument and evidence. The other set of questions examines the author's conclusions. (The summary and the detailed questions are based on material from *Critical Thinking*, Fowler and Aaron, and Schmidt, et al.)

Summary Checklist for Reading or Writing Critically

Below is a checklist for students to use in checking their arguments as well as those of other authors.

1. Has the author stated the central point or assertion of the essay, article, or book in a thesis sentence?

2. Does the body of the work demonstrate the validity of the thesis sentence by breaking it down into other statements or assertions?

3. Has the author reasoned inductively or deductively?

4. Is the evidence provided varied, representative, relevant, and inclusive of facts, examples, and expert opinion?

5. Are there areas where the argument exhibits problems of faulty reasoning or where the author did not face the question posed?

Detailed Set of Questions to Ask About
the Author's Argument and Evidence:
(Adapted from *Critical Thinking....,* Ruggiero, pp. 54-64, 149-157)

Issues

A.   Look for an explicit reference to the issue. Often authors will use subjective language to introduce the issue and their point of view. For example, here is a statement: "Should flag desecration be a crime?"
    1.   Students should ask what is the author's definition of flag desecration and which forms of flag desecration is the author concerned about.
    2.   Students should ask under what conditions would misuse of the flag be considered punishable or not punishable, according to the author.
B.   Look for implicit references to the issue.
    1.   This may involve examining the closing or concluding remarks of the author.
    2.   Authors will often use words that sum up or suggest relationships in the conclusion that imply what issue has been examined in the work.

Reasons

A.   Authors are obligated to give readers reasons why their points are true or valid.

B.   Students should look for clues in the literature to identify the evidence.
1.   Look for identifying words such as because, since, for one thing, also.
2.   Look for ordered paragraphs starting with first, second, third, finally.
3.   Look for statistics, graphs, or tables.

Ambiguity

A.   Look for words or phrases which may seem obvious but have multiple meanings.

B.   Look for ambiguous or abstract words.
1.   Words such as liberal, conservative, freedom, equality, and justice are abstract and lack specificity.
2.   Be sure you know how such words are being used. Look for qualifying references and definitions.

C.   Understand all the terms, concepts, and phrases used, including professional jargon.

D.   Beware of tautologies or truisms.
1.   Tautologies or truisms are statements that are always true and cannot be disproved by any evidence or data.
2.   One example of a truism is that people will either vote or they will not. Whether people vote or do not vote does not matter because either way the statement remains true.

Value Assumptions

A.   Look for the author's stated ideas or beliefs about what influences behavior or choices.
1.   Does the author base points and arguments upon values concerning the desirability of competition, justice, freedom of speech?
2.   Does the author make assumptions about behavior or choices that are generally true?

B.   Look for the author's unstated beliefs about what influences behavior or choices. Read between the lines.

C.   Realize what your personal values and biases are and be prepared to accept defeat in light of a well reasoned, factually based argument made by someone else.
1.   Identify the stated and unstated value assumptions that are consistent with your own.
2.   Identify the stated and unstated value assumptions that conflict with your own.

Evidence

A.   If empirical (quantitative) data are used as evidence then examine the data fully.
   1.   Are the data representative (in size, breadth, and randomness) of the target population being studied?
   2.   Look for misleading use of percentages: comparisons of percentages and reporting especially large percentages are often suspect.
   3.   Be sure you know the size on which the percentages were based. Small sample sizes often produce misleading results.
   4.   Remember that correlation is not the same thing as causation. When two things are correlated (occurring at the same time) they may not necessarily be causally related (one thing causing the occurrence of the other thing).
B.   If the evidence is qualitative then examine the context of the evidence.
   1.   Be sure that the evidence is from an objective and respected authority.
   2.   For example, a recommendation by the American Medical Association for action concerning a disease would be an appropriate piece of evidence. However, a recommendation by the American Medical Association concerning National Health Insurance is suspect because that organization has a personal stake in the outcome and cannot be considered an objective authority.
   3.   Be cautious of one compelling example used as evidence. Remember, as data, the example would be a non-representative sample composed of one data point.

Logical Errors

A.   Be sure that the evidence fits the conclusions.
   1.   Form your own conclusions from the data and check them against the author's conclusion.
   2.   If the author's conclusion differs from your own conclusion, go back and check the author's reasoning, value assumptions, and qualifying terms and definitions.
B.   Reject evidence when it exhibits the following flaws:
   1.   Attacks an individual's character rather than the issue.
   2.   Creates a false dilemma by oversimplifying the choices or alternatives.
   3.   Diverts the reader's attention by changing subjects within the argument.
   4.   Begs the question by using a reason that repeats the conclusion in different words.

Omissions

A.   Has more than one viewpoint been presented?
   1.   Have credible contrary views been acknowledged?
   2.   Have the contrary views been explained and reasons given why they are not acceptable?
B.   Is the evidence supporting the argument or thesis overwhelming? Can you think of anything that has been left out?

C.   Has the author examined the underlying reasons concerning an issue?
D.   Has the author gone beyond his or her argument and added a normative idea?
1.   A positive argument deals with an issue, provides reasons, and concludes based on those reasons.
2.   A normative argument goes beyond the reasons presented and prescribes a solution about what should be done. This prescription is based on value assumptions and biases that require a separate analysis.

READING CRITICALLY TO WRITE CRITICALLY

So far, we have examined specific examples of arguments and evidence used to support an opinion. Rarely are arguments so contrived to fit the evidence or is the evidence clearly presented. In the following pages is an example of an editorial concerning the controversy over funding art that is politically unacceptable to a political majority of citizens. Read the essay; mark the text to find the critical point made by the author using the suggestions presented on this and the previous pages. Then look at the annotated examination of the essay immediately following the essay. By reading the annotations of the essay, you should have a better understanding of the elements of expository writing in political science.

In particular, reading critically simply means asking questions as you are reading and noting where the arguments, evidence, and conclusions are weakest or strongest. Not all information must be remembered verbatim or memorized. Use shorthand symbols to mark in the margins of personal copies of books, articles, and essays for easy retrieval of information. You should be able to identify at least the important points, the hypothesis, the evidence, and the conclusion in a piece of literature.

Here are some suggestions for identifying critical points in a piece of literature.

1.   Use a "T" to identify the theory, hypothesis, or thesis sentence.
2.   Use a star (*) to identify an important point. The more important the point, the more stars you put in the margin.
3.   Use an "E" to identify quantitative evidence and information that is proven or known to be true.
4.   Use an "S" to identify suggestive or qualitative evidence.
5.   Use a "V" to indicate where the author has used a value assumption to make a point.
6.   Use a question mark (?) to indicate where the author's reasoning is unclear or use of evidence is suspect.
7.   Use an "X" to indicate where the author's evidence or point is not valid.
8.   Use a "C" to identify a conclusion based on an assertion about the relationship between the author's hypothesis and the evidence presented.

AN EXAMPLE OF A POLITICAL ARGUMENT
(Reprinted by permission)

FEDERAL FUNDING FOR NEA

AND
THE ROLE OF THE ARTS IN A DEMOCRACY

By
Alan G. Schmidt

The controversy over federal funding for the arts has moved to center stage again, as Congress--faced in an election year with the possibility of having to raise taxes--considers the budget for the National Endowment for the Arts (NEA). Emotions run high on both sides of the issue, and there are valid arguments to support both sides. On the one hand, it can be argued that culture is something that rises naturally out of the common values of a community and not something that can be dictated from a centralized bureaucratic source. It follows from that argument that America would not suddenly be without culture if a budget cut forced a trim in the NEA's funds. On the other hand, when artists are subsidized, they should not be subjected to political censorship and denied their First Amendment rights as a condition for public funding. Although public funding of the arts is not a cultural necessity, denial of funding for artists who express politically unpopular views erodes the value of important constitutional guarantees of equal protection, free speech, and minority rights.

One of the important issues in the debate over funding politically offensive art is whether public funds should support undesirable activities. This issue, however, obscures a hidden problem of equal protection. Public funds have been and are used to support undesirable activities. For example, tobacco farmers are given public subsidies to produce a crop that will kill half a million people every year. These tobacco farmers are given subsidies in spite of acknowledged government and public support for banning smoking as an undesirable, socially unacceptable activity.

Another important issue in the debate over public funding targets is not socially undesirable activity but politically oriented activity that may or may not be politically unacceptable. The crux of this argument stems from a desire to prevent tax dollars from being spent by individuals engaging in political debate. Unfortunately, this argument is flawed and inconsistent with standard tax subsidies provided to non-profit organizations. For example, according to this argument, the tax-exempt status for churches should be abolished. The Catholic Church spends over a million dollars a year on political lobbying against abortion and yet it pays no taxes. A tax exemption has the same effect as a tax subsidy--money from taxes which could be used for other public purposes is given (not collected) to churches for private use. No one seems to be asking Cardinal O'Connor or Jerry Falwell or Pat Robertson to stop engaging in politics as a condition of their organizations' tax-exempt status. Political expression, even that which is espoused by leaders of tax-exempt churches, is protected by the First Amendment.

At the very least, it seems that some consistency in what is considered protected rights and obligations is in order for examining public funding for the arts. There is one argument against funding the NEA, however, that could prove dangerous for all Americans, no matter what their feelings about the current controversy. Jonathan Yardley of *The Washington Post* has argued that public funds should not be granted to artists who engage in political expression. Although it was not clear who would judge an artist's work as political or apolitical and because assessing the content of a work is a subjective process, what Yardley apparently meant was that funding should be withheld for artists whose political agendas do not agree with his political agenda.

Again, constitutional provisions establishing equal protection and minority rights which inhibit arbitrary and subjective government activities help diffuse but not disarm this argument. Yardley's idea is disturbing because he expects artists who live in an open, democratic society to produce work totally devoid of democratic ideas. Much, if not all American art--from the poetry of Walt Whitman to the films of Frank Capra to the music of Elvis Presley--is inherently political. If American arts do not reflect the ideals and the conflicts in society, what purpose would they serve in society? Tolerance of statements about government and society, as promulgated by political philosopher J.S. Mill, is necessary for the maintenance of a democratic society and is at the very heart of the American experiment with democracy.

The basic artistic values and ideals of American culture were inherited from the ancient Greeks, for whom art (along with politics and good citizenship) was considered an essential act of public service. To refuse to fund works by artists for budgetary reasons is vastly different from refusing to fund works because they reflect political values. An artist has just as much right to express political ideas as anyone else. How can Americans promote their experiment to the world as an exemplary model of democratic government if they refuse to allow political discourse in the publicly funded arts?

The debate over tax-supported arts is one that may be on the public agenda for a long time. It is difficult to predict how it will resolve. Judging from Yardley's arguments, the debate will be centered on confusing rhetoric and a manipulation of emotions. Nonetheless, artists have just as much right to use their skills to influence political outcomes as anyone else. Public funding for NEA has helped to secure the right to political expression for artists whose activities are not often valued monetarily. Some federally funded art may indeed be offensive and objectionable to the majority of Americans, but to deny funding to the arts because of their political nature should be offensive and objectionable to all Americans.

AN ANNOTATED ANALYSIS OF A POLITICAL ARGUMENT

The material below is an annotation of the political argument immediately preceding this page. The essay has been critically reviewed based on the validity of the arguments and evidence presented below. Although a diagram of the reasoning would help to evaluate questionable parts of the argument, I have only concentrated on those problems or errors which correspond to the material discussed in Sections One and Two. The author of the essay uses many kinds of evidence discussed in Section One and types of arguments examined in Section Two. The essay is broken down into logical development of the argument, uses of evidence, and conclusions based on induction or deduction.

ANALYSIS OF *FEDERAL FUNDING FOR NEA AND THE ROLE OF THE ARTS IN A DEMOCRACY*

Introduction to the Problem

"The controversy over federal funding for the arts has moved to center stage again, as Congress--faced in an election year with the possibility of having to raise taxes--considers the budget for the National Endowment for the Arts (NEA)."

- The introduction quickly identifies the issue of federal funding for the arts as controversial.
- As a critical thinker, you should be wondering what the controversy is about and why it is important.

Context of the Problem

"Emotions run high on both sides of the issue, and there are valid arguments to support both sides. On the one hand, it can be argued that culture is something that rises naturally out of the common values of a community and not something that can be dictated from a centralized bureaucratic source. It follows from that argument that America would not suddenly be without culture if a budget cut forced a trim in the NEA's funds. On the other hand, when artists are subsidized, they should not be subjected to political censorship and denied their First Amendment rights as a condition for public funding."

- The author explains what the controversy concerns. He does this in two ways. First, with deductive reasoning he establishes the first side of the argument in the following way:

Premise 1:	(*implied*) All art is culture.
Premise 2:	Culture arises from common values of the community.
Conclusion A:	(*implied*) All art arises from common values of the community.
Premise 3:	Common values cannot be dictated from government.
Premise 4:	Culture exists without public funding.
Conclusion B:	(*implied*) All art will exist without public funding.

- Conclusion B is one side of the controversy. Yet, premise 1 is overstated. The word 'all' makes this statement apply to all cases. It is an unstated value assumption that all art is culture. Because premise 1 is weak, this weakens conclusions A and B.

- The author also sets up the second side of the argument. Unlike the first side of the controversy, the second side is mostly implied.

  (***all implied***)

Premise 1:	Art that conforms to politically correct values receives funding.
Premise 2:	Art that does not conform to politically correct values does not receive funding.
Premise 3:	Denying funds for political reasons is censorship.
Premise 4:	Censorship is a violation of First Amendment Rights.
Premise 5:	Violating First Amendment Rights is unlawful.
Conclusion:	Denying funds to artists for political reasons is unlawful.

- The author now has established the second view, that denial of public funding is unlawful.

Thesis

"Although public funding of the arts is not a cultural necessity, denial of funding for artists who express politically unpopular views erodes the value of important constitutional guarantees of equal protection, free speech, and minority rights."

- The author establishes his perspective on the issues.
- He is implying that although the first view has some validity, it misses the point. The real problem is that denial of funding for political reasons violates the constitution.

Assertion 1: An expressed opinion

"One of the important issues in the debate over funding politically offensive art is whether public funds should support undesirable activities. This issue, however, obscures a hidden problem of equal protection. Public funds have been and are used to support undesirable activities."

- In this first assertion, the author begins his defense of his thesis and a further examination of the important issues in the controversy.
- He presents one issue and proceeds to show through inductive reasoning that the objection to public funding is inconsistent with other kinds of public funding.

Evidence supporting Assertion 1: A Statistic

"For example, tobacco farmers are given public subsidies to produce a crop that will kill half a million people every year."

- The author is supplying a statistic to support the implied assertion that tobacco consumption is an undesirable activity.
- As a critical thinker, you should be asking, where did this figure come from? Is it a fact that tobacco kills people? Could this be a case of begging the question by treating a debatable theory as a fact? Could this be a case of a false analogy between politically offensive art and tobacco consumption?

Evidence supporting Assertion 1: An Example

"These tobacco farmers are given subsidies in spite of acknowledged government and public support for banning smoking as an undesirable, socially unacceptable activity."

- The author argues that the public objects to tobacco consumption. But is this valid?
- He implies that all of the public objects to smoking. Is this true? Is this a case of a hasty generalization? Who acknowledges this support?

Assertion 2: An expressed opinion

"Another important issue in the debate over public funding targets is not socially undesirable activity but politically oriented activity that may or may not be politically unacceptable."

- In this assertion, the author expresses an opinion about what issues he believes contribute to the controversy.
- He is suggesting that the issue is not social but political activities that are defined as problems.

Assertion 3: Assertion 2 interpreted

"The crux of this argument stems from a desire to prevent tax dollars from being spent by individuals engaging in political debate. Unfortunately, this argument is flawed and inconsistent with standard tax subsidies provided to non-profit organizations."

- Without actually explaining the difference between social activities and political activities, the author re-defines the issue to focus on political activities. Is there a difference? Does differentiating between social and political debate create a false dilemma?

- He concludes that the issue is the use of public money to fund political activities. But who are the people who do not desire this? The author's reference to 'desire' is vague.
- Nonetheless, the author proceeds to show that such a desire is inconsistent with other policies.

Evidence supporting Assertion 3: A factual example

"For example, according to this argument, the tax-exempt status for churches should be abolished. The Catholic Church spends over a million dollars a year on political lobbying against abortion and yet it pays no taxes. A tax exemption has the same effect as a tax subsidy--money from taxes which could be used for other public purposes is given (not collected) to churches for private use."

- Using a conclusion resulting from deductive reasoning, the author argues that subsidizing church organizations that engage in political activities makes the separation between subsidizing only social activities and not subsidizing political activities invalid.

Evidence supporting Assertion 3: Example

"No one seems to be asking Cardinal O'Connor or Jerry Falwell or Pat Robertson to stop engaging in politics as a condition of their organizations' tax-exempt status."

- The author is using an appeal to emotions here.
- For appeal to be effective, the reader must know that the individuals referenced here are highly controversial, politically outspoken religious leaders.

Evidence supporting Assertion 3: Fact and Example

"Political expression, even that which is espoused by leaders of tax-exempt churches, is protected by the First Amendment."

- The author uses a fact to establish the credibility of his assertion that protection of political expression is applied to politically questionable people who receive public subsidies.
- If readers accept the previous evidence, then they accept assertion 3.
- By accepting assertion 3, readers concede acceptance of assertion 2.

Assertion 4: An expressed opinion

"At the very least, it seems that some consistency in what is considered protected rights and obligations is in order for examining public funding for the arts. There is one argument against funding the NEA, however, that could prove dangerous for all Americans, no matter what their feelings about the current controversy."

- Having set up his argument so that he has invalidated objections to public funding in principle and in particular instances where political expression is concerned, the author then questions the credibility of the key opponents asserting that one of them has ideas that are dangerous to the public.
- He then begins to present an example.

Evidence supporting Assertion 4: Example

"Jonathan Yardley of *The Washington Post* has argued that public funds should not be granted to artists who engage in political expression. Although it was not clear who would judge an artist's work as political or apolitical and because assessing the content of a work is a subjective process, what Yardley apparently meant was that funding should be withheld for artists whose political agendas do not agree with his political agenda."

- The author restates the opposition's case and identifies a problem with the opponent's position.
- The author implies that the danger is using subjective measure of political activity.
- He implies that this subjectivity could be abusive and self-interested.
- But who is Yardley anyway? Is his opinion worth noting? Can he act in any effective way on his opinion?
- As critical thinkers, we need to be certain that first, Yardley's view is representative of the opposition to public funding.
- Second, we need to decide whether we trust the author to interpret the opposition's intentions correctly.
- In this matter, the author personalizes the issue -ad hominem- by concentrating on imagined negative characteristics.

Assertion 5: An expressed opinion

"Again, constitutional provisions establishing equal protection and minority rights which inhibit arbitrary and subjective government activities help diffuse but not disarm this argument. Yardley's idea is disturbing because he expects artists who live in an open, democratic society to produce work totally devoid of democratic ideas."

- The author builds on the reader's acceptance of assertion 4 to continue interpreting the opposition's view as being unacceptable.
- He implies that Yardley's commitment to or understanding of democratic society is questionable.
- The author is attempting to cast doubt on the credibility of the opponent's view by suggesting that the opponent is not knowledgeable about the issue.
- Again, the author is appealing to the negative characteristics -ad hominem- of his opponent.
- To accept this as valid evidence, we must trust that the author is fairly representing the opponent's credentials.

Evidence to support Assertion 5: An Example

"Much, if not all American art--from the poetry of Walt Whitman to the films of Frank Capra to the music of Elvis Presley--is inherently political. If American arts do not reflect the ideals and the conflicts in society, what purpose would they serve in society?"

- The author is using a set of examples to show that the distinction between social and political activities is not valid when applied generally to art.
- He is implying that to reflect societal values is by definition a reflection of political values in society.
- The author supports this, however, by using what appears to be the beginning of a non-sequitur form of reasoning.
- He presents two ideas that have no obvious connection. The first idea questions what thing art reflects. The second idea is what purpose art serves in society.
- He is hoping to induce the reader to accept that art serves a role in society that is to reflect its ideals and conflicts. Yet, he did not say how reflecting an ideal relates to serving society.

Evidence to support Assertion 5: Expert Opinion

"Tolerance of statements about government and society, as promulgated by political philosopher J.S. Mill, is necessary for the maintenance of a democratic society and is at the very heart the American experiment with democracy."

- Now the author makes the connection for us by paraphrasing a famous political philosopher and commentator.
- Historical accounts of the early days of the framing of our constitution tell us that the framers were highly influenced by the teachings of Mill.
- The author is using an appeal to authority to convince the reader that tolerance of political statements serve to preserve democratic society.

Evidence supporting Assertion 5: A Fact

The basic artistic values and ideals of American culture were inherited from the ancient Greeks, for whom art (along with politics and good citizenship) was considered an essential act of public service.

> (This piece of evidence is being used as additional support for the connection between art, societal ideals, and preservation of democracy. It is also setting up the next assertion by appealing to the emotions -- to the romanticism and reverence held for those ancient cultures who were among the first to experiment with democratic government. It implies that to be against political art is to deny America's ancient and sacred cultural heritage.)

Assertion 6

"To refuse to fund works by artists for budgetary reasons is a vastly different matter than refusing to fund works because they reflect political values. An artist has just as much right to express political ideas as anyone else."

- The author is now granting that for non-political, civic, or objective reasons, refusing to fund the arts could be acceptable. It is the act of refusing funding for political reasons that is a denial of rights.
- The author is using a bandwagon approach akin to "everybody does it so why can't they?"
- He implies that political expression should not come with a political cost. Does everyone have the right to freely express himself or herself and be guaranteed protection from political costs?

Evidence supporting Assertion 6: An example

"How can Americans promote their experiment to the world as an exemplary model of democratic government if they refuse to allow political discourse in the publicly funded arts?"

- The author expresses a belief here and uses it as evidence supporting the notion that the American democratic experiment holds special historical significance in the preservation of democratic ideals.
- Again, the author appeals to the emotions, especially to patriotism, to induce support from the reader.
- There is no question, by now, about the author's understanding of democracy. Is this true? He has firmly established his appreciation of and commitment to democratic values. Or has he?

Conclusion 1

"The debate over tax-supported arts is one that may be on the public agenda for a long time. It is difficult to predict how it will resolve. Judging from Yardley's arguments, the debate will be centered on confusing rhetoric and a manipulation of emotions."

- The author now restates the problem and identifies the causes more clearly.
- By referring to Yardley, his first conclusion implies that emotional, not rational reasons, are used by opponents as evidence against public funding as a way of censoring views held by artists who are in the political minority.

Conclusion 2

"Nonetheless, artists have just as much right to use their skills to influence political outcomes as anyone else."

- The author re-asserts his contention that the problem with denying public funding to the arts is a matter of equal protection.

Conclusion 3

"Public funding for NEA has helped secure the right to political expression for artists whose activities are not often valued monetarily."

- The author re-asserts his position that public funding helps ensure minority rights and free speech.
- This is implied by the reference to artists who do not profit from their activities related to political expression and may not be able to pay the costs of expressing unpopular views.

Knowledge

"Some federally funded art may indeed be offensive and objectionable to the majority of Americans, but to deny funding to the arts because of their political nature should be offensive and objectionable to all Americans."

- What have we learned from this argument?
- In essence, the author has shown us that to be against funding art, especially if it is political in nature, is (at best) to be ignorant of American values or is (at worst) un-American!
- Are you convinced that this is true?
- If readers accept all the assertions made and evidence presented as valid, then they must accept this conclusion.

SECTION THREE

CHOOSING A TOPIC

CHOOSING A TOPIC:

Students should view open-ended writing assignments as opportunities to develop their long-term professional interests. Each subdiscipline in political science offers a set of rich and varied subjects for students to explore. Students may wish to combine one or more types of topics to limit the scope of their research. They can also limit the scope of their research by examining a characteristic of an object associated with a concept. The combinations are limited only by the nature of the course and constraints set by the instructor.

Objects: Things That Can Be Seen Physically

PLAYERS: these are people who are politically important. Presidents, members of Congress, interest group leaders, bureaucrats, and judges are examples of political players.

INSTITUTIONS: these are any body that engages in routinized interaction. Affiliations, association, alliances, and political organizations such as Congress, bureaucracies, political parties, interest groups, and even families are institutions.

EVENTS: these are occurrences or situations that led to political outcomes or consequences or are political outcomes. The Kent State Massacre, political assassinations, campaigns, the Great Depression, and the Nixon resignation are examples of events.

POLICIES: these are or can be any decision made by any public official in any branch of government which has the force of law. Policies also include custom as well as non-decisions on problems. Congressional legislation, bureaucratic regulations, presidential orders, judicial decisions, and common law are policies.

Concepts: Things That Are Believed, Acknowledged

DILEMMAS: these are undesirable situations or problems that seem to be difficult to resolve. They are often associated with unwanted and unsatisfactory conditions. They can also be related to a difficulty in achieving some preferred outcome. Political apathy, political intolerance, providing for social welfare during a recession, providing for cleaner air without devastating the coal industry, and reconciling individual liberties with the public good are examples of dilemmas.

PROCESSES: refers to observable patterns of political behavior in people and groups. They are associated with procedures and mechanisms for using, acquiring and distributing political power. The methods and structure of congressional, judicial, and bureaucratic decision-making are examples of processes. Democracy, Federalism, Confederation, oligarchy, monarchy, feudalism, socialism, and communism are all different processes for organizing government.

VALUES: These are outlooks, perspectives, and subjective or biased opinions. Values are often associated with irrational, moral, or ethical judgements. A value is a sentiment that may or may not be socially acceptable. For example, support for a political party or for racial supremacy are values which sustain vastly different levels of public support. Patriotism, individualism, collectivism, racism, and loyalty are examples of values.

BELIEFS: These each are a state of mind related to a conviction or unconscious trust in a statement which is not fact-based or based on objective evidence. They are often associated with faith or custom. Natural rights, liberty, justice, freedom, and self-sufficiency are examples of beliefs.

PRINCIPLES: these are doctrines or codes of conduct that are usually held in high esteem. Self-determination, limited government, constitutionalism, rule of law, and legitimacy are examples of principles.

IDEOLOGIES: these each has an integrated body of ideas, values, beliefs, and aspirations that constitute a socio-political program. They are associated with a desire, a need, a moral obligation, or a utopian vision. The ideas, beliefs, or values need not be socially acceptable; all that is needed is that the ideas, beliefs, and values are linked coherently. Liberalism, Conservatism, anarchism, authoritarianism, pacifism, imperialism, Marxism, fascism, Nazism, Libertarianism, and nationalism are examples of ideologies.

THEORIES: are sets of plausible statements or general principles offered to explain phenomena or events. Theories offer testable hypotheses or speculations about the causes of political outcomes. Theories are often modified or constrained by ideological perspectives. Democratic Theory, corporatism, the Downesian model of party competition, egalitarianism, the American Voter Model, the Domino Theory, feminism, elitism, and pluralism are all theories.

TIPS FOR CHOOSING A TOPIC

When choosing a topic, students must keep in mind that whatever they have chosen to write about must relate to the course material, be interesting to study, and adhere explicitly to the instructions and limitations set by the instructor. Failing to keep these three criteria in mind when choosing a topic will, in most instances, result in an undesirable grade. There are a number of ways that students can assure that their topics contain these characteristics.

Look at the Table of Contents in your course textbooks.

1.   Make a list of the people, institutions, or other objects that seem interesting to you.

2.   Make a list of any theories, ideologies, or other concepts that seem interesting to you.

- Do not waste time worrying about whether a concept fits into a particular category.

- If the thing is something that cannot be touched then it is a concept.

3.   Combine the list of objects and concepts in different ways.

4.   Choose the combination that most piques your curiosity.

5.   Use verbs and qualifiers to transform the combination of objects into a question.

Check the handout, syllabus, or whatever the instructor gave you that states the requirements for the assignment.

1.   Note any special information or questions that must be addressed in the written assignments.

2.   Use these in combination with the abstract and concrete topics you listed as interesting from your textbooks to pose your topic question.

3.   Focus the topic so that it clearly addresses the requirements of the instructor.

Limit the time frame so that the topic can be addressed within the page limits set by the instructor.

1.   A five-page paper can support only a very narrow topic. Combine an abstraction and a concrete topic and specify a short time frame to narrow the topic.

2.   A ten-page paper can support a focused but very specific topic. Combine two concepts or combine a concept and an object but limit the period to no more than a decade.

3.   A fifteen-page paper can support a complex topic. Combine two or more objects with a concept but be careful that the period or scope does not become all encompassing or historical.

4.   A twenty-page paper or longer can support a complex topic and endure some description of historical context. Combine several objects with one or more concepts and keep the period manageable.

EXAMPLE OF COMBINING OBJECTS AND CONCEPTS

AMERICAN GOVERNMENT

OBJECTS		CONCEPTS	
PLAYERS:	Jesse Jackson	**DILEMMAS**:	Reconciling government aid with balanced budget
INSTITUTIONS:	Presidency	**PROCESSES**:	Congressional voting
EVENTS:	Scandal	**VALUES**:	Individualism
POLICIES:	Job Training	**BELIEFS**:	Justice
		PRINCIPLES:	Limited Government
		IDEOLOGIES:	Libertarianism
		THEORIES:	Egalitarianism

POSSIBLE COMBINATIONS

Combination One: Jesse Jackson and Social Justice
Combination Two   Reconciling Government Aid With a Balanced Budget and Congressional Voting in Urban Areas
Combination Three: Job Training and Limited Government
Combination Four: Scandal and the Presidency
Combination Five: The Presidency, Libertarianism, and Justice
Combination Six: Jesse Jackson and the Presidency
Combination Seven: Libertarianism and Limited Government
Combination Eight: Scandal and Congressional Voting
Combination Nine: Job Training and Reconciling Government Aid With a Balanced Budget
Combination Ten: Jesse Jackson, Egalitarianism, and Individualism

EXAMPLE OF COMBINING OBJECTS AND CONCEPTS

INTERNATIONAL RELATIONS

OBJECTS		CONCEPTS	
PLAYERS:	Saudis	**DILEMMAS**:	Presidential authority to deploy troops in peacetime
INSTITUTIONS:	United Nations	**PROCESSES**:	Communism
EVENTS:	Mideast crisis	**VALUES**:	Patriotism
POLICIES:	War Powers Act	**BELIEFS**:	Liberty
		PRINCIPLES:	Rule of Law
		IDEOLOGIES:	Nationalism
		THEORIES:	Democratic Theory

POSSIBLE COMBINATIONS

Combination One: Mideast Crisis, the United Nations, and Presidential Authority to Deploy Troops in Peacetime
Combination Two: Communism and Patriotism
Combination Three: The United Nations and Nationalism
Combination Four: The War Powers Act and Rule of Law
Combination Five: The Secretary of State and the United Nations
Combination Six: Communism and Democratic Theory
Combination Seven: Liberty and the Mideast Crisis
Combination Eight: Patriotism and Liberty
Combination Nine: Presidential Authority to Deploy Troops in Peacetime and the United Nations
Combination Ten: Nationalism and Patriotism

EXAMPLE OF COMBINING OBJECTS AND CONCEPTSOBJECTS

COMPARATIVE POLITICS

OBJECTS		CONCEPTS	
PLAYERS:	M.Thatcher	**DILEMMAS**:	Political Intolerance
INSTITUTIONS:	Parliament	**PROCESSES:**	Parliamentary Decision-Making
EVENTS:	Falklands War	**VALUES**:	Patriotism
POLICIES:	G.B Poll Tax	**BELIEFS**:	Natural Rights
		PRINCIPLES:	Legitimacy
		IDEOLOGIES:	Conservatism
		THEORIES:	Elitism

POSSIBLE COMBINATIONS

Combination One: Margaret Thatcher and the Growth of Political Intolerance
Combination Two   Parliament, the Falklands War, and Natural Rights
Combination Three: Margaret Thatcher, Poll Tax, and Elitism
Combination Four: Parliamentary Decision-Making, Margaret Thatcher, and Legitimacy
Combination Five: The Falklands War and Patriotism
Combination Six: Political Intolerance, Natural Rights, and Parliament
Combination Seven: Conservatism, Elitism, and Margaret Thatcher
Combination Eight: Britain's Poll Tax, Legitimacy, and Parliament
Combination Nine: Parliament and Parliamentary Decision-Making
Combination Ten: Poll Tax and Political Intolerance

EXAMPLE OF COMBINING OBJECTS AND CONCEPTS

PUBLIC ADMINISTRATION

OBJECTS		CONCEPTS	
PLAYERS:	Jack Kemp	**DILEMMAS:**	Reconciling bureaucratic discretion with accountability
INSTITUTIONS:	Congress	**PROCESSES:**	Bureaucratic decision-making
EVENTS:	HUD scandal	**VALUES**:	Loyalty
POLICIES:	Revenue Sharing	**BELIEFS**:	Liberty
		PRINCIPLES:	Legitimacy
		IDEOLOGIES:	Liberalism
		THEORIES:	Elitism

POSSIBLE COMBINATIONS

Combination One:	Congress and Reconciling Bureaucratic Discretion with Accountability
Combination Two	Jack Kemp, Congress, and the HUD Scandal
Combination Three:	Revenue Sharing and Reconciling Bureaucratic Discretion with Accountability
Combination Four:	Congress, Revenue sharing, and Bureaucratic Decision-making
Combination Five:	Jack Kemp, Loyalty, and Legitimacy
Combination Six:	Congress, Loyalty, and Bureaucratic Decision-making
Combination Seven:	Jack Kemp, HUD Scandal, and Bureaucratic Decision-making
Combination Eight:	Revenue Sharing, Liberty, and Liberalism
Combination Nine:	Congress, Loyalty, and the HUD Scandal
Combination Ten:	Congress, Elitism, and Bureaucratic Decision-making

EXAMPLE OF COMBINING OBJECTS AND CONCEPTS

PUBLIC LAW

OBJECTS		CONCEPTS	
PLAYERS:	Earl Warren	**DILEMMAS**:	Political Intolerance
INSTITUTIONS:	The Family	**PROCESSES**:	Judicial Decision-making
EVENTS:	Civil Rights March	**VALUES**:	Racism
POLICIES:	Abortion	**BELIEFS**:	Liberty
		PRINCIPLES:	Limited Government
		IDEOLOGIES:	Conservatism
		THEORIES:	Egalitarianism

POSSIBLE COMBINATIONS

Combination One:	Justice Warren and Egalitarianism
Combination Two	Justice Warren, Racism, and Limited Government
Combination Three:	Civil Rights Marches, Political Intolerance, and Liberty
Combination Four:	Abortion, The Family, and Limited Government
Combination Five:	Judicial Decision-making, The Family, and Abortion
Combination Six:	Political Intolerance, Abortion, and Conservatism
Combination Seven:	Civil Rights Marches, Racism, and Justice Warren
Combination Eight	Racism, Limited Government, and Civil Rights Marches
Combination Nine:	Abortion, Conservatism, and Liberty
Combination Ten:	Judicial Decision-making and Racism

EXAMPLE OF COMBINING OBJECTS AND CONCEPTS

POLITICAL THEORY

OBJECTS		CONCEPTS	
PLAYERS:	M. Gorbachev	**DILEMMAS:**	Reconciling Liberties with the Public Good
INSTITUTIONS:	Congress	**PROCESSES:**	Democracy
EVENTS:	Russia Renounces Socialism	**VALUES:**	Collectivism
POLICIES:	Perestroika	**BELIEFS:**	Freedom
		PRINCIPLES:	Self-Determination
		IDEOLOGIES:	Nationalism
		THEORIES:	Corporatism

POSSIBLE COMBINATIONS

Combination One:	Mikhail Gorbachev and Democracy
Combination Two	Congress and Reconciling Individual Liberties with the Public Good
Combination Three:	Perestroika and Reconciling Individual Liberties with the Public Good
Combination Four:	Mikhail Gorbachev, Perestroika, and Self-Determination
Combination Five:	Perestroika and Corporatism
Combination Six:	Renouncing Socialism: Mikhail Gorbachev and and Self-Determination
Combination Seven:	Corporatism and Freedom
Combination Eight:	Perestroika, Collectivism, and Democracy
Combination Nine:	Democracy, Reconciling Individual Liberties with the Public Good, and Congress
Combination Ten:	Congress, Reconciling Individual Liberties with the Public Good, and Freedom

SECTION FOUR

RESEARCHING USING INTERNET AND TRADITIONAL SOURCES

CHOOSING MATERIALS:
THE WRITER'S BURDEN OF PROOF

A well-written paper is only part of what determines whether a manuscript is a good effort or a poor effort on the part of the student. A paper must be well documented to be a good professional effort.

- The materials chosen as evidence to convince the reader that the writer is correct *support* an argument or a hypothesis.

- Students should remember that the quality of their work depends on the quality of the materials they used in their research.

- The highest quality of materials comes from sources that are objective; most scholarly research and government documents are considered high quality sources.

- STUDENTS SHOULD NEVER NEVER NEVER BASE THEIR RESEARCH ENTIRELY ON ONE SOURCE, THE INTERNET, NEWSPAPERS, OR POPULAR MAGAZINES.

Students must learn to synthesize and provide a new perspective on a topic or issue when writing a research paper. They can do this by:

- collecting a variety of materials

- sorting the information

- relating ideas from many sources

- adding their own insights and interpretations

Students must decide on what kinds of information they need for their research project. There are two kinds: primary and secondary sources.

- **Primary** sources are original research where students collect raw data (such as from a student authored survey), conduct an interview, analyze newspaper coverage over time, or evaluate a set of historical documents (such as presidential letters or a congressional hearing report).

- **Secondary** sources are published reports or discussions of primary research. These include journal articles, books, Internet sites, newspaper articles, agency reports, and Gallup polls.

PRIMARY RESEARCH

For primary research, students should identify the data they need for their research. If it is not available in secondary form, they then must collect it either from original documents, a questionnaire, or personal interview. If such research is being done on human beings and in conjunction with coursework or campus activities, students generally must obtain permission to do the research from their campus Human Subjects Committee.

Original Documents: To research in original documents, students may want to conduct a content analysis.

A **content analysis** is a system for defining categories of information and coding the basic units of each category. To do so, students must do the following:

- ◆ First, students must formulate a research question, theory, and hypothesis. These identify the relationships involved in the political event.

- ◆ Second, students must select a sample of the documents. The collection of documents should be manageable for the period of the student's coursework.

- ◆ Third, students must define categories of the information that are to measure the relationships. These categories are evaluated based on *validity*, *reliability*, and *objectivity*.

    Validity is determined by whether the category measures what it is supposed to measure.

    Reliability is determined the ability to reproduce the results.

    Objectivity is determined by whether the results are unbiased.

- ◆ Fourth, students then read and code the documents on data sheets.

- ◆ Fifth, students then count the frequency of the occurrences in category.

- ◆ Finally, students make an interpretation of the findings as they relate to their hypothesis.

Questionnaires: Questionnaires are just structured surveys of public opinion. Those being asked the questions are called respondents. Some questionnaires are designed with questions that are close-ended (with fixed answer choices). Some are designed with questions that are open-ended (with space for the respondent's own words). To conduct such a survey, students must:

- ◆ First, students must formulate a research question and hypothesis that identifies the nature and variety of information needed to study political problems, political actors, and/or public policies.

- ◆ Second, students must decide what kind of factual and/or attitudinal data must be obtained.

    Factual information generally consists of demographic data about the respondent (occupation, age, sex, education, income, etc.).

Attitudinal information includes how people think or feel about public policies or societal problems.

♦ Third, students must identify the target population for the survey. A target population is the portion (sample) of the public whose attitudes are important to the study. There are various ways to gather a sample:

Representative sample: this is a random selection of the target population where the proportions of each type of respondent in the sample are reasonably close to their proportions in the general population. This means that if women comprise 52 percent of the target population, the sample should contain approximately 52 percent women. The result is a relatively objective survey. The sample results can be used to describe attitudes in the target population.

Nonrandom sample: this is where respondents are not selected randomly and/or the sample does not include respondents in the same proportion as they occur in the general population. One example of this is to sample the first 100 people you see in a shopping center. The result is a biased survey. Such a survey may be used only to describe the sample population and cannot be used to describe the attitudes in the target population.

♦ Fourth, students must decide on how the respondents are to be contacted. Surveys may be mailed, conducted door-to-door, or by telephone. The costs and the response rates (percentage of survey responses completed) are lower for mailed surveys than they are for the other formats. The expected range for responses for mailed surveys is between less than 50 percent. For telephone surveys the expected range is less than 75 percent. For face-to-face surveys it is less than 90 percent.

♦ Fifth, students must decide on the questionnaire format. Open-ended questions require a content analysis and a coding scheme. Students using close-ended questions should consider whether the questions must elicit nominal, ordinal, or interval data. Regardless of the question type, questions should include an option for "don't know" or "no opinion." This allows the question to filter out those respondents who do not know how they feel about subject.

Nominal: These questions ask for information with closed-ended answers of two or more choices that may be "yes" or "no," 1=Democrat, 2=Republican, 3=Other, or "Agree" or "Disagree."

Interval: The answers to these questions have exact and constant values. They are often associated with questions asking for age, income, number of children, etc.

Ordinal: These questions ask for information where the close-ended answers are scaled or rank ordered to measure the direction and intensity of the opinion.

- A **Likert** scale provides choice options from *Strongly Agree* to *Strongly Disagree*.

  EXAMPLE:

  Would you strongly support, somewhat support, somewhat oppose, or strongly oppose rules that would restrict smoking on campus?

  > <1> Strongly Support
  > <2> Somewhat Support
  > <3> Don't Know
  > <4> Somewhat Oppose
  > <5> Strongly Oppose

- A **Guttman** scale provides options for a series of statements arranged from most general (tobacco consumption should be regulated) to the most specific (cigarette smoking should be banned in public places).

♦ Sixth, students must write short questions that address one issue at a time and use value neutral terminology. This means using words that are as objective as possible, using about 20 words or less per question, and keeping the total questionnaire to fewer than about six pages. Personal questions should be done at the end of the questionnaire. A pre-test of the questionnaire before distributing to the target population can help identify problems in the construction of the questionnaire.

♦ Seventh, once the questionnaire is distributed, students should analyze the data by at least describing the frequency of answer chosen per question. These summary results (often referred to as descriptive statistics) can then be presented graphically or in table form. For more sophisticated analysis of answers chosen by different types of respondents (cross-tabulation), students should use a statistical processing program to calculate the mean, standard deviation, adjusted error, and significance tests for the cross-tabulations. Many computer spreadsheets are capable of calculating these statistics, creating tables, and graphing data.

♦ Eighth, when writing about the data results, students should report the total number of respondents in the sample, the response rate, and when, where, and how the sample was distributed. Students should report the mean, standard deviation, the error, and significance tests if they were calculated.

Personal Interviews: Personal interviews are face-to-face unstructured interviews with targeted respondents. Personal interviews are valuable for providing background information, individual perspective, and insider information about political events. To conduct a personal interview, students must:

- First, students must formulate a research question and hypothesis that identifies the nature and variety of information needed from a particular respondent. This requires prior research not only on the topic of the student's research, but on the respondent as well.

- Second, always call or write for permission to do the interview. Tell the respondent about the purpose and focus of the interview.

- Third, students must identify the substance and nature of the information they need from the respondent. The information may include facts that cannot be otherwise found in public documents. The information may also include the respondent's opinions about trends, events, or remedies for problems related to the subject of the student's research. The information could also provide context or background information known only to insiders in the organization the respondent represents. Whatever the case, students should identify what information they expect from the respondent.

- Fourth, students should have questions written down and in order from vague to specific questions. The vague or more general questions should be asked first, and then progress to the most specific questions. Students should be prepared to ask follow-up or explanatory questions based on the respondent's answer to the question asked. More detail is better than less detail! All responses should be recorded either by a tape recorder or through student note-taking. Students must get permission from the respondent to tape record the interview.

EXAMPLE:

Question: Who helped you get the director's position in the National Labor Relations Board Regional Office in St. Louis, MO ?

Follow-up: What credentials were most helpful in securing this position?

Follow-up: Since taking the position, what kinds of organizational problems arose most frequently?

Follow-up: Do you sense antagonism between the national office and your staff?

Follow-up: Do you sense antagonism between your legal and nonlegal staff?

- Fifth, students should transcribe their notes or recordings as soon as possible.

- Sixth, students should write a thank you note to each of the respondents.

- Seventh, students then must conduct a content analysis to classify and analyze the responses.

SECONDARY RESEARCH

Most of student research is based on secondary sources. Students must formulate a research question, theory, and preliminary hypothesis before they begin the research process. Ideas for papers do not magically appear. Ideas come from exposure to information about political events; such exposure is usually in the context of class readings and lectures. Consequently, student research should satisfy a desire to clarify relationships, create explanations for why events occurred, provide solutions for problems, and understanding of political processes. So, before researching their topics, students should use class materials to guide them in formulating their research plan.

For secondary source information, students should look in abstracts and indexes to social science, political science, public affairs, and legal publications.

- Students should use these indexes and abstracts to locate scholarly works on their topics.

- Many libraries have "on-line" computer generated abstracts and indexes for social science books and journals that provide easy access to materials.

- The Internet provides an alternative source for information outside of standard library indexes and abstracts. Many public agencies and non-profit organizations provide direct access to their data bases, resource, and reports on-line.

Students should make the most of the services offered by the reference librarian.

- Reference librarians for social science and for government documents have specialized training in locating quality materials by general topics in these areas.

- Ask a reference librarian for assistance in locating appropriate indexes, index headings, and alternative sources both in the library and on-line.

- Be sure to bring in a description of the assignment when consulting reference librarians. This will help them fulfill your requests efficiently.

- Have a clear idea of your topic and the focus of the research investigation.

- Write a preliminary hypothesis. Show the reference librarian your research question and specific topic.

- Ask the reference librarian for help in decoding indexes and locating materials listed in the index. They can help with both library indexes and on-line indexes.

- Do not be afraid or reluctant to request help several times during your collection of research materials. As you become more knowledgeable, you will be able to ask questions that are more specific about data and other materials.

- Most of all, develop a working, collegial relationship with the reference librarians. Refrain from blaming them when it is difficult to locate materials. Work with them until the appropriate source or sources can be located.

Students should take advantage of any assistance the instructor is willing to provide for locating materials.

TIPS FOR LOCATING SECONDARY SOURCES FOR A RESEARCH PAPER

Students should be aware that there is a hard way and an easy way to locate source materials for a research paper.

The hard way: read everything you can find that is connected to your topic.

The easy way: let the experts guide you.

1.   Look for references to your topic in your textbooks.

- Note any authors referenced more than once: these are probably the leading scholars in the field.

- Copy down the citation and note name of the sources, especially the names of the academic journals.

2.   Go to the most current (no more than two years old) indexes and abstracts in paper and electronic (on-line) forms.

- Look for references to any of the authors listed in your textbook.

- Look for sources that examine topics in your textbook.

- Because materials are often replaced or updated on the Web, always printout or save any electronic source material. Be sure to write the full citation of the source on the material including the author/organization, title of the site, date, time, and place of posting.

3.   Go to the library shelves to retrieve your materials:

- For the books: examine the table of contents and index for each book one shelf above and one shelf below the book you came to take out.

- Look for any reference to your topic.

- Keep the ones that treat your topic with more than one page.

- For the journals: examine the Table of Contents in the previous and more current volumes of the journal you came to take out which date one year before and one year after.

- Keep the ones that have articles with topics close to yours.

4.   Look at the bibliographies of all the sources you have taken from the shelves or retrieved from the Web.

- Note the authors and titles of materials that are used in every one or many of the books or articles. These are usually the classic publications on the topic.

- Note the sources for the evidence or data used to support the authors' arguments.

5.   Repeat steps 2 through 4 until you have collected a rich and varied pile of resources. Then sort and process the information you have collected.

- For the books: before reading the entire book, read a review of the book. Look these up in the:

      Perspective or *Social Science Index*

      Book Review Digest or *Book Review Index.*

- For articles: read the abstract if it has one. Read only the articles that suggest some information in the abstract that might be useful to your project.

- For all sources: read selectively, actively, and take notes about the authors' arguments, methods, and conclusions.

- Code each set of notes by the topic or category of information it provides for each component of your research paper.

LOCATING SECONDARY SOURCES USING THE INTERNET
(Written with the assistance of Leila Niehuser)

The Internet has become a useful tool when searching for research sources. When used correctly, the Internet can reduce research time. When used incorrectly, the Internet can be at best a waste of time, and at worst can provide students with false or misleading information. Because it is unregulated, information provided through an Internet source (Web site) can be as reliable as information found in government documents or as unreliable as information provided in terrorist propaganda—and just as dangerous. To use the Internet efficiently, students must first understand what it is and is not. Second, students must become proficient in Internet search techniques. Third, students must learn how to evaluate Internet sources for quality and reliability.

THE INTERNET DEFINED

The Internet (also called the Net) is not like any other known information providing or processing entity. As a worldwide system of computer networks linked together, the Internet provides a forum for sharing information and resources. It is not free. There are real costs and implicit costs. The real costs are the costs to set up an Internet account and any fee the information provider wishes to charge. The implicit costs are found in how the information is collected and the time it takes to retrieve information. Because no one authority controls the Internet, each network is free to set its own standards and rules. Although no one controls the Internet, there are some common requirements.

♦ All Internet connections require software providing protocols, an Internet service provider, and a modem to provide the connection to the computer.

♦ Information on Web sites is stored in files often referred to as Web pages. These Web pages are structured by HTML, or Hypertext Markup Language.

♦ Access to the World Wide Web is gained through a browser such as *Netscape Navigator* or Microsoft's *Internet Explorer*.

♦ Each information source has a unique electronic mail address called a Uniform Resource Locator (URL). The format is generally as follows:

   • <protocol://domain.name/directory/subdirectory/filename.ext

   • This URL is sensitive to errors and must be typed in precisely as given.

   • All URL have protocol and domain names.

   • Some URL will not have directories, subdirectories, or filenames.

♦ Each URL contains a protocol (type of link) or service made. Each service requires a different piece of software. These protocols include:

   • World Wide Web service is **http://**

   • Telnet service is **telenet://**

   • FTP for file transfer service is **ftp://**

   • Gopher service is **gopher://**

   • News service is **news://**

   • Email service is **mailto://**

   • WAIS service is **wais://**

♦ Each URL contains a domain name that identifies the owner of the Web site. These include:

   • .org for nonprofit organizations

   • .com for commercial organizations

   • .gov for government institutions

   • .net for networking services

   • .mil for military sites

- .us for United States

♦ Some URL contain a directory path that is the address of the Web site.

♦ If the URL for a Web site is not known, most Web sites can be accessed by using a search engine to *surf* (explore, search) for information. Search engines use 'spiders' or 'robots' to retrieve individual Web pages or documents, either because the author of the engine prefers to list the Web site, or because the Web site owner has asked to be listed. Search engines tend to "index" (record by word) all of the terms on a given Web document. Or, they may index all of the terms within the first few sentences, the Web site title, or the document metatags.

♦ Here is a list of some of the search engines currently being used on the Internet.

- AltaVista [http://www.altavista.digital.com]

- Excite [http://www.excite.com]

- Looksmart [http://www.looksmart.com]

- Hotbot [http://www.hotbot.com]

- Infoseek [http://www.infoseek.com]

- Lycos [http://www.lycos.com]

- Magellan [http://www.mckinley.com]

- Mining Company [http://www.miningco.com]

- NetFind (AOL) [http://www.aol.com]

- Northern Light [http://www.nlsearch.com]

- Yahoo [http://www.yahoo.com]

- Bigfoot [http://www.bigfoot.com]

♦ The best way to find information fast is to conduct a meta-search. Meta-search engines combine several search engines simultaneously. Often referred to as parallel search tools, these meta-search engines do not build their own databases. These tools use the search engines and directories created by others. The meta-search tools identify the most relevant sites for the information requested. Here are some popular meta-search tools:

- Go2Net [http://www.go2net.com]

- Dogpile [http://www.dogpile.com]

- Google [http://www.google.com]

- WebCrawler [http://www.WebCrawler.com]

- All-in-One Search Page [http://www.albany.net/allinone]

- Internet Sleuth [http://www.isleuth.com]

- Search.Com [http://www.search.com]

- SavvySearch [http://www.cs.colostate.edu/~dreiling/smartform.html]

EFFICIENT INTERNET SEARCH TECHNIQUES

Know Your Topic. Students should **not** begin surfing the Net before they have done any prior research or serious thinking about the research project. Students should identify a specific topic for the research project before searching the Internet, preferably using the method discussed earlier in this chapter.

- ♦ Before students begin searching, they should have identified an object and a concept to limit their topics.

- ♦ After selecting the object and concept, students should read, ***at least***, any class materials related to the topic chosen and/or visit the Reference section of their libraries for general reference articles and books on the topic.

- ♦ Using classroom notes and texts, identify terms and key words that are related to the topic.

  - Searches done without this step are generally a waste of time.

  - A search using concise, precise, and relevant terms and keywords allows for combining information to narrow the search.

  - **Example**: If you were doing a research paper on the National Labor Relations Board you would want to know that words such as labor, labor law, industrial relations, and oversight were important terms to help control the search.

Find a Search Engine. Unless students already have the URL to the Web site they wish to visit, students must first choose a search engine from those available on their computers. All search engines are not alike. One search engine might not produce any results on a particular topic but another search engine will provide many hits (items found containing something about the topic). A thorough search will enlist several search engines.

Keyword Searching. Using a search engine, students will need to conduct a keyword search using the terms they have identified as relevant to their topics. A keyword search looks for any document containing the keyword or words entered in the search box. The problem with keyword searches is that they can bring back many irrelevant documents or no documents at all.

- ♦ Imagine doing research on the National Labor Relations Board and typing in just the term *labor*. The result will necessarily include thousands of hits, many of which will have no relevance to the topic. The word *labor* could arise in an article about child labor or slave labor. It would be a waste of time and energy to scroll the thousands of results to find useful information.

♦   Sometimes a keyword will give no results. A keyword search resulting in no hits does not mean that there is no information on a chosen topic. It generally means one of two things: either the keyword is not broad or common enough for the engine to locate items that match that word or the search engine chosen does not list Web sites using the keyword. Just choose another related term and/or choose another search engine.

Efficient Searching With Boolean Operators. To improve the search effort and reduce the chances of getting too many or too little hits in the search, Boolean operators are used to either broaden or narrow the search.   Boolean Logic refers to the connectors or operators including *plus signs, minus signs, asterisk, parentheses, AND, OR,* and *NOT.*

♦   **Plus signs**: placed directly in front of the keyword will assure that the search will result in documents that include that keyword. By placing additional plus signs in between a list of keywords, students may further limit the search to documents that contain only the terms listed. Example: +child+sex+abuse.

♦   **Minus signs**: placed directly in front of the keyword will assure that the search will result in documents that do not include the keyword. Using the minus sign in conjunction with the plus sign will remove unwanted documents from the hit list. Example: +child-sex-abuse.

♦   **AND:** Use AND to narrow your search and locate articles that contains multiple search items or concepts. Example: Congressional Laws AND labor.

♦   **OR:** Use OR to broaden the search and to take synonyms or various forms of spelling into account. Example: industrial relations OR labor relations.

♦   **NOT:** Use NOT to eliminate words with many connotations and to narrow the search. Example: If the research topic was President Bill Clinton's economic policies but previous searches included unwanted documents about Monica Lewinsky, just type in: Bill Clinton NOT Monica Lewinsky.

♦   **Parentheses**: Use parentheses for grouping complex search terms together to further narrow the search. Example: NLRB AND (labor OR Congress OR law).

♦   **Asterisk:**   Another important operator is truncation using an asterisk (*). Truncation is yet another way to broaden the search. It broadens by producing documents that incorporate all the variations on the ending of a word. Example: *child** will result in hits containing all the words that started with child as the root of the word. Words like *children* and *child's* would be included in the documents found.

Getting Stuck: What can students do for more information?

♦   Sometimes a limited search of a directory of Internet resources can help stimulate some new ideas or keywords for searching. Students should be careful when using these directories. Such Web sites can often cost more in time searching than they yield in documents or information. Try the following:

•   Academic Info Political Science: An Annotated Directory of Internet Resources http://www.academicinfo.net/polisci.html

- Political Resources on the Net: political sites sorted by country. http://www.agora.stm.it/politic

◆ A useful way to get more information is to use the information already retrieved. Use information from the references for bibliographies at the end of the documents. Search for authors commonly used in those documents. Search for keywords commonly used in the titles of the sources referenced in the documents

Internet Sensitivity: When typing in keywords it is **VERY** important to use the correct spelling. When a search engine comes across a misspelled word, it tries to find a match to that exact word. Unless the word is misspelled in all the documents, the search results will be unsatisfactory.

Saving Materials from the Web: It is important to save and/or print any materials you plan to use in your research project. Internet materials, unlike any other sources available, are subject to frequent revisions (minute by minute, daily, weekly, monthly, annually) that make George Orwell's *1984* an easier world for research than ours! In Orwellian fashion, not only are Web sites updated, they can be re-written with new information that is different, even contrary, to that which was posted earlier. "Here today, gone tomorrow" is common for Web sites. Unlike books and articles that are available through interlibrary loan if not available at your location, Web sites removed temporarily or permanently cannot be reconstructed just for your research project. Because the Internet information is so unstable, students should print or save the material to a disk to preserve it. For the purposes of their research, students must be able to produce the materials they used for instructors who ask for them. Many instructors randomly check student sources. For books and articles, instructors can check the library. For Web materials, that is not always possible when the source of the materials has been discontinued or changed. It is the student's responsibility to provide evidence of the validity and reliability of the Web materials.

To save the entire Web page:

- Insert a floppy disk into the computer.
- Select *File*
- Select *Save As*
- Select the drive the floppy is in
- Give the file a name
- Select *Plain Text*
- Select *OK*

To save part of a Web page:

- Click and hold the left mouse button at the beginning of the text and drag the cursor over the range of text to be saved. Release the button.
- From the menu bar, select *Edit*

- Select *Copy*
- Open a word processing application
- From the menu bar of the word processing application, select *Edit*
- Select *Paste*
- Save the file with a filename

To save a Web address with a title:

- Click and hold the left mouse button at the beginning of the address in the box marked **Netsite** and drag the cursor over the range of text to be saved. Release the button.
- From the menu bar, select *Edit*
- Select *Copy*
- Open a word processing application
- From the menu bar of the word processing application, select *Edit*
- Select *Paste*
- Repeat process for the title of the Web page
- Edit and change the font of the text
- Annotate (write about) the site with any other descriptive information or notes about the site.
- Save the file with a filename

EVALUATING THE QUALITY AND RELIABILITY OF INTERNET SOURCES

As it is with all materials retrieved for a research project, Internet material must be evaluated before it can be used. Regardless of whether students are using books, articles, or Web materials, each item should be evaluated based on the author's credentials, accuracy of the information, objectivity, timeliness, focus, audience, and origins of the evidence. Students may want to access the "Web Evaluation Menu" from Widener University at http://www.science.widener.edu/~withers/webeval.html for an evaluation of a site or use the guidelines below.

Credentials: Students should be wary of any Web site that does not have an identifiable author. Sometimes the author is listed as an organization, sometimes as a series of individuals, and sometimes as a single individual. Some of the questions student should ask about the author of the materials include:

- ◆ If the author is an individual, what are the author's credentials and educational background?

- ◆ Who supports the Web site—a government agency, a nonprofit institution, a university, etc.? For example, sources in Web sites with a domain name ending in .gov, .us, or .edu have higher credibility than unknown individuals or some obscure organization.

- ◆ Read the source carefully. Some Web sites will try to confuse the researcher by using domain names that sound like governmental or university organizations but are really owned and maintained by individuals.

- ◆ If there is any doubt about the origins of the Web site, find out who operates it by going to http://www.rs.internic.net. Click on the "Whois" search database of registered domain names. Type in the domain name of the Web site.

- ◆ A tilde (~) in the Web site address generally means that it is an individual's home page. Be very careful of these types of home pages. Even some .gov and .edu Web sites will include these. Remember that an individual home page regardless of the domain still represents just the individual's viewpoint.

- ◆ Web sites with long complicated addresses are also suspect. Such Web sites are generally so imbedded and distant from the Web site owners that the researcher cannot easily find out who is the owner of the site. For such sites, start by deleting parts of the address from right to left until the domain name and home page appear. This is like peeling an onion; the purpose of this is to get to the owner of the Web site.

Accuracy of the information: Just because it is on the Web does not make information true or accurate. All information from the Web needs verification. Just because a credible Web site lists additional sites does not mean those sites are equally credible.

- ◆ One way to assess the accuracy of the information is to find it in two different sources. If it can be found in two places, preferably at least one government, academic, or university source, the information is probably accurate.

- ◆ Another way to assess a resource is to look for relative balance in the information presented. Does the author present alternative views? Is the author associated with an organization with an interest in the outcome?

- ◆ Web sites with hyperlinks (links to sites) that only link the user to the same author or server are also suspect. Hyperlinks in Web sites should direct the user to additional information and corroborating sources not authored or provided by the same server.

- ◆ Web sites that refer users to resources in print form (books and journals, for example) have a higher credibility than those that refer users to nothing else or to their own servers.

- ◆ Web sites with frequent grammatical and spelling errors are also suspect. Credible servers/authors professionally maintain their Web pages.

Objectivity: Assessing objectivity is difficult if the researcher is unfamiliar with general information about the topic. Until the researcher is better informed about the topic, using verbal clues and cues will help determine the value of the Web information. Value laden, manipulative, belief driven, baseless information is of very little value in academic research. Other than being used as an example of a type of opinion or perspective, the information contained in such sources is often tainted by the author's biases. Assess the information using the following questions:

- Is the language used in the information neutral or persuasive?

- Are the terms used value neutral or value laden?

- Are the author's assertions based on beliefs or quantifiable, reliable data?

- Does the author express opinions with or without factual evidence?

Timeliness: Timeliness is an important characteristic if the research project requires current information or data. All data and facts in the Web source should contain a date collected and/or some indicator of the context in which it was collected.

- Check statistics and any numerical facts for a date collected or compiled. If there is no indication of when the data were collected, do not use the data.

- Make sure to record the date the material was accessed on the Web. Often, Web sites are frequently changed, updated, corrected for errors, removed, etc.

- Examine when the last Web site was last updated. Assertions about current trends based on Web information that has not been updated for years will not be valid.

Focus: The focus of the information is important. Web searches identify *any* source that has a word matching the keyword requested. Such searches result in sources that have the research topic as the focus as well as sources that may mention the keyword in a footnote or as an aside. The better sources are those that have the research topic as the focus of the information.

- Does the source have the keyword in the title?

- Does the source include material unrelated to the keyword?

- Does the source discuss the topic in depth?

Purpose: The best sources are those that are compiled for educational, scholarly, academic, and informational purposes. Expectations for such sources are high. If the purpose of the material is popular, entertaining, recreational, or promotional, the value of this source diminishes and it is not appropriate for student research.

- Does the material include data professionally presented in charts and graphs or with glitzy icons, music, flashing characters etc. Scholarly information rarely incorporates glitzy presentations.

- Does the material provide references in the form of parenthetical citations, footnotes, or endnotes? Scholarly material, as a rule, provides full disclosure of where and how evidence used was collected.

- Does the material include a request for money, product offerings, membership invitations, or other inducements? Scholarly material rarely includes any such inducements or advertisements.

Origins of the Data: Web site information may include primary or secondary data or evidence. If the Web site uses primary (original) data or resources, students must examine how, when, where, and why the data or resources were collected. Personal interviews, survey data, and content analyses of newspapers are a few examples of primary sources. The author collects primary information. Secondary information is derived from the work of others. Evidence based on data collection and description performed by others, books, and encyclopedias are examples of secondary sources. While with primary data or resources the researcher must investigate the methods of collecting the information, with secondary data or resources the researcher must investigate how the material has been used or manipulated from its intended purpose.

- ◆ Does the author discuss the methods of data or resource collection? Are the methods reasonable, understandable, and conform to generally accepted practices?

- ◆ Does the author reference work by other researchers without discussing the context of the work? If so, look at the original work before referencing or using any assertions by the author about that work.

Addition Information

Ackerman, Ernest and Karen Hartman. 1998. *Searching and Researching on the Internet and the World Wide Web*. Wisonville, OR: Frankin, Beedle, & Associates, Inc.

Basch, Reva. 1998. *Researching Online for Dummies*. Dummies Technology Press.

Paul Gilster. 1997. *Digital Literacy*. Wiley Computer Publishing.

Harnack, Andrew and Eugene Kleppinger. 1998. *Online! A Reference Guide to Using Internet Sources*. NY: St. Martin's Press.

COMMONLY USED INDEXES, ABSTRACTS, DIRECTORIES, AND ELECTRONIC DATA BASES

Here is a list of reference sources that provide a good start to finding materials. These indexes, abstracts, and directories exist in either paper or electronic form. Often, some of these exist in both forms. Most often, the older editions of some of the indexes/abstracts exist in paper form or on CD-ROM and the newer ones exist in electronic form. A little knowledge of these sources can go a long way. *Caution: the electronic addresses are active at the time of publication. If you try to access one that has gone off-line or its address has changed, just search for the name of the site using a meta-search engine. If the site still exists anywhere, it should appear in a search.*

SCHOLARLY RESEARCH

ABC Pol Sci: This indexes a broad spectrum of recent and past political science research articles. It can be used for finding articles dating back five years or longer depending on the library holdings. This indexes major journals and books in political science, related fields, and government. It is easy to use and is a good place to begin research.

Academic Search (on-line): This library version indexes a broad spectrum of articles from all disciplines and subjects. It is generally limited to current material, often no older than three years since publication. It is best used for finding recent sources. It provides full text articles from popular and scholarly journals.

Academic Universe (on-line): This is a library version of *Lexis-Nexis*. It often provides full text of articles from all subjects. It indexes articles and newspapers.

CQ Researcher: This provides information congressional reports

CQ Library (on-line): This provides Web access to *CQ Researcher* reports.

Index to Legal Periodicals: This indexes law journals. This is a good place to start research on legislation or constitutional questions about public policy.

International Political Science Abstracts: This abstract indexes political science journals published worldwide. The abstracts are printed in English or French depending on the origin of the article.

Lexis-Nexis (on-line): This is a professional index, sometimes provided to libraries as *Academic Universe*. It often provides full text of articles from all subjects. It indexes articles and newspapers.

PAIS (Public Affairs Information Service **on-line**): This indexes a variety of sources beyond scholarly journals and books. It is interdisciplinary and usually annotated. This index specializes in policy sources.

Sage Public Administration Abstracts: This abstract specializes in public administration sources.

Social Sciences Citation Index: this is a thorough yet complicated index to social science journals, books, and book reviews. The advantage to using this source is that it indexes important words in titles, the citations used in articles, and who referenced these articles elsewhere. This index is a good secondary source. Students should use this to identify other scholarly works that address some of the same issues as in one of their important sources.

Social Sciences Index: This index is a thorough and easy guide to a broad range of scholarly work. It is a good place to start research that has been addressed by many disciplines besides political science. The index is interdisciplinary and easily accessible.

United States Political Science Documents: This abstract also indexes the major political science journals of the U.S. It is a narrow, yet thorough guide that includes abstracts of the works indexed.

BOOK REVIEWS

Book Review Digest: This indexes book reviews published in popular and some scholarly journals. It contains multiple references to books reviewed more than once. It is a good place to start for less scholarly reviews of books across disciplines.

Perspective: This does not index book reviews. The book reviews are by subfield political science scholars and are published in the volume. The reviews are highly selective and emphasize the books' contribution to the subfield and the study of political science.

Political Science Reviewer: This source contains thoughtful book review essays that examine issues and philosophical questions identified in the books. Although not a good source for an elementary understanding of a book, it can help students think about the issues raised and concepts addressed in the book.

GOVERNMENT PUBLICATIONS

CIS/Index to Publications of the U.S. Congress: This indexes and analyzes government documents such as congressional hearings, agency reports, and special congressional investigations. This is an excellent place to start research on legislative and public policy issues.

Federal Web Locator: [http://www.law.vill.edu/fed-agency/fedwebloc.html] This helps locate web sites in the U.S. federal departments and agencies.

Government Printing Office Access: [http://www.access.gpo.gov/su_docs/] This helps locate bills, documents, reports, budgets, public laws, and much more.

Monthly Catalog of United States Government Publications: This indexes government publications that are sent to depository libraries. Most major state and private universities have depository libraries. This source is usually helpful as a backup to the CIS.

Monthly Checklist of State Publications (State Publications): This source indexes state publications. Although not as thorough as the Monthly Catalog of U.S. Government Publications, it provides students with access to reports and pamphlets published at the state level. This is helpful for comparative state and local research.

The Great American Website: [http://www.uncle-sam.com/unclesam/]

Thomas: [http://thomas.loc.gov/] This provides excellent legislative information about bills etc.

U.S. Federal Government Agencies Page: [http://www.lib.lsu.edu/gov/fedgov.html]

U.S. Government Information Sources: [http://www.nttc.edu/gov_res.html]

UNDOC Current Index (United Nations Publications only): This source indexes United Nations publications. It is an excellent source of country-specific information and is helpful for work involving comparative or international relations issues.

LEGAL RESEARCH

Federal Reporter: This source lists rulings and decisions of the president and the federal bureaucracy. This is a good source of current information about executive branch decisions.

Index to Legal Periodicals: This is the best source for articles in law journals. Law journals examine and explain the reasoning behind legal decisions. It is a good place to start when examining judicial decision-making.

United States Code: This source indexes federal legislation passed by Congress. It is a good place to start when examining legislation. It does not index state legislation. Each state has its individual version of these volumes.

GENERAL AND STATISTICAL DATA

ABI/Inform Ann Arbor: This covers economic and business articles.

American Statistics Index: This source indexes all U.S. government statistical publications. It is a good source for economic and demographic data. It is a good place to start when seeking data because it is annotated.

Black Studies: This covers publications by African-Americans.

Book of the States: This is a rich, dense source of information about the institutional structure and financing in each state. It is a good source of data on budget expenditures as well as summary statistics related to laws and regulations.

Census Bureau: [http://www.census.gov/population/socdemo/voting/votetab2.txt] This provides data on voting turnout rates for the 1996 presidential election.

CIA World Fact Book: [http://odci.gov/cia/publications/factbook/index.html] This provides information about geography, politics, and military power for every country in the world.

Congressional Quarterly's VoteWatch:
[http://search.cnet.com/Single/0,7,100-350494,0200.html] This is a database for House and Senate votes.

Congressional Research Reports: [http://www.senate.gove/~dpc/crs/] This provides access to congressional reports.

County and City Data Book. This provides census data for every county and for large cities in the United States.

County and City Data Book: This source is a companion to the Statistical Abstracts of the U.S. The data are disaggregated by population, by industry, by city and county, by geographic region, and by states. It is a rich source of data for studies of comparative state demographic and economic data.

County and City Data Books: [http://fisher.lib.virginia.edu/ccdb/]

County and City Extra: This updates the County and City Data Book.

Criminal Justice Abstracts: This covers the field of criminal justice.

Encyclopedia of American Public Policy: This provides a discussion of a broad spectrum of policy areas. It includes a historical context and list of major legislation in each areas.

ERIC: This covers articles in the field of education.

Europa Yearbook: This source provides data that is multi-national and detailed on a large number of countries. It contains data on international institutions as well as comparative institutional and political structures. It is a good source of data for comparative or international relations projects.

Federal, State, and Local Data: [http://census.gov/govs/www/index.html]

Fedworld Guide: [http://www.fedworld.gov/] This provides a guide to federal Web sites.

Findlaw: [http://www.findlaw.com]

Full-text State Statutes and Legislation on the Internet: [http://www.prairienet.org/~scruffy/f.htm]

Gallup Opinion Index: This source lists the survey results of the Gallup Poll organization. This is an excellent source of demographic, political, and social opinion data. The companion volumes, The Gallup Poll: Public Opinion 1935-1971, 1972-1981, and subsequent volumes, contain the actual poll results.

Gallup Poll Organization: [http://www.gallup.com] This provides access to Gallup Poll information.

General Periodicals Index (InfoTrac) (on-line): This indexes business, social science, and humanities publications.

HAPI: This covers articles related to U.S. Hispanic and Latin American subjects.

Harris Center: [http://www.techsetter.com/harris] This provides access to Harris public opinion data.

Human Resources Abstracts: This covers articles related to social and labor problems.

Information Please Almanac: This provides a variety of data about the United States and the world.

Municipal Year Book. This provides articles and data relating to urban affairs.

National Election Studies: [http://www.votelink.com] This covers national election data.

Periodical Abstracts: This indexes scholarly journals and popular magazines.

Policy.com: [http://www.policy.com] This provides a directory for policy information.

Project Vote Smart: [http://www.vote-smart.org] This site is about politics.

Public Policy Institutes: [http://www.dir.yahoo.com/social_science/political_science/public policy_policy/organizations/]

Reader's Guide to Periodical Literature: This indexes popular magazines.

Roper Center: [http://www.lib.uconn.edu/] This provides access to Roper public opinion data.

Sociofile: This covers social policy.

State and Local Governments: [http://www.lcweb.loc.gov/global/state/stategov.html]

State and Metropolitan Area Data Book: This provides statistics on health, education, employment etc. for cities and states.

Statistical Abstract of the United States: This is a summary annual publication that has economic, political, and demographic data. Although most of the data are national level, some of the tables are disaggregated by state or region. The tables are fully referenced by original source. This is a good place to start when looking for summary statistics.

Statistical Abstract Webpage: [http://www.census.gov/statab/www/rank.html] This is the Census Bureau's Statistical Abstract webpage with links to tables on the economy, labor, socioeconomic data, and more.

Think: **Opinions, Ideas, and Commentary** [http://www.opinion-pages.org/] This provides links to Op/Ed pages from English language print media from around the world.

Women's Resources International: This abstracts articles relating to women.

World Almanac: This source lists data on a broad spectrum of comparative information about different countries. It contains statistics about politics, the economy, society, etc. It is a good place to start for examining data for comparative research.

World Elections: [http://www.psr.keele.ac.uk/election.htm]

NEWSPAPERS AND PERIODICALS

Christian Science Monitory Index: This indexes articles written in the *Christian Science Monitor* and is especially good for thoughtful examinations of public events.

Ethnic Newswatch: This covers ethnic and minority news articles.

Facts on File: This source summarizes current events by category. Although it is not fully referenced, it provides a concise description of world events.

National Newspaper Index (InfoTrac): This covers the major newspapers in the United States.

New York Times Index: This is an index to stories written in *The New York Times*. It is an excellent source of current event information because of the thoroughness and depth of national news coverage. The index is annotated and completely referenced.

NewsBank Index: This covers only the major news articles of value in research.

Newspaper Abstracts: This covers the major national, regional, and international newspapers.

Reader's Guide to Periodicals: This indexes popular magazines from both the left and right wings of the political spectrum. It is a good source of information related to important current events.

Wall Street Journal Index: This source is good for information concerning economic institutions and studying issues of political economy.

Washington Post Index: This is an index to stories written in *The Washington Post*. It is an excellent source of information about national current events, especially involving those taking places in Washington, DC.

LIST OF POLITICAL SCIENCE SOURCES (ABRIDGED)

ACADEMIC JOURNALS

Administration and Society: This journal covers public and human service organizations.

Administrative Science Quarterly: This is the premier journal in organizational theory.

American Journal of Comparative Law: This journal covers legal issues.

American Journal of Economics and Sociology: This journal is interdisciplinary and covers policy and social welfare issues.

American Journal of International Law: This is a premier journal that includes articles by scholars and summaries of court and tribunal decisions.

American Journal of Jurisprudence: This journal specializes in issues concerning natural law.

American Journal of Political Science: This journal covers a broad spectrum of subfields. Material in this journal is generally of high quality.

American Journal of Sociology: This journal publishes articles on social science issues.

American Political Science Review: This journal is considered the premier journal in American government. Although it covers a broad spectrum of subfields, it is best used for locating cutting edge, methodological research.

American Politics Quarterly: Material in this journal is limited to issues of American government.

American Review of Politics: This journal covers most American government topics.

American Review of Public Administration: This journal specializes in public administration issues.

American Sociological Review: This journal specializes in social processes.

Annals of Regional Science: This journal is interdisciplinary and publishes articles on regional issues.

Armed Forces and Society: This journal specializes in military issues.

Asian Affairs: This journal specializes in Asian studies.

Australian Journal of International Affairs: This is a premier Australian journal covering a broad range of subfields.

Australian Journal of Public Administration: This journal covers all topics in public administration.

Boston College International and Comparative Law Review: This law journal covers international law issues.

British Journal of Political Science: This journal covers a broad spectrum of subfields, is of high quality, and is internationally respected.

California Law Review: This law review covers a broad spectrum of legal issues.

California Management Review: This journal covers issues in management of interest to scholars and practitioners.

Canadian Journal of Development Studies: This journal covers a wide range of development issues.

Canadian Journal of Political Science: This journal covers all areas in political science.

Canadian Public Administration: This journal covers issues of public administration and public management.

China Quarterly: This journal publishes high quality research on modern China.

Columbia Law Review: This law review publishes articles on national and international law.

Communist and Post-Communist Studies: This journal examines issues in communist and formerly communist countries.

Comparative Political Studies: This interdisciplinary journal covers all aspects of comparative research.

Comparative Politics: This is a quality publication limited to comparative political studies. It is a good source for area studies and cross-national research.

Comparative Strategy: This journal specializes in strategic decision-making.

Conflict Management and Peace Science: This journal publishes articles on foreign and defense policy.

Congress and the Presidency: This journal specializes in presidential and congressional studies.

Contemporary Security Policy: This journal specializes in security issues.

Cooperation and Conflict: This journal specializes in foreign policy and international research.

Cornell Law Review: This journal specializes in contemporary legal issues.

Crime, Law, and Social Change: This journal specializes in the political economy of crime.

Critical Review: This journal specializes in the nature and politics of political order.

Critical Social Policy: This journal specializes in understanding welfare.

Daedalus: This journal is devoted to political theory issues.

Development and Change: This journal is devoted to analysis of development issues.

Diplomacy and Statecraft: This journal specializes in international affairs.

Dissent: This journal specializes in critical analysis and European politics.

East European Politics and Societies: This journal focuses on social, economic, and political issues in Eastern Europe.

Economic and Industrial Democracy: This journal focuses on the quality of the workplace and workplace democracy.

Economic Development and Cultural Change: This journal examines noneconomic variables in the development process.

Education and Urban Society: This journal focuses on education as a social institution.

Electoral Studies: This is an international journal covering all aspects of voting.

Emory Law Journal: This journal covers a range of legal issues.

Ethics: This journal specializes in theory articles.

Ethnic and Racial Studies: This is the leading international journal on race and ethnic issues.

European Journal of Industrial Relations: This journal specializes in European industrialization developments.

European Journal of International Relations: This journal specializes in normative and formal theories of international relations.

European Journal of Political Economy: This journal specializes in theoretical and empirical research on economic events.

European Journal of Political Research: This journal focuses on issues of broad theoretical and comparative value.

European Journal of Social Theory: This journal focuses on contemporary social thought.

European Urban and Regional Studies: This journal focuses on ways that space has determined political, economic, and social change.

Foreign Affairs: The material in this journal is written by scholars and non-academic experts in foreign policy. The material is generally topical and focused on current affairs related to foreign policy.

Foreign Policy: This journal is an influential journal on foreign affairs.

Governance: This journal specializes in an international approach to public policy and public administration.

Growth and Change, A Journal of Urban and Regional Policy: This journal specializes in development issues and regional policy.

Harvard International Journal of Press/Politics: This journal specializes in the relationship between the press and public policy.

Harvard International Law Journal: This journal specializes in international and comparative law.

Harvard Journal of Law and Public Policy: This journal is dedicated to libertarian and conservative analyses of policy and legal issues.

Harvard Journal on Legislation: This journal focuses on legislative reform and legislative process.

Harvard Law Review: This journal publishes legal scholarship.

Hastings International and Comparative Law Review: This journal specializes in international and comparative law.

History of Political Thought: This journal specializes in political ideas.

Human Rights Quarterly: This journal specializes in law, social science, and philosophy.

India Quarterly: This journal specializes in foreign affairs.

India Journal of Political Science: This journal covers political science and public administration.

Industrial and Labor Relations Review: This journal specializes in labor law and labor relations.

International Affairs (Russia): This specializes in Russian foreign affairs.

International and Comparative Law Quarterly: This journal covers international legal issues.

International Journal: This journal covers international affairs.

International Journal of Comparative Sociology: This journal focuses on comparative culture.

International Journal of Middle East Studies: This journal actually covers more than the Middle East, it also covers southern Europe and Eastern Europe.

International Journal of Public Administration: This journal focuses on American theory and practice of public administration as well as developmental issues.

International Journal of Public Opinion Research: This journal focuses on the methodology of public opinion research.

International Journal of Urban and Regional Research: This journal focuses on global and local issues.

International Journal on World Peace: This journal focuses on all issues, politics, and cultures.

International Organization: This journal publishes articles on policy, international relations, and institutions.

International Peacekeeping: This journal covers areas related to peacekeeping policy and organizations.

International Political Science Review: This journal covers a broad spectrum of political science topics.

International Politics: This journal focuses on transnational issues.

International Regional Science Review: This is a multidisciplinary journal examining regional issues.

International Relations: This journal provides articles on a wide spectrum of political and international issues.

International Review of Administrative Science: This journal publishes articles on administrative process and reform.

International Security: This journal covers contemporary issues in control and use of force.

International Studies: This journal focuses on Indian foreign affairs.

International Studies Quarterly: This journal publishes articles on policy and international affairs.

Issues and Studies: This journal publishes articles on Asian affairs.

Journal of Applied Behavioral Science: This journal focuses on policy and social change.

Journal of Common Market Studies: This journal focuses on European integration.

Journal of Commonwealth and Comparative Politics: This journal is devoted to studies of Commonwealth countries.

Journal of Conflict Resolution: This is devoted to both intergroup and international conflict resolution.

Journal of Contemporary History: This journal covers international history.

Journal of Criminal Law and Criminology: This journal covers criminal justice issues.

Journal of Democracy: This journal covers issues in maintaining democracy.

Journal of Developing Areas: This journal focuses on development issues.

Journal of Development Studies: This journal is an interdisciplinary approach to development issues.

Journal of Health Politics, Policy, and Law: This journal is devoted to health policy issues.

Journal of Interamerican Studies and World Affairs: This journal publishes articles on Latin American relations.

Journal of Interdisciplinary History: This journal covers all geographical areas and periods of history.

Journal of International Affairs: This journal focuses on international issues.

Journal of Latin American Studies: This journal focuses on Latin American issues.

Journal of Law and Economics: This journal focuses on regulations and law.

Journal of Law and Society: This journal focuses on interdisciplinary and cross-cultural research.

Journal of Management Science and Policy Analysis: This is a public management journal.

Journal of Peace Research: This journal covers issues of conflict resolution.

Journal of Policy Analysis and Management: This journal focuses on public management issues.

Journal of Policy Modeling: This journal covers issues of international policy.

Journal of Political Economy: This journal covers labor, business, and economic policy.

Journal of Political and Military Sociology: This journal covers a broad spectrum of issues related to military policy and its societal effects.

Journal of Political Philosophy: This journal publishes articles on legal, moral, and political life.

Journal of Politics: This journal covers a broad spectrum of subfields. Material in this journal is generally of high quality and exhibits diversity in issues addressed.

Journal of Public Administration: This journal publishes empirical research on public administration.

Journal of Public Policy: This journal publishes articles on political, economic, and social policy.

Journal of Social Issues: The focus of this journal is on the human condition and its problems.

Journal of Social Policy: This journal focuses on the implementation of social policy.

Journal of Social, Political, and Economic Studies: This journal publishes articles on international issues.

Journal of Southeastern Asian Studies: This journal publishes articles on Asian issues.

Journal of Southern African Studies: This journal publishes interdisciplinary articles on African issues.

Journal of Theoretical Politics: This journal focuses on all perspectives of political theory.

Journal of Urban History: This is an interdisciplinary journal of policy and history.

Latin American Research Review: This journal focuses on Latin American issues.

Law and Policy: This journal focuses on the role of law in public policy.

Law and Society Review: This is an interdisciplinary journal that crosscuts law, social science, and the humanities. This is a good source for material related to legal issues in a broader framework than found in law journals.

Legislative Studies Quarterly: This journal is multi-cultural yet focused on institutions. It is a good source for legislative analyses, especially those examining international institutions or requiring comparative research.

Modern Asian Studies: This journal focuses on interdisciplinary research on Asian issues.

Modern China: This journal focuses on interdisciplinary research on China issues.

Natural Resources Journal: This is a policy journal.

New Political Science: This journal is devoted to issues of social change.

New York University Journal of International Law and Politics: This journal focuses on international legal topics.

Pacific Affairs: This is an interdisciplinary journal on Asian affairs.

Philosophy and Public Affairs: This journal examines social and political issues.

Policy and Politics: This is a multi-disciplinary journal focusing on origin, impact, and evaluation of policy.

Policy Sciences: This journal focuses on conceptual articles about policy issues.

Policy Studies Review: This journal publishes a wide range of articles on public policy.

Policy Studies Review: This is a broad-spectrum journal on general issues in public policy. It is a good source of review articles and highly focused research on topical policy issues.

Political Behavior: This is an interdisciplinary journal focusing on political behavior, institutions, and policy.

Political Communication: This journal covers issues of mass media and politics.

Political Geography: This journal covers the impact of region on political issues.

Political Psychology: This journal is devoted to the relationship between psychological and political processes.

Political Quarterly: This journal is devoted to issues of political and social reform.

Political Research Quarterly: This journal publishes on a wide range of political science topics.

Political Science: This journal publishes on a wide range of political science topics.

Political Science Quarterly: This journal is a good source for normative and descriptive analyses of a variety of subfields.

Political Studies: This journal publishes on a wide range of political science topics.

Political Theory: This is an international journal focusing on political though.

Politics and Society: This journal publishes articles on the social roots of politics.

Politics and the Life Science: This journal publishes interdisciplinary articles on life science.

Polity: This journal covers a broad spectrum of subfields. Material in this journal is generally of good quality.

Presidential Studies Quarterly: This journal focuses on presidential politics.

Public Administration: This journal publishes national and international articles on public management and administration.

Public Administration and Development: This journal focuses on local, regional, and international development.

Public Administration Review: Material in this journal is written for and by academics and nonacademics. It focuses on topical issues of interest to the administration of public policy.

Public Budgeting and Finance: This journal focuses on public finance.

Public Choice: This journal publishes articles on the intersection between political science and economics.

Public Opinion Quarterly: This journal focuses on issues related to public opinion and opinion research. It usually contains both analyses of the effect of public opinion on political outcomes as well as effectiveness of instruments measuring public attitudes.

Public Personnel Management: This journal focuses on human resource issues.

Public Productivity and Management Review: This journal focuses on issues in public management and non-profit management.

Publius, the Journal of Federalism: This journal publishes the latest research on federalism.

Regional and Federal Studies: This is an international journal on policy issues.

Review of Politics: This journal covers a broad spectrum of subfields.

Science and Society: This is an interdisciplinary journal focusing on Marxist scholarship.

Signs, Journal of Women in Culture and Society: This is an international journal of women's studies.

Social Choice and Welfare: This journal focuses on social choice and social welfare issues.

Social Forces: This is a journal of social research.

Social Science Journal: This journal covers a broad spectrum of social science topics.

Social Science Quarterly: This is an interdisciplinary journal that covers a broad range of socio-political issues. The material in this journal is of good quality.

Social Science Research: This journal covers substantive issues in all social science fields.

Social Theory and Practice: This journal publishes philosophical research.

Socio-Economic Planning Sciences: This is a planning journal.

Southeastern Political Review: This journal is devoted to studies of the American south.

Stanford Journal of International Law: This journal is devoted to international legal issues.

Stanford Law Review: This journal covers a broad spectrum of legal issues.

State and Local Government Review: This journal focuses on politics, policy, and management.

Studies in Comparative International Development: This journal is devoted to development theory and practices.

Urban Affairs Quarterly: Material in this journal is structured for urban research.

Urban Affairs Review: Material in this journal is publishes articles on urban planning.

Urban Studies: Material in this journal focuses on for urban and regional research.

Western European Politics: This journal is devoted to the study of Western European political issues.

Women and Politics: This journal publishes gender studies.

World Development: This is an interdisciplinary journal of development studies.

World Politics: This journal is a prestige journal in political science and international relations. The material is of high quality.

GOVERNMENT DOCUMENTS

Agency Reports: These materials are generally published under the name of the department and agency making the report. They are a good source of information about programs and policies administered by the federal bureaucracy.

Congressional Hearings: These publications originate from committee hearings. This is a good source of information regarding the intent of Congress and the problems identified with a bill.

Congressional Record: This publication provides an account of every speech made on the floor of Congress. Members of Congress may add material to the record as well. It is a good source of information related to the nature of debate in Congress over policy.

Congressional Reports: These types of publications originate from committee investigations. This is a good source of information regarding the issues involved in a piece of legislation.

Reports of the President: These types of publications originate from the president's office. The Economic Report of the President is one such report that is rich with economic data and executive statements about the health of the economy.

QUALITY PUBLICATIONS

Congressional Quarterly Weekly Reports: This publication is a rich and highly respected source of data and other information about congressional and presidential activities.

National Journal: This publication is a good source of commentary on current activities in all branches of government. In a clear, concise style, it provides analysis of issues and controversies occurring in U.S. institutions.

Congressional Digest: This publication examines the controversial issues pending in Congress. It includes commentary by scholars and experts on the issues under consideration.

MASS PUBLICATIONS

The New York Times: This publication is often touted as the premier newspaper in the U.S. It contains broad ranging news coverage, thoughtful investigative reporting, and provocative commentary on national and international events and features. It often contains sources of original data regarding mass attitudes. It has been known to reflect liberal to moderate perspectives.

Newsweek: This is one of the better weekly news gathering publications. It contains broad news and feature coverage, social commentary, and analyses. It is not significantly different from *Time*. It is known as reflecting moderate views.

Time: This is one of the better weekly news gathering publications. It contains broad news and feature coverage, social commentary, and analyses. It is not significantly different from *Newsweek*. It is known as reflecting moderate views.

The Wall Street Journal: This publication is often touted as the premier newspaper for economic news and analysis. The focus is both economic and political. It has been known to reflect conservative perspectives.

The Washington Post: This publication is considered the heartbeat of the Washington, DC community. Although its coverage is broad, it is known for its investigative reporting on problems in the U.S. government. It has been known to reflect liberal to moderate perspectives.

SECTION FIVE

PROPERTIES
OF
ESSAYS
AND
RESEARCH PAPERS

PROPERTIES OF A GOOD ESSAY OR RESEARCH PAPER

A well-written, well-documented essay or research paper has three basic parts: an introduction, a body, and a conclusion.

The **introduction** must include a thesis sentence that structures and focuses the paper on an assertion or a hypothesis about the relationship between concrete and/or abstract political objects.

The **body** of the paper must include arguments, assertions, or points that provide reasons why the thesis sentence is true and counter-arguments against the thesis. The body also includes evidence to back up each reason or assertion. There is no absolute number of reasons required for supporting a thesis. The diagram below shows the thesis supported by three arguments with evidence for illustrative purposes only.

The **conclusion** generally summarizes the main supporting points and clarifies the functional or logical relationships between the evidence and the inferences made by the author.

PROPERTIES OF AN ESSAY OR PAPER

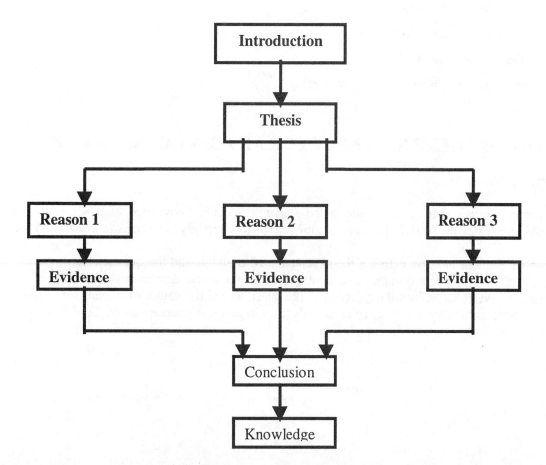

RECOGNIZING AND WRITING A GOOD THESIS SENTENCE

Functions of a Thesis Sentence

- A thesis sentence sums up the main ideas that the writer wants to make.

- A thesis sentence asserts something about the topic.

- A thesis sentence conveys the writer's purpose.

- A thesis sentence acts as a working guide to organize the writer's points.

- A thesis sentence provides a concise preview of the major subtopics addressed in the written work.

Requirements of a Thesis Sentence

- Does it make an assertion about your topic?

- Does it convey a purpose?

- Is it limited to an assertion of only one main point?

- Is the assertion specific?

- Does it suggest a plan for the paper or essay?

WRITING A THESIS SENTENCE FOR AN ESSAY OR ESSAY TEST

Definition of Terms

Essay exams are designed to demonstrate the student's specific knowledge of a subject. Students are responsible for choosing the right facts and organizing them coherently to demonstrate what they know.

An essential element in constructing a thesis sentence is to understand the question being asked. Students must first read the question thoroughly and identify the key words that determine the meaning of the question. Very often, the verb determines the meaning of the question and the nature of the answer. Here is a list of important terms and definitions that are commonly used in political science essays (Corder and Ruszkiewicz, p. 631).

Analyze: give main divisions or elements

Classify: arrange into main divisions

Compare: point out the likenesses

Contrast: point out the differences

Criticize: give your perspective on good and bad features

Describe: name the features of or identify the steps

Discuss: examine in detail

Evaluate: give your perspective on the value or validity

Explain: make clear, give reasons for

Illustrate: give one or more examples of

Interpret: give an explanation or clarify the meaning of

Justify: defend, show to be right

Review: examine on a broad scale

Significance: show why some something is meaningful

Summarize: briefly go over the essentials

Common Problems in Answering Essay Questions

Here are some common problems that students have experienced in writing opinion essays or essays for exams. An instructor may use an acronym to signify these problems. An example of each problem follows each explanation based on the following question:

Question: Describe the important changes which would occur in the structure of power relationships in Congress if the outcomes of the House and Senate elections resulted in a change in party dominance.

Answer: If the Republicans were to recapture control of either chamber, the changes would not be nearly as radical in the Senate as they would be in the House because the Democrats have dominated the House leadership positions for a very long time.

Reason: This sentence answers the question directly by describing the changes as radical in the House and less radical in the Senate. In particular, it provides reasons why this would be true.

Begs the Question

BQ: These types of thesis sentences do not answer the question asked. They typically make assertions about some small aspect of the question without really answering the question at all.

Example: There would be a dramatic change in the structure of power relationships in Congress if the outcome of the Senate elections resulted in a change of party dominance.

Problem: This sentence begs the question by answering only a small part of the question. It does not address the comparison between the House changes and the Senate changes.

Ambiguous or Vague

AV: These types of thesis sentences typically need clarification and/or limiting. They usually lack specific detail about the topic. Such thesis sentences result in the reader asking such questions as, "So what? So why should we worry about that?"

Example: If the outcome of the elections resulted in a switch from one party to another, some say it would have little impact.

Problem: This sentence is vague. It does not tell the reader why such a change would not have much of an impact. In addition, it does not say who says that a change in party dominance would not have much of an impact.

Descriptive or Historical

DH: These types of answers are typically factually correct but do not provide a critical or analytical response to the question. Very often, these thesis sentences prepare the reader for a chronology of events without addressing the controversy associated with the events or relationships.

Example: Party dominance has changed from one party to another in both chambers and has changed the structure of power relationships in them many times, yet Congress continues to function.

Problem: This sentence, while it may appear to answer the question, actually prepares the reader for a chronology of elections where the party dominance has changed in one or both chambers. It does not address the comparative intent of the question.

WRITING A THESIS SENTENCE FOR A RESEARCH PAPER

Research paper assignments help students demonstrate their ability to organize their thoughts about a topic or subject. Such assignments help students clarify their understanding about political phenomena. A research paper requires students, more than any other assignment, to synthesize and integrate information and opinions.

- Research papers require students to organize material coherently to support an argument or statement.

- Research papers are most often assigned without any particular question to answer.

- Research papers require students to think critically and formulate an opinion or a perspective about their topics that is both interesting and supportable within the scope of the assignment.

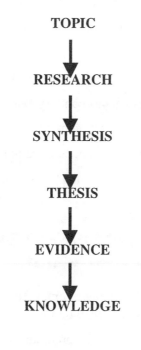

TOPIC

RESEARCH

SYNTHESIS

THESIS

EVIDENCE

KNOWLEDGE

Understanding the function of the thesis sentence in a research paper

Students often have trouble understanding the reason for having a clearly stated thesis sentence for their papers. The thesis sentence is usually found in the first paragraph. This thesis lays out the plan for the paper by incorporating the major subtopics or points within the statement. The function of the thesis sentence is to provide a preview of the main supporting ideas and the order in which the writer will address these ideas. One way to think of the function of a thesis sentence for a research paper is to:

1. Visualize the thesis as a defendant in a murder case.

2. Visualize yourself as Clarence Darrow presenting a classic legal defense.

3. In your opening statement to the jury, after presenting some background information, you declare a thesis sentence. Your thesis sentence is that your client is not guilty because of the following reasons:

    -   he has exhibited a lifetime commitment to nonviolence.

    -   he had no motive.

    -   he was with someone else at the time of the murder.

4. The thesis sentence is on trial for being a false statement. It is up to you to defend it through:

    -   sound reasoning.

    -   presentation of material supporting your point.

    -   defending your point against contrary evidence.

5. The jury can reasonably expect the summary:

    -   to summarize every valid point asserted in the thesis.

    -   to summarize every point refuted but asserted in the thesis.

STEPS TO FORMULATING A THESIS SENTENCE FOR A RESEARCH PAPER

1. **Once students have picked out their topics, they must do some preliminary research to narrow and limit the focus of their papers**.

    -   Only after students do this preliminary research can they begin to develop a preliminary thesis sentence or hypothesis.

    -   This hypothesis is a statement which can be tested and confirmed (or disconfirmed) through the presentation of empirical evidence.

- Here is one *example* of a hypothesis that is testable through the presentation of information and data. "Women's issues have a greater chance of getting on to the congressional agenda when Democrats control the White House and the Congress."

2. **Once students have formulated their preliminary thesis, subsequent research should either lend support or disprove their assertion**.

   - Students should expect to refine and revise their thesis sentences many times throughout the course of their research.

   - As the thesis is narrowed and focused, it takes on a more controversial tone.

   - An increasing knowledge base allows students to ask more sophisticated and critical questions about the topic.

   - The more knowledgeable students become about their topics, the more focused they should become with their assertions about the topic.

3. **For most student papers, a thesis statement with one main idea supported by three subtopics is usually sufficient and preferable to more complex and complicated thesis sentences**.

   - The rule of thumb is to keep the thesis sentence simple, narrow, and specific.

   - The best way to do this is to capsulize and state succinctly the causal relationships between the main point and the subtopics.

   - *A word of caution*: The length of the manuscript and the nature of the topic will influence the structure and desirability of having more or less than three subtopics in the thesis statement.

EXAMPLE OF NARROWING AND REFINING A THESIS

To give students a better idea of how a thesis can be revised over time, the following are examples of revisions, from start to finish, of one thesis sentence. As you read each revision, notice how each statement further refines and focuses the main idea. Each subsequent statement also reflects a greater and greater sophistication and mastery of the material. (Hairston and Ruszkiewicz, pp. 688-690.)

1. **Labor union leaders, during the past decade, have been less effective than business leaders in mobilizing worker or political support**.

   - This thesis sentence, though narrow enough, is vague. What does effectiveness mean? Political support from whom? Why have they been less effective?

2. **Lane Kirkland is not the leader Walter Reuther was in safeguarding his union against economic blackmail upheld by the NLRB, market fluctuations, and a union-busting president**.

- This thesis sentence is focused too narrowly on one person and one union and is vague about the causal relationship between the variables. The thesis does not specify what economic blackmail is nor does it refer to any specific time period.

3. **Labor unions, as political-economic groups, have fallen onto hard times in the past decade due to a hostile presidential administration, the recession, and new techniques in union busting.**

   - This thesis sentence is more specific about the causal relationship between the variables but does not identify the important political actors or the intervening relationships that help produce this political problem.

4. **Next to management's advanced, state-of-the-art techniques for busting unions with the support of the Reagan administration appointees to the NLRB, efforts by union leaders such as Lane Kirkland dwarf in comparison when conducting organizing campaigns during the worst U.S. recession since the Great Depression.**

   - This thesis sentence, while quite complex, fully describes the context, the players, and the variables associated with problems in union organizing.

TIPS FOR WRITING A THESIS SENTENCE FOR PAPERS WITH SPECIFIC REQUIREMENTS

Sometimes students are given a paper assignment for which the instructor has provided the reading materials, a question to be answered, and/or that requires certain types of questions to be answered within the text of the paper. This should not alter the student's ability to construct an effective thesis statement. It does, however, limit the range of ideas and points that can be made in the paper.

1. To construct a thesis sentence for a paper assignment in which the instructor has provided the reading materials and a specific question to answer:

   - use the essay test thesis sentence format.

   - answer the question directly and reference the reading material to support the main points of the thesis.

2. To construct a thesis sentence for a research paper that must answer specific questions within the text:

   - reflect the paper's main idea in the thesis sentence and subdivide the paper so that it reflects the answers to the questions.

   - structure the paper's main arguments to comply with the requirements of the assignment.

COMMON PROBLEMS IN CONSTRUCTING A THESIS

Here are some common problems that students have experienced in writing a thesis sentence for a research paper. An instructor may use an acronym to signify these problems.

Ambiguous or Vague (Not Specific)

AV: These types of thesis sentences are usually worded very generally and typically need clarification and/or limiting. They often lack specific detail about the topic.

> **Example 1:**   "Labor union members have different voting patterns than non-union workers."
>
> - Such thesis sentences result in the reader asking questions like "How are they different and why is this information important to know?"
>
> **Example 2:**   "Many men and women do not fully participate in the political system."
>
> - These types of statements result in the reader asking questions such as, "So what? So, why should we worry about that? How many? What is considered full participation? Which political system?"

Not Unified

NU: These types of thesis sentences typically attempt to link two different ideas without suggesting how they are related.

> **Example**:   "Workplace participation can help reinforce democratic values even if people do not vote."
>
> - Such thesis sentences result in the reader asking questions like "What does this mean? Does one part cause the other?"

Too Factual or Obvious

TF: These types of thesis sentences typically declare or assert some opinion or perspective that is not controversial.

> **Example**:   "Automatic voting registration would require the government to spend money."
>
> - Such thesis sentences results in the reader asking questions like "What will the rest of the paper be about? So, tell me something I do not know!"

RECOGNIZING AND WRITING A GOOD PARAGRAPH: FUNCTIONS OF A PARAGRAPH

Paragraph construction in expository or argumentative writing is both similar to and different from other kinds of writing, such as technical or creative writing styles. They both use the same grammatical rules for sentence and paragraph structure. Nevertheless, the paragraphs and the sentences in a paragraph constructed for expository writing must logically and functionally relate to one another. This is not always the case for creative or even technical writing.

All paragraphs do not function in the same way nor do they have the same properties.

There are three types of paragraphs

> Introductory paragraphs
>
> Supporting or explanatory paragraphs in the body
>
> Concluding or summary paragraphs

Each of these types of paragraphs has a special job to do in communicating the writer's goals and ideas to the reader. There is no absolute number of paragraphs required for supporting an introductory paragraph. The diagram below shows the introductory thesis paragraph supported by three explanatory paragraphs for illustrative purposes only.

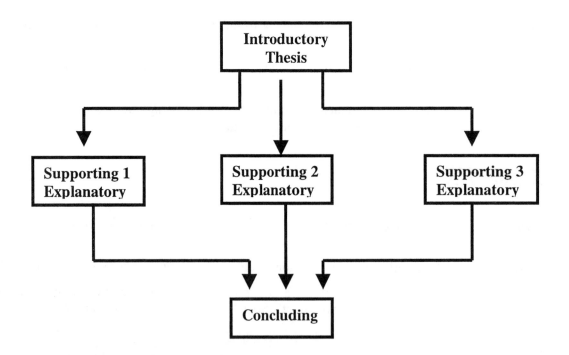

PROPERTIES OF AN INTRODUCTORY OR OPENING PARAGRAPH

♦ An opening paragraph should capture the reader's attention and interest in the topic, specify what the writer will be discussing, and set the tone, direction, scope, and content of the essay or paper.

♦ An opening paragraph should contain at least three sentences: these sentences include

- a general statement (a topic or thesis sentence).

- a clarifying sentence.

- an explanatory sentence.

♦ The best opening paragraph begins with a general statement, followed by a clarifying statement or two, and ends with the thesis sentence.

Advice for Constructing Introductory Paragraphs

Try one of these ways of constructing the first paragraph:

- State the subject.

- Use a meaningful or thought-provoking quotation.

- Ask a question.

- Make a historical comparison or contrast.

- State an important fact.

- Do not use these methods in an introductory paragraph

- Do not use vague generalities.

- Do not use "The purpose of ..." in the first line.

- Do not use the title of the paper in the first line.

- Do not use "According to...." in the first line.

- Do not use truisms and statements of the obvious.

EXAMPLE OF AN INTRODUCTORY PARAGRAPH

The political dynasty, in the American context, is an organization usually centered on a family that transcends traditional norms in campaign and voter perception. By transcending these norms, the dynasty develops the image of American "royalty." The Kennedy and Rockefeller families have evolved as the most dominant examples of political dynasties in the twentieth century. The phenomena, as evidenced in these examples, appear to center around one individual and build from there. Once established, this mutation of American politics becomes its own organization, nearly independent of their respective parties in power and strategy (Salmore 39). Even though the later elements of the dynasty benefit from their link to the overall public perception, they are, at times, mistakenly associated and credited with the dynasty's accomplishments as well (Granberg 504-516).

PROPERTIES OF A CONCLUDING PARAGRAPH

♦ A concluding paragraph is not just the last paragraph; it concludes or summarizes the author's main points, completes the writer's thoughts about the topic, and ties the ending to the beginning of the paper or essay.

♦ The concluding paragraph must contain at least three sentences:

  • a general statement.

  • a clarifying sentence.

  • an explanatory sentence.

♦ The best concluding paragraph restates the thesis and summarizes the evidence.

Advice for Constructing Concluding or Closing Paragraphs

Use these methods to construct a closing paragraph:

  • Summarize the paper's main assertions or points.

  • Clarify, qualify, and restate the main issues.

  • Answer the question asked in the introduction.

  • Suggest a course of action based on your evidence.

DO NOT use these methods to construct a closing paragraph:

- Do not provide new arguments or information.

- Do not restate your introduction.

- Do not conclude more than you reasonably can from the material and arguments you presented in the paper.

- Do not apologize for materials or views presented.

EXAMPLE OF A CONCLUDING PARAGRAPH

The success of the Kennedy and the Rockefeller families, as two prime examples of American dynasties, exemplifies the primary political dynamics that are essential to being part of American political life. These dynamics are instant name recognition for family members, instant empathy from the electorate for the family member's position on issues, nonrational voting based on residual biases associated with the family, and ability to exhibit independence from party politics. The practical effect of establishing a political dynasty is political survival. The societal effect is much less noticeable; political dynasties package political change as familial continuity and thus provide for the survival of their family's influence as well as goals for society. Because of this, political dynasties built in the past shape present political life and have uncommon influence over the America's destiny.

PROPERTIES OF A PARAGRAPH: FOR THE BODY OF THE PAPER

The paragraphs in the body of the written work function to support the thesis sentence and explain the writer's perspective on the topic in detail.

- The paragraphs in the body of the work help to break down the thesis sentence into subtopics and ideas.

- The paragraphs in the body of the work break down the central point or thesis into manageable parts, discuss each part, and relate each part to each other.

- Because the writer makes a commitment to the reader in the thesis sentence, paragraphs that follow must inform readers by filling in details, supporting claims, and giving examples.

Each Paragraph Must Contain Three Types of Sentences

- A general statement or topic sentence.

- A specific or clarifying and limiting sentence.

- A sentence which provides details or examples.

EXAMPLE OF A PARAGRAPH FOR THE BODY OF THE PAPER

Each political dynasty, however, is different; each dynasty has its own dynamics that separates it from the rest of the political community. The Kennedys, for example, are a nationally recognized political family even though the family center or core is in Massachusetts. The Rockefellers, while equally nationally known, have spread their political dominance over the governor mansions in New York, Arkansas, and West Virginia (Salmore 125). While both families exhibited a drive for dominance, the political bases of their influence span the spectrum from highly centralized to decentralized (Clinch x).

PROPERTIES OF A TOPIC SENTENCE

Every paragraph needs a topic sentence except the paragraph that holds the thesis sentence. Like a thesis sentence, a topic sentence states the central idea and the writer's perspective about it. Topic sentences, however, elaborate on parts of the thesis sentence in the body of the paper. In particular, the topic sentence states the main idea of the paragraph and every sentence following it supports that one idea.

Where to Place the Topic Sentence

Most of the time the topic sentence is placed at the beginning of the paragraph. Sometimes, writers put the topic sentence at the end of the paragraph. The structure of the rest of the paragraph depends on where the topic sentence is placed.

Try thinking of a paragraph as a car, a stick shift vehicle to get your idea or point to the reader. If you place the topic sentence at the beginning, you would downshift. If you place it at the end, you would shift up. If you know anything about cars with stick shifts, you know that upshifting without enough speed results in the car losing power. Downshifting too fast results in grinding the gears and may damage the transmission.

A VISUAL OF THE TWO PATTERNS OF PARAGRAPH CONSTRUCTION

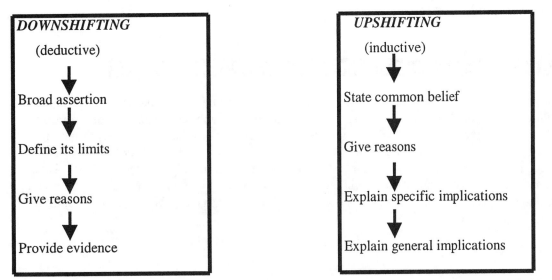

Writing a good explanatory paragraph takes as much skill and attention as shifting a car. Just as a car's transmission can be damaged by improper shifting, the "transmission" of your argument from your head to your reader can be equally damaged by improper shifting from idea to evidence to conclusion. Clearly state your idea in a topic sentence, support the topic sentence with explanatory and supporting sentences (at least one), and resolve the paragraph.

Be careful! If you shift from an idea or belief to your resolution without explaining your point clearly, you will weaken your assertion and your general argument will lose power. If you shift from a broad assertion to a resolution without limiting your assertion and backing it up with evidence, you may bring your argument to a grinding halt. Political scientists are in the business of communicating and evaluating information. As a writer, you must be careful that ideas or points are not lost in the transmission due to poor explanatory paragraph development.

TIPS FOR REASONING ONCE THE TOPIC SENTENCE HAS BEEN PLACED IN A PARAGRAPH

When It is Placed at the Beginning of a Paragraph:

- It is the first sentence when it introduces a general point or idea.

- It is the second sentence when the author has made a transition from one point to the next. The first sentence in this case is a transition sentence.

- Writers must use deductive reasoning for constructing the rest of the paragraph.

- This means that the topic sentence will make a broad statement that is then supported, enriched, and expanded by other sentences.

EXAMPLE OF A TOPIC SENTENCE IN THE BEGINNING OF THE PARAGRAPH.

Although political dynasties may benefit similarly from the same sources of power, the political bases of their influence span the spectrum from highly centralized to decentralized (Clinch x). Each political dynasty is different. Each dynasty has its own dynamics that separates it from the rest of the political community. The Kennedys, for example, are a nationally recognized political family even though the family center or core is in Massachusetts. The Rockefellers, while equally nationally known, have spread their political dominance over the governor mansions in New York, Arkansas, and West Virginia (Salmore 125).

When It is Placed at the End of a Paragraph:

- It is the last sentence when it makes a general statement about the implications of an idea or point.

- Writers must use inductive reasoning for constructing the rest of the paragraph.

- This means that the topic sentence will make an assertion about how some specific idea applies generally.

- This method requires a climactic order, from least important to more important, from most familiar to least familiar, or from simplest to complex supporting reasons or examples.

EXAMPLE OF A TOPIC SENTENCE AT THE END OF A PARAGRAPH.

Each political dynasty, however, is different. Each dynasty has its own dynamics that separates it from the rest of the political community. The Kennedys, for example, are a nationally recognized political family even though the family center or core is in Massachusetts. The Rockefellers, while equally nationally known, have spread their political dominance over the governor mansions in New York, Arkansas, and West Virginia (Salmore 125). While both families exhibited a drive for dominance, the political bases of their influence, however, span the spectrum from highly centralized to decentralized (Clinch x).

ADVICE FOR CONSTRUCTING PARAGRAPHS

Use a commitment and response pattern for your paragraphs.

1. Make a commitment in your topic sentence to a main idea.

2. Then, make sure each sentence in the paragraph contributes to explaining and supporting that idea.

3. DOWNSHIFT!!!! When all else fails, start general and get specific.

ALWAYS ALWAYS ALWAYS use a topic sentence.

1. Make a point in one sentence and stick to it.

2. In the draft copy of your paper, highlight what you think is your topic sentence in every paragraph.

3. Then make sure each sentence says something about the point you made in the topic sentence in each paragraph.

Use transition sentences and transitional words or phrases to keep the paragraph unified and coherent. These link ideas together between sentences or between paragraphs. (See List of Transitional Expressions.)

1. Use varying sentence structures and styles by using transitional words and phrases to keep the ideas in the paragraph coherently linked together.

    -   repeat important words, use synonyms.
    -   use connecting words such as, *however*, for example.
    -   use pointer words such as *first*, *second*, and *finally*, to keep track of supporting ideas.

2. Transitional sentences provide a bridge between the current paragraph and the previous paragraph.

    -   Transitional sentences help the writer make a change in direction without losing the reader.
    -   Transitional sentences point back to the previous idea and forward to the new one at the same time.
    -   For a major change in direction, it may take more than one transitional sentence.
    -   The topic sentence then comes after the transitional sentence.
    -   All supporting information comes after the transitional sentences.

LIST OF TRANSITIONAL EXPRESSIONS
(Fowler and Aaron, pp. 95-96)

TO ADD OR SHOW SEQUENCE: again, also, and, and then, besides, equally important, finally, first, further, furthermore, in addition, in the first place, last, moreover, next, second, still, too

TO COMPARE: also, in the same way, likewise, similarly

TO CONTRAST: although, and yet, but, but at the same time, despite, even so, even though, for all that, however, in contrast, in spite of, nevertheless, notwithstanding, on the contrary, on the other hand, regardless, still, though, yet

TO GIVE EXAMPLES OR INTENSIFY: after all, an illustration of, even, for example, for instance, indeed, in fact, it is true, of course, specifically, that is, to illustrate, truly

TO INDICATE PLACE: above, adjacent to, below, elsewhere, farther on, here, near, nearby, on the other side, there, opposite to, to the east, to the left

TO INDICATE TIME: after a while, afterward, as long as, as soon as, at last, at length, at that time, before, earlier, formerly, immediately, in the meantime, in the past, lately, later, meanwhile, now, presently, shortly, simultaneously, since, so far, soon, subsequently, then, thereafter, until, until now, when

TO REPEAT, SUMMARIZE, OR CONCLUDE: all in all, altogether, as has been said, in brief, in conclusion, in other words, in particular, in short, in simpler terms, in summary, on the whole, that is, therefore, to put it differently, to summarize

TO SHOW CAUSE OR EFFECT: accordingly, as a result, because, consequently, for this purpose, hence, otherwise, then, therefore, thereupon, thus, to this end, with this object

COMMON PROBLEMS IN CONSTRUCTING PARAGRAPHS

Here are some common problems that students have experienced with paragraphs. An instructor may use an acronym to signify these problems.

NOT UNIFIED

(NU): Paragraphs exhibiting this problem usually include an idea or point that is unrelated to the topic sentence.

- These paragraphs are not focused on a central point.
- The reader will typically ask the question, "how does this contribute to the central point (topic sentence)?"

EXAMPLE: The structure of our federalist government has influenced the ways people act in society today. It helps to set the standards that influence people's lifestyles. It is not only one person who enforces these rules but a set of institutions. In our society, the people elect representatives to these institutions that shape and enforce the rules of the government.

PROBLEM: It includes points and ideas that are unrelated to the topic sentence.

SOLUTION: Take out all sentences and information which does not directly contribute to the central point made in the topic sentence. In this case, that is everything after the second sentence.

INCOHERENT

(IC) Paragraphs exhibiting this problem usually have sentences that do not establish a clear relationship between ideas or points.

- These paragraphs are generally confusing because the author has not linked the sentences together logically or functionally.
- The reader will typically ask the question, "how do the sentences relate to the main topic or to one another?"

EXAMPLE: The goal of regulating national powers became mandatory for the framers. The national government, like the state and local government, has three law making bodies: the executive, the legislative, and judicial branches of government. The president makes up the executive branch. Congress makes up the legislative branch, and the Supreme Court makes up the judicial branch.

PROBLEM: The sentences do not establish a clear relationship between the ideas or points.

SOLUTION: Use transitional expressions to link important ideas and sentences together. In this case, we could say "that one way the framers sought to achieve this goal was to divide....For example...."

TOO LONG IN LENGTH

(LG)   Paragraphs exhibiting this problem usually encompass more than one idea in a paragraph.

- The writer will fail to communicate the main point of the paragraph clearly and will confuse the reader.
- The reader will generally ask the question, "which point does the information support?"

EXAMPLE: The U.S. constitution and tradition provide the office of the presidency with many powers and responsibilities. His role represents a fusion of the stature of a king and the power of a prime minister. While his role as the symbolic leader of the nation provides him societal support, the president's veto power also gives him much influence over the Congressional agenda. The persuasive ability of the individual holding the office of the presidency also contributes to the president's power. The ability of the president to harness and focus competing groups inside and outside of the government, especially in Congress, greatly influences his effectiveness in promoting his agenda. To be effective, the president must be able to persuade others to follow his lead.

PROBLEM: It tries to cover more than one main idea in a paragraph.

SOLUTION: Break up the paragraph where the sentences change in time, place, direction, focus, or emphasis. In this case, break the paragraph before the sentence concerning the president's persuasive abilities.

TOO SHORT IN LENGTH

(ST)   Paragraphs exhibiting this problem fragment an idea among two or more paragraphs. Often these paragraphs are only one or two lines long.

- The writer will fail to establish the main point of the paragraph and/or will not support the point with sufficient evidence or limiting information.
- The reader will generally ask the question, "what is the point of giving me this information?"

EXAMPLE: Media, interest groups, and political parties become important political influences on mass attitudes. Even if at times they are criticized, our political system would not work as well without them.

PROBLEM: The paragraph is too short. It does not make a point, nor it does not follow through with evidence and supporting information.

SOLUTION: Expand on the central idea expressed in the topic sentence by including additional limiting information, evidence, or examples. In this case, expand on the desirable and undesirable ways that media, interest groups, and political parties similarly influence mass attitudes.

FIRST AID FOR BAD PARAGRAPHS!

Break up long paragraphs wherever the sentences in the paragraph shift in time, place, direction, focus, or emphasis.

1. Remember: only one main point or idea per paragraph.

2. A unified, coherent paragraph is usually no longer than a half of a typed, double spaced page with one inch margins.

3. A quick way to tell visually if your paragraphs are too long:

   - Measure--if a paragraph is longer than five inches of the page, then it is too long. Keep an 8" by 5" index card handy to use as a template to measure as you revise.

   - There should not be less than two paragraphs on a typed, double spaced page.

Develop the ideas in a short paragraph or combine the paragraph with adjacent paragraphs.

1. If the paragraph makes a point which is different from those of previous and following paragraphs then:
   - develop the idea sufficiently by narrowing your assertion.
   - provide evidence to support the topic sentence.

2. If the paragraph does not make a point that is different from those of previous and following paragraphs then:
   - identify the topic sentence in each of the previous and following paragraphs.
   - identify which topic sentence would be best supported by the information provided in the short paragraph.
   - merge the short paragraph with that paragraph..

3. A quick way to tell visually if your paragraphs are too short:
   - if a paragraph is smaller than the width of two fingers placed side by side, then it is too short.
   - there should not be more than three paragraphs on a typed, double spaced page.
   - if a paragraph is only three lines long, then it is too short.
   - if a paragraph does not contain at least three sentences (a topic, a specific, and an explanatory sentence), then it is too short.

SECTION
SIX

COMMON
PROBLEMS
WITH
WRITING

COMMON STYLISTIC PROBLEMS

Although some stylistic problems are particular to the writer, many are common to even some of the best writers. Good writing requires diligence and persistence in learning to recognize functional errors. While stylistic problems are not the primary cause of poor communication of ideas, they interfere in the relationship between the author and the reader. Stylistic problems create confusion at best, and at their worst, they reflect negatively on the writer's credibility.

MISINTERPRETING THE AUDIENCE FOR THE STUDENT'S WORK:

Students must define their audience before writing even one word on a page. Letters written to a friend, a Senator, a parent, and a judge differ in tone, content, and mutual expectations. This is true of academic writing as well.

Students should avoid the following in written assignments:

- Students should not assume that the audience is composed of their friends or relatives. This encourages familiar, informal, and pedestrian writing.

- Students should not write for themselves. This encourages incomplete thought and shallow explanations.

Students should target the following audiences when writing a paper for a class:

- Students should write for scholars in the field. This encourages students to approach the assignment in a professional way.

- Students should write for the professor and keep in mind what his or her expectations and objectives are for the assignment.

- Students should write for the class as well as for the professor. This will keep the student's approach at a less pompous level than it might be if written for the professor alone.

USING THE WRONG VOICE

Students should approach their assignments in a serious, thoughtful, respectful, and professional way. The voice for an assignment should be formal unless the professor directs the student otherwise.

Students should avoid the following in written assignments:

- Students should not use colloquial language, such as "The senator gave the majority leader the slip on that piece of legislation."

- Students should not address their opinions or assertions by using a first person reference. Statements such as "It is my opinion that..." or "I believe that..." or "I can only conclude that..." are inappropriate and weaken the student's arguments.

- Students should not use contractions in their written work. Such words as "don't, won't, didn't, she'd, and can't," while technically correct, reduce a student's writing to an informal or pedestrian level.

- Students must never use vulgar, profane, or obscene language or references in their written work. Statements such as "The senator really kicked butt on the floor" have no place in professional writing. This type of language weakens the credibility of the author as well as the argument.

LINGUISTIC BIAS

Race, class, and sexual stereotyping have no place in academic writing. These kinds of linguistic biases demean individuals and weaken the author's arguments. Unfortunately, it is difficult to break old habits. Although linguistic biases may not be intentional, students should carefully edit their work to avoid linguistic biases which are most obvious (see Ward, pp. 1-5, 29-32, and her Appendix number 4).

Students can avoid problems with linguistic bias if they:

1. **Refer to race by a socially acceptable reference**.

    - attach the word "American" to the reference of an individual's heritage. For example, use African American to refer to U.S. citizens of African heritage.

    - black is still an acceptable reference to people of African heritage.

    - "minorities and people of color" are acceptable references to people who are not of Caucasian heritage residing in the United States.

2. **Refer to the problems of the poor or disadvantaged as a problem of society, not as a character flaw in individuals belonging to that class**.

    - avoid overgeneralizing about preferences and characteristics of individuals classified based on social or economic criteria.

    - avoid attributing problems experienced by one set of people as a class problem.

3.   **Change the structure of sentences and terminology to reflect gender neutral language**.

- substitute a plural for a gender pronoun or alternate between female and male pronouns.

- substitute the words someone, anyone, person, or people for references to men and women generally (such as, "people who become police officers...").

- refer to people by occupation or role only (such as, "parents are concerned about child care...").

- use more specific terms rather than using the suffix of "man" to refer to people's occupations (such as, members of Congress rather than Congressmen).

- avoid using the term 'man' as a catch-all term to refer to a group (such as all men were created equal).

- avoid descriptions that imply stereotypical behavior (such as rugged men and delicate women).

PUNCTUATION

Issues of punctuation plague us all. The best way to properly punctuate is to keep your sentences simple. Long, complex sentences are difficult to read and comprehend. Sometime it is necessary though, to create complex sentences. Punctuation, then, provides the mechanism for helping the reader absorb the complexities of the thought the sentence represents.

Capitalization: Capitalize proper nouns (names of people, places, and things, i.e., *Alabama*) and proper adjectives (adjectives created from proper nouns (i.e., *American flag*). In general, capitalize titles of anything, any geographic location, names of organizations, names of types of people (race, ethnicity).

Colon: Use a colon in a sentence after which you list or describe items. Whenever possible, students should make the list or description using a complete sentence.

Semi-colon: Use a semi-colon in a sentence whenever you wish to connect two complete thoughts directly. Both parts of the sentence must be complete sentences as well.

Commas: Use a comma to break up complex sentences that either have descriptive clauses or a series of information.

Apostrophes: An apostrophe is used for two reasons. Either to show possession for a noun (i.e., dog's bone) or to indicate a contraction (i.e., *won't*). Pronouns (such as *she* or *it*) never have apostrophes showing possession. The only time a pronoun has an apostrophe is to indicate a contraction (*she's* for *she is*, *it's* for *it is*).

COMMON ERRORS: PROOFREADING THE MANUSCRIPT

Proofreading manuscripts is essential for catching typographical, spelling, usage, and grammatical errors. But proofreading can also catch omissions and errors related to the standards and requirements set by the instructor.

- ♦ Complying with the specific requests of the instructor is important for receiving full credit for the students' research and writing efforts.

- ♦ Good writing skills and good presentation skills are not the same things.

  - Writing is a creative activity.

  - Good presentation is a mechanical activity--it is simple compliance and attention to detail.

- ♦ Poor presentation of the written material diminishes the quality of the manuscript as a product of the author.

  - A poorly proofed manuscript impinges on the credibility of the author.

  - A sloppy manuscript implies sloppy research as well.

  - Attention to detail implies that the author is thoughtful and thorough.

TIPS ON PROOFING PAPERS

Choose someone, preferably from class, to be a draft partner.

- Make a common list of the requirements for the assignment.

- Trade drafts of manuscripts and read them in the presence of one another.

- Check for compliance to the minimum requirements.

- Check the logical development of arguments and presentation of evidence.

- Discuss inconsistencies with each other.

Re-read your own manuscript for the above as well.

- Address all criticisms by draft partner.

- Ask the instructor for clarification of requirements and issues on which you and your partner disagree.

Once the minimum requirements are met, proofread for typographical, spelling, usage, and grammatical errors.

1.   Read the corrected draft aloud. Typographical, spelling, usage, and grammatical errors are more noticeable when you read the text aloud. Reading the text aloud and from the last sentence to the first sentence, (if you can stand it!) allows the students to disconnect from the substance of the paper and focus on proper usage, spelling, and grammar.

2.   Spelling is a talent, not a skill. Those less talented in spelling should take heart in the following quotation from Mark Twain and then, do the following:

> *"To spell correctly is a talent, not an acquirement.*
> *There is some dignity about an acquirement, because it*
> *is a product of your own labor...[To] do a thing merely*
> *by [grace] where possibly it is a matter of pride and*
> *satisfaction,...leaves you naked and bankrupt (Twain, p.*
> *27)."*

- If using a word processor, use the spell checker. Spell checkers identify typographical or spelling errors as long as the error is not a real word. Spell checkers are not fool proof but generally keep you from making a fool of yourself with typographical and spelling errors!

- The most common spelling error is found in words containing "ei" or "ie," Remember that the letter "i" comes before the letter "e" except when these letters follow the letter "c." The word is spelled with an "ei" when the letter "c" precedes this vowel combination.

- Keep a list of your most common spelling errors. Search the text for these words and double-check the spelling.

- Keep a dictionary and a thesaurus handy. If you cannot find the word in the dictionary, look up a synonym (a word that has a similar meaning) in a thesaurus. Usually, the word will be listed in the thesaurus.

- For students who have great difficulty with spelling but cannot use a spell checker, there are several handy spelling aids. Buy the following inexpensive tools:

    ✓ A *Bad Speller's* or *Misspeller's Dictionary*. These dictionaries list the words as they are commonly pronounced (or mispronounced) phonetically, or as they are most commonly misspelled; then they provide the correct spelling.

  ✓ A *Word Book* or *Expression Locator.* A *Word Book* is simply a list of words spelled and divided. An *Expression Locator* has the words spelled, divided, and in the context in which they are frequently used.

 • If none of these tools are available or useful, either ask someone or choose a synonym to replace the word! Do not purposely leave a spelling error uncorrected.

3. Usage problems are different from spelling problems. These are errors in word choice.

 • For example, students often use the word "since" to suggest a reason and as a substitute for "because." This is incorrect.

  ✓ The word "since" is used to designate a time dependent or temporal relationship.

  ✓ The word "because" is used to designate a causal relationship.

 • For example, students often use the word "affect" and "effect" interchangeably. This is incorrect.

  ✓ The word "affect" is a verb that means "to influence."

  ✓ The word "effect," as a verb, means "to bring about, accomplish."

  ✓ The word "effect," as a noun, means "result."

 • Students who are unsure of the correct usage of a word should do the following:

  ✓ Buy a copy of *The Elements of Style* by William Strunk, Jr. and E. B. White. This book is a short but thorough guide to usage.

  ✓ Many publishers have desk reference materials that include a usage glossary. Buy one that is concise. For example, Houghton-Mifflin Publishers has one entitled *The Written Word.*

  ✓ Avoid fancy, big words when small common words express your ideas as clearly. Usage problems are common with words that are not used frequently in communication.

  ✓ Use an Expression Locator to match the context in which you want to use the word with the most common context in which it is used.

 • If none of these tools are available or useful, either ask someone or choose a synonym to replace the word! Do not purposely leave questionable usage uncorrected.

4.   Clean up questionable grammar. Good grammar is an acquired skill. It is acquired through careful attention to placement of commas, tense agreement, and verb-noun agreement.

- If using a word processing program, use the grammar checker. Grammar checkers identify usage errors in sentence structure. They are not fool proof but they identify long sentences, wordiness, sentence fragments, improper punctuation, improper word use, and verb-noun disagreements.

  ✓ Caution: not every error identified by these programs is really an error. Students must know what is proper usage and what is not.

  ✓ In general, even when the program identifies a problem in a sentence that is not really a problem, usually some awkward, vague, or ambiguous language triggered the program's response. Take a serious look at any sentence targeted by the program and find a way to re-write the sentence so that it does not trigger an error anymore.

- Commas are required between two or more words modifying a noun, lists of items in a series, compound sentences, transitional words, and descriptive phrases.

  ✓ A rule of thumb when reading the text aloud: if you paused in reading the sentence, the sentence probably needs a comma wherever you paused.

  ✓ Usage guides typically have sections on punctuation rules for commas, periods, and other forms of punctuation. When in doubt, look it up.

- A common problem in writing is switching from the present to the past or future tense in the middle of a sentence or paragraph.

  ✓ Make the usage of verbs such as, *was, is, were, have, had,* and *has* agree with the tense chosen for the paragraph or paper.

  ✓ Make sure words ending in "ed" agree with the tense of the paragraph or paper.

- Verb-noun agreement is essential to clarity of expression. Verb-noun agreement occurs where the activity associated with the noun is clearly one that can be done by the noun.

  ✓ For example, students often write that "our government makes policies..." or "the institution produced ..." This is incorrect. Governments and institutions are things that are acted upon, they cannot act. People make policies but policies are made in government institutions.

✓ A rule of thumb: people act; things and places are acted upon. If the noun is a thing or place, then avoid language that suggests that things and places are responsible for some action.

HOW TO USE A WRITING CENTER

Most universities have a writing center or lab for students who need assistance in completing their writing assignments. Knowing what the writing center can do and what it cannot do helps students use the resource efficiently (Leahy 1990).

What Writing Centers Do:

- Writing centers offer limited assistance for students who need help in picking topics and structuring papers.

- Writing centers can help students prepare for research by showing them ways to organize their thoughts.

- Writing centers assist students in the writing process.

What Writing Centers Will Not Do:

- Writing center staffs are not proofreaders. They can show a student how to proofread but they do not proofread papers.

- Writing centers typically do not offer remedial help for students who lack basic skills. Students with severe writing problems should take remedial classes in basic skills.

Using the Writing Center:

All students should use the Writing Center at least once during the writing process. Professors are often too busy or too close to the assignment to give sufficient attention to students' individual writing problems. Students can best benefit when the Writing Center staff is seen as a partner in a collaborative learning process.

1.   Visit the Writing Center when you are in the discovery phase of your research project. Ask the Writing Center to give you suggestions on how to work through an idea or freewrite about a topic.

2.   Construct your thesis sentence. Ask the Writing Center tutor to critique it for focus and specificity.

3.   Construct your topic outline. Ask the Writing Center tutor to critique it for logical development.

4.   Write a first draft. Ask the Writing Center tutor to critique it for logical development, coherence, and unity.

On-line Writing Centers (OWL)

The Internet hosts numerous sites on writing research papers. While many of these sites are useful for quick information about referencing, usage, grammar, and style, some are not much more than *fronts* for term and research paper sales.

♦ There are numerous sites offering term and research papers for "free" or for sale. **Do not use these**. To acquire a paper from the Internet is inviting a poor grade at best and trouble for plagiarism at worst.

•   These are generic papers and will be easily spotted by the instructor. Most instructors have specific guidelines and topics for the assignments.

•   Even those supposedly 'custom ordered" are easy to spot because the context of the research materials and resulting paper does not reflect the instructor's course specific context. Because students have been taught the course material within the context of the instructor's individual style and perspective, students' written papers generally unwittingly reflect such a style and perspective.

•   Many instructors are now acquiring software specifically designed for identifying Internet plagiarism (cheating). Not only can the software detect plagiarism in commercially produce papers, but can also detect material that has been take in whole or in part from the Internet.

♦ There are numerous sites offering ideas for term and research papers. Be very careful using these. If you decide to use an idea, ask the instructor *before you do any research* if the topic or idea is appropriate for the assignment. There is nothing wrong with getting ideas from others.

♦ Here are some useful sites for information about writing and editing.

•   **Researchpaper.com**. This site provides help with term paper topics and ideas, plus writing assistance for term papers and research reports.
<http://www.researchpaper.com/writing.html>

•   **Indispensable Writing Resources**: This site provides information about resources on the Net that will help you write or research a paper. It includes links to reference materials, writing labs, and related sites. <http://www.stetson.edu/~rhansen/writing.html>

- **OWL Handouts (listed by topic)**: OWL Handouts Indexed by Topic Writing (Planning/Writing/Revising/Genres). It also has information on Planning/Starting to Write, Effective Writing Revising/Editing/Proofreading Types/Genres of Writing Sentences. <http://owl.english.purdue.edu/writers/by-topic.html>

- **Paradigm Online Writing Assistant**: This site provides information about discovering, organizing, revising, and editing. <http://www.powa.org/>

- **Academic Writing**: This site provides information on writing literature, research, and reviews. <http://www.wisc.edu/writing/Handbook/AcademicWriting.html>

WHAT TO DO FOR WRITER'S BLOCK

Writers of every variety, at one time or another, experience trouble getting started on their manuscripts. Starting the manuscript, with those first few words on the page is often a frustrating experience. Here are a few tips for breaking your writer's block.

1.   **Work with your research materials.**

- Talk about your research and your topic with a friend.

- Freewrite about your topic. Do not worry about organization, grammar, punctuation, or style. Write in a stream of consciousness style--write anything that comes to mind about your topic.

- Examine the result of your freewriting. Using a cut and paste method, group ideas, arguments, and evidence together into broadly defined categories. Try to find at least three categories. Two categories are too broad and more than four are too narrow.

2.   **There is no substitute for good research organization.**

- Using the three or four broadly defined categories from your freewriting exercise, write a scratch outline, then a topic outline, and then a sentence outline.

- On your sentence outline, match your research notes to your ideas, arguments, and evidence. Write the citation next to each of these.

- By the time you are done you will have reviewed, organized, integrated, and synthesized your materials to coordinate with your ideas and arguments.

3.   **Now you are ready to write.**

- Use your first paragraph to quickly sketch a framework for your thesis sentence.

- Do not linger on the first paragraph. If necessary, skip it altogether. Write your thesis sentence and begin a new paragraph with the first explanatory paragraph for the body of the work. You can and should always return to the introduction and rewrite it after you have completed the conclusion.

- Write without editing and critiquing your work as you go along. Forget about grammar, structure, usage, and spelling. Concentrate on expressing your ideas.

- Work as though you are writing a timed, in-class essay. Do not stop to mull over a point. If you are stuck on expressing a point, write a note to yourself in the text to address this issue later and continue with the next point.

- Continue working until you have completed a draft with a conclusion.

- If there is enough time between the date you finished the draft and the date the assignment is due, put the assignment away for at least a day.

- Examine your research materials and supplement them, if necessary, to address the issues, arguments, and evidence you had problems addressing.

- Examine your draft for logical development of ideas, be sure your paragraphs exhibit a commitment and response pattern, expand paragraphs which are too short, break up paragraphs which are too long, and then write your introduction.

- Now correct your grammar, usage, and spelling.

- Now, using your draft checklist, make sure you have complied with the instructor's requirements.

- You should be ready now to type the second draft copy.

5.   **Using the second draft, proofread for the final copy using the tips for proofreading to correct for common errors described in the preceding pages.**

SECTION SEVEN

FORMAT FOR MANUSCRIPT TEXT AND REFERENCES

PROPERTIES OF
STANDARD MANUSCRIPT PRESENTATION:

Although professors have their own preferences about how a paper should be presented, students should observe a few standards. Students should check their syllabus or handout concerning their written assignments for specific details.

WHAT THE MANUSCRIPT SHOULD LOOK LIKE

1.   **Text**: Assignments should be typed, double-spaced, with one-inch margins.

   - Do not justify the right hand margin. It is difficult to read and distracting.
   - Do not double space between the lines in your bibliography but only between references.
   - Each page should be numbered except the title and the abstract pages.

2.   **Printing**: The paper should look presentable.

   - The paper should be printed or typed on white bond or computer paper with the edges clean and smooth.
   - Do not use erasable bond paper. Erasable bond smears easily and the assignment could be destroyed.
   - Tear off all tractor edges and separate each page of a manuscript printed on computer paper.
   - Use a new or dark ribbon in your typewriter or set your printer on near-letter quality.
   - Never purposely turn in an assignment in which the type is barely readable.

3.   **Binding**: The paper should be bound sensibly.

   - The simplest and best method of binding the paper is with a staple in the left-hand corner.
   - Unless the instructor tells students otherwise, do not use paper clips, folders, multiple staples along the edge, or binders of any kind.

TIPS ON THE PRESENTATION OF AN ASSIGNMENT

1.   **Always always always** make a photocopy of your paper--papers get lost.
2.   Write and re-write your work at least once before you turn in your paper.
3.   Learn to use a word processor and type your draft, then revising is easy.
4.   **Never never never** wait until the night before to type your paper. Typewriter ribbons that break and computer files that get lost at the stroke of midnight are common and unconvincing excuses for late papers.

5.   Avoid overquoting. A rule of thumb: do not use more than two quotes for every ten pages of text.

6.   Make sure that your work is well documented. A rule of thumb: make sure every paragraph of substantive secondary information has at least two references.

FORMAT AND PLACEMENT OF ITEMS IN THE PAPER OR ESSAY

A description of each of the items below can be found in the following pages. The descriptions of the format and placement of each item reflect the standard form across style guides. Check the style guide preferred or required by the instructor to verify that these suggestions conform to the standards set by your guide.

THE MANUSCRIPT SHOULD INCLUDE:

- A TITLE PAGE

- AN ABSTRACT

- TABLE OF CONTENTS

- LIST OF TABLES AND FIGURES (RARELY NECESSARY)

- HEADINGS AND SUBHEADINGS

- AN APPENDIX (WHEN NECESSARY)

- TABLES AND FIGURES (WHEN NECESSARY)

- PARENTHETICAL, FOOTNOTE, OR ENDNOTE CITATIONS

- EXPLANATORY NOTES (WHEN NECESSARY)

- QUOTATIONS (ONLY WHEN ABSOLUTELY NECESSARY)

- A BIBLIOGRAPHY OR REFERENCE PAGE

Placement of Items in the Manuscript

1. Title Page

2. Abstract Page or Executive Summary (if required)

3. Table of Contents and/or List of Tables and Figures

4. Text: (Identify parts of text by using subheadings)

   - Introduction

   - Explanation or Background or Literature Review

   - Method or Test of Argument or Reasons

   - Results or Linking of Argument with Evidence

   - Conclusion or Summary

5. Appendix (after last sentence of the body)

6. Explanatory notes

7. References

8. Tables

9. Figures

FORMAT FOR THE TITLE PAGE

1. The title of the paper should be centered and two inches above the middle of the page (the title should not be longer than 12 words).

2. The student's name should be two inches from the bottom of the page.

3. The course number and professor's name should be under the student's name.

4. The date should be under the professor's name.

EXAMPLE OF A TITLE PAGE

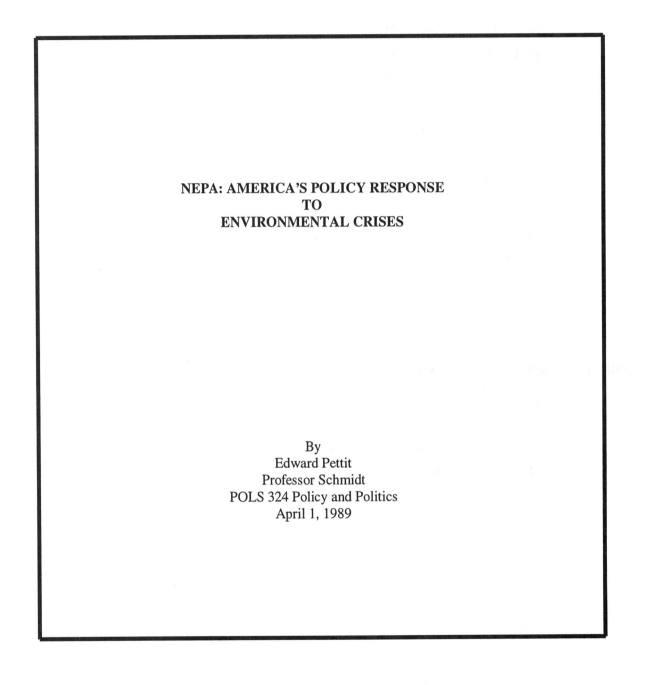

**NEPA: AMERICA'S POLICY RESPONSE
TO
ENVIRONMENTAL CRISES**

By
Edward Pettit
Professor Schmidt
POLS 324 Policy and Politics
April 1, 1989

FORMAT FOR AN ABSTRACT

1. The abstract should be on a separate page following the title page. (For student papers, the abstract can be on the title page -- refer to instructor's directions.)
2. Do not number the abstract page.
3. There are only two parts to an abstract: the title and the text.
4. The word **Abstract** is used as a title and is centered at the top of the page. Double space before writing the text of the abstract.
5. The abstract should summarize the paper in 150 words or less in one paragraph that is at least four sentences long.
6. The abstract is not an introduction. It should include, in order:
    - A description of the nature of the problem
    - A description of the major points and thesis
    - A description of the methods or evidence used
    - A description of the major conclusions reached
7. The abstract should not contain direct quotations from the text.
8. The abstract must use proper sentence structure and grammar.
9. Keep the ideas and main points identified in the abstract in the same order as they are presented in the paper.
10. The abstract may be double or single spaced. Usually, it is double spaced.

Tips for writing an abstract

- Read your paper carefully.
- Summarize in one sentence the focus of the introductory paragraph.
- Write down the main points.
- For each point, write down the evidence used to support the point.
- Summarize in one sentence the focus of the concluding paragraph.
- Use this information to write the abstract
- Use transitions to link the ideas together.

FORMAT FOR AN EXECUTIVE SUMMARY

1. The executive summary should be on a separate page following the title page.
2. Do not number the executive summary page.
3. There are only four components to an executive summary: the title, the purpose, the methodology, and the findings.
4. The words **Executive Summary** are used as a title and are centered at the top of the page. Double space before writing the descriptions of purpose, methodology, and findings sections.
5. The executive summary should summarize the paper in about a single-spaced page.

6. The executive summary is not an introduction. It should include, in order and *identified by subheadings*:
    - A description of the purpose of the study—about one paragraph.
    - A description of how the study was conducted—about two paragraphs
    - A description of the major findings—a one to two sentence generalization with the specific findings *listed with bullets or numbering*.
7. The executive summary should not contain direct quotations from the text.
8. The executive summary must use proper sentence structure and grammar.
9. Keep the ideas and main points identified in the executive summary in the same order as they are presented in the paper.
10. The executive summary may be double or single spaced. Usually, it is single spaced.

Tips for writing an executive summary

Read your paper carefully.
- Summarize in one sentence the focus of the introductory paragraph.
- Write down how the study was conducted.
- For each finding, list the evidence used.
- Summarize in one sentence the focus of the concluding paragraph.
- Use this information to write executive summary
- Use transitions to link the ideas together.

FORMAT FOR HEADINGS AND SUBHEADINGS

1. Use headings and subheadings when assignments call for specific information and questions to be answered, or when the paper topic is complex.
2. There are three kinds:
    - **major** headings: A major heading should be centered or left justified (to the left margin), in bold and capital letters. These are generally used to identify the major parts of the paper such as the introduction and conclusion.
    - **primary** subheadings: A primary heading should be left justified, in bold letters, and the first letter in each word capitalized. These are used to identify transitions between points or arguments within major parts of the paper.
    - **secondary** subheadings: A secondary heading should be left justified and in bold italic letters or bold and underlined. They are generally the first words in the paragraph, they are usually phrases (not complete sentences), and end in a period. These are used to distinguish a between subsections of one of the primary parts of the paper.
3. Double space between the major heading or primary subheading and the following paragraph.
4. For papers that are twenty pages or less, only major headings and primary headings are used.
5. Major headings should be used when the paper is longer than five pages and develops identifiable points and arguments.

FORMAT FOR THE TABLE OF CONTENTS OR
LIST OF TABLES AND FIGURES

Most students will never use a Table of Contents or need a List of Tables and Figures. The Table of Contents is generally produced for papers longer than 25 pages, with several parts or chapters. The List of Tables and Figures are usually only used when the paper is produces with many figures and/or tables embedded in the text of the paper.

1. The Table of Contents and the List of Tables and Figures are placed on separate pages after the abstract or executive summary and before the introduction.
2. On a page by itself, the Table of Contents lists all the headings used in the paper and provides a page number for each heading and subheading used. The headings are left justified and listed in the order they appear in the text. The page numbers where the headings can be found are right justified.
3. On a page by itself, the List of Tables and Figures lists all the tables and figures used in the paper and provides a page number for where each can be found. The table/figure numbers and names are left justified and listed in the order they appear in the text. The page numbers where the table/figure numbers and names can be found are right justified.
4. Do not number the Table of Content or List of Tables pages.

FORMAT AND PLACEMENT OF APPENDIX

1. If the paper has an appendix, put it after the last page of text and before the endnotes (if any), the reference page, and any tables or figures.
2. The appendix must be on a separate page.
3. An appendix is used mostly to present background information not in tables or figures.
4. It should be identified in the text with a parenthetical reference such as (see Appendix).
5. If there is more than one appendix, identify them as Appendix A, Appendix B, and so on.

FORMAT AND PLACEMENT OF TABLES AND FIGURES

1. Place the tables, if any, after the references.
2. Place the figures, if any, after the tables or after the reference page when there is no table.
3. Tables and figures should be numbered, placed on separate pages, and fully referenced with a complete citation.
4. The writer should address information found in the table or figure in the text by phrases, such as "as seen in Figure 1..." or "as the data in Table 1 shows..."
5. After the table or figure has been mentioned in the text, a direct reference to the table or figure is placed on a centered separate line.

EXAMPLE OF REFERENCING A TABLE IN THE TEXT

Importantly, as seen in Table 1, most of his nominees were confirmed.
(Table 1 About Here)
The data in the table show that the Democrat's large majorities, ranging from 57 percent to 75 percent in the 73rd –77th Senate, combined with Roosevelt's adherence to traditional selection methods, resulted in very few unconfirmed or rejected nominees.

FORMAT AND PLACEMENT FOR CITATIONS:

What to Cite: All secondary research material that has been quoted, paraphrased, or summarized must be acknowledged. The author's own material and information that is common knowledge does not need to be cited.

- Quotes are an author's words copied verbatim.
- Paraphrases are restatements of an author's ideas or information in your own words.
- Summaries condense an author's idea, argument, or information into a sentence or two.

Structure for All Types of Citations.

1. Research papers may include footnotes, endnotes, or parenthetical references to sources. Unless otherwise directed by the instructor, students should choose one form of citation and stick with it.

2. Parenthetical, endnote, or footnote citations should be used to identify the source of quotations and all controversial, obscure, or significant facts.

    - *Rule of thumb*: each paragraph in the body of the paper which deals with evidence or ideas borrowed from others should contain at least two citations.

    - *Rule of thumb*: when in doubt, reference the information.

3. All forms of citations must include a specific page number when quoting directly or paraphrasing a fact or data from a source.

STYLES OF CITING OR REFERENCING MATERIALS

Structure for Parenthetical Citations

For All Styles:

1. Parenthetical citations are references to sources that appear in the text.
2. The parenthetical citation is generally placed before the period at the end of a sentence.
3. The reference is placed between parentheses.
4. Multiple references to the same author are indicated with the same format, regardless of how many times the author is cited.
5. Ideas attributed to more than one author are identified by listing the reference together. The references are separated by semi-colons and enclosed together by parentheses.
6. The reference should include a page number if it is a direct quote or paraphrase.
7. References to works with multiple authors are listed the first time with all the authors' last names, but the second time only the first author's name followed by a comma and et al. (Such as: Smith, et al.)
8. References with titles only should be referenced with an abbreviated title followed by three periods. (Such as: "How Environments....")

AN EXAMPLE OF A PARENTHETICAL CITATION

The public is primarily exposed to new information about labor unions through the media. Media are generally seen as agenda setters and in some cases actually shape public opinions (Graber 1984; Iyengar 1987). While the citizens' views may come from their considerations of the political environment, the meaning of events tends to be defined for them by the media. In this sense, media act as agenda setters when pre-existing attitudes are strong and may change attitudes when pre-existing attitudes are weak (Iyengar 1987, pp. 815-820).

Structure for Endnote and Footnote Citations

1. Endnotes and footnotes are substitutes for each other and cannot be used together. They differ from each other only by where they are placed.
   - Footnotes are placed at the bottom of the page in which they were referenced.
   - Endnotes are listed on a page by themselves entitled with the word 'Notes' centered on the first line of the page. Double space between the title and the first citation.
   - The endnote page is placed after the appendix or last page of text if there is no appendix.
2. The text format for footnotes and endnotes is the same and should be indicated in the text by a raised number.
   - They should be listed in ascending order.
   - The first time a source is cited the endnote or footnote contains all reference information.
   - Subsequent citations to the same source immediately following the first citation can be designated by the term 'ibid.' Some styles guide rules suggest that the source of the

citation referenced after the first time include the last name of the author and the year and no other indicator such as 'ibid.' (check with your instructor or the required style guide)

- Ideas attributed to more than one author are identified by listing the authors together separated by semi-colons.

3. The reference format for footnotes and endnotes should be left justified except for the first line, which should be indented by five spaces.

4. The title of the book, journal, or Internet site must be formatted differently than the rest of the text. Most often the title is underlined or placed in italics.

5. Footnotes and Endnotes should include the following information separated by commas (adapted from Kalvelage, et al. 1984; Harnack and Kleppinger 1998):

Books:

- the raised number
- the author's full name, first name first
- the complete title (underlined or in italics)
- the editor's name (if any)
- the edition (if it is not the first)
- the name and number of the series (if any)
- the place of publication
- the name of the publisher
- the date of publication

Articles:

- the raised number
- the author's full name, first name first
- the title of the article (in quotation marks)
- the name of the periodical (underlined or in italics)
- the volume number of the periodical
- the date of the periodical
- the page numbers of the article

Internet:

- author's name (if available)
- title of the document (in quotation marks)
- title of the complete site (underlined or in italics)
- date of the posting or last revision
- volume number (if any)
- date of access
- URL in angle brackets

EXAMPLES OF FOOTNOTES AND ENDNOTES

Here is a sample of footnote/endnote style formats based on *The Chicago Manual of Style*. The information is separated by commas until the end of the sentence.

For a book.

[1]Jay M. Shafritz, *The Dictionary of American Government and Politics*, (Chicago, IL: Dorsey Press, 1988): 41.

For a journal article paginated by volume (page numbers begin at 1 for the first issue and continue in the next issue with the ending page number from the first issue).

[2]Edmond Costantini, "Political Women and Political Ambition: Closing the Gender Gap," *American Journal of Political Science*, 34 (August 1990): 741-770.

For a journal article paginated by issue (page numbers begin at 1 for each issue).

[3] James Coast, "Environmentally Safe Insecticides," *Consumer Digest*, 23, no. 2 (1974): 25-32.

For an article in an edited book.

[4]Hugh Heclo. "Issue Networks and the Executive Establishment," in *The New American Political System*, edited by Anthony King, (Washington, DC: American Enterprise Institute For Policy Research), 1978.

For an article with three authors in an edited book that is part of a series.

[5]Werner Gunth, Wolfgang Leininger, and Gunther Stephen,"On Supergames and Folk Theorems: A Conceptual Discussion," *Game Equilibrium Models*, vol. 2, ed. Reinhart Selten, Game Theory in the Behavioral Sciences no. 19, (Germany: Bielefeld University Press, 1988): 21-22.

For multiple works by an author:

[6]John E. Chubb, "Politics, Markets, and the Organization of Schools," *American Political Science Review*, 82 (September 1988): 1065-87.
[7]John E. Chubb and Terry Moe, *Politics, Markets, and America's Schools*, (Washington, DC: Brookings, 1990): 47, 70-80.

For a government document:

[8]U.S. Congress, House, Committee on Foreign Relations, *Report on Aid to South Africa*, 98th Cong., 2nd sess., (Washington, DC: Government Printing Office, 1985): 1.

For a newspaper or magazine article:
[9]Robert S. Greenberger, "Hottest Labor Consultant in Washington Adopts New Right Techniques to Bolster Union's Image," *The Wall Street Journal*, (October 23, 1981): 56.

For a source with no author:

[10]"Dr. King's Widow Testifies in a Civil Trial," *New York Times*, (November 17, 1999): A17.

For an Internet Source:

General Web site:
[11]Raymond Agius, "Quality and Audit in Occupational Health*,"* *Health, Environment and Work*, May 1999, <http://www.med.ed.ac.uk.HEW/quality.html> (8 June 1999).

Organizational Web site:
[13]AFL-CIO, W*orking Families Need a Voice: Who's Behind It?,* 14 January 1999, <http://www.aflcio.org/silence/behind.html> (19 July 1999).

Electronic Journal Web site:
[14]"Clinton Proposes Increased ChildCare Subsidies," *Amarillo Business Journal*, 3, no. 2 (1999), <http://businessjournal.net/stories/020698/child.html>(25 August 1999).

Electronic Magazine Web site:
[15]Debra Rosenberg, "More Than Just a Kiss: Hillary's Conflicted Life as First Lady and Candidate," *Newsweek*, 22 November 1999, <http://www.newsweek.com/nw-srv/printed/us/na/a55101-1999nov14.htm>) 17 November 1999.

Government site:
[16]National Labor Relations Board*, National Labor Relations Board Members*, 17 February 1999, <http://www.nlrb.gov/members.html> (14 July 1999).

Personal site:
[17]Jon Brown. "Homepage," 24 October 1998, <http://www.polsci.swms.edu/brown/personal.htm> (8 July 1999).

For Electronic Databases:

[18]National Labor Relations Board, (April 1997), Impact of Budget Cuts, Washington, DC: Author. Retrieved from SIRS database (SIRS, Government Reporter, CD-ROM, Spring 1997 release).

For Personal Interviews:

[19]Paul Simon, Personal Interview, 12 August 1998.

EXPLANATORY NOTES

1. Explanatory notes are put in the same place as footnotes or endnotes.
2. These are typically used to comment on the context of a fact or opinion, to explain a source, to elaborate on an idea, to define a term, or to provide background on an idea or methodology used.
3. Explanatory notes can be used in papers that have parenthetical citations.
4. If explanations are needed when the paper has footnote or endnote citations, explanatory information can be added after the citation or can stand alone with its own raised number.
5. All endnotes or footnotes must be identified with a raised number in ascending order regardless of whether they are explanatory or merely reference a source.

AN EXAMPLE OF AN EXPLANATORY NOTE

Media influence on political behavior has become increasingly noticeable.[1] For example, by analyzing a set of opinion polls, Lipset and Schneider show that news coverage shapes peoples attitudes about important political actors as well as people's perspectives on political events. The poll results suggest that people have lost confidence in big government, big business, and big labor due to exploitative news coverage about each.[2]

---

[1]The major point of debate over how media influences political behavior is over how information is processed. Some studies show that people read selectively and absorb very little of the news. See Doris Graber, *Processing the News: How People Tame the Information Tide*, NY: Longman, 1984.

[2]Seymour Martin Lipset and William Schneider, *The Confidence Gap: Business, Labor, and Government in the Public Mind*, Rev. Ed., MD: Johns Hopkins University Press, 1987.

FORMAT FOR QUOTATIONS

1.   Quotations are sets of information which have been copied verbatim from a source.
2.   Quotations should be used very very very sparingly and only when absolutely necessary.
     - Rule of thumb: avoid quotes altogether.
     - Rule of thumb: do not use more than two quotations for every ten pages of text.
3.   Quotations must be cited with an exact page number.
4.   Quotations that are shorter than three lines long should be placed between quotation marks (at the beginning and the end) and the citation placed after the ending quotation mark.
5.   Quotations that are longer than four lines long should be single spaced and indented 10 spaces on the left and right margins. The citation is placed after the last sentence of the quotation.
6.   Quotations should never be used as a substitute for writing or synthesizing information.
7.   Quotations must be introduced or framed into the text in some way.
     - one way is to identify the author or work directly or indirectly.
     - another way is to explain why the words that are being quoted are significant.
8.   Use quotes:
     - when the exact wording of a statement or point is crucial to the meaning of it.
     - to preserve distinctive phrasing or eloquence of a point.

EXAMPLE OF A SHORT QUOTE

Media influence on political behavior has been argued to be minimal until recently[1]. Some scholars argue that news coverage shapes people's attitudes about important political actors as well as people's perspectives on political events. For example, Lipset and Schneider (1987) found that, "...interest group leaders had an incentive to maintain a high level of criticism..." in the media to justify their positions (p. 405). Lipset and Schneider conclude that people have lost confidence in big government, big business, and big labor due to exploitative news coverage about each of them.

---

[1] The major point of debate over how media influences political behavior is over how information is processed. Some studies show that people read selectively and absorb very little of the news. See Doris Graber, *Processing the News: How People Tame the Information Tide*, NY: Longman, 1984.

EXAMPLE OF A LONG QUOTE

Media influence on political behavior has been argued to be minimal until recently[1]. Studies show that media is the major source of political information. Lipset and Schneider (1987) suggest that television carries with it a special consideration and influence in providing information to the public.

> The special impact of television is that it delivers the news to a much larger and 'inadvertent' audience than was the case before television, when only a limited segment of the population chose to follow news about politics and government. When people read newspapers and magazines, they edit the information by skipping over articles about subjects they are not interested in. Television watchers however, are exposed to everything. (Lipset and Schneider 1987, p. 405).

They conclude that people's attitudes have changed toward big government, big business, and big labor due to exploitative news coverage about them.

------

[1]The major point of debate over how media influences political behavior is over how information is processed. Some studies show that people read selectively and absorb very little of the news. See Graber 1984.

FORMAT FOR THE REFERENCE PAGE

1. Place the reference page (Bibliography or Works Cited) after the endnotes or after the last page of text in the absence of an appendix or endnotes.
2. A bibliography is the same as a works cited or reference page.
3. Do not separate the books from the articles. All references should be listed together in alphabetical order by the last name of the author.
4. All sources used for the assignment must be listed on the reference page.
5. All the sources listed should be typed using a hanging paragraph. A hanging paragraph has the first line flush with the margin (left justified) and all remaining lines indented five spaces.
6. Stylebooks differ on the order and punctuation of the source information, so check with the instructor for suggestions on which stylebook to use.
7. For multiple sources by one author, use a line five spaces in length instead of the author's name on the subsequent entry.
8. Citations listed on a reference page must have the following information separated by periods (adapted from Kalvelage, et al. 1984; Harnack and Kleppinger 1998):

Books:
- the author's full name, last name first
- the complete title (underlined or in italics)
- underlined the editor's name (if any)
- the edition (if it is not the first)
- the name and number of the series (if any)
- the place of publication
- the name of the publisher
- the date of publication

Articles:
- the author's full name, last name first
- the title of the article (in quotation marks)
- the name of the periodical (underlined or in italics)
- the volume number of the periodical
- the date of the periodical
- the page numbers of the article

Internet:
- author's name (if available)
- title of the document (in quotation marks)
- title of the complete site (underlined or in italics)
- date of the posting or last revision
- volume number (if any)
- date of access
- URL in angle brackets

EXAMPLES OF COMMON BIBLIOGRAPHIC REFERENCES

Here is a comparison of bibliography style formats for three popular style guides: these guides are *The Chicago Manual of Style* which is used by the American Political Science Association, *Publication Manual of the American Psychological Association,* and *MLA Handbook for Writers of Research Papers.* **Once a format is chosen, students must use the same format throughout the references.** For formatting information concerning document types not listed below, please see the following Web sites or books.

Chicago Manual

Chicago Manual of Style FAQ, <http://www.press.uchicago.edu/Misc/Chicago/cmosfaq.html>
Chicago Manual of Style. 1993. 14th ed. Chicago: University of Chicago Press.

APA

American Psychological Association. <http://www.apa.org/journals/faq.html>
Publication Manual of the American Psychological Association. 1994. 4th edition. Washington DC:
    American Psychological Association.

MLA

Modern Language Association (MLA). *Publication Manual FAQ* <http://www.mla.org/main.stl.htm>
Modern Language Association. *How to Cite Information From the World Wide Web*. (MLA)
    <http://www.apa.org/journals/webref.html>
Gibaldi, Joseph. 1995. *MLA Handbook for Writers of Research Papers*, 4th ed. NY: The Modern Language
    Association of America.

For a book.

Chicago Manual
Shafritz, Jay M. 1988. *The Dictionary of American Government and Politics*. Chicago, IL: Dorsey Press.

APA
Shafritz, Jay M. (1988). *The Dictionary of American Government and Politics*. Chicago, IL: Dorsey Press.

MLA
Shafritz, Jay M. *The Dictionary of American Government and Politics*. Chicago, IL: Dorsey Press, 1988.

For a journal article paginated by volume (page numbers begin at 1 for the first issue and continue in the next issue with the ending page number from the first issue).

Chicago Manual
Costantini, Edmond. 1990. "Political Women and Political Ambition: Closing the Gender Gap," *American
    Journal of Political Science*, 34: 741-770.

APA
Costantini, Edmond. (1990). Political Women and Political Ambition: Closing the Gender Gap, *American
    Journal of Political Science*, 34, 741-770.

MLA
Costantini, Edmond. "Political Women and Political Ambition: Closing the Gender Gap," *American Journal
    of Political Science*, 34 (1990): 741-770.

For a journal article paginated by issue (page numbers begin at 1 for each issue).

Chicago Manual
Coast, James. 1974. "Environmentally Safe Insecticides," *Consumer Digest*, 23, no. 2: 25-32.

APA
Coast, James. (1974). Environmentally Safe Insecticides, *Consumer Digest*, *23*, (2), 25-32.

MLA
Coast, James. "Environmentally Safe Insecticides," *Consumer Digest*, 23.2 (1974): 25-32.

For an article in an edited book.

Chicago Manual
Heclo, Hugh. 1978. "Issue Networks and the Executive Establishment." In *The New American Political System*. Edited by Anthony King. Washington, DC: American Enterprise Institute For Policy Research.

APA
Heclo, Hugh. (1978). Issue Networks and the Executive Establishment. In Anthony King (Ed.), *The New American Political System* (pp. 51-84). Washington, DC: American Enterprise Institute For Policy Research.

MLA
Heclo, Hugh. "Issue Networks and the Executive Establishment." *The New American Political System*. Ed. Anthony King. Washington, DC: American Enterprise Institute For Policy Research, 1978.

For an article with three authors in an edited book that is part of a series.

Chicago Manual
Gunth Werner, Wolfgang Leininger, and Gunther Stephen. 1988. "On Supergames and Folk Theorems: A Conceptual Discussion." In *Game Equilibrium Models*. Vol. 2, *Game Theory in the Behavioral Sciences,* no. 19, edited by Reinhart Selten. Germany: Bielefeld University Press.

APA
Gunth Werner, Wolfgang Leininger, and Gunther Stephen. (1988). On Supergames and Folk Theorems: A Conceptual Discussion. In Reinhart Selten (Ed.), *Game Equilibrium Models: Vol. 2. Game Theory in the Behavioral Sciences no. 19.* Germany: Bielefeld University Press.

MLA

Gunth Werner, Wolfgang Leininger, and Gunther Stephen. "On Supergames and Folk Theorems: A
    Conceptual Discussion." In Reinhart Selten (Ed.), *Game Equilibrium Models*. Vol. 2. Game Theory
    in the Behavioral Sciences no. 19. Germany: Bielefeld University Press, 1988.

For multiple works by an author:

Chicago Manual

Chubb' John E. 1988. "Politics, Markets, and the Organization of Schools," *American Political Science
    Review*, 82: 1065-87.
Chubb' John E. and Terry Moe. 1990. *Politics, Markets, and America's Schools*. Washington, DC:
    Brookings.

APA

Chubb' John E. (1988). Politics, Markets, and the Organization of Schools, *American Political Science
    Review*, 82, 1065-87.
Chubb' John E. and Terry Moe. 1990. *Politics, Markets, and America's Schools*. Washington, DC:
    Brookings.

MLA

Chubb' John E. "Politics, Markets, and the Organization of Schools," *American Political Science Review*, 82
    (1988): 1065-87.
Chubb' John E. and Terry Moe. *Politics, Markets, and America's Schools*. Washington, DC: Brookings,
    1990.

For a government document:

Chicago Manual

U. S. Congress. House. Committee on Foreign Relations. 1985. *Report on Aid to South Africa*. 98th Cong.
    2nd sess. Washington, DC: Government Printing Office.

APA

U. S. Congress. House. Committee on Foreign Relations. (1985). *Report on Aid to South Africa*. 98th
    Cong. 2nd sess. Washington, DC: Government Printing Office.

MLA

U. S. Congress. House. Committee on Foreign Relations. *Report on Aid to South Africa*. 98th Cong. 2nd
    sess. Washington, DC: GPO, 1985.

For a newspaper or magazine article.

Chicago Manual

Greenberger, Robert S. 1981. "Hottest Labor Consultant in Washington Adopts New Right Techniques to
    Bolster Union's Image." *The Wall Street Journal*, 23 October, 3.

APA

Greenberger, Robert S. (23 October 1981). Hottest Labor Consultant in Washington Adopts New Right
    Techniques to Bolster Union's Image. *The Wall Street Journal*, p. 3.

MLA

Greenberger, Robert S. "Hottest Labor Consultant in Washington Adopts New Right Techniques to Bolster
    Union's Image." *The Wall Street Journal*, 23 October 1981: 3.

For a source with no author.

Chicago Manual

"Dr. King's Widow Testifies in a Civil Trial" 1999. *The New York Times*, 17 November, A16.

APA

"Dr. King's Widow Testifies in a Civil Trial," (1999, 17 November). *The New York Times,* p. A16.

MLA

"Dr. King's Widow Testifies in a Civil Trial," *The New York Times* 17 November 1999: A16.

For an Internet Source:

General Web site:

Chicago Manual

Agius, Raymond. 1999. "Quality and Audit in Occupational Health." *Health, Environment and Work*. May.
    <http://www.med.ed.ac.uk.HEW/quality.html> (8 June 1999).

APA

Agius, Raymond. (1999, May) Quality and Audit in Occupational Health. *Health, Environment and Work.*
    <http://www.med.ed.ac.uk.HEW/quality.html> (8 June 1999).

MLA

Agius, Raymond. "Quality and Audit in Occupational Health." May 1999. *Health, Environment and Work.*
        <http://www.med.ed.ac.uk.HEW/quality.html> (8 June 1999).

Organizational Web site:

Chicago Manual

AFL-CIO. 1999. *Working Families Need a Voice: Who's Behind It?* 14 January.
        <http://www.aflcio.org/silence/behind.html> (19 July 1999).

APA

AFL-CIO. (1999, January 14). *Working Families Need a Voice: Who's Behind It?*
        <http://www.aflcio.org/silence/behind.html> (19 July 1999).

MLA

AFL-CIO. *Working Families Need a Voice: Who's Behind It?* 14 January 1999.
        <http://www.aflcio.org/silence/behind.html> (19 July 1999).

Electronic Journal Web site:

Chicago Manual

"Clinton Proposes Increased Child Care Subsidies." 1999. *Amarillo Business Journal*, 3, no. 2.
        <http://businessjournal.net/stories/020698/child.html>(25 August 1999).

APA

Clinton Proposes Increased ChildCare Subsidies. (1999). *Amarillo Business Journal*, 3, no. 2.
        <http://businessjournal.net/stories/020698/child.html>(25 August 1999).

MLA

"Clinton Proposes Increased Child Care Subsidies." *Amarillo Business Journal*, 3, no. 2. (1999).
        <http://businessjournal.net/stories/020698/child.html>(25 August 1999).

Electronic Magazine Web site:

`Chicago Manual`
Rosenberg, Debra. 1999. "More Than Just a Kiss: Hillary's Conflicted Life as First Lady and Candidate,"
        Newsweek, 22 November. <http://www.newsweek.com/nw-srv/printed/us/na/a55101-
        1999nov14.htm> (17 November 1999).

`APA`
Rosenberg, Debra. (1999, November 22). More Than Just a Kiss: Hillary's Conflicted Life as First Lady and
        Candidate, *Newsweek*, <http://www.newsweek.com/nw-srv/printed/us/na/a55101-1999nov14.htm>
        (17 November 1999).

`MLA`
Rosenberg, Debra. "More Than Just a Kiss: Hillary's Conflicted Life as First Lady and Candidate,"
        Newsweek, 22 November 1999. <http://www.newsweek.com/nw-srv/printed/us/na/a55101-
        1999nov14.htm> (17 November 1999).

Government site:

`Chicago Manual`
National Labor Relations Board. 1999. *National Labor Relations Board Members*. 17 February.
        <http://www.nlrb.gov/members.html> (14 July 1999).

`APA`
National Labor Relations Board. (1999, 17 February). *National Labor Relations Board Members*.
        <http://www.nlrb.gov/members.html> (14 July 1999).

`MLA`
National Labor Relations Board. *National Labor Relations Board Members*. 17 February 1999.
        <http://www.nlrb.gov/members.html> (14 July 1999).

Personal site:

Chicago Manual

Brown, Jon. "Homepage." 1998. 24 October. <http://www.polsci.swms.edu/brown/personal.htm> (8 July
    1999).

APA

Brown, Jon. Homepage. (1998, 24 October). <http://www.polsci.swms.edu/brown/personal.htm> (8 July
    1999).

MLA

Brown, Jon. "Homepage." 24 October 1998. <http://www.polsci.swms.edu/brown/personal.htm> (8 July
    1999).

For Electronic Databases.

Chicago Manual

National Labor Relations Board. 1997. Impact of Budget Cuts. April. Washington, DC: Author. Retrieved
    from SIRS database. SIRS. Government Reporter. CD-ROM. Spring 1997 release.

APA

National Labor Relations Board. (1997, April). Impact of Budget Cuts. Washington, DC: Author. Retrieved
    from SIRS database. SIRS. Government Reporter. CD-ROM. Spring 1997 release.

MLA

National Labor Relations Board. Impact of Budget Cuts. April 1997. Washington, DC: Author. Retrieved
    from SIRS database. SIRS. Government Reporter. CD-ROM. Spring 1997 release.

For Personal Interviews.

Chicago Manual
Simon, Paul. 1998. Personal Interview. 12 August.

APA
Simon, Paul. (1998, 12 August). Personal Interview.

MLA
Simon, Paul. Personal Interview. 12 August 1998.

SECTION EIGHT

FORMAT AND EXAMPLES FOR ACTIVITIES TO ENHANCE COMPREHENSION AND SYNTHESIS OF CLASS MATERIALS

ENHANCING COMPREHENSION AND SYNTHESIS OF CLASS MATERIALS

Instructors often require special kinds of assignments to help prepare students for professional research and to develop analytical skills. Rather than simply reading the material and taking a test on the facts, or writing a descriptive term paper or essay, students are asked to process the information in some way that will help them to synthesize the material for use later on. Sometimes the assignments just enhance comprehension and understanding of a particular concept or theory. In particular, the assignments are structured to help students develop research and problem solving skills. Developing such skills encourages students to integrate and synthesize the material in a meaningful and productive way.

Although many of the standards and rules that apply to research papers and essays apply to special assignments, there are some differences. These differences are generally found in the purpose and properties of each kind of activity. The following descriptions encompass a traditional approach to each assignment. Be sure to consult your instructor for specific requirements that are additional to those described in this section. Each description is followed by a written example.

List of special activities described in this section

ANALYTICAL ESSAYS

ANALYTICAL MULTIPLE CHOICE QUESTIONS

ESSAY EXAMS

LITERATURE REVIEW PRESENTATIONS

WRITING AN ANALYTICAL ESSAY

Analytical essays are usually very limited assignments. Like essay exam answers, they are meant to be brief but well reasoned and thorough examinations of some political theory, phenomenon, or behavior. Like a research paper, the evidence used to support an argument in an analytical essay should be source based. Most often, the instructor provides sources material in a reader or class packet. Sometimes instructors provide students with a particular question to answer or debate using course materials. The students are to take a position and support it using expert opinion. Here is a description of how to construct an analytical essay.

1. **Examine the limits and expectations stated by the instructor for the assignment**.

   - If a particular question must be answered, be sure you understand the context, limitations, and focus of the question before researching.
   - If a particular set of readings is required as sources for the essay, be sure that you have read it at least once while focusing on the issues required by the instructor.
   - Before using any materials other than those required or suggested by the instructor, ask the instructor if it is permissible to include additional sources.

2. **After reading the material, formulate an answer to the question.**

   - Use the introduction for briefly describing the context in which you are answering the question.
   - State your position clearly in a thesis statement.
   - Summarize the answer to the question in one sentence.
   - Be sure that the thesis sentence provides both an answer and a justification or reason.
   - Avoid vague or ambiguous thesis sentences.
   - Be bold, be obvious, be direct but do not be rhetorical!

3. **Use the assigned material as evidence supporting each reason you stated in your position.**

   - Do not outline the articles or materials used as a source.
   - Assert one idea or one justification of your position per paragraph.
   - Use the assigned material to support your assertion.
   - Use the assigned material to provide examples if necessary.
   - Avoid quoting altogether.
   - Summarize the sources' viewpoints in two or less sentences.

4.   **Write a conclusion that re-asserts your position.**

- Briefly review the main reasons why your position is valid.
- Offer some suggestion about the value of examining the issue identified in the assignment or question given to you by the instructor.

5.   **A standard two page analytical essay should be no longer than six paragraphs.**
- The essay should have an introduction, an explanatory paragraph for each reason given, and a conclusion.
- Be concise and do not waste words.

EXAMPLE OF ANALYTICAL ESSAYS

"WHY SHOULD WE WORRY ABOUT A JUDGE'S IDEOLOGY IF JUDICIAL DECISIONS ARE BASED ON PRECEDENT AND THE CONSTITUTION?"

AN ANALYTICAL ESSAY

By
Jean M. Schuberth
Professor Schmidt
GEB 114, SEC. 3
NOVEMBER 29, 1990
(Reprinted with permission)

Judicial review has been considered a political issue since the framing of the constitution. Supreme Court justices interpreted policy and used judicial discretion to define law and to set or overturn precedents. As a nation of people who believe in limited government and equal protection, discretion with which a judge makes decisions is at the source of concern over judicial power. In particular, if well harnessed by an ideological coalition, the act of interpreting law leaves significant opportunity for abuse of judicial power and the introduction of political bias.

Alexander Hamilton believed that the judicial system was the least powerful of the three branches of government. He argued that the court's power did not outweigh the other branches by interpreting the law because it was bound to interpretations that are consistent to the constitution. Hamilton stated that the legislative branch had controlled the money and "prescribes" the laws and rights of the community (Hamilton, 567). This statement, however, was irrelevant to the power of interpreting law. Interpreting laws prescribes laws and rights to the people as well by ruling what can and cannot be done constitutionally. American history reflects an important change in rights and obligations when judicial decisions over-rule precedent as being unfair and unconstitutional (Marbury v. Madison, 573).

A judge's ideology is significant from the standpoint that the Supreme Court makes law. Because judges are empowered to interpret the law, they have the opportunity to substitute their personal interpretation of laws. They control not only how laws are interpreted but also when precedents apply to a case. Only when judicial self-restraint is being utilized for the sake of non-confrontation and non-intervention will a judge's views seem unbiased (Roche, 577). Even then, it is questionable that precedent in this case, as interpreted by justices, does not exist. Self-restraint allows the opportunity for a coalition of judges to interpret policy again later when a stronger case representing their ideological viewpoints can be used to overturn decisions. A passive attitude by the judiciary can reflect as much ideological input as one which is dominated by an activist court (Roche, 581).

Supreme Court decisions are supposed to be reasoned by precedent and constitutionality. Unfortunately, interpretation of the constitution depends on individual justices to put aside their individual perspectives. Justices are obliged to overcome personal needs, use authority responsibility, and at the same time reinterpret, give new definition, reword, and revise the law (Brennan, 583). This is nearly impossible to do. Consequently, judicial decisions reflect a personal ideology based upon individual moral and ethical beliefs experienced as a member of society. Because the role of the Supreme Court judge involves not only interpretation but choosing which issues to try under law (Brennan, 585), the choice and processing of cases often reflect judges community or environmental experiences. Based upon the legitimate excuse that the thousands of cases received are too many to handle, judicial discretion is necessary for managing and controlling the judicial agenda. In this process, a decision to rule on a case or not necessarily will reflect a judge's ideology, if not biases.

The American constitution, as the law of the land, is a remarkable document with elaborate checks to constrain particular interests abusing power or exhibiting political favoritism at a minority's expense. The judicial branch has not special exemption to these checks. Unfortunately, judicial decisions are as difficult to question as they are to overturn. Individual biases are masked by the aura of an interpreted constitutionality and enhanced by coalitions within the Supreme Court who set, decide, and pursue political agendas reflecting their individual moral and political beliefs. A judge's ideology is as important to safeguarding political rights and protections because, in coalition, a judge's ideology is the mechanism that helps to define what the constitution means as well as what principles and precedents apply to interpreting the constitution.

WORKS CITED

(All references taken from Peter Woll, ed., *American Government: Readings and Cases*, 10th ed., Glenview, IL: Scott Foresman/Little Brown Higher Education, 1990.)

Brennan Jr., William J. "How the Supreme Court Arrives at Decisions," pp. 603-613.
Hamilton, Alexander. " Federalist 78," pp. 566-570.
"Marbury v Madison (1803)," pp. 571-575.
Roche, John P. "Judicial Self-Restraint," pp. 576-582.

WRITING POLITICAL EDITORIALS

Editorials, like analytical essays, are usually very limited assignments. Also like analytical essays, they are meant to be brief but well-reasoned examinations of some specific phenomenon or behavior. Unlike an analytical essay or a research paper, the evidence used to support an argument in an analytical essay need not be source based. Unlike the analytical essay, the tone and language used is casual, emotive, and value ladened. Most often, editorials are composed of more opinion than fact in the evidence and reasoning. In other words, they are thoughtful expressions of the author's **views** on political phenomena. The purpose of the editorial is not only to express views but also to persuade others to adopt the same views. Writing editorials, even if they are not published, helps students work on critical thinking and political argument techniques without the constraints of sources and secondary evidence. The students are to take a position and support it using reasons, logic, and, yes, even facts if necessary! Here is a description of how to construct an editorial.

Formulating an Opinion

1. **Identify and research an important salient issue.**
   - The best editorials are those that exhibit knowledge, authority, and passion about issue.
   - Use course materials for background information.
   - Talk to people and read about the issue in a variety of sources.
   - Gather ideas and viewpoints; analyze them on the bases of credibility.
2. **Formulate a *reasoned* opinion.**
   - Students must have a reason for every assertion they make in the editorial.
   - Every assertion must have a justification.
   - Assert one idea or one justification of your position per paragraph.
   - Assertions without reasons and justifications can be easily ignored.
3. **Keep in mind most editorials are only about 300 to 600 words.**
   - Use a highly emotive, assertive, active voice with a tone of conviction.
   - Avoid jargon and formal language.
   - Keep the paragraphs and sentences short and simple.

Format for the Editorial

While there is no set format for an editorial, most editorials generally follow a pattern. The order and number of the paragraphs can be changed a bit with the exception of the first and last paragraph. Often, people read only the first and last paragraphs of editorials in the newspaper. Because of this, the first and last paragraphs contain a concise but compelling assertion about what the issue is (the first paragraph) and what should be done about it (the last paragraph). All the material between these two important paragraphs serve as justification for the assertions.

1. **First paragraph:**
    - Begin the editorial with a controversial or compelling example or comment.
    - State succinctly what is wrong or right about a decision made or action taken concerning the issue.
    - Tell what should be done.
2. **Second paragraph:**
    - Provide context or background information about the event.
    - Focus on what happened before the event.
    - State why what happened before was better or worse than the event at issue.
3. **Third paragraph:**
    - Tell how the current situation is in opposition or contrary to the previous situation.
    - Explain concisely how the current situation differs from the past practices.
4. **Fourth paragraph:**
    - Provide more contextual examples.
    - Provide more examples that are illustrative of the issue at its worst.
    - Provide a compelling anecdote.
5. **Fifth paragraph:**
    - State strongly why you believe that this situation (policy, etc.) is good or bad.
    - Provide reasons for your assertions.
    - Provide a solution to help resolve the issue.
6. **Sixth paragraph:**
    - Forecast or suggest what will happen because of this situation.
    - Tell what the future will look like if the situation is left unchanged.
7. **Seventh paragraph:**
    - Restate why the result of an unchanged situation is good or bad.
    - Provide reasons for why it is good or bad.
8. **Last paragraph:**
    - Restate the issue.
    - Restate your opinion about how to resolve the issue.
    - End with a compelling statement or rhetorical question.

EXAMPLE OF AN EDITORIAL

YOUNG VOICES

JUST A HOUSEWIFE? THINK ABOUT IT A BIT LONGER!

What's your impression of this ad? CEO wanted for nonprofit organization: Duties: budget planning and administration, task delegation, scheduling of activities, training and teaching, implementation of the nutrition program plus miscellaneous duties. Prerequisites: enormous patience, organizational skill, flexibility, ability to handle emergencies efficiently, and an abundance of love and devotion. This position is voluntary, unpaid, and not highly regarded by society.

Who in their right mind would work for no pay? Believe it or not, there are millions of women out there who do this every day. Their title may not be CEO; on the contrary, they all too often refer to themselves as "just a housewife." Why is this honorable profession so terribly underrated in our society? It may just be envy.

Like so many moms on campus, we try to do it all yet we always feel inadequate. Somehow, it is never enough. Besides, it is very unfashionable to admit that what some of us really want is a family old-fashioned style; it's almost like saying a dirty word.

Women have made great strides for equality and shouldn't face any societal barriers to reaching their full potential. But I think the scale has tipped to where we have to do it all in order to be appreciated.

Just look at the Republican-crafted Welfare Reform Bill. All it accomplishes is forcing mothers out of the home away from small kids who are still in their most impressionable years. Mostly single mothers are affected by this and are not considered in the Republican emphasis on family values.

This implies that it's more acceptable for a mother to have a career than to be a housewife and mother, regardless of marital status. This sentiment even includes men. With few, but very notable exceptions, men on the average don't want to solely provide for a family. It seems to trigger the "fight or flight response," just like the M-word. What contributed to this? Do they feel that women have expectations they can't fulfill?

Maybe we as a group portray that image by chasing after high-paying/high-prestige careers—like the one I am chasing out of pure necessity.

A satisfying career has its definite rewards, but it still falls short of the joys of full-time motherhood. I had a glimpse of that during my maternity leave.

My daughter is now 3 years old and I'm used to this rat race, but I still long for baking cookies with Santa Faces, ironing a crease into a pair of suit pants right where it belongs (I do know how to do that stuff), cooking a meal that appeals to adult taste buds and is not yet another variety of Hamburger Helper, and asking a stressed-out, grumpy, traditional male prototype how his day went.

I'm not advocating the burning of Betty Friedan's "Feminine Mystique," nor have I just discovered that my childbearing years are down to single digits or overdosed on gender studies.

This doesn't come from an escapee from the conservative camp, but from a woman who benches 175 pounds, has fired a machine gun for a living, and hopes for the cloning of Hillary Rodham Clinton. Now that I have confessed and come out of the closet, the National Organization for Women will probably put a contract out on me.

It's just about choices. Choices subtly diminish once the maternal side kicks in, and one soon discovers that the day really has only 24 hours.

I'm far from saying that the three Ks (Kinder, Kueche, and Kirche) are for all women, but defying nature carries a cost that I'm getting tired of bearing.

Christine N. Rueda-Lynn is a columnist for *The Southwest Standard* at Southwest Missouri State University.
Reprinted in
Springfield News Leader
Dec. 1, 1997, p. 8a
(Reprinted by permission)

ANALYTICAL MULTIPLE CHOICE EXAMS

Although taking exams is not considered a special assignment, taking an analytical multiple choice exam is different from the average multiple-choice exam. Performing well on an analytical multiple choice exam, students must use the same skills they use in essay writing.

- These exams require knowledge, good reading habits, and critical thinking skills.
- In analytical multiple choice questions, there are no funny answers, no "all of the above," no "none of the above," and no questions where students must find the wrong answer in the group.
- Students must differentiate between closely related information or concepts.
- Students must understand how information, concepts, and explanations of political behavior or events are influenced by the context in which they are examined.
- The answers to analytical multiple-choice questions can rarely be guessed.
- The answers require well-reasoned responses and rarely exhibit a pattern.

Tips for Answering Analytical Multiple Choice Questions

The questions used in an analytical multiple choice exam are typically either factual, definitional, conceptual, or are practical applications. They are best approached as essay questions! Do the following before answering the question.

1.   **Determine what kind of question is being asked.**

2.   **Identify the important modifiers and qualifiers in the question.**
     - If you are allowed to write on the exam question sheet, underline the key words or concepts and circle the modifiers and qualifiers.
       - Exact words such as *always, never, none, must, necessarily*, and *without exception* mean there is no exception. If you can think of one exception, statements including these are false.
       - Indefinite words, such as *rarely, usually, seldom, some, sometimes, often,* and *frequently* suggest that the statement is true in context. How often it is true depends on the degree connoted by the indefinite word used.
     - Think about how these words change or influence the meaning of the concepts or facts listed.

3. **Cover the answers or do not look at them until you think of an answer.**
    - ♦ If you are allowed to write on the exam question sheet, make a quick list of the properties of the concept, theory, document, or whatever is the focus of the question. At least visualize the answer.
    - ♦ Use critical thinking skills and logic to reason the answer if you are unsure of the correct answer to the question.
      - • Do not let personal value judgements and ideology sway you.
      - • Often these questions provoke biased responses and those responses are usually wrong!
      - • Visualize an answer that conforms to what the instructor intended.
    - ♦ Then look at the list of responses available.
      - • Match your answer with the list of responses.
      - • If your answer does not match exactly with one of the choices then find the choice that most closely approximates your answer.
      - • If you are still in doubt, re-read the question and use logical reasoning to find the answer.
      - • If you are still in doubt, use a process of elimination by considering the deficiencies in each choice available. Choose the one with the fewest problems.

4. **Never leave a question blank unless you will lose more points for answering questions wrong than for answering them correctly. This is generally not true of political science course exams.**

5. **Do not hurry but do not linger too long. Answer the question and move on. Make a note to return to questions with doubtful answers after you have finished the exam.**

EXAMPLES OF ANALYTICAL MULTIPLE-CHOICE TEST QUESTIONS

FACTUAL

> The Constitution establishes three policy making institutions:
>
> A. the House, the bureaucracy, and the presidency.
> B. Congress, the presidency, and the courts.
> C. Congress, the presidency, and the presidential cabinet.
> D. Congress, the presidency, and the bureaucracy.

This question requires both depth and breadth of understanding about what the constitution establishes and what bodies make public policy. The important modifiers are the words establishes and policy making. A and D are incorrect because the bureaucracy was not established by the constitution as a policy making institution. C is incorrect because the presidency includes the cabinet. B is the answer because all three institutions make decisions that result in policy.

DEFINITION

> _____ is a means of selecting policy makers and of organizing government so that policy represents and responds to the majority of the people's preferences.
>
> A. Populism
> B. Pure Democracy
> C. Socialism
> D. Representative Democracy

This question requires an understanding of theoretical concepts. The important modifiers in this question are "means of selecting," "organizing government," "represents," and "responds to." A is incorrect because populism is an ideology not a system of government. C is incorrect because socialism is really an economic system and does not help to organize representative government. B is incorrect because pure democracy does not organize representative government. Only D is correct because under representative democracy policy makers answer to an electorate.

CONCEPTUAL

In the American electorate, the majority of voters are:

    A. moderately liberal.
    B. moderates.
    C. moderately libertarian.
    D. moderately conservative.

This question taps into the reader's personal ideology, value system, and the median voter concept. The important modifier is majority. For some students, the answer may seem to be a matter of perspective. Unfortunately, the answer, which is supported by numerous studies of the voters, is B. Answers A and D are a matter of degree. C is incorrect because libertarians are a very small portion of the electorate.

APPLICATION

It is up to political elites in public office to actually make policy choices for the majority because American government is _____ rather than a pure democracy.

    A. majoritarian
    B. representative
    C. pluralist
    D. elitist

This question asks students to apply what they know about who makes decisions in different kinds of democracies. The important modifiers are "actually make policy choice." The words "elites" and "majority" are not modifiers, they identify who is doing what for whom. The answer requires that the student understand the four terms well enough to apply them. C and D are incorrect because they are different theories of politics; they are not theories of the organization of government and decision making. Although our government is majoritarian, in a majoritarian government, the majority makes the rules. In our system, representatives make decisions for the majority. This means B is the answer.

ESSAY EXAMS

Many students are uneasy with essay exams. Although they may write well, they are reluctant to take essay tests because it may not be clear what is expected. Essay exams are another way of synthesizing information. Here are a couple of suggestions for reading and interpreting an answer to an essay question.

1. **An essay question may contain one or more important terms. (See Writing a Thesis for an Essay) For example, here is an essay question concerning the congressional budget process:**

> "Describe and analyze the budget process.
> Provide reasons why each step exists."

   In this case, the student must be careful to address **all** parts of the question. Just listing the information is not enough; the student must also demonstrate knowledge of why each step is important.

2. **Students must be careful, especially when answering questions that ask for criticisms or evaluations, that each assertion (or point) is supported with evidence or examples.**

3. The question should be answered directly. Underline the key verbs and modifiers which structure or limit the scope of the question.

4. The thesis sentence of an answer to this essay question should repeat the key terms of the question and lay out the writer's main points.

   - In short essays, the thesis sentence should be the first sentence.
   - In longer essays, the thesis should be in the first paragraph.

5. Address only one idea per paragraph.

   - Be sure to use a topic sentence, an explanatory sentence, and a summary sentence in each paragraph.
   - Use transitional words, such as *first, second, in addition*, or *thus* to organize and link ideas from paragraph to paragraph.
   - Most importantly, be obvious--do not be obtuse. Make your points clearly, simply, and directly.

6.   Time and space are usually limited during an essay exam so students must use them efficiently.
- If each essay contributes equally to the grade, then divide the number of essays by the number of minutes and allot equal amounts to each.
- If each essay does not contribute equally to the grade, determine the amount of time to spend on each by the proportion of each essay's contribution to the grade.

SAMPLE ANSWER TO AN ESSAY TEST QUESTION
(Reprinted with permission)

> Group theorists argue that public policy can be defined as the equilibrium that is reached in a group struggle. Explain this theory and offer an alternative, competing explanation of how public policy can be defined. Which one is preferable? Why?

By
Edward Pettit

Group theorists argue that public policy can be defined as the equilibrium that is reached in a group struggle. Explain this theory and offer an alternative, competing explanation of how public policy can be defined. Which one is preferable? Why?

Pluralist theory is only one of numerous such theories about how public policy is formulated. Though pluralist theory has its strong points, it does not explain how institutional structures constrain possible policy outcomes. Institutions theory offers a competing explanation about how policy is formulated. Unfortunately, institutions theory does not explain why public policy reflects the values of groups who are not part of the policy-making institution. Because of this, institutions theory can be considered less preferable than the pluralist theory for explaining policy making.

Pluralist theory essentially states that group struggle is the central force of politics, and that policies, including the goals, the means, and the outcomes, are directly attributable to group conflict. This theory states that individuals are important only when working in a group. Policy is defined, according to pluralist theory, as the compromise between competing groups and reflects the relative influence of each group. Although it does not account for why policy varies from institution to institution, it does explain why policy content reflects a dominant group's values.

In institutions theory, policy only results when a policy proposal is stated, adopted, implemented, and enforced by an institution. The institution provides a policy legitimacy, universality, and the coercive force necessary to enforce it equally across the populace. The structure of the policy-making institution provides both the means and constraints to formulating policy responses to public problems.

This policy definition is vastly different from the pluralist view because institutions, not people or groups, legitimize policy. It is, however, deficient because it does not state anything significant about policy content. Because policy content and institutional structure are not logically related, the institutional theory cannot explain why policy content benefits some more than others in society do. In the pluralist theory, policy content represents group struggle and the dominant group's influence over the policy response and related benefits. Thus, pluralist theory explains variations in policy responses and why some groups benefit at the public expense.

Both the pluralist and institutional models of policy formulation offer explanations of policy responses, but the pluralist model is more comprehensive because it explains, to a certain extent, not just how policy is made but why it was made. While the institutional model explains the formal processes of public policy making, it does not account for variations in policy content. Hence, although the process of policy making is important, pluralist theory models explain policy outcomes more directly and clearly than the institutional model.

SCHOLARLY LITERATURE REVIEW PRESENTATIONS

Class presentations on scholarly literature provide students the opportunity to examine different approaches and controversies not covered in the lectures or textbook. Often, the subject of the presentation is a scholarly article or book that provided a pathbreaking method or conceptual examination important to building a knowledge community in political science.

A literature review presentation typically includes the same material as a research presentation except that the expectations for a clear grasp of the content is somewhat lower than it would be for a description of a student's own research findings.

A literature review typically includes:

- a statement of the author's purpose.
- an identification of the author's hypothesis.
- a description of the issue context and assumptions.
- a description of the controversy.
- an explanation of how the controversy was examined.
- a description of the author's findings.
- a concluding statement about the significance of the work..

A literature review presentation is generally graded with the same criteria used to grade written assignments.

- Students' grades usually reflect the quality and thoroughness with which they presented the material contained in the categories listed.
- A literature review presentation is frequently graded on the degree to which the student identified the critical information provided in the scholarly book or article.
- A solid performance by the student demonstrates depth and breadth of understanding the significance of the work related to the subfield or topic area.

To write your presentation, outline the article or book using the above categories.

- The length and degree of detail in the presentation outline will depend on the time allotted for the presentation or the page limit set by the instructor.
- In general, the outline should be approximately two and a half pages typed in outline form.

Exhibit poise and confidence (try rehearsing).
- Be prepared to answer questions of clarification.
- Vary the voice level, make eye contact with other students, and use gestures.
- Do not read word for word from outline. Address the audience in a causal, conversational tone but avoid rambling from point to point.

LITERATURE PRESENTATION FORM

Purpose: a clear statement of the purpose and focus of the article or book.

Hypothesis: A clear statement of the controversy identified by the author and the hypothesis tested. State the causal relationships clearly in terms of dependent and independent variables.

Background: A brief discussion of the context and background related to the controversy or the assumptions used to justify the model. Note any value assumptions that are controversial in nature.

Method: An explanation of the method used for testing or examining the hypothesis.
- Describe the source materials used.
- Point out any problems identified by the author related to the gathering of data.
- Be sure to relate the data and source materials to the hypothesis.

Results: A summary of the results of the examination or test.
- If data were used, reproduce illustrative charts, graphs, or tables as visual aids.
- Use a table or chart to summarize the author's main points.
- Use an overhead projector to present the material or make copies of a visual aid for everyone.

Conclusion: This statement explains how the goals of the author were accomplished. In particular, this statement summarizes how the results relate to the author's stated goals.

Significance: A statement that applies the results appropriately to an expansion of knowledge about the subject.

EXAMPLE OF SCHOLARLY LITERATURE PRESENTATION

AN ARTICLE REVIEW

I.   **Purpose**: to review classic innovative article on voting.
      A.   **Source**: Gerald Kramer. 1971. "Short-term Fluctuations in U.S. Voting Behavior 1896-1964," *American Political Science Review*, 65: 131-143.
      B.   **Author's purpose**: to provide a quantitative analysis of short-term fluctuations in voting share for U.S. House of Representatives election with respect to the impact of economic conditions, incumbency advantage, and the presidential coattails effect.

II.   **Hypothesis**: Tests several competing and complementary hypotheses about influences on electoral outcomes. He argues that economic fluctuations have a greater impact on voting in House elections than political influences, such as coattail effects.

III. **Background:**
      A.   Author reviews some of the literature about influence on voting behavior.
            1.   Institutional advantage of the incumbent or incumbency advantage theory is problematic. Only an advantage when expectations are low for benefits. Could be a liability if expectations of voters' personal incomes not realized.
            2.   Party popularity may influence outcomes. House races come closest to Downesian model of anonymous candidates competing as members of a common team. Variations in overall popularity of the party could be a major factor in producing fluctuations in short-term voting behavior.
            3.   Incumbent party is usually defined, as the party of the president because the president's influence over the policy agenda is greater than that of an individual member of congress.
            4.   A vote for the minor party is considered an anti-incumbent vote and is counted as part of the major opposition party vote.
            5.   The coattails effect of a presidential race is reflected in the party as a team.

      B.   Author makes several assumptions about behavior.
            1.   An individual vote represents a choice between teams in the national election.
            2.   People base their decisions on past information.
            3.   People's expectations are based on the preceding year's events; they are retrospective not prospective voters.

IV.   **Method:** Uses statistical analysis to test relative impact of different influences on vote choice based on the literature review and methodological assumptions.
      A.   Model: States that the Republican party's share of a two-party vote is a function of incumbency, the difference between the actual and the expected performance, and net institutional advantage.
      B.   Creates a formal, testable model of voting behavior using the following variables.
            1.   Dependent variable: Republican party share of votes.
            2.   Independent variables: monetary income, real income, unemployment rate, time period, and coattails term.

    C.   Uses data gathered from 1896-1964.
        1.   Data collected from various government documents.
        2.   Left out years 1912 (inability to explain progressive votes) and 1918, 1942, and 1944 (wartime distortion of income and prices).

V.   **Results**: Used six different forms of the model as an equation to test his hypothesis.
    A.   The variables measuring expected prices and unemployment have an inverse relationship to the dependent variable.
    B.   All forms of the model explain a large portion of the variance in voting behavior.
        1.   Two-thirds of the variance explained by time variable.
        2.   Explanatory power of the model is weaker without the time variable. Only half of the variance is explained.
        3.   The income variable was significant and powerful in all the equations.
        4.   The price variable was only significant with the monetary variable but not with real income variable.
        5.   The unemployment variable was not significant and the direction of influence is counter to theory. Author proposes that unemployment variable is distorted because unemployed people are disproportionately less active politically.
        6.   Coattails variable was not significant. Author proposed that result was biased because the minor party vote was included in the measure because of split ticket voting. When minor party vote removed from coattail variable, it became significant.

VI.   **Overall finding** was that approximately one-third of the votes gained or lost in a presidential race are carried over into congressional candidate races.
    A.   Finds limits of the model. Model cannot identify or predict turning points in an election but can predict Republican vote shares.
    B.   The most important determinant of vote choice is income not incumbency advantage or coattails effect. A ten percent decrease in real income will lead to a four to five percent loss of votes for the incumbent party.
    C.   Coattails effect helps only when there is a strong presidential candidate. Can increase vote share by thirty percent.
    D.   The incumbent party only has advantage when the economy is doing well.

VII.   **Significance:**
    A.   Economic fluctuations are important to congressional elections. An upturn helps the incumbent and a downturn helps the challenger.
    B.   Found that election outcomes are more responsive to objective changes occurring under the incumbent party than to political changes.

SECTION NINE

FORMAT AND EXAMPLES OF ASSIGNMENTS FOR MANAGING AND PROCESSING INFORMATION

ASSIGNMENTS FOR MANAGING AND PROCESSING INFORMATION

> "We start out stupid. All we have at the beginning is the built-in wisdom of the body, which tells us which end to eat with...and not much more. But we are put here to do battle with entropy, and entropy equals stupidity. Therefore, we are obliged to learn. Our job is to process information and gain control of it: that is to say, to grow wiser as we go along" (Silverberg, p. 225).

As suggested by this quote, the soul of investigation is to control information. It is not enough to collect information for the sake of it. To become professionals, students must acquire the skills necessary for managing and processing information of interest to political scientists. A paper written by someone without a method, without good research skills, without problem solving skills, or without the ability to synthesize the information available, is not much better than amateur journalism.

To prepare students for more complex research, instructors often require students to do special kinds of assignments to help them prepare for professional research and develop analytical skills. Rather than simply reading the material and taking a test on the facts or writing a descriptive term paper or essay, students are asked to process the information in some way that will help them synthesize the material for use later on or just to enhance comprehension and understanding of a particular concept or theory. In particular, the assignments are structured to help students develop research and problem solving skills. More importantly, developing such skills encourages students to integrate and synthesize the material in a meaningful and productive way.

Although many of the standards and rules that apply to research papers and essays also apply to special assignments, there are some differences. These differences are generally found in the purpose and properties of each kind of assignment. The following descriptions encompass a traditional approach taken to complete each assignment. Be sure to consult your instructor for specific requirements that are additional to those described in this section. Each description is followed by a written example.

List of special assignments described in this section

> **ANNOTATED BIBLIOGRAPHIES**
> **BOOK REVIEWS**
> **BRIEFING CASES**
> **OUTLINES**
> **PRESENTATIONS**
> **RESEARCH PROPOSALS**

ANNOTATED BIBLIOGRAPHIES

Purpose of an Annotated Bibliography

An annotated bibliography is essentially a list of sources or materials (books, articles, etc.) that have been annotated and which relate to one topic. An annotation is a description of the purpose and significance of a source. More importantly, an annotated bibliography helps the student identify the thesis and the significance of research material in political science. It is often used to help students develop pre-writing skills. The research for the assignment should reflect a balance of sources. In addition, it should include scholarly books and articles.

Four Properties of an Annotated Bibliography

1. **Title Page**: The title page must be inclusive of the topic or subject of the annotated bibliography, the name of the student, the course number, the professor's name, and the date.
2. **Topic Paragraph**: On the second page, there must be a paragraph, at least three sentences long, that states the purpose of the annotated bibliography and a general summary of the sources' ideas.
3. **Sources**: The sources or entries are constructed with the same information as a standard bibliography, reference page, or works cited page and are listed in alphabetical order.
4. **Annotation**: An annotation is placed after the citation, skipping one line, and contains at least two full sentences stating:
    *   one sentence describing the purpose or thesis of the article or book.
    *   one sentence describing the significance of the findings and conclusions reached in the book or article.
    *   This assignment may be double spaced or single space. In general, the topic paragraph is single spaced. Students should double space between sources. The annotation to the reference should be single spaced.

AN EXAMPLE ANNOTATED BIBLIOGRAPHY

MEDIA AND POLITICS

Over the years, the media has grown in power and influence in the society and politics. This annotated bibliography lists sources that examine the relationship between media coverage of political events, freedom of the press, and changes in public opinion. In general, the literature shows that intrusive media coverage, while protected by the constitution, has the potential to shape the political outcomes.

Bennett, W. Lance. 1983. *News: The Politics of Illusion*. NY: Longman.
This author conducts an extensive examination of the impact of news coverage on political attitudes. He presents evidence that news coverage shapes the political agenda as well as people's perspectives on political events. He concludes that media, as political elites, influence what people think about.

Graber, Doris. 1984. *Processing the News: How People Tame the Information Tide*. NY: Longman.
This author conducted a study of news coverage of a campaign and changes in people's political awareness. She found that people accessed and remembered information selectively from news coverage depending on their personal interests.

Hallin, Daniel C. 1984. The Media, the War in Vietnam, and Political Support: A Critique of the Thesis of Oppositional Media, *Journal of Politics*, 46: 3-23.
This paper examines media as an institution that can be used to challenge political authority. He found that media shifted in the 1960s and 1970's toward an oppositional stance toward government.

Iyengar, Shanto. 1987. Television News and Citizen's Explanations of National Affairs, *American Political Science Review*, 81: 815-831.
This author argues that research into citizens' political explanations is an important new field for public opinion research. Iyengar found that citizens are able to identify the causes of complex national issues based on television coverage.

Keane, John. 1989. Citizenship and the Freedom of the Media, *The Political Quarterly*, 60: 285-296.
This author argues that policy decisions about the media are increasingly shaped by ideological views on individual choice, deregulation, and market competition. He presents evidence that competition among groups determines the definition of constraints on media freedom.

BOOK REVIEWS

Purpose of Book Review Assignments:

- To help students develop analytical skills in reading the primary literature in the field of political science.

- To provide an opportunity for students to identify main ideas of the book and help them examine the author's reasoning and evidence.

How to Write a Book Review:

1. Provide a complete reference inclusive of name, title, place of publication, publisher, and date.
2. Describe the subject, scope, and purpose of the book.
3. Summarize the author's thesis or hypothesis.
4. Identify the evidence used to support the thesis.
5. Summarize the author's conclusion.
6. Critique the argument.
   - is it logically sound?
   - is there a fair balance of opposing viewpoints?
7. Critique the evidence.
   - is it adequate?
   - is it factual or merely opinion?
   - is it based on respectable authorities?
   - is there substantive information?
8. Critique the author's conclusion.
   - does it follow from the evidence presented?
   - does it generalize beyond the evidence?
9. Suggest how the book fits into the real world--how does the book relate to current issues or other books on the subject?
10. Suggest how the book relates to the material covered in the course--how does it contribute to the body of knowledge in the field?

Tips for writing a book review

1. Most books assigned in classes for book reviews have already been reviewed by scholars.

    ♦   Look in one of these indexes to find a review:

        •   Perspective

        •   Social Science Citation

        •   The Political Science Reviewer

        •   Book Review Digest

    ♦   Read a review or two before reading the book.

        •   Reference any ideas borrowed from the review.

2. Look at the table of contents, index, reference pages, preface, introduction, and conclusion carefully before reading the text.

        •   note patterns in the presentation of the ideas.

        •   note the tone of the author.

3. Read with the purpose of answering and fulfilling the requirements of a book review.

4. Assert your perspective or viewpoint about the book but avoid stating your opinion with shallow words of praise or condemnation.

5. Do not use phrases such as "I think..." or "He thinks..." Offer only as evidence examples that can be identified explicitly.

6. Be sure to answer any questions the instructor has explicitly asked to be addressed in the book review in addition to the requirements for a book review.

7.   For books that include edited works, summarize the focus of the work in general and use specific examples from individual author's contributions to support particular hypothesis, theories, or arguments that embellish or explain the focus.

AN EXAMPLE OF A SINGLE AUTHOR BOOK REVIEW

A
BOOK REVIEW
OF
THE POLITICS OF CONGRESSIONAL ELECTIONS

By
Christopher Walka
Professor Schmidt
POLS 318
December 15, 1990
(Reprinted by Permission)

The Politics of Congressional Elections by Gary C. Jacobson (Boston, MA: Scott, Foresman, and Co. 1987), documents the many concerns and corresponding actions candidates undertake in order to gain political office. The book reduces these myriad factors into three sections: the historical background of the campaign process, the many elements comprising the actual campaign process and the role of the national party in this election process. Combining statistical tables, graphs, and other informative devices with "real-life" examples candidates have employed, the book balances both parties and their importance to the candidate.

Arguably, the single most important factor to candidates is the electorate. Without their support, the candidate has little or no chance of being elected. This fact Jacobson makes poignantly clear. He provides and explains the uses of a wide range of tactics candidates use to convey their image and issue agenda to the people. Included among these as particularly effective is the use of mass media to emphasize issues important to certain demographic voting areas. Likewise, Jacobson examines incumbency and how it can factor so heavily into the campaign success. Jacobson cites and examines statistics about the re-election rates of particular candidates and corresponding campaign expenditures to show that campaign success heavily depends on incumbency status. He also illuminates efforts of incumbents to quell any challengers, via the use of advertising campaigns well in advance of the traditional election period.

Though advertising serves an important role in the campaign, news coverage is nonetheless important, providing substantive reinforcement to an incumbent's claim of constituency service, or, ammunition for a challenger's heralding claims that the office holder and the voters are not well matched. Elementary to the media's functioning is that of a watchdog over government. Media serve to help winnow out candidates before the nomination process, as well as serving as the medium by which the candidate's agenda is conveyed to the people. Why Jacobson did not address the "news side" of the media and its relation to the candidate remains unexplained.

Similarly, the issue of campaign finance is also important to the candidate. Jacobson sheds considerable light on this issue, examining funding of both parties, how political action committees factor into this, and how incumbents benefit from prior service. Funding the campaign can be a very demanding venture, both from the generation of those funds and the expenditure of those funds. Jacobson illustrates the fact that campaigns have steadily increased in expense with graphics and statistics. This fact, coupled with regulations concerning contributions to candidates, brings out why campaign finance has dramatically increased in its importance to a campaign's viability.

Jacobson also examines the respective national parties and accompanying benefits available to the candidates recognized by the parties. Party affiliation provides many benefits to the candidate, ranging from resources to constituencies who identify and vote based on their identification with the party. Definitely not a toothless entity, the party helps lend credence to the campaign and the candidate. Similarly, facilities for the production of campaign literature, and other messages to the electorate, can be produced at substantially less cost than private firms charge. Additionally, Jacobson points out that the party helps establish a candidate to the voters: endorsements from other prominent members of the same party lending valiant support to the candidate. Ultimately, voters believe the candidate to be "for real" -- worthy of their attention and worth a vote on Election Day.

Jacobson's book examines many aspects of campaigns, the scope limited to those of Congressional positions but nonetheless applicable to lesser offices too. The book balances statistics with actual, documented cases, the balance serving to maintain reader interest. Jacobson concludes that the road to election on the federal level is multi-faceted, facets as complex as the positions themselves.

EXAMPLE OF A BOOK REVIEW: EDITED WORKS

THE REAGAN ADMINISTRATION'S POLICIES
ON
SOCIAL WELFARE SPENDING: ADVANTAGEOUS OR OTHERWISE

By
Edward M. Pettit
Professor Schmidt
POLS 324
February 22, 1990
(Reprinted By Permission)

Historically, spending for social welfare programs has been the basis for controversy in the political arenas of many countries, especially in the capitalist world. American social spending, and the modern American welfare state in particular, have been no exception to this trend, serving as a solid foundation for debate in this country for decades. Since the New Deal policies of President Franklin Delano Roosevelt, the controversy surrounding the American welfare state has increased in intensity, placing welfare policies among the more crucial issues in American politics.

One can easily understand, therefore, how the welfare state has come to play such an integral role in the political platforms of many of the recent leaders of the United States. Some presidents, such as Franklin D. Roosevelt (FDR), have sought policies in support of the welfare state, while others, such as Ronald Reagan, have pursued policies to the contrary. Each of these presidents has held strong convictions regarding his stance on the issue, and each has been both praised and criticized for his position. *The Mean Season: The Attack on The Welfare State* (NY: Pantheon Books, 1987), edited by Fred Block, Richard A. Cloward, Barbara Ehrenreich, and Francis Fox Piven, offers numerous criticisms of the Reagan administration's attitude toward the welfare state. Through their individual contributions, the authors provide a variety of criticisms of arguments against the necessity of welfare policy response.

Fred Block offers an interesting perspective to one such criticism when he argues that the Reagan administration's attitude toward the welfare state rests almost predominantly on a blind acceptance of the "realist" view of American politics. Under this notion, Block explains, welfare expenditures are considered to be directly responsible for reducing economic efficiency, and thus weakening our national economy. Block disagrees with this view, claiming that ". . .social justice [welfare expenditures] and the pursuit of economic efficiency are compatible" (Block: 155), and that by strengthening the welfare state, the Government of the United States could, in essence, ". . .promote equality, democracy, and a stronger economy" simultaneously (Block: 155). To Block, therefore, the policies of the Reagan administration aimed at reducing welfare spending to insure economic stability were misled and deserving of criticism.

Block's criticism certainly captures one's attention, but in many ways can be considered one dimensional. With regard to the economics in question, however, one person's dimension or perspective is as good as another's. Following from this, then, increasing the purchasing power of the disadvantaged (Block's dimension) might very well turn out to be as healthy for the national economy as providing incentives for increasing big business investment at the expense of the disadvantaged (Reagan's dimension). In this regard, Block's criticism can be considered reasonably relevant, in the abstract, and therefore worthy of further testing.

Barbara Ehrenreich adds an additional criticism of the Reagan administration's attitude toward the welfare state by uncovering what she considers to be its disguised intent. Ehrenreich discusses the Reagan administration's attempts to link the notion of "permissiveness" with the welfare state and its advocates as a means of undermining popular support for social welfare. Ehrenreich contends that by associating social welfare with the notion of "permissiveness" and its connotations of decadence and moral breakdown, the Reagan administration was essentially masking social welfare under the guise of a moral issue. In this regard, she claims the welfare state became shrouded beneath a cloud of value judgments, presenting, to a certain degree, its objective consideration by much of the American populace, and thus undermining its support.

Ehrenreich's criticism, on an ethical level, certainly warrants consideration because associating the welfare state with a moral issue could very well have denied it objective consideration. In reality, however, such clandestine intentions have come to be commonplace in political arenas worldwide, and disguising an issue in such a manner has been a trick of politicians for years. One would imagine that, under scrutinizing observation, similar tactics could most likely be found underlying many American policy issues.

Francis Fox Piven and Richard A. Cloward provide the focus of the book. They criticize the Reagan administration's attitude toward the welfare state based on its myopic perspective, particularly concerning the societal implications of relief giving. In the opinions of Piven and Cloward, the Reagan administration associated the problems of poverty and the poor directly to welfare programs, contending that welfare choices among the poor are ultimately attributable to material calculations, or the want of money. As such, the authors are quick to point out, Reagan and his subscribers openly neglected "...to consider an array of important changes in American Social institutions that ought reasonably to be investigated for their impacts on the lives of the poor" (Piven and Cloward: 83). Such changes, the authors add, might include the impact of the displacement of multitudes of southern agricultural workers during the years following WWII and the more recent impacts of rapid deindustrialization in this country.

In any event, Piven and Cloward continue by stating that by limiting its consideration of the welfare state solely to an economic agenda, the Reagan administration made ". . . the most basic societal processes that affect poverty and the poor seem peripheral" (Piven and Cloward: 73). As such, the Reagan administration created a model of the welfare state, and its relationship between relief giving and social behavior, which was far too simple. Certainly, as a means of criticism, this argument seems quite reasonable, since establishing a simple causal relationship within a complex social and political setting, such as that which the Reagan administration created, is virtually impossible. Therefore, by demonstrating the Reagan administration's negligence in considering numerous significant variables in the relationship between the welfare state and society, other than that of a mere economic calculus, Piven and Cloward, to a certain degree, expose a definite deficiency.

Throughout *The Mean Season: The Attack of The Welfare State*, Block, Cloward, Ehrenreich, and Piven offer numerous different criticisms of the Reagan administration's attitude toward the welfare state. These criticisms themselves, whether accepted or not, represent the long history of controversy which in recent years has come to play an increasingly important role in the American political arena. In their approach, these authors may very well be on the forefront of numerous changes in national opinion regarding the welfare state, especially in light of recent changes in the global economy.

Today, as will be the case in the future, the economies of the world are being fueled more and more by human talent. Therefore, investments in social welfare programs, essentially being investments in human capital, will become increasingly vital to the economic self-interests of the countries of the world and especially America. In turn, arguments in support of the welfare state, such as those of the authors of *The Mean Season: The Attack of The Welfare State*, may become increasingly influential. Despite this, however, the dispute over welfare spending will most likely continue to pepper American political discourse for many years to come.

BRIEFING CASES

Purpose of Briefing a Case

Preparing a case brief is a helpful way to summarize and analyze a court decision. Courts are political institutions and, therefore, decisions they make have political ramifications. Briefing a case helps students ascertain issues involved in important court cases and the justifications of the decisions.

Understanding Court Decisions:

The first step to briefing a case is, obviously, to read the case. Once court justices, such as Supreme Court members, have made a judgement in a case, they provide justifications for their determinations in documents called *decisions*. These *decisions* are bound in volumes called *reporters*. For briefing the case, students must locate specific information in these published decisions.

- **Name of the case**: The name of the case is distinguished by two names of participants in the case separated by a *v.* (such as Washington v. Davis). The first name is always the party bringing the case to the court for review; this party is generally referred to as the plaintiff or petitioner. The second name is always the target of the lawsuit; this party is generally referred to as the defendant or respondent. The plaintiff or the respondent could be an individual citizen, a representative of an organization, or a government.

- **Citation**: The citation is the location of the *decision* in the *reporter*. For example, the Washington v. Davis decision is cited as 96 S.Ct. 2040 (1976). This means that the decision is published in volume 96 of *The Supreme Court Reporter* on page 2040 in 1976. Sometimes the case citation will include references to other places where the case is published.

- **Decision**: The justices vote on whether to support the plaintiff or the defendant in the case. Their votes will either be split between the majority (usually at least five members) and minority, or they will be unanimous. The majority vote provides the winning decision. The decision will either affirm (agree with) or overturn (disagree with) the lower appellate court decision in cases brought to the court on appeal. In case of original jurisdiction, just the vote is recorded.

- **Majority opinion**: One of the justices in the majority will write the justification for the decision.

- **Concurring opinion**: One of the justices in the majority may write an alternative justification that provides additional or different reasons for the decision.

- **Dissenting opinion**: One of the justices in the minority may write a rebuttal to the majority opinion that identifies the problems and weaknesses in the justification by the majority.

A case brief is essentially an extended annotated reference. It is important to identify:

- the purpose of the case.
- the significance of the case.

Students should answer the standard questions of who, what, when, where, why, and how with a particular focus on legal and political costs and benefits. They need to focus on:

- who is claiming harm or paying political costs?

- who is benefiting at the cost of someone else?

- what legal issues were involved?

- what other earlier cases (precedents) were involved?

- when did the court make the decision?

- where did the decision take place?

- why did the court make the decision it rendered?

- how did the justice arrive at the decision?

- how much support was there for the decision among the justices?

There is nothing difficult or mystical about writing briefs. Although written court decisions look like and sometimes are imposing prose, the justifications, written by justices, are nothing more than analytical essays. Supreme Court decisions provide:

- a brief description of the context of the case.

- an opinion agreed to by the majority of justices supported by evidence from previous cases, the constitution, or legal theorists.

- dissenting opinions supported by previous cases, the constitution, or legal theorists.

Tips for Briefing a Case

For historical, landmark Supreme Court decisions, it is often not necessary for students to brief the case from the court records to understand the purpose, reasoning, and significance of the case. A standard text on constitutional law, civil rights and liberties, or American government can provide most of the information necessary for understanding the case. Cases that are more recent are usually examined or analyzed in law journals. Nonetheless, students may need to brief less known cases to support their arguments or assertions about the legality of an activity.

A legal brief can be a concise set of notes or an extensive set of notes depending on the reason researching a case. Instructors of public law courses often have students briefing cases so that they may understand the more complex issues and reasoning in landmark cases. Students of public policy, however, may need to brief cases that have only been addressed by judicial decisions. In any event, a standard legal brief should be no shorter than the front side of an 8" X 5" index card. It should be no longer than it takes to fill both sides of an 8" X 5" index card. Here are some simple guidelines for briefing a case:

1. State the name of the case.

2. State the full citation including the volume of the U.S. Reports, the page number, and the year.

3. Identify the important facts in the case--describe objectively what happened to whom.

4. Identify the issue--what was the problem.

5. State the decision (holding)--find out who won.

6. List the vote margin--how many voted yes and how many voted no.

7. Identify the reasons stated why the majority of the court voted the way they did.

8. Identify particular reasons given by individual justices for their concurring votes.

9. Identify particular reasons given by individual justices for their dissenting votes.

10. Identify and summarize the rule of law or outcome.

11. Identify and evaluate the importance of the case to your research or public policy.

AN EXAMPLE OF A BRIEF

NAME OF THE CASE: Washington v. Davis

CITATION: 426 U.S. 229, 96 S.Ct. 2040, 48 L.Ed. 2d 597 (1976)

FACTS:

All federal service employees, including police recruits, were required to take a standard literacy test. The number of black applicants who failed the test was four times that of white applicants. A discrimination case was filed in District Court that found no intent of discrimination. The Court of Appeals overturned that decision based on Griggs v. Duke Power Co. (1971) as it applied Title VII of the Civil Rights Act of 1964. This court held that the absence of proof that the test was an adequate measure of job performance and the high number of blacks who failed the test, regardless of intent, rendered the test unconstitutional.

ISSUE:

The first issue concerned the constitutionality of a literacy test that has an unintentional but apparent adverse impact on the employment of a protected class of people. The second issue concerned whether the literacy test should be invalidated under job performance standards of Title VII of the Civil Rights Act of 1964 set forth by Congress.

DECISION:

Overturned the Court of Appeals decision.

VOTE: (7 to 2), Justice White wrote the opinion.

JUSTIFICATION:

The court considered the second issue first. The Court of Appeals decision was overturned because it was based on Title VII that allows the impact rather than the intent to be sufficient cause for invalidating a non-job related employment test. The court said that Title VII is not a constitutional rule and invites more judicial probing and review than is justified under the Constitution. Therefore, because the decision was based on Title VII, the Court did not examine the literacy test at all.

CONCURRING:

Justice Stevens concurred but for different reasons. He argued that a literacy test was relevant to police work and because it was given throughout the federal service without the same impact on blacks, the test met Congressional standards and was not unconstitutional.

DISSENT:

Justices Brennan and Marshall argued that every district court except the one in this case had ruled such tests were discriminatory. The employers should have to demonstrate that the test measured skills related to performance.

RULE OF LAW:

The court stated clearly that it will not recognize impact instead of purpose of an act as a standard for establishing invidious racial discrimination, even though Congress established this criteria through legislation.

EVALUATION:

The court blatantly ignored congressional intent.

CONSTRUCTING OUTLINES

PURPOSE

Outlines help to organize ideas, arguments, and evidence into a coherent statement. Ideas must be presented in an ordered sequence and in chunks. Outlines help writers formulate a controlling pattern for presenting their ideas. Outlines help the writer to:

- order main and minor points.
- balance the introduction, body, and conclusion.
- place arguments with evidence.

Writers use several types of outlines.

Scratch outlines: a series of ordered notes about how to proceed with the paper.
Topic outlines: a list of ideas showing the order and relative importance of each idea in brief words or phrases.
Sentence outlines: a list of ideas showing the order and relative importance of each idea in complete sentences.

HOW TO CONSTRUCT A TOPIC OR SENTENCE OUTLINE

1. Topic outlines are structured to show relative importance, so before writing the outline:
    - Write out a thesis sentence.
    - List all the ideas.
    - List all the evidence.
    - Categorize the ideas and evidence so that they form separate chunks of information relating to the points made in the thesis sentence.
    - Order the chunks of information by strength and importance.

2. The parts of an outline are hierarchically ordered.
    - General ideas precede specific points.
    - Each point should have corresponding evidence.

3. Each division is numbered in ascending order.
    - General sections are ordered in Roman numerals.
    - Subsections are ordered by capital letters.
    - Supporting sections are ordered in Arabic numbers.
    - Explanatory sections are ordered by small letters.

4. Each Subsection, supporting section, and explanatory section must have at least two parts.

EXAMPLE OF A SCRATCH OUTLINE
(Reprinted with permission)

A POLICY FOR WELFARE REFORM

BY
THOMAS MITCHELL

1.   Issue of controlling poverty rate

2.   Economic Opportunity Act of 1964

3.   Employment conditions in 1964 vs. present

4.   Contributing public commentary

5.   Cash Support programs and controversies

6.   Remedial job skill training

7.   Programs for children to break poverty at an early age

8.   Employment programs for the non-working poor

9.   Techniques for measuring success

10. Conclusion

A POLICY FOR WELFARE REFORM

BY
THOMAS MITCHELL

Thesis statement: A multi-generational program that is both curative and remedial in structure will provide training and opportunity to the working poor, the non-working poor, and their families.

I.   Introduction or Executive Summary
- A.   Issue
  1.   Stagnant productivity of American workers
  2.   Goals of remedial training and quality education
- B.   Recommendations
  1.   Multi-generational policy
  2.   Specific recommendations of analysis

II.   The Issues
- A.   Past Strategies
  1.   Preventative, Punitive, and Alleviative
  2.   Goals of each strategy
- B.   History of Issue
  1.   Economic Opportunity Act of 1964
  2.   Employment conditions in 1964 vs. present
  3.   Reasons for change in conditions

III.   The Goals and Objectives
- A.   Goal of Welfare Policy
  1.   Security for those deemed worthy
  2.   Vehicle to self-sufficiency
  3.   Discourage welfare dependence
- B.   Demands of the Labor Market
  1.   More skills needed presently than ever before
  2.   Higher levels of education for even entry-level jobs
- C.   Public Commentary
  1.   John Kenneth Galbraith's (1957) *The Affluent Society*
  2.   Michael Harrington's (1962) *The Other America*
  3.   Martin Anderson's (1978) *Welfare*
  4.   George Gilder's (1981) *Wealth and Poverty*
  5.   Charles Murray's (1984) *Losing Ground*

IV.   Past Policy Responses
- A.   Cash Support programs
  1.   Examples including OASDI, AFDC, SSI, and GA
  2.   Assistance in adding to income level

        3.   Controversial due to loss of government authority
    B.   Direct Provision of Necessities
        1.   Examples including Medicare, food stamps
        2.   Political feasibility of direct provision
    C.   Preventive and Compensatory Efforts for Children
        1.   Rationality for focusing upon education
        2.   Problem of equally affordable education
        3.   Creation of Upward Bound and Head Start programs
    D.   Employment Related Programs
        1.   Explanation of the Family Support Act of 1988
        2.   Focus upon JOBS program and its goals
        3.   Problems of job creation, costs, and child care
V.   Recommendations
    A.   Explain Multi-Generational Program
        1.   Provide remedial training to presently impoverished
        2.   Create and further educational programs for youth
    B.   Continuation of Employment Programs
        1.   Need for programs due to welfare stigma
        2.   Poor less able to compete for jobs
    C.   Remedial Job Skill Training Programs
        1.   A means of welfare recipients acquiring skills
        2.   Upon completion, recipients enter employment programs
    D.   Continuation of Cash Support Payments
        1.   Allows millions of people to be kept off of welfare
        2.   Must participate in Skill Training to receive cash
    E.   Curative Programs Aimed at All Youth
        1.   Children of various income levels drop out of school
        2.   Children drop out before the legal age
        3.   Head Start, Upward Bound, and elementary programs for all high-risk youth
VI.   Measuring Success
    A.   Time Frame
        1.   Measure variables every three years
        2.   Several years before remedial training can be reduced
    B.   Employment Programs
        1.   Percentage of recipients securing employment
        2.   Average duration of employment
        3.   Securing of wages above welfare benefit level
    C.   Remedial Job Skill Training
        1.   Percent completion in program
        2.   Percent who enroll in employment programs
        3.   Number in program should lower over time as skills of youth increase due to educational programs

        D.   Cash Assistance Programs
             1.   Cash assistance outlays should lower as number in remedial lowers over time
             2.   Cash assistance outlays should lower as number in employment programs lowers over time
        E.   Curative Programs Aimed at High-Risk Children
             1.   Defining high-risk youth by each school district to lower cultural and regional bias of standardized tests
             2.   High school graduation rates should increase

VII.   Conclusion
        A.   Social Condition of Poverty
             1.   New demands on labor market
             2.   Resources of workers go untapped
        B.   Past Poverty Strategies
             1.   Past strategies have been unsuccessful
             2.   Restate thesis
        C.   Recommendations
             1.   List the four recommendations
             2.   Programs are integrated and mutually re-enforcing
             3.   Need for a true welfare reform as these recommendations would provide

A POLICY FOR WELFARE REFORM

BY
THOMAS MITCHELL

Thesis statement: A multi-generational program that is both curative and remedial in structure will provide training and opportunity to the working poor, the non-working poor, and their families.

I.   The percent of the population below the poverty level has continued to increase since 1979.
- A.   In order that the issue of increasing poverty rates be controlled, legislative development must be undertaken.
  - 1.   Provide remedial training to the working and non-working poor.
  - 2.   Ensure quality education as a curative strategy to poverty by breaking the cycle of poverty at an early age.
- B.   These goals can be achieved through specific policy recommendations.
  - 1.   Continuation of employment programs for the non-working poor.
  - 2.   Provide remedial job skill training and education programs to provide skills to the working and non-working poor and to induce the poor to enter the job market.
  - 3.   Continue to use cash support payments as a means to keep millions of individuals out of poverty.
  - 4.   Create and further curative programs aimed at high-risk children of all income and educational levels.

II.   As a relative concept, poverty will always exist because inequality is a constant problem.
- A.   Welfare policy has traditional taken one of four forms.
  - 1.   Preventive strategies are designed to ensure that certain groups do not enter poverty.
  - 2.   Alleviate strategies provide assistance to those impoverished.
  - 3.   Punitive strategies discourage assistance to those capable of work.
  - 4.   Curative strategies aim at controlling poverty by attacking its causes.
- B.   To comprehend the issue of poverty, one must understand its history.
  - 1.   The Economic Opportunity Act of 1964 attempted to guarantee to everyone the opportunity to live in decency and dignity.
  - 2.   However, the employment conditions that were in existence in 1964 are no longer the same today.
  - 3.   American businesses are now service oriented and demand more skills and education from its laborers.

III.   The goals and objective of welfare policy must be considered before constructing a policy.
- A.   There are three goals of welfare policy.
  - 1.   Welfare is an attempt to provide some level of security to those deemed worthy.

        2.   A lesser goal of welfare is to assist individuals in becoming self-sufficient.

        3.   A third goal of welfare policy is to discourage welfare dependence.

   B.   Today's labor market is demanding more of its labor force than ever before.

        1.   A skilled labor force is necessary in a service sector.

        2.   As the need for skilled labor increases, so does the requirement of higher levels of education.

   C.   The issue of poverty gained public attention due mainly to commentary.

        1.   John Kenneth Galbraith called attention to the existence of poverty amongst plenty in the United States.

        2.   Michael Harrington noted the issue of regional poverty.

        3.   Martin Anderson provided specific guidelines for welfare reform.

        4.   George Gilder theorized that poor people remain poor because welfare benefits are greater than work incentives.

        5.   Charles Murray argued that the expansion of welfare policies in the 1960s only increase poverty.

IV.   Past federal programs in aid of the poor have fallen into four categories.

   A.   Cash support programs provide the foundation for federal assistance to the poor.

        1.   Two groups included in the Social Security Act were social insurance and public assistance programs.

        2.   Because the income of the working poor is often not enough to raise them above the poverty level, cash support programs could add to their income.

        3.   Cash support payments are often disliked by policy makers for they have little authority in how the aid is spent.

   B.   Welfare policy also includes programs that deliver goods and services directly to the needy.

        1.   These programs include Medicare, public housing, and food stamps.

        2.   Direct provision of necessities is more politically feasible than cash assistance.

   C.   The federal government has focused on protecting children from poverty with preventive and compensatory programs.

        1.   Schools play an important role in socializing and educating children for the labor market.

        2.   The opportunity for an education is not equally affordable.

        3.   Upward Bound was created to motivate and assist poor students early in high school.

   D.   In an effort to help the non-working poor, employment programs were created to help them find work.

        1.   The Family Support Act of 1988 follows the idea that training and work experience will lead to self-sufficiency.

        2.   JOBS programs requires states to provide comprehensive education, training, and employment services for welfare recipients.

        3.   Employment programs have problems of job creation, costs, and childcare facilities.

V.   To propose a welfare reform, policies must be established addressing the present economic structure of the U.S.

    A.   A multi-generational program that is both curative and remedial in structure is needed.

        1.   This program would provide remedial training and education to the presently impoverished.

        2.   It would also create and further educational programs for the youth.

    B.   In order to assist recipient in finding work, the JOBS program needs to be continued.

        1.   The welfare stigma attached to recipients has handicapped them in the labor market.

        2.   The poor are not equally able to compete for jobs with non-welfare recipients.

    C.   A program is needed to deal with the millions of adults currently impoverished.

        1.   Remedial training programs can provide a means for recipients to acquire the skills needed by the labor market.

        2.   Upon completion of remedial training, recipients could enroll in employment programs.

    D.   Cash assistance programs can help individuals attain an income level above the poverty line.

        1.   This type of program would allow millions of persons to stay off welfare.

        2.   Legislation could be enacted that would require employable recipients to participate in remedial training programs in order to attain cash assistance.

    E.   Curative programs should be aimed at high-risk children of all income and educational levels that are in need of additional educational support.

        1.   Children of various income levels are represented in the high school dropout rate.

        2.   Many students essentially drop out of school before the legal age.

        3.   Programs including Head Start, Upward Bound, as well as similar elementary programs need to be expanded for all high-risk children.

VI.   To assess the success of this policy, each recommendation must be defined and evaluated.

    A.   The establishment of a time frame will allow for the monitoring of progress towards our established goals.

        1.   The variables involved in each recommendation shall be evaluated every three years.

        2.   It will require several years before remedial training funds can be lowered.

    B.   Since the goal of employment programs is to assist recipients in securing work, two measures of that success can be examined.

        1.   The percentage of recipients attaining employment should remain high each year if program is to be considered a success.

        2.   The duration of employment should not be short or temporary.

        3.   Wages secured in employment through JOBS should reflect wages above benefits from welfare assistance.

    C.   Remedial job skill training will eventually become less necessary because those who are participating in youth educational programs should not require the service if these programs are successful.

        1.   One measure of success for remedial training programs is the percentage of recipients who enroll as well as complete the program.

        2.   The number of participants in these programs should lower over time as the skills of youth increase because of educational programs.

     D.   Cash assistance programs are recommended to be directly linked to the participation in job skill training or employment programs by employable recipients.
1. Cash assistance outlays should lower over time as the number of recipients in remedial training lowers over time.
2. Cash assistance outlays should lower over time as the number of recipients in employment programs lowers over time.

     E.   To implement curative programs, high risk must first be defined and then programs made available to all high risk children.
1. The definition and classification of high-risk youth should be done by means of testing prepared by each individual school district to lower the cultural and regional bias associated with standardized tests.
2. These programs are successful if the graduation rates for all high-risk youth show an increase as compared to past policies.

VII.   **Conclusion**
     A.   In recent years, the poverty rate has been steadily increasing.
1. As the labor market has had to adapt to a recently established service sector, new skills and higher levels of education are being demanded.
2. However, the productivity of American labor has remained stagnant as the resources of millions of workers go untapped.

     B.   Past poverty strategies have proven unsuccessful in controlling the rise in poverty.
1. Therefore, this policy analysis recommends that a multi-generational program that is both curative and remedial in structure be implemented.
2. This is to provide training and opportunity to the working poor, the non-working poor, and their families.

     C.   This policy analysis consists of four parts:
1. Continuation of employment programs for the non-working poor accompanied by increased funding;
2. Remedial Job Skill Training and Education programs for the working and non-working poor and to induce the poor to enter the labor market;
3. Continuation of cash support payments to keep millions of individuals out of poverty;
4. Curative programs aimed at high-risk children at all educational levels that are in need of additional educational support.

     D.   These programs are integrated and mutually re-enforcing.
1. Each recommendation is to build upon each of the others as to provide a structured and directional welfare policy.
2. The implementation of this multi-generational program will represent a true welfare reform in which major strides can be made toward reducing the social condition of growing poverty rates.

RESEARCH PRESENTATIONS

Research presentations generally have two purposes. Presentations give students the opportunity to describe their research verbally to their classmates and respond to questions directly. The subject of the presentation is based on the student's research. (This outline style is very similar to the format used for research proposals.)

A standard professional presentation typically includes more than a description of research. It includes:

- a statement of student's purpose.
- a declaration of student's position.
- a description of relevant background on the topic.
- a description of the controversy.
- an explanation of how the controversy was examined.
- a description of the student's findings.
- a concluding statement regarding the significance of the research project.

A class presentation is generally graded with the same criteria used to grade written assignments.

- Students' grades usually reflect the quality and thoroughness in which they presented the material contained in the categories listed.
- Sometimes an instructor will request a copy of your presentation, so write a outline.
- A quick way to begin writing your presentation outline is to re-organize the topic or sentence outline for your research paper to fit into these categories.
- The length and degree of detail in the presentation outline will depend on the time allotted for the presentation. Generally, a presentation is two and a half (or less) pages typed in outline form.

Class presentations are frequently graded on the degree of professionalism exhibited by the student during the presentation. A solid performance by the student demonstrates depth and breadth of subject area knowledge.

- Exhibit poise and confidence (try rehearsing).
- Answer questions succinctly.
- Vary the voice level, make eye contact with other students, and use gestures.
- Do not read word for word from your research paper. Use an outline.

STANDARD PRESENTATION FORM

Purpose: A clear statement of the purpose and focus of the student's research.

Hypothesis: A clear statement of the controversy examined and hypothesis tested. If possible, try to identify the causal relationship between independent and dependent variables.

Background: A brief discussion of the context and background related to the controversy examined and assumptions behind the students research motives.

- Be sure to present the background so that it supports your purpose and relationships specified between the variables.
- Work from weakest to strongest assertions.

Method: An explanation of the method or how you tested your hypothesis.

- If you used quantitative data, describe how the data or source materials were collected.
- Fully disclose any problems in information gathering.
- Be sure to relate the data and source materials to the hypothesis.

Results: A summary of the results of the examination or test.

- If data were used, make charts, graphs, or tables to use as visual aids.
- Use a table or chart to summarize your main points.
- Use visual aids for complex material or highly descriptive material. For example, use maps to help the audience understand the context of boundary disputes between nations.
- Use an overhead projector to present your material or make copies of a visual aid for everyone.

Conclusion: This statement explains how the goals of the research were accomplished. In particular, this statement summarizes how the results relate to the goals of the student's research endeavor.

Significance: A statement that applies the results appropriately to an expansion of knowledge about the subject.

WELFARE REFORM PRESENTATION

By
Thomas Mitchell
Dr. Schmidt
POLS 444
July 1, 1991
(Reprinted with permission).

WELFARE REFORM PRESENTATION NOTES

I. Purpose is to examine manpower programs that are designed to increase the marketability of impoverished citizens and propose a new course of action that will help diminish the number of citizens requiring such aid in the future.

    A. Controversy:
1. Productivity of American workers stagnant.
2. The percent of the population below the poverty level has continued to increase since 1979.

    B. Thesis statement: A multi-generational program that is both curative and remedial in structure will provide training and opportunity to the working poor, the non-working poor, and their families.

    C. Goal: To address the issue of increasing poverty rates, legislative action must be undertaken.
1. Provide remedial training to the working and non-working poor.
2. Ensure quality education as a curative strategy to poverty by breaking the cycle of poverty at an early age.

    D. These goals can be achieved through specific policy recommendations.
1. Continuation of employment programs for the non-working poor.
2. Provide remedial job skill training and education programs to provide skills to the working and non-working poor and to induce the poor to enter the job market.
3. Continue to use cash support payments as a means to keep millions of individuals out of poverty.
4. Create and expand curative programs aimed at high-risk children of all income and educational levels.

II. Brief description of the context or background:

    A. Past strategies.
1. Preventative, Punitive, and Alleviative.
2. Goals of each strategy.

    B. History of Issue.
1. Economic Opportunity Act of 1964.
2. Employment conditions in 1964 vs. present.
3. Reasons for change in conditions.

III. Explanation of research method:

    A. Analyzed explicit goals of welfare policies and employment policy.

    B. Examined and evaluated past and present programs used to address goals.

    C. Used secondary sources, primary sources, and expert opinion.

IV.   Findings on Welfare Policies:
    A.   Welfare policy goals.
        1.   Security for those deemed worthy.
        2.   Vehicle to self-sufficiency.
        3.   Discourage welfare dependence.
    B.   Welfare policy responses-evaluated.
        1.   Cash Support programs: Examples OASDI, AFDC, SSI.
        2.   Direct Provision of Necessities: Example Medicare.
        3.   Preventive Efforts for Children: Example Headstart.

V.   Findings on Employment Programs:
    A.   Goals and problems in labor market.
        1.   More skills needed presently than ever before.
        2.   Higher levels of education for even entry-level jobs.
    B.   Employment related programs:
        1.   Explanation of the Family Support Act of 1988.
        2.   Focus upon JOBS program and its goals.
        3.   Problems of job creation, costs, and child care.

VI.   Recommendations:
    A.   Explain multi-generational program.
        1.   Provide remedial training to presently impoverished
        2.   Create and further educational programs for youth.
    B.   Continuation of employment programs.
        1.   Need for programs due to welfare stigma.
        2.   Poor less able to compete for jobs.
    C.   Remedial job skill training programs.
        1.   A means of welfare recipients acquiring skills.
        2.   Upon completion, recipients enter employment programs.
    D.   Continuation of cash support payments.
        1.   Allows millions of people to be kept off of welfare.
        2.   Must participate in skill training to receive cash.
    E.   Curative programs aimed at all youth.
        1.   Children of various income levels drop out of school.
        2.   Children drop out before the legal age.
        3.   Head Start, Upward Bound, and elementary programs for all high-risk youth.

VII.   Conclusion:
   A.   Social condition of poverty.
         1.   New demands on labor market.
         2.   Resources of workers go untapped.
   B.   Past poverty strategies.
         1.   Past strategies have been unsuccessful.
         2.   Restate thesis.
VIII.   Significance:
   A.   Summarize four-part recommendation.
   B.   Four parts: are integrated and mutually re-enforcing.

RESEARCH PROPOSALS

For upper level classes, scholarships, grants, and other professional level work, students may be asked to submit a research proposal. A research proposal is a synopsis of the main elements of a research paper. It should be brief, concise, and specific. This means that students must complete the preliminary research before writing the proposal. The length varies with the research question and design. A research proposal should be no shorter than two typed double-spaced pages and no longer than five typed double-spaced pages. A research proposal generally includes the following:

A title page: that includes the title of the research project and the name of the student.

An essay: allocating at least one paragraph to each item, a discussion of the following:

Topic: Describe the focus of the research project, clearly, succinctly.

Purpose: Describe the purpose of the research project.

Hypothesis: Clearly express, in one or two sentences, the question or controversy you are seeking to examine. One of these sentences should be your thesis sentence. You may need to follow the thesis sentence with qualifying, explanatory sentences that clarify or propose sub-hypotheses.

Justification: Provide a discussion of the background, context, or origins of the controversy. This may take more than one paragraph. For complex research topics, include a condensed but pertinent literature review on the subject and controversy.

Method: Describe the method and sources used to examine or test the research question.

- Be sure to specify whether qualitative or quantitative (or both) evidence will be used to support your assertions.

- If statistical tools or graphics will be used, be sure to specify the source of the data and how it will be transformed into tables and figures. If survey data are used, be sure to specify the source of the data.

- If the research is based on qualitative evidence, then identify the primary sources such as scholarly, mass publications, etc.

Expected Results: Describe, based on your preliminary research, what you believe you will find to support your hypothesis. If possible, indicate the strength of that support. Do not overstate.

Expected Significance: Describe what your research will contribute to the body of knowledge on the topic or subject. Be bold but not rhetorical. Avoid saying that your research will enlighten everyone. Keep your assertion carefully and narrowly focused on what can be understood about your subject or topic.

RESEARCH PROPOSAL: GRAMM-RUDMAN-HOLLINGS: PROGRESSIVE POLICY OR TROJAN HORSE?

By
Lowell Linder
POLS 324
Dr. Schmidt
June 21, 1991
(Reprinted with Permission)

RESEARCH PROPOSAL: GRAMM-RUDMAN-HOLLINGS:
PROGRESSIVE POLICY OR TROJAN HORSE?

The topic of this research paper is the Balanced Budget Act of 1985, also known as Gramm-Rudman-Hollings. This congressional act was designed to help eliminate the budget deficit by 1991. The focus of my research is to examine the origin, intent, implementation, and effectiveness of the act.

The purpose of this paper is to evaluate the effectiveness of the Gramm-Rudman Hollings (GRH) Act. GRH has become a source of controversy for many reasons. Its constitutionality has been questioned, and consequently its legitimacy, due to a damaging decision concerning it by the Supreme Court. Another source for controversy is the issue of the fairness of automatic budget cuts authorized by the bill. Thus, the major focus of this research will be to examine the feasibility, constitutionality, and controversies surrounding GRH.

More specifically, I will test the hypothesis that GRH is an adequate but limited solution to the deficit problem. To do so, I will first examine what is meant by a budget deficit and how great a problem it is. Second, given that the deficit is perceived to be a grave public problem, I will examine the alternatives available to Congress other than GRH. Finally, I will examine who benefits most from GRH.

The justification of the research question is very simple. Not long ago, the nation braced itself for the GRH automatic budget cuts to begin. GRH grabbed the spotlight as Congress failed to meet the budget deadline. Many federal workers faced layoffs and the social welfare and defense programs faced huge funding cuts. Many have already forgotten the panic these cuts brought about, but there is still reason for concern. GRH forces Congress and the President to make difficult as well as politically unpopular decisions about the allocation of scarce public resources.

For my method of examination, I will use both quantitative and qualitative analysis. Because the size of the deficit will be relative to the question of how much to cut from the budget, I will examine budget figures from 1980-1991. I have collected data on the deficit from the Government Accounting Office publications, Congressional Quarterly, and the President's Economic Report. I will also examine arguments by supporters and nonsupporters concerning the desirability and effectiveness of the automatic cuts. I will gather these arguments from both scholarly and mass publications.

Expected results of this research project are difficult to predict. In some aspects, I expect to find that GRH is unconstitutional. I also expect to find convincing arguments suggesting that, in reality, the goals of the GRH are not feasible. Most importantly, I expect to find that policymakers have given the goal of balancing the budget a highly visible yet symbolic place on the institutional agenda. Finally, because achieving the goals of GRH will come at the expense of both high and low cost programs, I expect to find that it hurts government programs differentially.

The expected significance of the finished project should tell us much about our commitment to national priorities, especially by Congress and the President, and about the viability of enacting legislation which mandates unpopular and politically unacceptable activities. Hopefully, some insight will be gained into how the U.S. got into this dilemma and the limitations of the budget policy process. Finally, I hope to discover what important ramifications of the GRH success and failures will have for future legislation mandating government fiscal responsibility.

SECTION TEN

FORMAT AND EXAMPLES OF CONVENTIONAL RESEARCH PAPERS

FORMULAS FOR ORGANIZING STANDARD RESEARCH PAPERS

In the following pages, there are three examples of standard undergraduate research papers exhibiting a range of writing styles, topics, and research methods.

First Paper: A Comparative Paper

"The Kennedys and the Rockefellers: Political Dynasties' Effects on the American Electorate" uses qualitative data and is a simple comparative or case study.

The Second Paper: An Analysis

"Youth Influence in Political Outcomes" uses a mixture of qualitative and quantitative data to examine the reasons why young people participate in politics and suggest a theory about the impact of this activity. This paper is an example of an analysis.

The Third Paper: A Position Paper

"Chief Justice Rehnquist: Does He Lead the Court?" is empirical research that tests a hypothesis using quantitative data and statistical methods. This is an example of a position paper that supports a theory about political influence and leadership in the judicial branch.

These papers exhibit the standard qualities for a research paper in political science where students were not required to address specific criteria or questions. An explanation of the form for each type of paper precedes the examples.

FORMAT FOR A COMPARATIVE STUDY

In many political science courses, especially in Comparative Politics or International Relations, instructors will ask students to compare government responses to issues, problems, or political phenomena. Comparison papers may use qualitative evidence, quantitative evidence, or a mixture of both. Here are three simple frameworks to organize your research and ideas (Lester 1990, p. 74).

For comparative papers on two or more objects or people:

1. In the introduction, briefly identify and compare the items. State the central point of the comparison. In your thesis sentence, present your perspective on the relevance of the comparison or why the comparison is important.

2. In the body:

    - Examine the first item's characteristics thoroughly.
    - Next, examine the second item's characteristics thoroughly.
    - Next, identify characteristics that are similar and offer an explanation/evidence of why they are similar.
    - Next, identify characteristics that are different and offer an explanation/evidence of why they are different.

3. Discuss the significant differences and similarities. Suggest why it was important to identify these differences and similarities.

For comparative papers on two or more ideas or theories:

1. In the introduction, briefly identify and compare the items. State the central point of the comparison. In your thesis sentence, present your perspective on the relevance of the comparison or why the comparison is important.

2. In the body:

    - First, identify characteristics that are similar and offer an explanation/evidence of why they are similar.
    - Next, identify characteristics that are different and offer an explanation/evidence of why they are different.
    - Next, discuss and evaluate the central issues or characteristics that differentiate the items.
    - Present arguments that rank one item over the other.

3.   Reiterate the major differences and strong points of each item. Suggest why it was important to identify these differences and similarities. Conclude by identifying and supporting the reason why one item is preferable to another.

For papers that compare responses to issues by two subjects or objects:

1.   In the introduction, briefly identify and compare the items and the issues. State the central point of the comparison. In your thesis sentence, present your perspective on the relevance of the comparison or why the comparison is important.

2.   In the body:

- First, identify the first issue. Discuss the differences and similarities between the items' treatment of the issue. Present arguments about why the differences and similarities exist.
- Next, identify the second issue. Discuss the differences and similarities between the items' treatment of the issue. Present arguments about why the differences and similarities exist.
- Next, identify the third issue. Discuss the differences and similarities between the items' treatment of the issue. Present arguments about why the differences and similarities exist.
- Present arguments that rate one item's treatment over the other.

3.   Reiterate the major differences and similarities in each item's treatment of each issue. Suggest why these differences and similarities exist. Conclude by identifying and supporting the reason why one item's treatment is preferable to another.

EXAMPLE OF A COMPARATIVE PAPER

**THE KENNEDYS AND THE ROCKEFELLERS:
POLITICAL DYNASTIES'EFFECTS ON THE AMERICAN ELECTORATE**

By
John T. Sullivan
Professor Schmidt
POLS 318
December 1, 1988
(Reprinted with permission)

ABSTRACT

One of the most intriguing phenomena in American politics is that of the so-called "dynasty" and its effects on the voters. These political dynasties appear to create irrational tendencies in voting patterns. The dynasty also appears to be akin to a candidate centered campaign on a greater magnitude. In particular, a political dynasty is an unpredictable anomaly on the political scene, but it is relatively easy to identify. The specific examples of the political families, the Kennedys and the Rockefellers, provide evidence that political dynasties influence the careers of family members and give them extra political influence.

Introduction

The political dynasty, in the American context, is an organization usually centered on a family which transcends traditional campaign and voter perception. By transcending these norms, the dynasty develops the image of American "royalty." The Kennedy and Rockefeller families have evolved as the most dominant examples of political dynasties in the twentieth century. The phenomena, as evidenced in these examples, appear to center around one individual and build from there. Once established, this mutation of American politics becomes its own organization, nearly independent of its respective parties in power and strategy (Salmore: 39). Even though the later elements of the dynasty benefit from their link to the overall public perception, they are, at times, mistakenly associated and credited with the dynasty's accomplishments as well (Granberg: 504-16).

Each political dynasty, however, is different; each dynasty has its own dynamics that separate it from the rest of the political community. The Kennedys, for example, are a nationally recognized political family although the family center or core is in Massachusetts. The Rockefellers, while equally nationally known, have spread their political dominance over the governor's mansions in New York, Arkansas, and West Virginia (Salmore: 125). While both families exhibited a drive for dominance, the political bases of their influence span the spectrum from highly centralized to decentralized (Clinch x).

The Kennedy Dynasty

The Kennedys and their episodic saga in American politics are the premier political dynasty in evidence. The roots of the Kennedy dynasty began with John F. Fitzgerald who was the mayor of Boston and a U.S. Congressman (Davis 41). The figure who is the symbol of the Kennedy mystique, however, is John F. Kennedy (JFK), 35th President of the United States. JFK's popularity and successful election have created a standard by which the Kennedy heirs were measured. Because of JFK's success and characteristic demeanor, Kennedy heirs were perceived as intellectually keen, eloquent, and youthful (Wills: 153). Those virtues were even more firmly associated with the Kennedy family due to efforts by his successor, Lyndon Johnson, to immortalize Kennedy in public for political purpose to gain public support for the presidential agenda (Schuyler: 503-4).

The first tests of the Kennedy dynasty's effects on the electorate came soon after JFK's assassination. In 1964, Robert F. Kennedy (RFK), brother of the former president, challenged President Johnson and the Democratic Party regulars for the presidency. RFK sought to build on the foundations of residual grief over his slain brother. In particular, RFK promised to return to the values and programs of JFK. RFK became a rallying symbol for disenfranchised party opposition to Johnson (Halberstam: 5). Johnson feared, as did other Democratic party leaders, "that the country would turn to Robert Kennedy . . . as the successor to the throne, as the rightful heir to the Kennedy tradition . . ." (Schuyler: 506). Even though the Kennedy campaign started late, party supporters won their first primary with the help of the Kennedy family "machine" which used its own network and popularity to sidestep the party apparatus (Halberstam: 161).

The reincarnation of the Kennedy dynasty had dramatic effects as fate again lent a hand. RFK, broadening the reformist, intellectual style of the Kennedys (Halberstam: 162), contributed his final piece to the puzzle as he was assassinated following a crucial 1968 California primary. Until his death, RFK's candidacy was gaining momentum by the day. Voters, especially young people, flocked to his campaign. There is little doubt that such voting behavior was caused by the Kennedy dynasty; RFK was a late entry, a freshman senator, and opposed to the policies of his own incumbent president. These factors would destroy other contenders for the oval office.

RFK's assassination event merely further magnified the Kennedy mystique as the promises of two Kennedy family politicians would go unfulfilled (Halberstam: 209). Because of this, the public looked to the last heir apparent in Senator Edward M. Kennedy. The subsequent trials of Ted Kennedy are the best examples of the Kennedy dynasty. Because the Kennedy image had been firmly entrenched by liberals in the original Kennedy administration (Matusow: 153) and enhanced by the revival of that liberalism by RFK's run in, much was expected of Ted Kennedy. Despite a divorce and a highly controversial accident in which a woman he was with died, Ted Kennedy had been easily re-elected to the Senate and was a serious candidate for the presidency. His past electoral successes and near success for president occurred in part because of the Kennedy name. In addition, he has forged an impressive senatorial record in keeping with family tradition, and he has echoed the rhetoric of his deceased brothers at two national conventions (Wills: 294).

Even with the Kennedy's success, the "ghosts" of the Kennedy family's past have forced Ted Kennedy into ill fought contests for the presidency (Wills: 295). The public's perception of him is still linked to the Kennedy legacies. Ted Kennedy's popularity is due in part to a public perception that he is more liberal than his record indicates (Granberg: 504-16). The public has a rigid perception of the Kennedy dynasty that is evident in the emerging popularity of a new Kennedy. Joseph P. Kennedy III, oldest son of Robert, is running for his third term in Congress as he and the Kennedy machine reclaimed the seat held by his great-grandfather, uncle, and former House Speaker Tip O'Neil. Young Joseph Kennedy defeated a field of 10 candidates to win the seat ("Liberals Rebuffed": 28). Thus, the Kennedy dynasty continues with young Joe, 37 years old, maintaining and rejuvenating the family.

The Rockefeller Dynasty

Like the Kennedy dynasty, the reign of the Rockefellers in the United States has been one of philanthropy and public service. The Rockefellers are presently in their fourth generation of public service. The Rockefeller dynasty began with the billions of dollars made by John D. Rockefeller in the late nineteenth century and early twentieth century through his success in founding Standard Oil (Ensor Harr: xiii). Unlike the Kennedys, the Rockefellers established themselves as a political dynasty more through philanthropic causes than public service (Lundberg: 329). Although the Rockefellers' public image is associated with being ruthless businessmen, (Collier: 4) it is estimated that by the third generation of Rockefellers, a staggering 5 billion dollars was donated to the philanthropic causes by John D. Sr., John D. Jr., and John D. Rockefeller III (Lundberg: 329).

More importantly, the Rockefeller dynasty has produced one Vice-President and former governor, a U.S. Senator and a former governor, and another governor--all from different states (Salmore: 125 & Ensor Harr: 8-9). The Rockefellers first entered the political arena in 1958. Nelson Rockefeller, son of John D. Jr., ran for and won the governor's seat in New York (Collier: 330). From there, Nelson used his reputation as a base to run for the presidency. In 1968, Nelson ran for the nomination of the Republican Party without entering the primaries (Halberstam). He did this to use polls to boost his popularity and bypass any losses in primaries that would diminish his chances of success. Although Rockefeller lost to Nixon, the Rockefeller machine continued to churn.

In 1964, Winthrop Rockefeller, brother of Nelson, ran unsuccessfully for the governor of Arkansas, but he won in 1966 and 1968 (Lundberg: 285). Winthrop re-shaped the new Rockefeller political mold by supporting issues important to blacks and impoverished citizens. Likewise, Nelson was very popular with black voters in his campaign for president. Winthrop became Arkansas' first Republican governor in a century (Lundberg: 285). Winthrop, long regarded as the "black sheep" in the family, retired from the governor spot when his term ended in 1970 (Ensor Harr: 5).

The Rockefeller political spotlight has also shone on the nephew of Nelson and Winthrop. John (Jay) D. Rockefeller IV has gone where no Rockefeller has gone before. Though Nelson was appointed as Vice-President for the troubled Ford administration, no Rockefeller had served in Congress. Jay, following two terms as the Democratic Governor of W. Virginia, ran and won a senate seat in 1984 ("King of the Hills and Hollers": 22-24). Although, the Rockefeller dynasty has been accused of buying elections (Salmore: 125) with the election of "J.D. IV," the Rockefeller name has secured its place in the elite American political arena.

Conclusion

The success of the Kennedy and the Rockefeller families as two prime examples of American dynasties exemplifies the primary political dynamics that are essential to being part of American political life. These dynamics are instant name recognition for family members, instant empathy from the electorate for the family member's position on issues, nonrational voting behavior based on residual biases associated with the family, and ability to exhibit independence from party politics. The practical effects of establishing a political dynasty are political survival. The societal effect is much less noticeable; political dynasties package political change as familial continuity and thus provide for the survival of their family's influence as well as goals for society. Because of this, political dynasties built in the past shape present political life and have uncommon influence over America's destiny.

Works Cited

Clinch, Nancy Gager. 1973. *The Kennedy Neurosis*. New York: Grosset & Dunlap..

Collier, Peter and David Horowitz. 1976. *The Rockefellers: An American Dynasty*. New York: Holt, Rinehart and Winston.

Davis, John H. 1984. The Kennedys: Dynasty and Disaster 1848-1983. New York: McGraw-Hill Book Company.

Ensor Harr, John and Peter J. Johnson. 1988. *The Rockefeller Century*. New York: Charles Scribner's Sons.

Granberg, Donald. 1985. "An Anomaly in Political Perception," *The Public Opinion Quarterly* 49: 504-16.

Lundberg, Ferdinand. 1975. *The Rockefeller Syndrome*. Secaucus, New Jersey: Lyle Stuart Inc.

"King of the Hills and Hollers," 20 Oct. 1984. *The Economist*: 22-24.

Halberstam, David. 1968. *The Unfinished Odyssey of Robert Kennedy*. New York: Random House.

"Liberals Rebuffed." 20 Sept. 1986. *The Economist*: 20.

Matusow, Allen J. 1983. "John F. Kennedy and the Intellectuals," *The Wilson Quarterly*, Autumn: 140-53.

Salmore, Barbara G., and Stephen A. Salmore. 1989. *Candidates, Parties, and Campaigns*. Washington D.C.: Congressional Quarterly Inc.

Schuyler, Michael W. 1987. "*Ghosts in the White House: LBJ, RFK, and the Assassination of JFK*," *Presidential Studies Quarterly*, 49: 503-18.

Wayne, Stephen J. 1990. *The Road to the White House*. New York: St. Martin's Press.

Wills, Garry. 1982. *The Kennedy Imprisonment*. Boston: Little, Brown and Company.

WRITING AN ANALYSIS

In some courses in political science, instructors prefer students to examine political events or phenomena critically. Writing an analysis of an event is part descriptive, part historical, part journalistic, and part imagination! An analysis involves identifying and differentiating between relevant and irrelevant information. It is specifically focused on the causal relationship between variables. In other words, an analysis provides an examination of the causes of political events. It involves asking not just who, what, when, and where, but also who benefited politically, who paid the political costs, what were the motivation or incentives, and when was the impact of the event realized. An analysis is typically, but not always, supported with both qualitative and quantitative evidence. Here is a standard formula for political event analysis (Lester 1990: 73.)

1.   **Describe the event. In particular, briefly describe the context in which the event occurred.**

- Identify specific activities that lead up to the event.
- Identify any perceived reactions to the event or arguments about its impact.
- State your thesis about why the event occurred.
- Be sure your thesis sentence clearly identifies the important causal variables associated with the event.

2.   **For the body, using your thesis sentence to guide you:**

- Examine critically, all important activities preceding the event.
- Using evidence, show how each activity is linked to the event.
- Rank order the events by importance to the outcome. Support this ranking with evidence.
- Provide evidence that describes the political consequence of the event or outcome.

3.   **Summarize the causal relationships and emphasize the important determinants of the event or outcome.**

- Show how the evidence supported your thesis sentence.
- Reaffirm your explanation of the event's impact on politics in society.

YOUTH INFLUENCE IN POLITICAL OUTCOMES

BY

PATRICK J. BROWN
Professor Schmidt
POLS 318
October 9, 1990
(Printed with Permission)

ABSTRACT

The youth in this country have had a direct influence on electoral outcomes by adding new voters to the voting block in 1972 and by taking part directly in the electoral process. Volunteering time to a candidate is the best way to get directly involved in an election. Also, if the youth vote in an election, they can add millions of votes to the outcome. In addition, if the majority of the youth movement is voting for a particular candidate, they can really make the difference in the election results. Although voter turnout of the youth has always been the lowest of the voting blocks, the youth movement can still make a difference. A good example of this occurred in the presidential election of 1968. The youth in the 1980s have identified with the Republicans and in the 1970s with the Democrats. This report will show that when the youth coalesce, they can make a difference in electoral outcome.

INTRODUCTION

According to the Twenty-sixth Amendment of the Constitution of the United States, citizens who are eighteen years of age or older have the right to vote. This Amendment was the turning point of the youth movement of the late 1960s. Now, the youth of this country can not only protest against our government, they can vote to change the representatives to govern it. Even before 1972, when the Amendment was approved, the youth (18-24) in the United States have made a difference in the electoral process and the outcomes. The youth can and have made a difference on electoral outcomes by adding a new voting block with millions of new voters and by taking part directly by working and volunteering for candidates.

TRENDS IN STUDENT ACTIVISM

In the 1960s, young people all over the world, particularly in the United States, seemed to develop a distinctive style of political dissent. Newspaper coverage about some youth organization holding a protest or political rally became increasingly frequent. According to Anthony Orum, there are three important conclusions that emerge from observing youth and their politics in the United States through historical perspectives. The conclusions are: the United States was not the first nation to experience vigorous political activity, it was uncommon to experience large-scale political activity by American youth until the 1960s, and most of the youth activists were well educated and wealthy.[1] A study of accredited four-year universities during the 1967-68 academic year found that only about two percent of the student population belonged to leftist student organizations and that an additional 8-10 percent were strongly sympathetic with the movement for social change and were capable of temporary activism depending on the issues.[2]

The activism of the 1960s had its origins in Berkeley, California, when in 1964 student activists were banned from political activities in an area of campus where they were formerly allowed. When the American involvement in Vietnam escalated, student unrest on campuses often became violent. According to Robert K. Landers:

> Student activists, to make a distinctive mark on their time, must overcome the thinness of their ranks and assert a plausible claim to represent in essence, the future. Hence, they must somehow arouse the sympathies of--and get occasional demonstrations of support from--the mass of students. During the 1960s, activists were able to accomplish this, but during the 1980s, they have been far less successful.[3]

The protests and the Vietnam War were both fought by young people. The unpopular war called more attention to the impact of government than any other event in this century.[4] Those who wanted to make a change had some alternatives. Some activists called for a revolution; however, others called for a non-violent means of expression.

TRENDS IN YOUTH VOTER TURNOUT

One alternative to revolution was to exercise the power of voting. Importantly, the Twenty-sixth Amendment, lowering of the voting age to eighteen in 1972, created a potential new influence on the outcome of elections. In addition, the post-World War II "baby boom" also resulted in many new voters entering the electorate in the late 1960s and early 1970s. Both of these factors drastically changed the electorate in this country. There were approximately 25 million new voters.[5] Many of these voters were more inclined to be less partisan and vote more along the lines of the issues.

Disappointing Youth Voter Turnout

There was, however, a surprise to those who advocated the Twenty-sixth Amendment: the trend of a declining youth turnout. In 1972, only about 48.3 percent turned out and voted. Although voting can be a powerful force for the youth agenda, only about 45.6 percent of that same group four years later voted.[6] Further, in the 1972 election, the percentage for 18-20 year olds who were not registered was 41.9 percent and for 21-24 year olds who were not registered was 40.5 percent.[7]

Nonetheless, in terms of non-voters, young people tend to be more interested in politics than older Americans. Among the population as a whole, older persons are more interested than the youth. The voting turnout by age characteristics of 18-20 year olds from the 1972 election to the 1984 election was considerably low compared with the rest of the voting classes. Since 1972, Democrats have outnumbered Republicans in terms of new voters by more than two to one.[8] The major reason was the Democrats' opposition to the war in Vietnam. Unfortunately, the Democrats, more than the Republicans, are inclined to not vote in an election. Together with youth identification with the Democratic party, this characteristic might help explain the low youth turnout.

More importantly, the tendency of the youngest voters to identify with the Republican Party may offer the greatest hope of increasing the size of the GOP. Although youth generally identify with the political party of their parents, increasingly young voters are aligning with the Republican Party regardless of their parent's party identification.[9] This change could help the party grow generational replacement. For example, in the 1984 election the younger voters supported the re-election of Ronald Reagan. This was a big change since the first youth election in 1972. The cause of this shift was not a move to the right among college students, but rather a shift to the middle ground or moderate positions in 1984[10]. Further, according to a New York Times-CBS News pole, Ronald Reagan won the support of full-time students by a margin of 51 to 48 percent. Again in the 1988 election, George Bush defeated Michael Dukakis in the youth category 52 to 47 percent.[11]

Inducing Youth Turnout

Although young people vote less than any other category, there are opportunities to change this trend. To induce voting among youth, candidates must advocate what young people perceive as their needs. In addition, the parties must change structurally to be more appealing and inclusive of young people. Finally, voting must result in identification benefits to youths.[12] Youth need to feel something when they vote. Young people must be persuaded to find efficacy and clear reasons for participating.[13] The foremost obstacle to increasing voting participation among youth is persuading them that their votes count.

Nonetheless, students and young people participate. Many of these activists volunteer in political campaigns because they feel strongly about the issues and candidates and because they want to make a difference. In conservative terms, there is a word to describe the effort of youth activism on college campuses to participate in the electoral process. The term is referred to as the Mass-Based Youth Effort.[14] The school that a potential activist can attend is called the Morton Blackwell Leadership Institute.[15] Based in Virginia, the Institute holds training seminars in central locations throughout the U.S. During this two-day seminar, activists learn how to conduct a canvass of the university's student population. Once activists locate the strong supporters for their candidate, they remind their supporters to go to the polls and vote. These activists also learn how to identify unregistered voters who agree with their party and how to register them to vote. Youths are taught how to get active and directly involved in the electoral process while showing young people how the election directly concerns them.

Another youth-based set of groups which mobilize students are the College Republicans and the College Democrats. Both the College Republicans National Committee and the Young College Democrats planned massive voter registration drives in the 1984 and 1988 elections. The Republicans concentrated on all fifty states compared with the seventeen-state effort in 1980. The College Democrats for the first time in 1984 worked in thirty states.[16] The College Republicans have a full time staff in Washington, D.C., and they have an annual budget of $250,000. The College Democrats have only a $12,000 budget and lack any central office of staff.[17] The main reason for the difference is because Morton Blackwell used to be the Executive Director of the College Republican National Committee, and the mass based youth effort concepts are used by the National Committee. The College Republicans now hold their own leadership training schools.

Impact of Youth Mobilization Programs

These youth movements have made a difference in electoral outcomes. In 1984, some 35,000 new student voters in Ohio helped to defeat three statewide referendums that would have raised the drinking age, and cut education funding.[18] Also, in New Orleans, at Xavier University in 1984, ninety-eight percent of the students are registered to vote.[19] Top priority was finally placed on voter registration by youth groups in 1984. Since then efforts are still going strong on campuses all over the country.

Students were also actively involved in Gary Hart's campaign for President in 1984. The students are credited with Hart's win in the New Hampshire primary because of the student canvassing effort. The students canvassed ninety percent of the precincts in the state.[20] The New Hampshire win placed Gary Hart in the race as a major contender. Many students joined the campaign as full time staff for the rest of the way. About half of Gary Hart's volunteers were students, compared with a third working for Jesse Jackson, and a fourth working for Walter Mondale.[21] All of the Democratic candidates made numerous campus campaign stops in 1984 because they believed that students could make a difference in many ways.

Probably the best example of a direct youth influence on the outcome of an election happened in the presidential election of 1968. Senator Eugene McCarthy was an early Democratic candidate for President of the United States. As president, Lyndon Johnson was favored in the race. The vote predictions in the New Hampshire primary by Gallup Polls had predicted in January that McCarthy had only twelve percent of the vote. When it was all over in March of 1968, McCarthy received 42.4 percent of the vote.[22] The students, most of who could not even vote yet, came to New Hampshire from Michigan, Wisconsin, Yale, and Harvard to work for their candidate, Eugene McCarthy. McCarthy gave the students the inspiration to care about politics and the Presidency. He also promised to end the war in Vietnam. It was estimated that as many as five thousand students campaigned on weekends and two thousand were full time.[23]

In particular, an important campaign stop for the Eugene McCarthy Campaign was in Wisconsin. Theodore H. White sums up what happened next during that visit.

> Student headquarters for McCarthy at the Wisconsin Hotel, a mile away, was explosive in contrast--eight thousand students were now roving over Wisconsin. Every town of five thousand had its student platoons, sleeping at friendly homes, in church basements, and still, on this Saturday they were pouring in, eight hundred from Michigan alone--and now the

students were veterans--volunteer specialists had broken the lists down into streets, blocks, and districts--assigned eighty calls to each volunteer. By two o'clock in the morning, Sunday, student headquarters were sending back the other busloads because they could not be used.[24]

When the votes were counted, Eugene McCarthy had 56.2 percent to Lyndon Johnson's 34.6 percent and Robert Kennedy's 6.3 percent.[25] Later, President Johnson gave a speech in which he withdrew his name from the electoral process and did not seek another term. The students in Eugene McCarthy's campaign worked many tasks from administrative to the most menial kinds of campaign work. The allure of the McCarthy campaign primarily centered on the treatment of youths in his campaign organization. His campaign staff did not distinguish between adult and the youth movement. They all worked together for a common cause.

Conclusion

The youth in this country, in terms of voting, have always had the lowest turnout. Nevertheless, youth can still make a difference in electoral outcomes. Youth groups major influence comes because of being the new voting block of 1972 and the impact of the numbers of "baby boom" votes cast in the elections. The candidates in the 1972 election had to appeal to the youth of this country. Because young people were protesting government policies, it was difficult to win over the youth vote in the late 1960s and the early 1970s. Most of those who were mobilized attached themselves to the Democratic Party. This continued to be the case until 1984, when the young people realigned to the Republican party during the re-election of Ronald Reagan. The youth vote has been largely Republican since that time. Part of the reason was a shift to more moderate positions by the youth and because of the Republicans' youth effort to attract votes, volunteers, and registration of new young voters in this country.

Perhaps the lowering of the voting age in this country did not have the impact in terms of increasing the number of young people that actually vote. It did, however, give millions of young people an incentive to use a nonviolent means of expressing opinions about policy decisions that impact them the most. Hard working mass-based youth movements can make a difference in this country like they did in the election for President in 1968. Theodore H. White describes that remarkable event in 1968 that best summarizes the potential impact of youth voting participation:

> It was not part of the script of history that Lyndon Johnson of the Pedernales should be brought down by a poet from Watkin, Minnesota. Hard working college students in nine weeks had brought down not a dean, not a president of a university, but the President of the United States.[26]

NOTES

[1]Anthony M. Orum, *The Seeds of Politics*, (New Jersey: Prentice-Hall, Inc., 1972), p. 2.

[2]Richard E. Peterson, "The Scope of Organized Student Protest," in Julian Foster and Durward Long, eds. *Protest! Student Activism in America*, (NY: Morrow, 1970) p. 78.

[3]Robert K. Landers, "Student Politics 1980s Style," *Editorial Research Reports*, 1986, p. 661; See also Louis M. Seagull, Youth *And Change In American Politics*. (New York: Franklin Watts Inc., 1977).

[4]William C. Mitchell, *Why Vote?*, (Chicago: Markham Publishing Company, 1971) p. 8.

[5]Mitchell, p. 8; see also, M. Kent Jennings and Richard G. Niemi. *The Political Character of Adolescence.* New York: Princeton University Press, 1974.

[6]David Hill and Norman Luttbeg, *Trends in American Electoral Behavior*, (Illinois: F.E. Peacock Pub, Inc, 1980).

[7]William J. Crotty, *Political Reform and the American Experiment*, (New York: Thomas J. Crowell Co., 1977), p. 54; see also Stanley Kelly and Richard E. Ayres and William G. Bowen, "Registration and Voting: Putting Things First," *American Political Science Review*, June, 1967, pg. 61.

[8]William H. Flanigan, *Political Behavior of the American Electorate*, (Boston: Allyn and Bacon, Inc., 1972), p. 26.

[9]1Everett Carl Ladd, "On Mandates, Realignments, and the 1984 Presidential Election", *Political Science Quarterly*, Spring, 1985, p. 18. See also, M. Kent Jennings and Richard G. Niemi, "The Transmission of Political Values From Parent To Child," *American Political Science Review*, March, 1968, pg. 171.

[10]Landers, p. 613; see also Frank J. Sorauf and Paul Allen Beck, *Party Politics In America*, (Glenview, IL: Scott, Foresman, 1987).

[11]Larry J. Sabato, *The 1988 Election in America*, (Glenview, IL: Scott, Foresman, 1989), p. 32.

[12]Curtis Gans, "Why Young People Don't Vote", *Educational Digest*, February 1989, p. 40.

[13]Gans, p. 43.

[14]This information is based on my field observation of the institution. See Morton Blackwell, *Leadership Source Manual*, mimeo, (Springfield, VA: Morton Blackwell Leadership Institute, 1990).

[15]Blackwell.

[16]Donna St. George, "Students Bone Up On Art Of Politics," *National Journal*, (April 7, 1984), p. 667.

[17]Larry J. Sabato, *The Party's Just Begun*, (Glenview, IL: Scott, Foresman, 1988), p. 81.

[18]St. George, p. 665.

[19]St. George, p. 665.

[20]St. George, p. 665.

[21]21St. George, p. 665.

[22]Eugene J. McCarthy, *The Year of the People*, (New York: Doubleday and Company, Inc., 1969), p. 89; see also Arthur Herzog, *McCarthy For President*. (New York: Viking Press, 1969).

[23]McCarthy, p. 70.

[24]Theodore H. White, *The Making of the President 1896*, (New York: Atheneum Publishers, 1969), p. 120.

[25]McCarthy, p. 108.

[26]White, p. 125.

BIBLIOGRAPHY

Blackwell, Morton. *Leadership Source Manual*. Mimeo. Springfield, VA: Morton Blackwell Leadership Institute. 1990.

Crotty, William J. *Political Reform and the American Experiment*. New York: Thomas J. Crowell Co. 1977.

Flanigan, William H. *Political Behavior of the American Electorate*. Boston: Allyn and Bacon, Inc. 1972.

Gans, Curtis. "Why Young People Don't Vote," *Educational Digest*, 54 (February 1989), pp.40-43.

Herzog, Arthur. *McCarthy For President*. New York: Viking Press. 1969.

Hill, David and Norman R. Luttbeg. *Trends in American Electoral Behavior*. Illinois: F.E. Peacock Publishers, Inc. 1990.

Jennings, M. Kent and Richard G. Niemi. *The Political Character of Adolescence*. New York: Princeton University Press. 1974.

_____. "The Transmission of Political Values From Parent To Child," *American Political Science Review*, 62 (March 1968), pp. 168-184.

Kelly, Stanley and Richard E. Ayres, and William G. Bowen, "Registration and Voting: Putting Things First," *American Political Science Review*, 61 (June 1967), pp.359-379.

Ladd, Everett Carl. "On Mandates, Realignments, and the 1984 Presidential Election," *Political Science Quarterly*, 100 (Spring 1985), pp.1-25.

Landers, Robert K. "Student Politics 1980s Style," *Editorial Research Reports*, 2 (1986), pp.609-628.

McCarthy, Eugene J. *The Year of the People*. New York: Doubleday and Company. 1969.

Mitchell, William C. *Why Vote?* Chicago: Markham Publishing Company. 1971.

Orum, Anthony M. *The Seeds of Politics*. New Jersey: Prentice-Hall, Inc. 1972.

Peterson, Richard E. "The Scope of Organized Student Protest," in Julian Foster and Durward Long, eds. Protest! Student Activism in America, NY: Morrow. 1970.

Sabato, Larry J. *The 1988 Elections In America*. Glenview, IL: Scott, Foresman and Company. 1989.

_____. *The Party's Just Begun*. Glenview, IL: Scott, Foresman and Company. 1988.

Seagull, Louis M. *Youth And Change In American Politics*. New York Franklin Watts Inc. 1977.

Sorauf, Frank J. and Paul Allen Beck. *Party Politics In America*. Glenview, IL: Scott, Foresman and Company. 1987.

St. George, Donna. "Students Bone Up To Art of Politics," *National Journal*, 16 (April 7, 1984), pp. 665-668.

White, Theodore H. *The Making Of The President 1968*. New York: Anteneum Publishers, Inc.. 1969.

WRITING A POSITION PAPER

Instructors in some upper level political science classes may assign a research paper which requires the student to do more than just research what other people say about a topic or controversy. A position paper takes the research process one step further than simple comparison or analysis. In a position paper, the student is required to construct a theory or position about an event, problem, or controversy and defend that theory or position using evidence. Position papers include, at minimum, scholarly qualitative evidence. Quantitative evidence and statistical methods are often used to provide further support for the author's theory or position. Here is a standard formula for writing a position paper.

1. **Describe a problem, event, or controversy. In particular, briefly describe the significance of the item you identified.**
   - Identify alternative explanations about why the problem/controversy exists or the event occurred.
   - In your thesis sentence, state your unique perspective about why the event occurred or why the problem/controversy exists.
   - Be sure you clearly separate your perspective from the others described.
   - Be sure your thesis sentence clearly identifies the important causal variables associated with the event, controversy, or problem.

2. **Trace the evolution of the event, problem, or controversy.**
   - Describe the context in which the event, problem, or controversy occurs.
   - Analyze the details, major identifiable issues, and minor underlying issues connected with the event, problem, or controversy.

3. **Identify the arguments or different important perspectives that have been used to explain the event, problem, or controversy.**
   - Be sure to justify why these perspectives are important.
   - Differentiate between the alternative explanations. How are they different? How are they similar?
   - Criticize the alternative explanations for errors in reasoning, omission, and/or facts.

4. **Describe your competing theory or position and justify it with evidence.**
   - State clearly how your perspective is different or corrects errors identified in other explanations.
   - Present evidence that strongly supports your theory or position.
   - Identify any evidence that appears to refute your theory or position. Explain why this evidence is not valid or how your theory must be adjusted to address the evidence if it is valid.

5. **Restate your theory or position and provide a concluding statement.**
   - Defend your theory or position by briefly recalling the evidence that supports your explanation and not the alternative explanations.
   - Make sure your analysis and arguments support your defense.
   - If possible, suggest a course of action or how the event, problem, or controversy could be addressed better in the future.

EXAMPLE OF A POSITION PAPER

**CHIEF JUSTICE REHNQUIST:
DOES HE LEAD THE COURT?**

By
Chris Kozenski

POLS 435
December 7, 1989
(Reprinted with Permission)

INTRODUCTION

The chief justice, as the head of the Supreme Court, is in both a good and bad position to lead and influence the members of the Courts. There are two limitations of power facing today's chief justice. As Laurence Baum (1986) indicates in his book *The Supreme Court*, the first limitation is that the chief justice is burdened with more administrative duties than ever. As the head of the federal court system, the chief serves both a powerful ceremonial and bureaucratic role, which keeps him very busy. According to Baum, one observer of the Court, Jeffery Morris, states that the Chief "may well stand at a relative disadvantage . . ." in the writing and arguing over opinions" because of the unique demands upon his time" (1986:153).

The second limitation of the power of today's chief justice is that present day justices are strong-minded, skilled individuals who are not likely to be controlled. Chief Justice John Marshall, in the early 1800s, had substantial control over his Court as seen by his writing of the Court's opinion in almost all cases. Rarely under Marshall did another justice's views win out over the chief justice. Yet, Chief Justice Rehnquist would never be able to lead the Court as strongly (Baum, 1986).

But the position of chief justice also has formal powers that strengthen his position as the leader of the court. In particular, there are three formal powers which can be quite important: 1) presiding over oral argument and conference, 2) creating the discuss list, and 3) opinion assignment (Baum, 1986). By presiding over conference, the chief justice opens the discussion on a case, he summarizes it, then gives his personal opinions on the case. He can also end discussion on the case. In this way, it might be possible for the chief to "frame alternatives, thus helping to shape the outcome of the discussion" (Baum 1986:153).

The discuss list is a set of petitions that will receive group judgment by the Court. The chief justice has the duty to make the first informal version of the list. By doing this, the chief plays an important role in determining which cases will be heard and decided on by the group (Baum 1986).

OPINION ASSIGNMENTS IN THE REHNQUIST COURT

The chief justice's third power--opinion assignment--that is by far his strongest leadership tool. The chief justice is, by position, the justice who assigns the writer of the Court's majority opinion. If the chief is not in the majority, then the next senior-most justice in the majority assigns the opinion (Baum 1986). What makes this power so important is that it is in these majority opinions where the Supreme Court establishes "controlling constitutional principles" and where "broader policy objectives beyond the immediate case are fashioned" (Slotnick, 1978: 219). So by assigning the opinions to the justice of his choice, the chief is in a good position to alter, even frame, the public policies that result from Supreme Court decisions.

Because of the importance of opinion assignment, it should be shown that certain factors do come into play when the chief justice makes an assignment. There are four factors, in particular, that have influence on the chief justice's assignment. The first is the equality of distribution. This means that the justices should have relatively equal workloads and if the chief assigns opinions disproportionately, he will upset those justices who do not have an equal share of the workload, and therefore an unequal share of opinions (Slotnick 1978). Ability and expertise are also important factors the chief takes into consideration when assigning an opinion. The fourth factor is the importance of the decision. If a decision is considered important, often the chief will self-assign the opinion. This is traditionally an unwritten norm of the court. As the "equal above equals" the chief lends his prestige to a decision when he is the author of the opinion (Slotnick 1978).

Still, there are four other things the chief justice must take into consideration when making an assignment. David Danelski tells us that whomever the chief justice designates to speak for the court may be highly influential in:

1) determining the precedent value of a decision (because the justice who authors the opinion often decides the grounds for the decision).

2) making the decision as publicly acceptable as possible.

3) holding a majority together when it is a close vote.

4) and minimizing the number of dissenting and concurring opinions (Danelski, 1986).

Often the assigner of the opinion will choose the justice who stands in the middle of the voting coalitions in order to gain support for the majority decision. For example, if a particular decision has the court divided, the chief must choose the justice with a moderate view in order to gain votes from the dissenting side of the court (Danelski 1986).

Equality of Assignments

There are two ways in which equality of opinion assignment can be examined. The first way is through measuring absolute equality; this is simply the equality of caseloads between the justices. Another way to examine equality is to look at it conditionally; this means that equality is based on the frequency of times a justice is available to write the opinion (Spaeth, 1984:300).

To see how fairly Chief Justice Rehnquist assigned opinions, I examined majority opinion assignments from both viewpoints of equality (Spaeth 1984:299-304), the same way Harold Spaeth studied court decisions. [1] Absolute equality was examined for the 1986, 1987, and 1988 terms. Table 1 displays the number of opinions that each justice wrote per term, regardless of who made the assignment or how often the justice was in the majority. It was measured using a mean (which is simply the average number of times a justice wrote an opinion for that year), a standard deviation (Std. Dev.), and a coefficient of relative variation (CRV) which standardizes a set of deviations based on different means.

(TABLE 1 ABOUT HERE)

Because the chief justice assigns a majority of cases, it was up to Rehnquist to assign fairly and equally if he wanted a record of distributive equality in opinion assignments. Table 1 shows an impressive equal distribution of opinion writing between the justices. Treating the terms as a whole ('86-'88) each justice wrote an average of 15.8 opinions. The number of times a justice varied by more than three assignments from the

---

[1] Opinion Assignment Ratio was used here in order to compare with Spaeth's findings of Burger and Warren. (The overall OARS are as follows: Rehn.=14.0, Bren.=17.3, White=14.8, Mar.=16.1, Blac.=13.6, Pow.=15.8, Stev.=15.8, O'C=14.2, Sca. 11.1, Ken.=12.6).

term average is only three (two occurring in 1986, Powell and Scalia; one occurring in 1988, Scalia). Rehnquist's CRVs are low in all three terms (1986: CRV .15; 1987: CRV .13; 1988: CRV .13).

Comparing Rehnquist to other chief justices only enhances his record of absolute quality. Rehnquist has an overall CRV of .12, while Burger's overall CRV is .179, and Warren's was .24. Stone, Vinson, Taft, and Hughes are all at least twice as high as Burger's, which makes Rehnquist's CRV the best of the last six chief justices of the Supreme Court (Spaeth 1984).

Rehnquist has a very good overall distribution record, but what happens when conditioned equality of assignments is looked at? To study this, opinion assignment ratios were used to see the overall picture. Again following Spaeth's study, Rehnquist's equality of assignments in "important" cases was compared to that of Burger and Warren. It is in these "important" cases where major public policy is made. To test whether Chief Justice Rehnquist is leading the Court's public policy, it is necessary to look at his opinion distribution practices in these important cases.

There have been many methods employed to define important cases. Sidney Ulmer deems a case important by the amount of times the "court cites the case within five years of the decision" (Spaeth 1984:303). This cannot apply here because of the recent data being used. Another approach uses constitutional casebooks, and if the case is discussed in several of these books, then it is considered as important. But because both of these methods have come under fire for various reasons, Spaeth's method was used. Spaeth's method defined a case as important if it appears within a rectangle on the front cover of the Lawyers Edition of U.S. Reports. Of these important cases (47 in all between 1986 and 1989) Rehnquist assigned 72 percent of the opinions. (He assigned 50 percent in 1986, 80 percent in 1987, and 82 percent in 1988).

As a norm of the Court, the chief justice is expected to disproportionately assign important decisions to himself, being the "first above equals." Yet Rehnquist's patterns of opinion assignments in important cases show huge disparities. Using an opinion assignment ratio (OAR), each justice was given a ratio for the '86-'88 terms. The OAR is "simply the percentage of times a given justice is assigned the majority opinion when he is in the Court's majority" (Slotnick, 199:63). Measuring a justice's OAR is important because "it is more sensitive than a simple average would be when dealing with a justice who is in dissent [or not sitting] a great deal of the time" (Spaeth 1984:304).

According to their OARs, as seen in Table 2, three justices had very high OARs and were at least 13.6 points above the mean; these justices were Rehnquist with an OAR of 29.4, White with an OAR of 37.9, and Powell with an OAR of 42.9.

(TABLE 2 ABOUT HERE)

There were also three justices who had OARs of zero, meaning that no time in the 1986, 1987, or 1988 term did Chief Justice Rehnquist assign them an "important" opinion to write. These justices were Brennan, Marshall, and Stevens. Blackmun also had a relatively low OAR of 6.7. The standard deviation is 15.1 and the CRV = .96. This is a tremendously high CRV, which shows that there are great differences in the number of opinions each justice wrote.

Comparing Rehnquist to other chief justices shows to what degree Rehnquist unequally assigned cases. Burger's overall CRV of important cases was .47 (Spaeth 1984:304). Stone's CRV was .40, Vinson's CRV was .55, and Warren's CRV equaled .44 (Spaeth 1984:304). Even if Slotnick's rule is followed, which excludes those justices who are available in less than ten cases (Brennan and Powell), Rehnquist's CRV is still .80, while Burger's declines to .34 (Spaeth 1984:304).

In sum, these results show that Rehnquist unequally assigns the opinions of important cases. In particular, he especially favored those justices who fit his ideology. Further, according to the data reported, his distributive inequality is the largest of the last five chief justices.

Self-Assignment

To see if this inequity came from Rehnquist's self-assignment practices, his OARs were compared to the average OAR of the Court. Following Slotnick's (1978) study Tables 3 and 4 show the results of the comparison.

(TABLES 3 AND 4 ABOUT HERE)

Rehnquist has a lower OAR than the Court average in the case universe, which means he writes .5 fewer opinions than does the average justice on the court when considering all cases. When only important decisions are examined does Rehnquist's OAR exceeds the court average by 13.6.

Table 4, however, shows that it is the norm for the Chief Justice's OAR to be substantially above the Court average. This confirms Slotnick's (1978) findings. Rehnquist is only 1.5 above the total for all justices from Taft to Burger. Thus these findings suggest Rehnquist's unequal distribution of opinion assignments in important cases is not due to his self-assignment practices.

IDEOLOGIES ON THE REHNQUIST COURT

To further test these findings on Rehnquist's leadership practices, the justices' judicial perspective was evaluated on an ideological spectrum. To address this same issue Harold Spaeth and David Rohde examined the conflicts between the liberal and conservative positions on the Court (Baum, 1986). Rohde and Spaeth break these issues of conflict down into three categories: 1) freedom, 2) equality, 3) New Dealism. Using these categories, it is easy to rank the justices on an ideological spectrum.

In order to say that Rehnquist is leading the Court, evidence is needed to show that he is assigning those opinions of important cases disproportionately to those who are most like him. In a study on the 1986 term, Rohde and Spaeth looked at the voting patterns on "freedom" cases in 58 non-unanimous decisions. Freedom cases are defined as involving "conflicts between individual freedoms and governmental action" (Baum 1986:138). They found that some justices were prone to vote liberally and others were prone to vote conservatively. This comes as no surprise. By using a scalogram, Rohde and Spaeth were able to rank the justices according to their number of liberal votes.

In 1986, according to the scalogram, Marshall, Brennan, and Stevens, in that order, had the most liberal votes. Blackmun also voted liberally more than conservatively. On the other end of the spectrum, Rehnquist, O'Connor, White, Scalia, and Powell had the most conservative votes.

Looking at the interagreement among justices, Baum (1986) uses a table for the median percentage of cases in which pairs of justices supported the same opinion in the 1985 and 1986 terms. Unlike the Rohde and Spaeth study, this table includes all cases in all issue areas. Baum finds that Rehnquist agrees with Powell 87 percent of the time, and White and O'Connor 81 percent and 85 percent of the time. Rehnquist had the lowest rates of agreement with Marshall 39 percent, Brennan 42 percent, and Stevens 49 percent of the time. This interagreement, along with the findings of Spaeth and Rohde, makes a very clear picture. These findings also clearly support what I have concluded from my study -- that is, Chief Justice Rehnquist assigns important opinions to justices who will fulfill his policy objectives--these justices often being Powell, White, and the Chief Justice himself.

DISCUSSION AND CONCLUSIONS

So far, this study has shown that Chief Justice Rehnquist has a fair overall opinion assignment rate. More importantly, this study has shown that Rehnquist has an unfair opinion assignment rate in important cases where most public policy is made. In particular, the findings show that Rehnquist favors conservatives, like himself, by giving them more politically significant opinions to write. Yet, it is important to mention that Rehnquist only assigned 73 percent of the total important cases in the three terms studied. Brennan assigned the other 27 percent of the cases, except for one assigned by Marshall. Thus, Justice Brennan appears to have assigned cases just as unfairly as Rehnquist did.

The OAR ratio should be used to examine the relative assignment behavior more closely. But because the numbers were so low, actual percentages of times Brennan assigned opinions to each justice is an adequate and meaningful substitute for an OAR ratio. Brennan self-assigned the opinion exactly 50 percent of the time. Stevens, Marshall, and Blackmun each were assigned 10 percent. Brennan only assigned 10 important cases in all, so of the ten, he assigned 80 percent (or 8) of them to liberals on the court.[2] Both O'Connor and Powell were assigned one opinion also. From these numbers it is plain to see that Brennan uses the 27 percent of the cases he assigns to promote liberal public policies. In this way he, too, is a leader of the court, although he is not as powerful as the chief justice is. Thus, this suggests that although the Chief Justice has a normal self-assignment rate, he self-assigns cases less than the average justice overall and is similar to higher chief justices in self-assignment on important cases.

FINAL REMARKS

Earlier in this paper, many different factors were mentioned, each having a possible effect on opinion assignment practices. Among the more important factors mentioned were expertise and holding the majority vote together. It is true that these factors work together and produce an effect on the Chief Justice's decision. Yet, it is apparent that chief justices, through the use of their power of assignment, also have wide discretion in pursuing their own public policy ideals (Slotnick, 1979). Chief Justice Rehnquist is no exception; in fact, he was shown to have possibly the widest discretion of the more recent chief justices. It will be interesting to see if this trend continues in his future terms as chief justice.

---

[2]The case of K-Mart vs. Cartier was not included because of the plurality of opinions.

REFERENCES

Altfeld, M.F., and H.J. Spaeth. (1984). Measuring influence on the U.S. Supreme Court. *Jurimetrics Journal*, 24, 236-247.

Baum, L. (1986). *The Supreme Court.* (3rd ed.) Washington, D.C.: Congressional Quarterly.

Brenner, S., and H.J. Spaeth. (1986). Issue specialization in majority opinion assignment on the Burger court. *Western Political Quarterly*, 39, 520-527.

Cannon, M.C., and D.M. O'Brien. (1985). *Views from the bench.* Chatham: Chatham House.

Chaper, J.H. (1987). *The Supreme Court and its justices.* Chicago: American Bar Association.

Goldberg, A.J. (1986). The Rehnquist Court. *Hastings Constitutional Law Quarterly*, 14, 21-24.

Danelski, David. (1986). The Influence of the Decisionmaking Process. In Murphy, W.F., and Pritchett, C.H. (eds.) (1986). *Courts, judges, and politics.* New York: Random House.

Slotnick, E.E. (1978). The Chief Justices and self-assignment on majority opinions: A research note. *Western Political Quarterly*, 31, 219-225.

Slotnick, E.E. (1979). Who speaks for the Court? Majority opinion assignment from Taft to Burger. *American Journal of Political Science*, 23(1), 60-77.

Spaeth, H.J. (1984). Distributive justice: Majority opinion assignments in the Burger court. *Judicature*, 67, 299-304.

Spaeth, H.J., and F.A. Michael. (1985). Influence relationships within the Supreme Court: A comparison of the Warren and Burger courts. *Western Political Quarterly*, 38, 70-83.

Steamer, R.J. (1986). *Chief Justice.* Columbia: University of South Carolina Press.

TABLE 1: DISTRIBUTION OF OPINIONS AND JUDGMENTS OF THE COURT

JUSTICE	*TERM*		
	1986	1987	1988
Rehnquist	17	15	16
Brennan	16	16	17
White	16	20	18
Marshall	15	15	15
Blackmun	13	15	15
Powell	20	--	--
Stevens	15	19	15
O'Connor	18	16	13
Scalia	12	16	11
Kennedy	12	7*	16
Mean	15.78	16.50	15.11
Std. Dev.	2.43	2.17	1.97
CRV	.15	.13	.13

Mean: the average number of times a justice wrote an opinion, Std. Dev: standard deviation from the mean. CRV: a coefficient of relative variation that standardizes a set of deviations based on different means.

* Kennedy did not participate in the entire 87-88 term, so he was excluded from the mean, std. dev., CRV. If Kennedy was included, the following data apply: mean = 15.44, std. dev. 3.44, CRV =.22.

Source: *Supreme Court Reporter*.

TABLE 2: REHNQUIST'S ASSIGNEES AND
THEIR OPINION ASSIGNMENT RATIOS IN "IMPORTANT CASES"

Assignees	Number of Assignments	Times Available	OAR
Rehnquist	10	34	29.4
Brennan	0	9	0
White	11	29	37.9
Marshall	0	10	0
Blackmun	1	15	6.7
Powell	3	7	42.9
Stevens	0	14	0
O'Connor	2	18	11.1
Scalia	4	29	13.8
Kennedy	3	19	15.8

Mean (for the court) = 15.8
Std. Dev. (for the court) = 15.1
CRV (for the court) = .96

TABLE 3: SELF-ASSIGNMENT RATES V. "OTHER" ASSIGNMENT

Unit	Rehnquist's OAR	OAR for Court
Case Universe	14	14.5
"important"decisions	29.4	15.8

TABLE 4: SELF-ASSIGNMENT V. "OTHER" ASSIGNMENT

| Chief Justice | Case Universe | | "Important"Decisions | |
	Self-Assign OAR	Court OAR	Self-Assign OAR	Court OAR
Taft	16.3	11.1	38.2	10.2
Hughes	15.5	11.8	34.8	10.8
Stone	16.4	13.0	19.4	13.7
Vinson	12.1	14.6	24.6	13.1
Warren	13.0	14.0	19.0	13.5
Burger	13.7	14.5	25.7	12.9
TOTAL	14.8	12.6	24.8	12.7
Rehnquist	14.0	14.5	29.4	15.8

SECTION ELEVEN

FORMAT AND EXAMPLES OF ASSIGNMENTS REQUIRING SPECIAL TECHNIQUES

ASSIGNMENTS REQUIRING SPECIAL ANALYTICAL TECHNIQUES

In the following pages, there are five examples of highly specialized undergraduate research papers that exhibit a range of writing styles and topics concerning public policy and decision-making. Like standard research papers, the ideas in the papers develop from a thesis sentence and present an argument about the significance of the findings. Unlike standard research papers, these papers require a special analytical structure where to be complete, the author must include specific details and information concerning the topic. Like standard research papers, these techniques are not specific to the study of American government. The study of comparative public policy and international agreements requires the same attention to the processes and details of making and implementing public policy. These papers exhibit the standard form and degree of thoroughness necessary for studying different kinds of policy at different points in the policy life cycle. The explanation and form for each type of paper precedes the examples.

First Paper: Analytical Case Study

"Dysfunctional Behavior in the FBI," examines the organizational practices of the Federal Bureau of Investigation. As a case study of administrative behavior, the paper focuses on the historical and contemporary organizational relationships between staff, administrators, and the public.

Second Paper: Problem-Solving Case Study

"Building Inspection Expense Analysis: Building Inspection Department," is a policy memorandum that provides a highly condensed analytical summary of budget expenditures and budget recommendations.

Third Paper: An Analysis of Legislation

"Education For All Handicapped Children Act of 1975," uses government documents and is limited to examining the initiation phase of public policymaking.

Fourth Paper: A Policy Evaluation

"NEPA: America's Policy Response to Environmental Crises," uses a variety of sources from political science to scientific research reports. It is limited to examining the initiation and expansion phase of public policymaking.

Fifth Paper: A Policy Recommendation

"A Hypothetical Policy Recommendation: Welfare Reform," uses a variety of literature and some statistical information to propose a re-evaluation and re-formulation of welfare policy. This paper analyzes the entire policy life cycle from the initiation to the expansion to the reformulation stages.

ANALYTICAL CASE STUDY

Analytical case studies provide students with the opportunity to apply theories learned in class to practical situations. The goal of an analytical case study is to examine behavior related to political decision-making and explain why and how that behavior influenced political outcomes. Importantly, the reason for doing case studies is to learn something about how the political *system* works by examining how a *component* of the system works.

- The usefulness of case studies is that the research provides intricate details about the structure of organizations, strategies used by decision-makers, and behavior of individuals at the individual level.

- The problem with analytical case studies is that they are not often generalizable across the political spectrum.

The best analytical case studies focus on aspects of political behavior that are applicable to the broader political spectrum while providing a compelling story about the idiosyncratic aspects of the subject being studied. At the end, the reader should know some interesting contextual information about the subject of the case study and understand more about the effect of particular structures and behavior on political outcomes.

How to Write an Analytical Case Study

1. **Title page**

2. **Executive Summary**

   - Use bullets to highlight the key problems.
   - Summarize the conclusions.

3. **Narrative of Historical Context**

   - Write the thesis as a statement of the specific objective of the case study (i.e., what is to be explained and how).
   - Identify when the organization was formed (cultural and political context).
   - Identify why the organization was formed (goals, mission).
   - Describe the structure of the organization.
   - Describe the external political pressures on the staff from interest groups, Congress, the president, other agencies, or courts.
   - Describe the internal political pressures on the staff from standard operation procedures, agency structure, distribution of authority, or agency mission.

4.   **Problem Identification**

- Write this section in short story form with descriptive and compelling language.
- Identify no more than 4 problems.
- If more than 4 problems exist, then classify or cluster the problems together into categories.
- Rank order the problems from most compelling to least compelling.
- Describe the most compelling problem first and then the rest in rank order.
- Provide an illustrative, compelling, descriptive example for each problem identified.
- Identify the characters involved in the problems.
- Describe how the characters are involved in controversy and/or conflict.

5.   **Analysis of the Problem**

- Suggest how the problems identified influenced political outcomes.
- Suggest how individual behavior influences the problems and the outcomes.
- Suggest how organizational structure influence the problems and the outcomes
- Identify any attempts to solve the problems.
- Suggest why attempts to solve the problems failed.
- Identify any solutions available but untried.
- Suggest why some available solutions have not been, or cannot be, used.

6.   **Conclusion**

- Restate the problems.
- Restate the effect of the problems on political outcomes.
- Suggest what is new knowledge about the organization.
- Suggest what is new knowledge about how the political system works.

EXAMPLE OF AN ANALYTICAL CASE STUDY

DYSFUNCTIONAL BEHAVIOR IN THE FBI

By
Steve Goard
Professor Diane Schmidt
POL 260A
December 1, 1998

EXECUTIVE SUMMARY

The primary mission of the Federal Bureau of Investigation (FBI) was to investigate federal violations such as bankruptcy fraud, anti trust crimes, and neutrality violations. The FBI, since the J. Edgar Hoover administration, has chosen the path of bureaucratic effectiveness over efficiency and equity. Though Congress granted authority to the FBI to investigate violations, the FBI became a bureau of corruption because of:

- unchecked personal power.

- corrupt standard operating procedures.

- legislative collusion.

- presidential collusion.

Within the context of these problems, the FBI became an effective agency in achieving more authority, creating fear, and ruining individuals. The lack of responsible oversight and accountability that was pervasive during the Hoover administration continues to taint the image of the FBI and the creditability of its agents.

ORIGINS OF THE FBI'S POWER

In July of 1907, the American born grandnephew of Napoleon I, Charles J. Bonaparte, approached Congress with the idea of creating a permanent detective force within the Department of Justice (DOJ). In July of 1908, upon authority of the United States Congress, the Federal Bureau of Investigation (FBI) was established. In 1910, Congress passed the Mann Act to help curb prostitution. The act inadvertently expanded the authority of the FBI and enabled the FBI to develop dossiers on criminals, elected officials, and wealthy socialists[4]. During the World War I era, Congress gave the FBI the responsibility to investigate espionage, sabotage, and draft violations. At this point, the FBI demonstrated their crude tactics on monitoring and catching such violators. During this period the FBI extended their perimeter of censorship and continued to violate more civil liberties. For example, German teachers and German music composers were prohibited from teaching and performing (Gentry 1991).

PROBLEMS IN THE FBI

In December of 1924, the young J. Edgar Hoover was appointed as the director of the FBI. Hoover's appointment was to correct the bureau's reputation as a corrupt national law enforcement agency (Turner 1970). Hoover acknowledged the orders from Congress publicly, but some historians contend that Hoover and the FBI never intended to correct but to continue the pre-1924 intelligence activity (Croog 1992).

Unchecked Personal Power

Faced with a corrupt FBI, Hoover publicly accepted the challenge and vowed to restore the values of the FBI. December of 1924 marked the beginning of a new era under the control of Director J. Edgar Hoover. Upon Hoover's appointment, the FBI's authority was limited to federal violations only (Charles 1997). But in 1934, FBI agents were given the power to make arrests and to carry firearms (Feinman 1991). This grant of authority prompted Hoover to create more government files on United States citizens.

Further, in 1936 the FBI was given the far-reaching authority to investigate possible Nazis. However, this authority was quickly abused by the Hoover administration (Felt 1979). Not surprisingly, the FBI's focus centered on radical activists, organization, and even influential personalities ranging from famous author Ernest Hemingway, civil rights activists Martin Luther King Jr. and Malcolm X, and even went so far to investigate First Lady Eleanor Roosevelt (Theoharis 1993).

Hoover, an influential and persuasive person himself, conned and convinced Congress into believing his investigations were needed in order to protect the national security. Yet, many believe that the primary motivation for the investigations was more related to controlling and containing dissent that it was to promote the public interest (Theoharis 1993).

Corrupt Standard Operation Procedures

In order for the FBI to continue such illegal investigation, Hoover and the FBI created the "secret file" system. The norm for the FBI was that agents would relay all information to the heads of the administration; they in turn would review the information and debrief the White House. The "secret file" system was carefully calculated technique to keep some illegal investigations from being exposed (Powers 1987). All information known to be sensitive would be labeled "personal and confidential." All information that entered the FBI with that label would end up on Hoover's desk. Hoover would then review all the information and would file it away for safekeeping (Jung and Thom, 1997). The "secret file" procedure kept all illegal politically motivated reports out of the FBI's central records system. This technique allowed Hoover to safely side step the Attorney General's ban and continue to investigate and monitor political activities (Theoharis 1993).

Perhaps there was an intended coincidence in the name of the "secret files"; it is everything the name implies. The FBI investigated and kept information on influential individuals, radicals and anyone thought to be a communist. The investigative approach the FBI took involved the gathering of information using sex as a tool. The FBI used the prostitution ring and other sexual decoys to infiltrate specific groups, and sometimes individuals (Marx 1992). In New York City, for instance, the FBI financed the making of pornographic films and had policewomen direct the on-camera sex acts.

Hoover's bulging files on individuals contained information on more than just sex and other improper acts (Marx 1992). In another example, the FBI came upon information that in Chicago there was a link between the organized crime ring and prostitution. Federal agents took over a credit card processing company and over a four year period processed $30 million in customer payments for sexual services. These transactions were recorded on credit card receipts as food, beverages, and office supplies, which could be taken as business tax reductions. The FBI-run agency paid, out of the FBI's bank account, for sex clubs. It provided $100,000 to bribe the local police agencies in order to stay open. The investigation did not lead to any arrests, but helped the FBI collect information on high profile individuals and political leaders who received bribes (Marx 1992).

All of this was in pursuit of information. Hoover was adept at this. The information gathered implied the threat of public ruin, threat of exposure, all which was used as a political tool. But the outlandish investigations did not stop there. Sex was used as an investigative toll, as well as other inappropriate methods in order to gather new information. The bureau investigated the sexual habits and many other elements of a person's private life. For example, the FBI investigated the Church Committee, instructing the informant to sleep with as many wives as possible (Croog 1992). The tactic here was to break up marriages and gather information.

The FBI's approach was to gather information and control that individual with the threat of public humiliation (Croog 1992). One clear example of the FBI's approach was the case involving a rather un-influential gossip columnist Inga Arvad. Arvad became the target of an intensive FBI investigation due to her political views and employment by the *Washington Times-Herald* (Theoharis 1993). Arvad was a target due to the FBI's tainted and over expanded definition of "communist." The FBI approached Arvad's place of employment and demanded an investigative interview. The fear of the public discovering that the *Washington Times-Herald* employed a communist, the *Washington Times-Herald* complied. When the interview turned up nothing, the FBI stepped up the investigation by adding wiretaps to Arvad's personal telephone. Although the investigation turned up nothing, Hoover used his persuasive tactics to convince the Attorney General to continue the investigation. After years of harassment, the FBI discontinued the investigation. With the information gathered, the FBI discovered that Miss Arvad was a strong isolationist but held nothing that reflected pro-axis or anti-axis information.

Legislative Collusion

The FBI's jurisdiction and authority is directly granted by legislation. The president, Attorney General, and Congress all decide the authority the FBI is given. Glancing back at the events described earlier, it appears that the FBI expands its authority and jurisdiction by creating and implementing new policy within the FBI.

For example, the FBI, with this new secret policy, avoided being limited by legislation. During the 1950s, the Cold War hit its fevered pitch. Senator Joseph McCarthy and the House of Un-American Activities Committee (HUAC) alerted the nation of the serious threat of a communist take over in the United States (Moore 1990). Congress granted the FBI the authority (known as the Responsibilities Program) to investigate communist subversives in the government. Hoover, the FBI, along with the president and Congress used the Responsibilities Program to go after suspected communists, influential people, organizations, political opponents and even people they plainly disliked (Jung and Thom 1997). With the Responsibilities Program safely in tact, the FBI created a very broad definition of communist.

Although this was the first time that legislation gave the FBI the authority to investigate suspected communists, the truth of the matter was, the FBI had been conducting these types of investigations since the 1930s (Feinman 1992). The FBI's definition of "communist" included almost any left-wing activity that could be interpreted as subversive. The Responsibilities Program was designed to investigate possible communist subversives employed in the government and public services (Croog 1992). All information was reviewed and the FBI secretly supplied governors and high-level municipal authorities with any information about the individual being investigated. The immediate problem with the program was confidential leaks. The Responsibilities Program quickly devolved into systematic tool of harassment providing irrelevant information on perceived subversives, which lead to many terminations of employment, particularly those in education.

To maximize total control of the new program, Hoover and the FBI insisted that FBI headquarters alone be the ones to determine the information to be divulged. This response was due to the questionable legality of the FBI's investigative techniques. The FBI established a plan in which FBI agents would see to it that those terminated from employment were not rehired somewhere else.

The fall of the Responsibilities Program came in the late 1950's. Some historians contend that the techniques employed by the FBI caused the destruction of the program. The confidential leaks to the media exposed some awful truths about the FBI's illegal investigations. There were 794 individuals investigated. 429 who were employed in education. Hoover claimed the FBI was effective in finding and removing communists that were in the position to poison the minds of the youth of this country. Of the 429 suspected communists employed in education, 429 were terminated from educational employment (Jung and Thom 1997). The FBI made it clear that they were outraged that those individuals who leaked this information could be retained in government employment.

There was a point in the FBI's history where Hoover ignored legislation and implemented his own program of continuing his secret policies. During the Ford administration, Hoover created an execution squad. The squad's job was to cause the permanent disappearance of individuals the FBI believed would never be brought to justice if proper policy and procedure were followed. The squad members consisted mostly of organized crime families, but also included military personnel and local police (Marx 1992). Hoover believed the squad would be more effective if the FBI and its agents were not directly involved.

The squad was considered a special force of assassins to take out any individuals the FBI named. Although there has been no official recognition of the squad, some historians contend some of the squad's victims included KGB agents, former Japanese officers, and Nazi war criminals. Some historians claim the squad offers some insight into the relationship that the FBI had with famous organized crime families (Turner 1970). The squad gives even further insight into why the FBI was so reluctant in going after organized crime families.

Presidential Collusion

The FBI was more than just an asset to the nation's people; the FBI was a political tool for several politicians. The FBI was the mortal enemy of anyone being investigated. The FBI demonstrated its bureaucratic survival skills and capacity to manipulate the press, Congress, and the President of the United States without revealing its hand. The majority of the authority and jurisdiction the FBI was awarded can be directly contributed to the relationship the FBI had with the presidential administration. Presidents, Roosevelt, Nixon, Carter, Ford, and Johnson all had a personal stake in the FBI.

With Roosevelt's election in 1932, the FBI no longer had to be so circumspect. In 1934, Roosevelt secretly ordered the FBI to investigate and monitor the activities of American Nazis and Nazi sympathizers. Between 1934 and 1936, the president requested investigative reports on all right-wingers. By 1939, Roosevelt ordered the FBI to conduct widespread surveillance on political opposition and critics of presidential policy (Jung and Thom 1997). During the Roosevelt administration, the FBI's illegal investigations primarily focused on foreign policy critics. The FBI had a favored relationship with the Roosevelt administration. Roosevelt supported the New Deal crime-control program, which gave the FBI more authority to go after "bad guys" without regard to personal and civil rights. The FBI investigated the lives and activities of political organizations, political opponents of the president, and critics of administrative policy. The FBI consistently sought potentially damaging information on individuals' personal lives (Feinman 1991). Carefully cultivated informants would relay sensitive information back to FBI headquarters (due to the FBI's secret file system, the information landed directly on Hoover's desk) Hoover would then leak this damaging information on to friendly journalists, presidents, and other politicians for the multiple purposes of destroying and discrediting those individuals.

The FBI's hit list included several members of the American Civil Liberties Union (ACLU), Charles Lindbergh, and several political opponents. Although several presidents used the FBI in their favor in order to achieve personal success, Hoover and the FBI was a feared bureaucracy (Watters and Gillers 1973). The FBI flexed its bureaucratic muscle by turning the game against those who played it. President Nixon publicly praised the FBI and Hoover for making the FBI the defender of Americans' precious right to be free from fear. But fear is what the FBI brought to President Nixon. Recorded on the White House tapes, Nixon expressed his concern about the FBI files and how the FBI had secret files on everyone, including him. Nixon feared the information the FBI collected on him. Nixon feared that the FBI could bring down the Nixon administration if Nixon ever restricted the FBI's authority.

Fear and the FBI's blackmail controlled several politicians and the way policy was enacted. While several people were successfully blackmailed, those who refuse to submit were often ruined by mysterious, and sometimes false, FBI press leaks. Some historians would contend death resulted for a few who refused to comply with the FBI. With Hoover as the head of the country's chief law enforcement agency, the president could investigate, monitor, and potentially destroy political opponents. Since 1936, the FBI catered to each of the succeeding administrations proving the FBI's political worth (Charles 1997).

EVALUATION OF PROBLEMS IN THE FBI

The secret investigations gave the FBI some persuasive power when it came to American politics. The secret files and the secret files system helped the FBI to become a powerful and experienced agency; an agency led by those committed to effectiveness. The unstoppable behavior of the FBI was directly influenced by the FBI's authority and secret power to control high profile figures, including presidents of the United

States. Despite so many obvious violations of civil liberties through illegal investigations, the FBI continued to operate under a crime-control fashion.

The secret file system, in particular, proved to be an asset for the FBI and the way Hoover ran the agency. The illegal investigations included wiretaps, prostitution, physical assaults, and blatant violations of constitutional rights. These investigations even sought out the individuals who controlled the FBI (i.e.: the president, Attorney General, and Congress). The FBI collected such a massive amount of damaging information on high profile figures that the threat of exposure kept the FBI's authority from being limited. The FBI became an effective agency in achieving more authority, creating fear, and ruining individuals. The FBI created several programs on its own authority and kept these programs centralized. These tactics employed by the FBI kept presidents and Attorney Generals ignorant, allowing the FBI to elude investigations into their own activity.

While the FBI initiated several of these programs on its own authority, it would be wrong to conclude the FBI was the only factor to their creation. Hoover and the FBI took advantage of the times. The Cold War, the threat of communism, and the civil rights demonstrations created an awkward tension between political freedoms and the right to rid the United States of the communist agents. At those times Hoover led the FBI on his own personal beliefs, convincing the appropriate people and manipulating them into believing there was a need for programs (Gentry 1991).

With Hoover as the director, the FBI became the bully agency that mastered the science of manipulation and used it in its favor. While following secret orders of the president to investigate his opposition and critics, the FBI secretly investigated those giving the orders. The FBI's investigations generally uncovered damaging information, which caused fear among those expected to control the FBI. With the threat of exposure, very few would monitor the activities of the FBI. The FBI acted like a pack of hyenas, seeking out and destroying whatever they desired. Some historians have reached various conclusions that the creation of programs like the Responsibilities Program, and the Squad, were a direct result of the inadequate supervision of the FBI (Jung and Thom 1997).

The threat of communism, the civil right demonstrations, and the subversive press were situations where the FBI manipulated the minds of members of Congress, the president, and the public. Situations described in the examples earlier demonstrate how the FBI took the opportunity to abuse and expand the FBI's power. Consequently, the FBI gained more power and authority while the monitoring of the FBI decreased substantially. This is just what Hoover and the FBI wanted-- no restriction and no limits.

CONCLUSION

Upon the authority of Congress, the United States in 1908 received its first permanent detective force, the Federal Bureau of Investigations. Charles Bonaparte succeeded with his idea and the FBI was granted the authority to investigate federal law violations. It was soon after the FBI's creation when the FBI began using illegal investigative tactics to gather information. Every time America was faced with a threatening situation, the FBI would receive greater jurisdiction and authority. The World War I era gave the FBI greater jurisdiction to investigate sabotage, espionage, and draft violators. With the insurmountable power and authority, the FBI continued to ignore the intended purpose of the FBI. The wave of corruption quickly spread through and consumed the FBI. The FBI continued to use illegal tactics that violated due process, civil liberties, and most of all, frayed the fabric of the FBI.

Faced with a corrupt law enforcement agency, the administration was pressured to make a change. With the appointment of J. Edgar Hoover, the problems became worse. Hoover publicly acknowledged the

FBI's problems and vowed to restore the FBI's dignity. Privately, Hoover's plans were to ignore efficiency and equity while rebuilding the FBI's reputation. Hoover wanted an effective agency and believed the only way to achieve complete effectiveness was to attack with full force.

Using these tactics, the FBI quickly confirmed its political worth. Deception and manipulation achieved effectiveness. The FBI created the secret file system and began the onslaught of investigations. The FBI investigated a broad spectrum of individuals, including the president's wife. The secret file system allowed the FBI to continue the hundreds of illegal investigations. The system's policy required all reports that included sensitive information to be labeled "personal and confidential." Those reports fell directly on the director's desk avoiding the FBI's central records system.

This paper clearly demonstrates through examples how the FBI chose bureaucratic effectiveness over efficiency and equity. The FBI currently continues to repair the reputation of a corrupt agency. Although death ended the career of the infamous Hoover, however, scandals like those of *Ruby Ridge and The Branch Dividians in Waco* continue to raise the ghost of Hoover's FBI. Some historians will contend there was a sigh of relief when Hoover's era ended. Yet, under specter of great Hoover's legacy, the FBI continues to receive more jurisdiction and authority while still conducting investigations that remain "personal and confidential".

WORKS CITED

Charles, Douglas M. "FBI political surveillance and the Charles Lindbergh Investigation*,*" *The Historian*, Summer 1997, Vol. 59 Issue 4, p831.

Croog, Charles. "FBI Political Surveillance and the Isolationist-Interventionist Debate, 1939 1941," *Historian*, Spring 1992, Vol. 54 Issue 3, p441.

Feinman, Ronald L. "The Rise and Fall of Domestic Intelligence*", Presidential Studies Quarterly*, Winter 1991, Vol. 21 Issue 1, p174.

Felt, Mark W. *The FBI Pyramid: From the Inside*. New York, G.P. Putman's Sons, 1979

Gentry, Curt. *J. Edgar Hoover: The Man and the Secrets*. New York, 1991.

Jung, Patrick and Cathleen Thom. "The Responsibilities Program of the FBI, 1951-1955," *Historian,* Winter 1997, Vol. 59 Issue 2, p347.

Marx, Gary T. "Under-the-Cover Undercover Investigations: Some Reflections on the Untied States use of Sex and Deception in Law Enforcement*," Criminal Justice Ethics*, Winter Spring 1992, Vol. 11 Issue 1, p13.

Moore, Richter H. Jr. "United States: Politics and Public Policy*," Perspectives on Political Science*, Fall 1990, Vol. 23 Issue 2, p109.

Powers, Richard G. *Secrecy and Power: The life of J. Edgar Hoover*. New York, Mcmillan Inc.,1987.

Theoharis, Athan. "The FBI, The Roosevelt Administration and the "Subversive" press," *Journalism History*, Spring-Summer 1993, Vol. 19 Issue 1, p3.

Turner, William W. *Hoover's FBI: The Men and the Myth*. Los Angeles, CA. Kingsport Press Inc., 1970.

Watters, Patty and Stephen Gillers. *Investigating the FBI: A Tough Fair look at the Powerful Bureau, Its Present and Its Future*. New York, Library of Congress, 1973.

PROBLEM-SOLVING CASE STUDIES

Unlike analytical case studies, problem-solving case studies provide students with the opportunity to go beyond problem identification to recommending a course of action. Importantly, the main reasons for doing problem-solving case studies is to identify a problem, to provide reasons for how the problem occurred, and to provide suggestions for resolving the problem most efficiently. Problem-solving case studies provide an analysis of no less than one page and no more than five pages.

- For narrowly defined problems, the case study report is a highly condensed, concise description of the problem, the causes, and recommended solutions of approximately two pages.

- For broadly defined or complex problems, the case study report is condensed into an executive summary, with supporting material attached, of approximately five pages.

The best problem-solving case studies focus on aspects of decision-making that are internal and specific to the target of the study. External factors are only important if they are responsible for influencing the target's decisions. At the end, the reader should know what the problem is, what possibly caused the problem, and what can be done to resolve the problem.

How to Write a Problem-Solving Case Study

1. Identify the target of the case study
2. Identify the objective of the case study
   - Summarize the problem in one or two sentences
   - Write concisely, clearly, and assertively
3. Provide a brief review of:
   - General conditions
   - Specific conditions
4. Identify the major problems and their causes
   - Rank order the problems
   - Investigate and report possible causes or causal relationships
5. Identify possible solutions for each problem identified
   - Rank order the solutions for each problem
   - Identify the benefits, costs, and unintended consequences of applying a solution
6. Make a recommendation
   - Choose a solution for each problem identified
   - Suggest how the solution can be implemented
7. Attach any data, supporting evidence, and references for additional information

MEMORANDUM

To: City Department Manager
From: Annette Allison
Date: October 5, 1999
Re: Building Inspection Department Expense Analysis

Objective:

This report analyzes the city's Building Inspection Department Budget to identify which expenditure items are responsible for budget increases. These increases have resulted in the department being over budget for two years. The report provides a recommendation for either budget allocation increases and/or reduction of spending in discretionary budget categories. Decisions to decrease spending should be based on further investigation of the relative spending efficiency in categories showing significant increases.

1.   **How well did the department spend what was actually budgeted?**
   - FY I was under budget by 9 %.
   - However, in FY II & III the budget was within 1% of its targets.
   - FY IV & V were both well over the budget targets (31% & 7% respectively).

2.   **Major spending categories over 5-year period:**
   - <u>Salaries</u> (158,712 in FY V) are the *largest* spending category during all five years.
   - <u>Capital improvements</u> (9,795 in FY V) are the *second largest* spending category during all five years and show significant increases in the last two years.
   - Travel expenses category show significant increases in the past two years
   - Smaller spending categories are office supplies, training, and dues and subscriptions.

3.   **Major variances (dollar and percent changes) from year to year:**
   - The total spent budget increased by 31% from FY III to FY IV.
   - The total spent budget increased 23% from FY IV to FY V.
   - <u>Capital improvements</u>, <u>printing</u>, and <u>travel expenses</u> were major spending categories during FY V.

4.   **Line-item changes & changes in budget shares over time:**
   - <u>Salaries</u> account for the *largest share* of the spent budget. During the past five years, salaries have accounted for between 81%-86% of the total spent budget.
   - <u>Travel expenses</u> accounted for the *second largest share* of the total spent budget in

both FY IV & V, accounting for 9% in those years.
- <u>Capital improvement</u> was the ***third largest share*** of the spent budget.
- <u>Car allowance</u> and <u>office supplies</u> are also ***large shares*** of the spent budget.

5.   **What changes are revealed when inflation is taken into account?**
- When inflation is taken into account, the spent budget still reveals that there has been a steady increase in the total spent budget over the past five years, with a sizable increase within the past two years.
- Although salaries have been steadily increasing over the past five years, employees are making much less over the past four years when inflation in taken into account.

6.   **What else might account for the specific changes?**
- The larger salary, training, and travel expenditures over the past five years might indicate the hiring of more staff.
- The large amounts spent on capital improvements might indicate that the building inspection department is growing and requires new or additional facilities.

7.   **Impact of spending trends on next year's budget:**
- Since the building inspection department has been over budget the past two years, it may reflect a need for more budget allocations for the following budget year.
- However, capital improvements and travel expenses should be looked at closely when allocating the following years budget, because these services may not be needed.

8.   **Ratio analysis:**
- Based on the per capita ratio in FY V, each resident spends approximately $4.27 to support the building inspection department.

Recommendation:
The results of this analysis suggest that while ***salaries are the largest spending item, they are not responsible*** for the department being over budget in the last two years. Increases in expenses related to ***capital improvements, travel, and office supplies significantly contributed the increases*** in the spent budget. This report recommends scrutiny of these expenditures particularly as they relate to the purposes and necessity for continued increased spending in each of these categories. Based on the results of an evaluation of these expenditures, the city should either increase the budget allocation and/or reduce spending on capital improvements, travel, and office supplies to reduce the likelihood of the department being over budget in the future.

Attachments: Expense Analysis

BUILDING INSPECTION DEPARTMENT
BUILDING INSPECTION EXPENSE ANALYSIS (EXERPT)

EXPENSE	YR 1 SPENT	YR 1 CONSTANT	YR 2 SPENT	YR 1-2 $ DIFF	YR 1-2 % CHANGE	YR 2 CONSTANT
SALARIES	$90,340	$90,340	$99,830	$4,375	5%	$94,715
TRUCK & CAR REPAIRS	4,286	$4,286	1,732	$(2,643)	-62%	$1,643
TRAVEL EXPENSE	546	$546	612	$35	6%	$581
SUPPLIES	1,092	$1,092	1,242	$86	8%	$1,178
OFFICE SUPPLIES	3,400	$3,400	5,500	$1,818	53%	$5,218
STREET LIGHTING	208	$208	0	$(208)	-100%	$-
TELEPHONE	146	$146	330	$167	114%	$313
GAS & OIL	0	$-	0	$-		$-
EQUIPMENT REPAIRS	0	$-	0	$-		$-
TOOLS & SUPPLIES	0	$-	0	$-		$-
CHRISTMAS LIGHTS	944	$944	6,662	$5,377	570%	$6,321
REAL PROPERTY LIGHTS	1,170	$1,170	840	$(373)	-32%	$797
EDUCATION & TRAINING	224	$224	1,190	$905	404%	$1,129
DUES & SUBSCRIP-TIONS	0	$-	0	$-		$-
UTILITIES	1,736	$1,736	1,400	$(408)	-23%	$1,328
PRINTING	236	$236	134	$(109)	-46%	$127
CAPITAL IMPROVE-MENTS	270	$270	0	$(270)	-100%	$-
COMMUNI-CATIONS	0	$-	0	$-		$-
TOTAL	$104,598	$104,598	$119,472	$8,753	8%	$113,351

ANALYSIS OF LEGISLATION

Purpose of an Analysis of Legislation

Analyzing a Congressional bill helps the student understand more about the legislative process. Unlike other policies, which can be custom, rulings by courts, regulations written by bureaucrats, or executive orders, legislation is made in Congress. To examine the legislative process, we need to identify the context within which the legislation was introduced, the goals of the legislation, supporters, the opponents, and the problems of passing the bill. (For more information, see Robert U. Goehlert and Fenton S. Martin, *Congress and Law-Making: Researching the Legislative Process*. 2nd. ed. CA: ABC-CLIO, 1989. See the section on tracing legislation pages 53-59.)

Writing an Analysis of a Legislative Bill

1. Choose a law that is of interest to you.
    *   find the public law number.
    *   choose one that is at least a year old.
2. Identify where the idea for the bill originated--Congress, bureaucracy, interest groups, or the executive office.
    *   sometimes an idea or draft has more than one source.
    *   find out who introduced the bill.
    *   examine the hearings.
3. Identify the objectives, targets, or goals of the bill.
    *   what was the legislation supposed to do exactly?
    *   who was supposed to benefit?
    *   does the bill expand or correct other policy action by government?
4. Identify the means or policy instruments used to achieve the goals or objectives.
    *   how was the legislation supposed to achieve its goals?
    *   policy tools---transfers? regulation? subsidy? spending?
5. Identify who supported and who opposed the bill.
    *   was it a partisan bill?
    *   did support come from an ideological coalition?
6. Examine the bill's success in passing.
    *   what constraints prevented it passing easily?
    *   what kind of problems did it encounter?
7. Using the above six steps write the paper with the following:
    *   an introduction, a description of the origins of the bill, the objectives and tools used to achieve the objectives.
    *   compare and contrast the various political arguments and forces supporting and opposing the bill.
    *   relate these political problems to any problems in passing the bill. Separate the political problems from institutional or structural problems that may exist and then provide a conclusion.

EXAMPLE OF A LEGISLATIVE ANALYSIS

EDUCATION FOR ALL HANDICAPPED CHILDREN ACT OF 1975

By
Amy Andrews
Professor Schmidt
POLS 321
November 16, 1989
(Reprinted with permission)

ABSTRACT

The purpose of this paper is to research the Education for All Handicapped Children Act of 1975, P.L. 94-142. How this piece of legislation came about, the goals or purpose of the law, and the path to passage have all been addressed in this paper. Also identified are the supporters and opposition to the bill at the time of its passage. The study found that this piece of legislation had the most significant influence on reshaping federal policy toward the education of handicapped children. Because of the extensive funding provided by the national government and the reinforcement of government intervention in educational matters, this Act is considered the most vital legislation passed concerning handicapped education.

INTRODUCTION

On November 29, 1975, President Gerald Ford signed into law a bill targeted to assure adequate and free public school education to America's eight million handicapped children ("Aid to Education of Handicapped Approved" 651). The Education of All Handicapped Children Act (P.L. 94-142, referred to as the Act throughout) is technically a series of amendments to the Education of the Handicapped Act (EHA). It is regarded as the most important legislation enacted since the landmark Elementary and Secondary Education Act of 1965 (Osman). The bill expanded the authorization of appropriations and required school districts to educate or provide equivalent appropriate services to all handicapped children aged 3 to 21 by 1980. The federal government by fiscal year (FY) 1982 would provided up to 20% of the additional cost of educating handicapped children at an estimated cost of $3.2 billion a year ("Aid..." 651).

Under this law, if a state submits an annual plan to the Bureau of Education for the Handicapped in the US Office of Education which conforms to procedures outlined in the Act, it can receive federal funds to supplement education of handicapped children (Rauth 2). This is a major step in governmental oversight and funding for a role that was traditionally left to the states. The Act assumed an independent identity as breakthrough legislation that drastically reshaped federal policy making it the most vital legislation for the education of handicapped children.

ORIGINS OF THE PROBLEM

The beginning of the Act can be traced to judicial and legislative decisions, principally at the state level, and the Congressional finding that a significant unmet education need among handicapped children continued to exist. According to the Office of Education, only about half of the nation's eight million handicapped children were receiving an adequate education, 2.5 million were receiving an inadequate education, and 1.75 million no education at all. ("Aid..." 651). In recent years, several state and federal courts have ruled that handicapped children are entitled to receive free public school education.

Current education rights of handicapped children were established initially in two major state level lawsuits, Pennsylvania Association for Retarded Citizens (PARC) vs. Commonwealth of Pennsylvania and Mills vs. D.C. Board of Education. Both of these suits addressed the exclusion of certain handicapped children from any educational instruction and the lack of appropriate educational programming for certain handicapped children (Fraas 1). It would appear that this right is a needless restatement of a basic human right of free public education (Boyer 299). Yet many handicapped children simply were not getting an appropriate education, mainly due to a lack of funding. It is a constitutional right that state and local funding be spent appropriately for handicapped children just like they are spent for nonhandicapped children ("The Teacher's Rights in P.L. 94-142"). It was due to this denial of a constitutional right that the Act was created.

Also, states and the local school districts had the principal responsibility for the education of school-aged handicapped children, and the court mandates had strapped already financially pressed schools (Osman). Parents, too, learned the hard way that appropriate education for a handicapped child costs more than public education could, or would, pay. Parents often had to assume the entire financial burden of private school regardless of whether they could afford it (Boyer 299). The National Educational Finance Project has estimated that the average cost of educating a handicapped child is 1.9 times that of educating a normal child ("Aid..." 652). A need for governmental assistance had definitely been established.

P.L. 94-142 amended EHA. This Act, as amended, is the primary federal legislation directed toward meeting the special educational needs of handicapped persons (Osman). Initially enacted in April, 1970,

EHA consolidated certain existing authorities and established new programs to serve the education needs of handicapped people. Within this legislative framework, the 1970 Act authorized one program of formula grant assistance to states (the Part B - Assistance to States for Education of Handicapped Children) (Osman). The Education Amendments of 1974 amended and extended the programs authorized under EHA. These modified the Part B for FY 1975, and required that Part B State plans assure all handicapped children the opportunity for needed special education services (Osman).

In the 94th Congress, the Education for All Handicapped Children Act of 1975 reauthorized and substantially amended all of the Part B requirements for states and local school districts and expanded the scope of authorized federal assistance (Osman). To give the states incentive to expand their educational services for handicapped persons and to help defray the costs, the Act would grant the states $300 for each handicapped child aged 3 to 21 who was receiving educational services. It was estimated that the $300 grant would cover about a quarter of the additional cost of educating a handicapped child (Gottron 1372).

To be eligible for the grants, each state would have to provide a free appropriate education to all handicapped persons between the ages of 3 and 17 by 1978 and to all handicapped people between the ages of 18 and 21 by 1980 (Gottron 1372). Priorities in the use of federal funds were established to ensure the funds were properly and fairly received. First were the identification, location, evaluation and provision of special education and related services to handicapped children not receiving any education; second was to provide the same to handicapped children within each disability with the most severe handicaps who are receiving an inadequate education. Finally, the other Act requirements were to be met (Rauth 2).

The Act expanded federal responsibility for handicapped children by requiring every state and local school district receiving federal funds to find and educate at public expense all handicapped children in its jurisdiction, regardless of the nature or severity of a child's handicap (Boyer 299). The Senate Labor and Public Welfare Committee justified this expansion by stating that the long-range results of inaction would be the expenditure by public agencies and taxpayers of "billions of dollars over the lifetimes of these individuals to maintain such persons as dependents and in a minimally acceptable lifestyle. With proper educational services, many would...become productive citizens, contributing to society instead of being forced to remain burdens. Others...would increase their independence, thus reducing their dependence on society" (US Senate Report).

GOALS OF LEGISLATION

The primary purpose of the Act as stated is to "assure that all handicapped children have available to them...a free appropriate public education which emphasizes special education and related services designed to meet their unique needs" (Section 3 (c)). This education must be at public expense and under public supervision and must meet standards of the state educational agency. Each child requiring special education must have an individualized education program as evidence that he/she is receiving a "free appropriate education" (Rauth 2).

The states were required to provide this education to the same age range as nonhandicapped students who receive a free public education. Federal grants would go to local school districts based on a complex formula that counted the number of handicapped children served multiplied by 50 percent of the average per pupil expenditure ("Aid..." 653). No state would receive a total grant less than $300,000. To avoid mislabeling students in order to receive a larger grant, no state could count more than 12% of its children aged 5 through 17. No more than one-sixth of the children counted could be those with specific learning disabilities (not caused by cultural, environmental, or economic disadvantages) (Gottron 2592). It is because of the provisions and the complexity of the grant requirements that the Act is considered such a breakthrough for federal education grants for the handicapped.

The second stated purpose of the Act was to "assure that the rights of handicapped children and their parents or guardians are protected" (Section 3 (c)). This is a direct response to the previous denial of the Constitutional right of handicapped children. It involved educating handicapped children with nonhandicapped children to the maximum extent possible and assuring that testing and evaluation materials are not racially or culturally discriminatory (Gottron 1373). This provision was made to "protect and promote the uniformity, conformity of the group" (Willhoite 668). Congress wanted to make sure to avoid as much discrimination and separation as possible.

The final two goals of the Act are also worth noting. The third stated an aid to states and localities in providing for the education for the children (Section 3 (c)). Authorized were sums as necessary for payments to educational agencies to assist with the removal of architectural features that barred full participation (Gottron 1670). To many schools, this major feat required extensive funding for remodeling. That the federal government was to assist with this was another important feature of the bill.

The final goal was to "assure the effectiveness of efforts to educate handicapped children" (Section 3 (c)). To receive its grant each local school district would be required to establish procedures for identifying handicapped children (clearly defined in Section 602 (1) of the Act) and then develop and maintain an educational program tailored to the needs of each child ("Aid..." 652). School districts also would be required to educate handicapped children in the least restrictive setting, preferably in a classroom. Those children that must be privately educated (as referred by the local school district) were to be educated at no cost to the parents (Gottron 1486). Again, another major impact on handicapped education in terms of federal expenses.

PROBLEMS OF PASSAGE

Senator Harrison A. Williams Jr. (D N.J.) wrote the bill and introduced it (along with 23 other Senators) on January 15, 1975 (Osman). Because of the Congressional organizational problems, the bill was not reported from the Senate Labor and Public Welfare Committee (in which Williams was chair) until June 2, 1975 ("Aid..." 651). Because that first session of the new 94th Congress contained more new members than had been sent to Washington in a single Congress in the past 25 years, the normal organizational process took longer than usual (this involved the allocation of office space, creation of staffs, committee selections, etc.) ("Recent Major Action in the Congress" 33). Large numbers of legislation proposals are usually introduced in the opening days of session, yet committee consideration does not begin in earnest until these other necessary preliminaries have been settled. In this case this process took even more time than normal, for the Senate was involved in a controversy over the rightful occupant of the junior New Hampshire seat ("Recent Major..." 65).

The Senate Subcommittee on the Handicapped's hearings included over 100 individuals lobbying for the bill's passage who represented every group which the bill affected (US Senate Report). Although education is considered a campaign-defined controversial issue causing lobbyists to be more floor oriented, the Subcommittee hearings were vital to the lobbyists because of the role the Committee played in shaping the content of the legislation (Bacheller 257). It was the Subcommittee that set the initial level of funding, and this was the most worrisome part for those to be affected by the bill. The Subcommittee easily approved the bill for full Committee consideration, which in turn unanimously approved it for floor consideration.

The Senate adopted substantive amendments by voice vote on June 18, 1975 (Osman). Usually a voice vote reveals splits along party lines, but this was not the case (Norporth 1156). Robert T. Stafford (R.

Vt.), ranking Republican on the Subcommittee on the Handicapped, and Edward M. Kennedy (D Mass.) offered the most important amendment (clearly showing that this issue was not based on strict party lines) (US Senate Report). It provided an additional $400 (for a total of $600) for each child aged 3-5 that the state served. Kennedy stated that a child's needs should be detected early or required teen-aged training could be too late (Gottron 1373).

The other important amendment adopted was by Richard Stone (D Fla.), providing that the state would not have to pass through funds to any agency if the grant amount was less than $7500 (Gottron 1374). The money instead would be distributed on a priority basis. This would keep the grants from being spread too thinly to serve any purpose (Gottron 1374).

Representative John Brademas (D Ind.), chair of the Education and Labor Select Education Committee and chief author of HR 7217 (the bill's House counterpart), introduced the bill with 24 other members (Osman). It too was voted unanimously out of the House Education and Labor Committee to the chamber (Gottron 1485). An amendment offered by Albert H. Quie (R Minn.) that would have scaled down the authorization was first adopted on a standing vote (18-16), but was later rejected on a recorded vote (116-308) ("Aid..." 654).

Six Republicans supported the bill "whole-heartedly" but felt that the level of spending that was called for was unrealistic and to expect it to be reached was "pure folly" (US HR Report). Quie, the ranking Republican on the Education and Labor Committee headed this group. They urged the budget and appropriations committees determine the spending level. This action could have drastically reduced the appropriation level.

Thomas P. O'Neill (D MASS.) proposed a second important amendment. This ensured that federal grants would not be cut off to those states that were already financing extensive handicapped education programs with their own funds. It also stipulated that states could not replace state or local funds with federal funds ("Aid..." 655). This "insurance" provision added another important clause to ensure that the federal funds were used for the purpose of the handicapped only. The House rejected a motion by John M. Ashbrook (R Ohio) to recommit the bill, but this measure was rejected by voice vote (Gottron 1611). HR 7217 was passed on a 375-44 vote. Eight Democrats and 36 Republicans opposed passage, primarily because of the extensive funding that was called for ("Aid..." 653).

FRIENDS AND FOES

After the Act was approved by the conference reports, it was reported back to both chambers. In the House the Act was adopted with a 404-7 vote, and in the Senate it passed with a 87-7 majority (Gottron 2593). The fact that only 14 Congress members out of 535 voted against the Act is worth noting. Those that did go on record as opposing the Act did so solely because they did not agree with the unusually high level of funding appropriated, not because they disagreed with the purpose or idea of the Act (Osman). In fact, the issue was not even party related, for those in opposition to the authorization level in the House were of both parties ("House Votes").

The Department of Health Education and Welfare (HEW) opposed the Act on the grounds that education was primarily the responsibility of the states and not the federal government ("Aid..." 653). The federal government's role should be one of "capacity-building and insurance of equality of opportunity" wrote then HEW secretary Casper W. Weinberger (Gottron 1372). Weinberger also stated that it was unlikely that appropriations would be anywhere near the authorization level. He said it was an impossibility to offer entitlements that are "nearly 12 times as great as the current appropriation level" ("Aid..." 653).

President Ford signed the bill reluctantly (Gottron 1372). He said that the "bill promises more than the federal government can deliver, and its good intentions could be thwarted by the many unwise provisions it contains. Even the strongest supporters of this measure know as well as I that they are falsely raising the expectations of the groups affected by claiming authorization levels which are excessive and unrealistic" if federal spending was to be brought under control ("Aid..." 653). Ford also rejected the administrative requirements that would assert federal control over traditionally state and local functions. Yet Ford knew that the overwhelming margins with which the bill was passed by both houses virtually guaranteed a veto override, so he was stuck signing a measure that he did not believe would turn out as planned.

Many groups and organizations favored the bill's passage. The two noted lobbyists were the Bureau of Education for the Handicapped and the National Advisory Committee on the Handicapped (Biehler 180). Also contributing their support was the Children's Defense Fund. (Biehler 179). These groups are national organizations that naturally advocate the betterment of handicapped conditions. Their approval and push for the bill unwavered.

CONCLUSION

The Act has opened the door to a host of promising practices for young handicapped children (Cohen 280). More children are being served thanks to federal government intervention. Although not approved by the republican administration, the bill passed with overwhelming majorities in both houses (only in the Senate were the seven opposing votes solely from Republicans) ("House Votes"). This legislation significantly altered the education practices of handicapped children and reinforced government intervention in these matters, principally because of the funding approved. Handicapped children were now guaranteed an appropriate public education that had been denied to many in the past.

Incidentally, the federal government has continued to appropriate the required spending levels for funding the Act. Currently Senator Tom Harkin (D Iowa), chair of the Subcommittee on the Handicapped, is planning to introduce legislation to reauthorize the discretionary programs of EHA, which are Parts C-G (Simon). Harkin stated that the reauthorization process "gives us the opportunity to reassess these programs to make sure they are doing what they were intended to do" (Harkin). These programs "support research and demonstrations, personal training, technical assistance and the dissemination of information, and address the particular needs of certain populations of individuals with disabilities" (Harkin). Part B of EHA (P.L. 94-142) has a permanent authorization, yet still holds a vital "continuing obligation" to Congress (Harkin).

BIBLIOGRAPHY

"Aid to Education of Handicapped Approved." *Congressional Quarterly Almanac*. 31 (1975): 651-656.

Bacheller, John M. "Lobbyists and the Legislative Process: The Impact of Environmental Constraints." The American Political Science Review. 71.1 (1977): 252-262.

Biehler, Robert F. and Jack Snowman. *Psychology Applied to Teaching*. Boston: Houghton Mifflin Company, 1986.

Boyer, Ernest L. "Public Law 94-142: A Promising Start?" *Educational Leadership*. 36.5 (1979): 298-301.

Cohen, Shirley, Marilyn Semmers, and Michael J. Guralnick. "Public Law 94-142 and the Education of Preschool Handicapped Children." *Exceptional Children*. 45.4 (1979): 279-280.

Fraas, Charlotte Jones. *Education of the Handicapped*. Washington D.C.: Congressional Research Service, 1985.

Gottron, Martha V. "Aid to Education of Handicapped Approved." *Congressional Quarterly Weekly Report*. 33.48 (1975): 2591-2593.

---. "Education for Handicapped." *Congressional Quarterly Weekly Report*. 32.28 (1975): 1485-1486.

---. "Education for Handicapped." *Congressional Quarterly Weekly Report*. 33.31 (1975): 1669-1671.

---. "Handicapped Children: Senate Expands Aid." *Congressional Quarterly Weekly Report*. 33.26 (1975): 1372-1374.

Harkin, Tom. "Letter to Senate Committee on Labor and Human Resources." Unpublished. U.S. Senate, Washington D.C., 1989.

"House Votes." *Congressional Quarterly Weekly Report*. 33.47 (1975): 2566-2568.

Norporth, Helmut. "Explaining Party Cohesion in Congress: The Case of Shared Policy Attitudes." The *American Political Science Review*. 39 (1977): 667-683.

Osman, David S. *Public Law 94-142 - Education for All Handicapped Children Act of 1975*. Washington, D.C.: Congressional Research Service, 1979.

Powell, Thomas H. "Educating All Disabled Children: A Practical Guide to P.L. 94-142." *The Exceptional Parent*. 8.4 (1978) L3-L6.

Rauth, Marilyn. *A Guide to Understanding the Education for All Handicapped Children Act (P.L. 94-142)*. Washington D.C.: American Federation of Teachers, 1983.

"Recent Major Action in the Congress." *Congressional Digest*. 54.2-3 (1975): 33. 65-66.

Simon, Paul. "Letter to the Author". U.S. Senate. 11 October 1989.

"The Teacher's Rights in P.L. 94-142." *Journal of Learning Disabilities*. 11.6 (1978): 4-14.

United States. House Committee on Education and Labor. *Report*. 94th Congress, 1st Session. 1-6 vols. Washington: GPA 1975.

---. ---. Senate Committee on Labor and Public Welfare. *Report*. 94th Congress, 1st Session. 1-3 vols. Washington: GPA 1975.

---. ---. Congress. *Education for All Handicapped Children Act of 1975*. 94th Congress, 1st Session. 1975.

Willhoite, Fred H. Jr. "Evolution and Collective Intolerance." *Journal of Politics*. 39 (1977): 667-683.

POLICY ANALYSIS:
EVALUATION OR RECOMMENDATION

Purpose of a Policy Analysis

The purpose of a policy analysis is to examine a public policy's impact on the political environment in which it was or is to be implemented.

- Not all public policies are made by Congress.

- Policies can be custom, rulings by courts, regulations written by bureaucrats, or executive orders.

- When examining a public policy, we want to identify the goals, the tools, and the outcomes so that we can assess whether it was or is a successful and worthwhile intervention by government.

Formats of a Policy Analysis

Policy analysis is usually found in one of two formats:

Policy evaluation is limited to evaluation of past or present policies. This type of policy analysis entails examining the characteristics of a current or past policy. To do this, we must identify and analyze the policy's origins, the policy's goals, who benefits, the instruments used to implement the goals of the policy, and its perceived or actual impact.

Policy recommendation involves proposing a new solution to a new or existing problem. This type of policy analysis may or may not involve an analysis of a current policy. To produce a policy recommendation, we must first evaluate current policy responses to the problem or similar to the problem identified. A policy recommendation, however, takes the analysis one step further. After evaluating past policy responses to similar problems, a policy recommendation then argues for the adoption of a new solution to the current problem. It provides both the rationale for the solution and a description of how it would be implemented, who it would benefit, who is likely to oppose it, and how we would evaluate its progress toward solving the problem.

RESEARCHING AND WRITING A POLICY EVALUATION

1. Identify a social problem or social condition.
    - ♦ Look in the newspaper for ideas.
    - ♦ Choose something of particular interest to you.
    - ♦ State clearly why you are interested the problem.
2. Identify indicators of the social condition.
    - ♦ Find one relevant quantitative indicator from each of the following:
        - • An almanac.
        - • A statistical yearbook.
        - • American Statistics Index.
    - ♦ Locate sources related to the topic or problem using a computer search system, the card catalog, abstracts, and indexes.
        - • Obtain two books on your subject.
        - • Locate five scholarly journal articles.
        - • Locate two articles from quality publications.
        - • Locate two articles from mass publications.
    - ♦ Locate one government publication related to your topic or problem from each of the following:
        - • Congressional Information Service Index.
        - • Monthly Catalog of U.S. Publications.
        - • Congressional Record.
3. Identify the nature of the problem.
    - ♦ Describe the problem.
        - • Explain clearly what the problem is.
        - • Explain clearly why the problem is public concern.
    - ♦ Present evidence of the existence of the problem.
        - • Quantitative (statistical or numerical) evidence.
        - • Qualitative (expert opinion, examples) evidence.
    - ♦ List the factors underlying the problem.
        - • Identify the broad underlying factors.
        - • Identify the specific underlying factors.
4. Find the public policy, if there is one, dealing with the problem.
    - ♦ Describe the different solutions proposed or available and the solution adopted.
    - ♦ Identify where the public policy originated--custom, Congress, bureaucracy, judicial, or executive policy.
        - • Examine how and where the policy was initiated.
        - • Sometimes a policy has more than one source.
    - ♦ Identify five important political actors or players who either supported or opposed the solution adopted.
        - • State the issue position of each player.
        - • State the power of each player.

- Identify at least two reasons why you included each player.
- Rank order the players by importance to implementing the solution.
♦ Identify whether the policy been expanded or adjusted over time.
- State the conditions for the change.
- State the reasons for the change.

5. Identify the objectives, targets, or goals of the policy.
  ♦ What was the policy supposed to do exactly?
  - What target population was supposed to benefit?
  - Is the solution curative? preventative? remedial?
  ♦ What were the means or policy instruments used to achieve the goals or objectives?
  - How was the policy supposed to achieve its goals?
  - Policy tools---transfers? regulation? subsidy?

6. Analyze who or what benefited and who or what was hurt by the policy.
  - Who seems better off, who is worse off?
  - Who paid the cost, who benefited?

7. Evaluate the success of the policy by examining whether the goals or objectives were achieved.
  - Match the goals with the outcomes.
  - How can you tell the policy is working?
  - Did the targets benefit as expected?
  - What constraints prevented it from working well?
  - What do the experts say about the policy?

8. When writing your evaluation, include a discussion, in order, of the following:
  ♦ An introduction which includes:
  - A brief description of the social problem.
  - The context.
  - Solution adopted to solve the problem.
  - A statement which assesses the usefulness of the solution for solving the problem.
  ♦ Subheadings identifying the discussion of :
  - The issue.
  - The historical context or background.
  - The objectives of the solution with justification.
  - The critique of the policy response in meeting the objectives with justification.
  - A cost-benefit analysis with justification.
  ♦ A conclusion which restates briefly the context of the social problem and the justification of your critique of the solution.
  ♦ Do not forget to include a list of sources for all borrowed ideas, arguments, and data. Use tables, charts, and graphs to illustrate data where necessary.

POLICY EVALUATION EXAMPLE

NEPA: AMERICAS POLICY RESPONSE
TO ENVIRONMENTAL CRISES

BY
EDWARD M. PETTIT
PROFESSOR SCHMIDT
POLS 324
APRIL 18, 1990
(Reprinted with permission)

ABSTRACT

As this country's primary public policy reaction to the environmental crisis, the National Environmental Policy Act of 1969 understandably has remained in the public eye since its inception twenty years ago. Analysis of the Act, and its general precepts regarding environmental management, suggests that although it has remained virtually unchanged over the years, NEPA has provided an overall statement of purpose within which several more specific environmental laws have been enacted. As such, it can be considered one of the most orderly, rational, and productive policy responses in United States history. In addition, as a declaration of a comprehensive national environmental policy, NEPA has marked not only a genuine American commitment to sound management of the natural environment, but also a possible shift in our dominant social belief structure regarding the relationship between humans and nature. NEPA, therefore, truly can be considered a success.

INTRODUCTION

In recent years, environmental concerns have become increasingly paramount in the eyes of the American populace. As the United States has become ever more aware of the dangers of a possible human-induced environmental collapse, the public has begun to question once again our motives in those activities which in any way affect the natural environment. To many, this represents a new awakening in ecological consciousness, but to others it is simply a resurgence of the concerns characteristic of the environmental movement of the 1960s, a movement which marked the era of American history most often credited with the implementation of environmental policy in this country.

The ten years between 1960 and 1970 did indeed constitute the decade when much of the body of current environmental legislation evolved. During this period, many Americans began to realize that the high standards of living associated with the American way of life had come at the expense of widespread, and in many cases irreparable, environmental degradation. As a result a growing concern for the natural environment developed, gaining momentum throughout the nation, and forming the foundation for what would become a very powerful, environmentally active constituency.

Eventually, the United States Congress heard the powerful voices of citizens with environmental concerns and began passing a series of landmark laws aimed at protecting the environment. It was not until the 91st Congress passed the National Environmental Policy Act of 1969, however, that our country could boast an actual environmental policy. This Act, commonly referred to as NEPA, proved to be the most orderly, rational, and constructive Federal response to environmental decision making in U.S. history, and as such, represented the true manifestation of America's commitment to environmental policy.

POLICY INITIATION

Even before the passage of NEPA in 1969, the years from 1960 to 1968 could be considered a very significant era in the development of United States environmental policy, primarily due to the unprecedented amount of environmentally oriented legislation passed then. Walt Westman is one of several observers who explains the motivation behind this ecologically sound legislative activity as "an aroused public [calling] on Congress to express the nation's environmental aspirations" (1985, p. 30). Sure enough, as Westman claims, the outcry was heeded, and Congress passed numerous pieces of legislation during the decade oriented toward soil and forest conservation, oceanography, air and water pollution abatement, protection of public lands, and numerous other areas of particular environmental concern ("Population: Will man succeed in destroying himself?", 1970).

Yet, because each piece of legislation typically dealt with a specific environmental problem, Federal responsibility for environmental protection remained "scattered through a number of different departments and agencies [lacking] clearly defined goals and overall planning" ("Nixon asks total mobilization to save environment.", 1969, p. 1274). Even President Nixon recognized this problem when he described the piecemeal development of federal institutions and legislation for dealing with the environment, the missions of which he felt tended to overlap and even conflict at times. ("Environmental policy", 1970). Environmental legislation of the period, though plentiful, was seen as being in a state of disarray, and a consensus developed among key policy makers, emphasizing the need to reorganize and coordinate the Federal Government's efforts to contend with the environmental problems at hand.

In response to this need, Congress passed the National Environmental Policy Act of 1969, as introduced by Senator Henry M Jackson (D-Wash), Chairman of the Senate Interior and Insular Affairs

Committee. Jackson and his colleagues recognized that "a wide and diffuse range of concerns is subsumed under the subject heading of environmental problems" (Lieber, 1970, p. 278), and that the disjointed and sometimes misguided pre-NEPA environmental legislation failed adequately to aggregate the concerns of all environmental issues. As a means of addressing this problem, the National Environmental Policy Act represented the culmination of years of efforts to establish an explicit national policy to guide all Federal activities affecting the natural environment. For the first time, environmental policy in the United States had a certain degree of cohesion, specifically in the form of a Federal guideline requiring "systematic, interdisciplinary, and interagency approaches to achieving or maintaining environmental quality . . . by all federal agencies" (Henning & Mangun, 1989, p. 20).

Much of NEPA, as introduced in the 91st Congress by Senator Jackson, had its roots in various measures introduced in previous Congresses, reaching as far back as the Resources and Conservation Act, introduced to the 86th Congress by Senator James E. Murray (D-Mont) in 1959 ("National Environmental Policy Act of 1969", 1969). The motivation behind NEPA thus rested on an earlier recognition of the need to reexamine the American approach to managing the natural environment. As Murray had advocated in 1959, the 1969 NEPA provided continuity in all governmental actions directly or indirectly affecting the environment, requiring that on the basis of existing knowledge, the possible ecological consequences of government or government-sponsored activities be taken into account (Lave, 1988).

Understandably, NEPA soon became heralded as the most significant piece of environmental legislation ever passed in the United States. By declaring its comprehensive national policy and goals, establishing a Council on Environmental Quality, and providing for review of all Federal programs for their impact on the environment, the Act permeated all levels of the Federal bureaucracy, providing the long overdue sense of unity needed in the effort to manage the environment (Lieber, 1970). With NEPA, many Americans felt that the nation had finally embarked on the long road toward sensible management of the environment (Vig & Kraft, 1990, p. 235).

EXPANSION

Some may find it surprising that since its passage roughly twenty years ago, NEPA has not been expanded or changed significantly. But with its primary purpose of "ensuring that environmental consequences be considered as a factor in all relevant policy decisions" (Anderson, Brady, Bullock, & Steward, 1984, p. 125), not much could really be done to elaborate the basic Act itself. Essentially, by making environmental protection in general a national policy, NEPA provided the bubble under which more specific environmental legislation could be implemented, in line with the general goals the Act itself set forward. Therefore, any expansion or changes that have occurred have come in the form of new or updated legislation dealing with specific environmental problems, such as with the Endangered Species Act of 1973 (Vig & Kraft, 1990, p. 396). By expressing a broad, national goal for the management of the natural environment, then, NEPA is concerned primarily with principle rather than detail, and subsequently has escaped the need for restructuring or expansion of its coverage.

TARGETS

In theory, by establishing a broad national environmental policy, NEPA was aimed at assuring for all Americans safe, healthful, productive, and aesthetically and culturally pleasing surroundings (Henning & Mangun, 1989, p. 198). Presumably, therefore, the Act was targeting all Americans as its beneficiaries.

Nevertheless, as Allen Kneese points out, environmental policy in the United States, for the most part, owes its inception to the 1960s, a decade when Americans "became increasingly aware that the fruits of economic development were infected by the rot of environmental deterioration" (Kneese, 1984, p. 1). This statement espouses the fundamental concept that environmental policy, like that initiated by NEPA, is one that pits the notions of economic development and environmental quality against one another. As such, NEPA's coverage can be thought to target two, readily discernable, opposing interests.

By providing the conditions for a harmonious and productive relationship between humans and nature, the coordinated rather than fragmented environmental policy put forth by NEPA has obvious benefits for ecologically conscious citizens (Lieber, 1970, p. 283). In a country of countless preferences and competing constituencies, NEPA lends itself most readily to environmental concerns. In this sense, the Act can be thought to cater predominantly to Americans who are predisposed to environment quality (Paehlke, 1989, p. 21).

On the other hand, in a modern industrial society, as in virtually any economy, there are inevitable tradeoffs. And though one can presumably ascribe to all Americans the desire for a clean environment, one must acknowledge a strong national desire for economic gain (Paehlke, 1989, p. 206; Fairfax 1978). Thus, in the case of any environmental legislation, a truly clean environment may come at a cost to those whose economic gain results from activities that in some way degrade our natural surroundings. In this sense, though NEPA represents a seemingly quintessential public interest piece of legislation, it has obvious deleterious effects for those who favor economic gain over environmental quality (Vig & Kraft, 1990, p. 220; Milbrath 1980).

EVALUATION

As with any piece of legislation, NEPA has both its faultfinders and its champions. Therefore, when attempting to determine the success of NEPA in achieving its goals, any analyst may end up wading through a virtual sea of conflicting evidence. For instance, in line with Murray Edelman's arguments regarding political quiescence (Edelman, 1964), one plausible criticism of NEPA is that by symbolizing a solution to America's environmental problems, without actually constituting one, the Act has served to pacify the demands of ecologically concerned citizens. Thus, by having the potential effect of "silencing critical ecofreaks" (Schindler, 1976, p. 632), NEPA, in many regards, may have actually impeded the efforts to better manage our natural surroundings.

On the other hand, the Act has often been praised, even based on its mere existence, which some feel is a testament to a more environmentally conscious America. Westman, for example, considers NEPA to be representative of an increased willingness on the part of many Americans to acknowledge our dependence on the natural environment for our own continued survival (1985). Jigs and Kraft offer a similar argument, especially with regard to the Federal government, when they state that despite any criticisms, "most studies show that [NEPA] forced greater environmental awareness and more careful planning in many agencies" (1990, p. 22).

Regardless of the unavoidable differences in opinion one may encounter when evaluating NEPA's success, however, the Act does represent an indisputable success in achieving its primary goal. As an official declaration of national policy, NEPA directs all Federal agencies to comply with its general precepts regarding improved management of the natural environment ("National Environmental Policy Act of 1969", 1969). This in itself is a mammoth victory, since seldom does a single policy pervade every level of the Federal bureaucracy, engendering the kind of sweeping guidelines as those of NEPA. By effecting such a comprehensive policy, therefore, NEPA adequately addresses the broad spectrum of environmental concerns facing our nation, and thus can be considered a true success.

CONCLUSION

The passage of the National Environmental Policy Act of 1969, without a doubt can be considered one of the most significant events in the history of the American approach to sound management of the natural environment. By establishing a comprehensive national environmental policy, NEPA is representative not only of the efforts of the foresighted, ecologically conscious Americans who inspired its passage, but also the beginning of this country's genuine devotion to the eradication of thoughtless and unnecessary environmental degradation. In this sense, NEPA truly represents an exemplary model of an orderly, rational, and productive national public policy.

In addition, however, NEPA may be indicative of an even more significant phenomenon in American society. As a representative of a new approach to managing the environment, NEPA could conceivably presage a major shift in the dominant social paradigm in America regarding the relationship between humans and nature. As a manifestation of greater concern and appreciation for America's natural surroundings, NEPA may have marked a change from a belief structure based on human domination of nature, to one that recognizes that the relationship ought to be symbiotic. As such, NEPA may very well have outlined the framework for a new collective consciousness regarding humans and the environment.

REFERENCES

Anderson, James E., David W.Brady, Charles S., Bullock III, & Steward, Joseph Jr. (1984) *Public policy and politics in America* (2d ed.). Monterey: Brooks/Cole. .

Edelman, Murray. (1964). *The symbolic uses of politics*. Urbana: University of Illinois Press.

Environmental policy. (1970, February 13). *Congressional Quarterly Weekly Report*, 28, pp. 394.

Fairfax, Sally K. (1978, February 17). A disaster in the environment movement. *Science*, 199, pp. 743-747.

Henning, Daniel H. & William R. Mangun (1989). Managing the environmental crisis: *Incorporating competing values in natural resource administration*. Durham: Duke University Press.

Kneese, Allen V. (1984). *Measuring the benefits of clean air and water*. Washington: Resources for the Future, Inc.

Lave, Lester B. (1988, Spring). The greenhouse effect: What government actions are needed? *Journal of Policy Analysis and Management*, 7, pp. 460-470.

Lieber, Harvey. (1970, May/June). Public administration and environmental quality. *Public Administration Review*, 30, pp. 277-286.

Milbrath, Lester W. (1984, March). The context of public opinion: How our belief systems can affect poll results. *The Annals of the American Academy of Political and Social Science*, pp. 472, 35-49.

National Environmental Policy Act of 1969. (1969, July 2 to July 14). *Congressional Record*, 115, pp. 19008-19013.

Nixon asks total mobilization to save environment. (1969, July 18*). Congressional Quarterly Weekly Report*, 28, pp. 1274.

Paehlke, Robert C. (1989*). Environmentalism and the future of progressive politics*. New Haven: Yale University Press.

Population: Will man succeed in destroying himself? (1970, January 30). *Congressional Quarterly Weekly Report*, 28, pp. 281.

Schindler, D. W. (1976, May 7). The impact statement boondoggle. *Science,* 192, pp. 632.

Vig, Norman J. & Michael E. Kraft. (1990). *Environmental policy in the 1990's: Toward a new agenda*. Washington: Congressional Quarterly Press.

Westman Walter E. (1985). *Ecology, impact assessment, and environmental planning*. New York: John Wiley and Sons, Inc.

RESEARCHING AND WRITING A POLICY RECOMMENDATION

1.   Identify a social problem by examining newspapers or observing your environment.
   ♦ Choose a new problem (aids).
   ♦ Or choose an old problem (homelessness).

2.   Conduct a policy evaluation of a policy addressing problems like or similar to the problem identified.
   ♦ For new problems, examine policies closely related to the problem or which indirectly address the problem identified.
   ♦ For old problems, examine policies currently enforced which directly or indirectly address the problem.
   ♦ Be sure to identify the inadequacies of existing government policies you examined.
      • This step will aid in preventing you from proposing a policy solution that is already in force.
      • This step provides you with the depth and breadth necessary to recommend policy solutions.

3.   Identify the goals or objectives to be achieved in an ideal solution to the problem you identified.
   ♦ What do you want to do about the problem?
   ♦ What do experts say should be done about it?
   ♦ Rank the objectives by order of importance.
   ♦ What desired outcome is most important?

4.   Identify alternative solutions proposed to solve the problem.
   ♦ What public actions do experts propose to deal with the problem?
      • Identify at least three alternatives.
      • Be sure you know the position and qualifications of each source.
   ♦ Identify which alternatives address the objectives and outcomes you stated as being most important.
      • Clearly distinguish between each alternative's objectives.
      • Be sure to identify undesirable objectives stated by the experts who are supplemental or complementary to those which are desirable.
   ♦ What are the proposed outcomes of the alternative solutions?
      • Identify the expected outcomes of each alternative.
      • Clearly distinguish between outcomes which are desirable and undesirable.
      • Match up the objectives you stated with the outcomes from each alternative.
   ♦ Rank order the alternatives by preferred objective and outcome.
      • Be able to justify which alternative best fits the objectives and outcomes you prefer.
      • Clearly distinguish between objectives and expected outcomes.

5.   Who do experts say should perform the actions?
   ♦ Identify the level of government that will be responsible for the policy.
   ♦ Identify the government agency that will implement the policy.

6.   Identify the costs and benefits of each alternative.
   ◆   Examine all the real and implied costs.
        •   Describe how you would measure the costs.
        •   Identify the data source used to measure costs.
        •   Identify and justify three real costs.
        •   Identify and justify three implied costs.
   ◆   Examine all the real and implied benefits.
        •   Describe how you measure the benefits.
        •   Identify the data source used to measure benefits.
        •   Identify and justify three real benefits.
        •   Identify and justify three implied benefits.

7.   Recommend the alternative that provides the greatest benefit for the least cost.
   ◆   Decide which benefits are necessary.
   ◆   Be able to justify all acceptable costs to achieve the benefits.

8.   Identify at least five important political actors or players who are likely to either support or oppose your solution.
   ◆   Be sure you identify some players that are supporters and some that are part of the opposition.
   ◆   Identify the issue position, the power, and priority of each player listed.

   ◆   When writing your recommendation, include a discussion, in order, of the following:
   ◆   An introduction or executive summary which includes:
        •   A brief description of the social problem.
        •   The context.
        •   Previous attempts to solve the problem.
        •   Your recommendation.
   ◆   Subheadings identifying the discussion of:
        •   The issue.
        •   The historical context or background.
        •   The objectives of the ideal solution with justification.
        •   The critique of available alternatives.
        •   Your complete recommendation with justification and cost-benefit analysis.
   ◆   A conclusion which restates briefly the context of the social problem and justification of your solution.
   ◆   Do not forget to include a list of sources for all borrowed ideas, arguments, and data. Use tables, charts, and graphs to illustrate data where necessary.

EXAMPLE OF A POLICY RECOMMENDATION

A HYPOTHETICAL POLICY RECOMMENDATION:
WELFARE REFORM

BY
THOMAS P. MITCHELL
PROFESSOR SCHMIDT
POLS 444
JULY 1, 1991
(Reprinted with Permission)

Report to: Secretary of Health and Human Services

From: Thomas P. Mitchell, Staff Policy Analyst

Regarding: Welfare Reform

Date: July 1, 1991

EXECUTIVE SUMMARY

Although the preamble to the Economic Opportunity Act of 1964 states that the goal of antipoverty programs "is to eliminate the paradox of poverty in the midst of plenty in the Nation by opening to everyone the opportunity to live in decency and dignity" (Levitan 1988: 112), the percent of the population below the poverty level has continued to increase since 1979 (U.S. Bureau of the Census 1980). The productivity of American labor remains stagnant as the resources of millions of workers go untapped and poverty continues to capture a growing percent of the American population. To address this issue:

1.   Provide remedial training to the working and non-working poor;

2.   Ensure quality education as a curative strategy to poverty by breaking the cycle of poverty at an early age.

The past strategies of punitive, preventive, and alleviative techniques have not been able to control this surge in the poverty rate that has occurred due in part to the economic shift in America from a manufacturing sector to a service oriented society. Instead, as this analysis advocates, a multi-generational program that is both curative and remedial in structure needs to be implemented to provide training and opportunity to the working poor, the non-working poor, and their families. By undertaking legislative reform in this area, strides can be made toward reducing the social condition of growing poverty rates and providing employment opportunities to all laborers in this service-orientated economy.

This policy analysis specifically recommends:

1.   Continuation of employment programs for the non-working poor.

2.   Remedial Job Skill Training and Education programs to provide skills to the working and non-working poor and to induce the poor to enter the labor market.

3.   Curative programs aimed at high-risk children of all income and educational levels that are in need of additional educational support.

4.   Continuation of cash support payment to keep millions of individuals out of poverty.

WELFARE POLICY ISSUES

As a relative concept, poverty will always exist because inequality is a problem in all societies at all times. The distribution of income in society is not equal, nor necessarily should it be (Levitan 1988: 1). However, the Great Society of Lyndon B. Johnson attempted to eliminate the presence of poverty in the United States by promoting opportunity among its citizenry (Levitan 1988: 112). As anti-poverty programs were implemented during the Great Society in the 1960s, the poverty rate fell from 22 percent of the total population in 1960 to 12 percent in 1969 (U.S. Bureau of the Census 1980). As the optimism of the Great Society dissolved in the late 1970's, however, poverty rates began to increase and are still steadily rising (Levitan 1988: 19).

Welfare policy has traditionally taken on one of four forms: preventative, alleviative, punitive, or curative. Preventive strategies are designed to ensure that certain groups of people do not enter poverty, including the elderly, the disabled, and the widowed. Alleviative strategies provide some assistance to those suffering from poverty. These strategies are typically referred to as "welfare" and include such programs as Aid to Families with Dependent Children (AFDC), Medicaid, and food stamps. The punitive strategy distinguishes between the worthy and non-worthy poor; those who are capable of work should not receive assistance because such assistance creates disincentives to work. Finally, curative strategies are targeted toward controlling poverty at an early age by attacking its causes with programs aimed at addressing poor education and the lack of job skills (Rushefsky 1990: 133-39).

To understand the existence of poverty as defined by a minimal level of income, the causes of poverty must be identified and the degrees of poverty must be clearly differentiated. In 1957, John Kenneth Galbraith's *The Affluent Society* distinguished between two types of poverty case poverty, which was a product of personal characteristics, area poverty, and economic deficiencies relating to a particular sector of the nation (Galbraith 1957: 288). William Julius Wilson, a noted sociologist at the University of Chicago, supports this view of area poverty by stating that the underlying problem and cause of poverty lies within the economic structure of the United States (Wilson lecture, 1991).

For example, the 1970's and early 1980's in the U.S. marked a period characterized by economic instability. Accompanied with inflation and recession, the United States witnessed the highest unemployment rates since the Great Depression (Harrington 1962: 431). As the cost of labor increased as a result of the combination of the recession and inflation, American businesses were forced to adopt strategies that were laborsaving. In particular, the United States evolved from a leading manufacturing nation to a service-oriented society (Wilson lecture; Stone 1988).

As the tertiary (service) sector grew, the primary (agriculture, mining, fishing, forestry) and secondary (manufacturing, raw materials processing) sectors have declined. In the 1960s when the Economic Opportunity Act was initiated, the primary and secondary sectors of our society entailed 42 percent of the labor force. In 1981, however, this number had fallen to only 30 percent (Hughes 1987: 522; Statistical Abstracts 1982-83). In addition, from 1977-82, employment in the service sector of the U.S.'s largest twenty cities grew 54.7 percent, while the rate of growth in the manufacturing sector increased only 1.4 percent (Statistical Abstract of the U.S. 1988). These figures reveal that the employment conditions that were in existence when the Economic Opportunity Act of 1964 was created are no longer the same today. American businesses are now demanding a skilled labor force and requiring a broad education for success (Hughes 1987: 522). Unskilled workers lack the marketable skills required by businesses, and therefore no longer have the opportunity to complete effectively for jobs. The result of this economic shift has been a continuous increase in the rate of poverty.

The American labor force is now confronting the existence of 32.4 million people below the poverty level of $11,600 for a family of four (Statistical Abstract of the U.S. 1988; Rushefsky 1990: 131). These individuals not only include those unemployed or unable to work, but also those whose wages do not provide an income above the poverty level. For these individuals, past anti-poverty programs have not been successful.

GOALS AND OBJECTIVES

The major goal of welfare policy is security (Rushefsky 1990: 130). Welfare policy is an attempt to provide some minimal level of assistance, whether temporarily or permanently, to those deemed worthy. Those deemed "worthy" include the elderly and the young. A lesser goal of welfare policy is to assist those who are capable of working in becoming self-sufficient. Third, a goal of welfare policy is the desire to discourage welfare dependence on the part of those capable of self-sufficiency (Rushefsky 1990: 130). As these goals have been developed over time, objectives have been created in the form of programs and policies to address poverty.

The 1964 Economic Opportunity Act, passed as one of Lyndon B. Johnson's Great Society programs, characterized the philosophy of the times--the belief that federal expertise and resources could be used to strengthen new government programs and strategies in the war on poverty (Katz 1986: 255). During this time, the issue of poverty regained its place on the policy agenda labeled as the War on Poverty (Anderson, J. et al. 1984: 138), much of this due to two important literary works. The first book, Galbraith's *The Affluent Society* (1957) not only distinguished between case and area poverty, but also called attention to the existence of poverty amidst plenty. Galbraith elaborated upon the existence of poverty in a nation rich in resources (Galbraith 1957: 1). However, as the public viewed America as a rich country, the acceptance of Galbraith's work was limited (Rushefsky 1990: 139).

The other literary source was Harrington's *The Other America* (1962). Harrington's work drew attention to poverty among blacks in the urban north and rural south, among whites in Appalachia, and among the aged. This work was published during the Kennedy administration: this administration was sensitive to its message and able to promote it (Rushefsky 1990: 139).

Thus, these two works prompted the War on Poverty, which was designed to provide support for the currently impoverished while at the same time attempting to alleviate poverty for the next generation. Although this strategy was sound, it also proved expensive (Levitan 1988: 136). As the presidency during the mid-1970s focused on restraining the growth of the federal budget, outlays for welfare policy dwindled, thus assuring that poverty would continue into the 1980s (Levitan 1988: 137).

During the past two decades, two differing views from experts as to what government should do to alleviate poverty have dominated public policy. Throughout the 1970s, the idea that society would be best served by encouraging welfare recipients to work without losing all of their welfare benefits characterized welfare policy. Provisions for combining work and welfare recognized that low-wage employment by itself often was not sufficient to raise larger families out of poverty, and that incentives for continued work efforts offer some hope from eventual escape from welfare dependency (Levitan 1988: 18).

In the 1980's, however, this view was rejected. During this era, sharp distinctions were made between the "truly needy" who cannot work and the "undeserving" poor who are presumably employable and capable of work (Levitan 1988: 18). Also, welfare was seen as a failure, costing too much and providing little, if any, work incentive to welfare recipients. The notion that government was the problem rather than the solution identified the prevailing theme in policy making (Anderson, J. et.al.1984: 142). In accordance with these themes, financial incentives for welfare recipients were reduced and assistance to the working poor with some income was cut dramatically (Levitan 1988: 18).

Just as the works of Galbraith and Harrington prompted experimentation with welfare policy in the late 1950's and early 1960s, literary sources again contributed to the issue of welfare policy reform in the early 1980's. Martin Anderson in Welfare (1978) provided guidelines for welfare reform which were adopted during the 1980's, including (1) assistance only for the needy; (2) increased emphasis on eliminating fraud; (3) workfare; (4) child support enforcement; (5) improved administration; and (6) shifting more responsibility to state and local governments and the private sector (Anderson, M. 1978: 159-164).

A second literary source was George Gilder's Wealth and Poverty (1981), in which Gilder theorized that poor people remained poor because they were paid to by welfare programs. This literary contribution asserted that because welfare programs were so generous, disincentives for work were created. Gilder also noted that a program to increase incomes by using transfer payments for less diligent groups is politically divisive because it creates a bitter resistance among the real working class (Gilder 1981: 6). In addition, notes Gilder, such an effort breaks the psychological link between effort and reward, which is important to upward mobility. These issues inspired Gilder to argue that the poor need jobs and incentives to look for employment, even if the jobs themselves were not well paying (Gilder 1981: 68).

Finally, Charles Murray's Losing Ground (1984) argued, as did Gilder, that welfare was counterproductive. Murray's argument was that the expansion of welfare policies in the sixties and seventies had the consequence of increasing poverty, rather than controlling it (Murray 1984: 68). Unlike Anderson or Gilder, Murray suggested that all welfare programs be eliminated because in implementation, the programs were counterproductive to their purpose (Murray 1984: 228).

These literary contributions meshed well with the Reagan administration and its banner of New Federalism. As New Federalism called for a decentralization of the federal role in administering and funding programs, states and localities were called upon to design and administer solutions to problems, including social welfare, in their own states in communities (Levitan 1988: 20). Following this philosophy of federal conservatism, financial incentives for welfare recipients to remain on welfare were reduced and assistance to the working poor with some income was dramatically cut under the rationale of targeting benefits to those most in need to control welfare costs (Levitan 1988: 19).

The recent shift to a predominantly tertiary sector reflects a labor market that now demands more skills and education of its workers than ever before. The opportunity to live free from poverty that was granted to all individuals within the Economic Opportunity Act of 1964 has been removed as a priority from the governmental agenda. Since the goals and objectives of welfare policy reflect security, assistance, and work, this opportunity needs to be reestablished in accordance with the Economic Opportunity Act in the framework of a service-oriented society.

Although welfare policy is still on the government agenda, it is not a priority. Even in the wealthiest of nations, difficult and unpleasant choices must be made among a range of public needs and national goals. The willingness to commit resources to the problem of poverty is a reflection of its priority among its citizenry (Levitan 1988: 145). Nonetheless, as poverty continues to encompass millions of Americans, resources devoted to welfare policy by means of strategies advocated in this analysis, namely remedial and curative policies, will be beneficial in controlling the increase in the rate of poverty.

PAST POLICY RESPONSES

Federal programs in aid of the poor fall into four categories: cash support, direct provision of necessities, preventive and compensatory efforts for children and youth, and employment-related programs and policies (Levitan 1988: 14).

Cash Support Programs

Cash support programs provide the foundation for federal assistance to the poor. Because poverty is usually defined by the lack of an adequate income level, it can be alleviated most directly by cash support (Levitan 1988: 15). The Social Security Act of 1935 is the most encompassing cash support program for both the poor and the nonpoor. Two groups of programs included in the act were (1) social insurance programs, including old age, survivors, and disability insurance (OASDI), and unemployment assistance; and (2) public assistance programs, including AFDC, AFDC with "unemployed parent" component (AFDC-UP), supplemental security income (SSI), and General Assistance. In 1982, an estimated 23.1 million persons were kept out of poverty by cash support programs alone (Levitan 1988: 25).

Lack of employment is a cause of poverty, but employment alone does not ensure self-sufficiency. Nearly 50 percent of the 7.6 million family heads who were above the poverty level in 1983 worked. For these working poor, income alone was not enough to alleviate them from poverty (Levitan 1988: 11). Because the income of the working poor is often not enough to raise them above the poverty level, cash support programs could add to their income level.

Cash support payments are often disliked by policy makers for two reasons. First, they have little authority in how the recipient spends the aid. Government officials argue they should ensure that welfare recipients spend their assistance properly. That is to say, assistance should only be spent on necessities (Levitan 1988: 16). Second, it is argued that cash assistance programs reduce work incentives for recipients. The public may be willing to support the poor as they participate in training programs, but be unwilling to support general relief for the poor (Levitan 1988: 15).

Direct Provision of Necessities

Welfare policy also includes programs that deliver goods and services directly to the needy as a supplement to their income. These programs include Medicare and Medicaid, public and subsidized housing, and food stamps. As the public is reluctant to provide general cash support to the poor, programs that control the usage of aid are more favorable.

In 1984, goods and services accounted for nearly three-fifths of total federal outlays in aid of the poor (Levitan 1988: 59). This is due in part to the fact that in-kind assistance is more politically feasible than cash assistance. Some argue that government is a better judge of needs and priorities than the welfare recipient is. Programs that directly provide necessities to welfare recipients offer a means of control and authority on behalf of the government as to what is considered essential. Further, in some instances the direct provision of goods and services is necessary because they are not available in the market. For example, welfare recipients need compensatory education and affordable health care, but the existence of establishments to provide these needs is limited in the public market. Lastly, in certain cases the government can provide these goods and services more efficiently than private enterprise, due to the economies of large-scale enterprise (Levitan 1988: 16).

Preventive and Compensatory Efforts for Children and Youth.

The federal government has focused programs on protecting the next generation from poverty by concentrating on three areas: (1) birth control to assist couples in keeping family size within their desires and financial means; (2) child care facilities to alleviate the pressures of poverty that bring the neglect of physical and social development during crucial years of a child's life; and (3) education as a means of equipping the children of the poor to compete in the job market (Levitan 1988: 92). Because of the service-orientation nature of the U.S. economy and the demand of the labor market for highly skilled and educated workers, educational institutions should play a crucial role in any welfare reform (Turner, et al. 1990)

A home environment of poverty can seriously impair a child's ability to learn. Impoverished children often experience great difficulties in school partly because of the lack of stimulation and motivation at home (Levitan 1988: 100). These conditions can result in learning disorders or behavioral problems that require special attention early in a child's education (Welfare and Housing Assistance...1989).

Due to an increasing demand for a highly skilled and technical work force, a high school education does not alone guarantee a life free from poverty (Anderson, J. et al. 1984; Hughes 1987). The demand for college education is growing for even an entry-level position. As the skills and education required by the labor market continue to increase, individuals must be equipped with the abilities necessary to secure gainful employment. These abilities can be developed and enhanced in post-secondary institutions (Levitan 1988).

But as post-secondary education provides the opportunity for a professional career, this opportunity is not equally affordable to everyone. According to U.S. Census data, only one-fourth of young people from families with incomes below $10,000 attend college, compared with over one-third from families with incomes between $10,000 and $20,000 and half of those from families with incomes above $20,000 per year (U.S. Bureau of the Census 1982; Levitan 1988: 106). This data indicates that those of lower incomes are being denied the opportunity to attend college.

The problems of insufficient income, lack of motivational support, and limited prior education combine to discourage children of the poor from attending college (Levitan 1988: 105). Because of these barriers, the Upward Bound program was designed to motivate students early in their high school career and to help them set their sights toward college (Levitan 1988: 105). Although Upward Bound has only been able to serve a small fraction of high school students who could benefit from this type of service due to costs, the results are still moderately encouraging. One out of every ten high school Upward Bound participants has entered college. Also, 60 percent of those in college were still enrolled two years later. This indicates that Upward Bound students are as likely to remain in college as those students from more affluent backgrounds (Levitan 1988: 106) are.

Similar to Upward Bound for high school youth, Head Start is a pre-school program for the children of low-income families. The premise of Head Start is that poor children entering school lack an enriching home and community environment and thus start school at a disadvantage. The program is intended to give these youth an early start in on their education (Rushefsky 1990: 134). As children participate in Head Start, they spend less time in their poverty stricken environment and are able to develop both social and learning skills that may be denied to them at home (Rushefsky 1990: 134; Turner 1990)).

These programs provide justification for devoting an increasing amount of resources to education. There is also a need, however, to develop policies which will serve to enhance education and address child care problems of the working poor (Shaping AFCD-Linked Child Care...1989). With the work incentive and requirement now set within most present welfare programs, many mothers are now entering the work force. Nevertheless, without establishing childcare facilities, many mothers are being neglected the opportunity to enter the labor market. Childcare responsibility is a formidable constraint in keeping parents, especially mothers, at home and out of the work force (Levitan 1988: 141; Abramovitz 1988).

Employment Related Programs

In an effort to help the unemployed and to induce the poor to enter the labor market, the federal government has created various employment and training programs to meet the needs of the poor (Levitan 1988: 113). The idea is that training and work experience will lead to self-sufficiency. The most recent and encompassing example of this type of employment and training program is the Family Support Act of 1988 (Gideonse and Meyers 1989).

The Family Support Act contains a provision for creating the Job Opportunities and Basic Skills Training Programs (JOBS). JOBS requires states to provide comprehensive state education, training, and employment programs for welfare recipients with children aged three and over, provided agencies can secure adequate child care and support services (Welfare and Housing Assistance 1983: 183). The goal is to have parents employed, thereby avoiding long-term welfare dependence (Gideonse and Meyers 1989: 33). The Family Support Act of 1988 has been labeled as a "welfare reform" (Lewis 1989: 42) and was described by President Reagan as a "real welfare reform--reform that will lead to lasting emancipation from welfare dependency." (Weekly Cumulation 1989: 1313 Walsh 1989).

Although the Family Support Act of 1988 was labeled as a welfare reform, it is marked with serious flaws that are typical of employment and training programs. Sponsors of the legislation expect the act to bring many parents, especially mothers, back into the labor force. The goal of the act is to supply welfare recipients with the skills necessary to enter the labor force (Gideonse and Meyers 1989: 33; Moynihan 1989; Kraus 1987). This expectation underlies the major problem with employment and training programs. It assumes the labor market will employ almost all able-bodied adults and pay them a living wage (Gideonse and Meyers 1989: 33).

This assumption is linked only slightly to the economic realities of American society. The problems of costs and lack of recipient skills hinder employment in the private sector (Gideonse and Meyers 1989: 33). The primary cost is that of providing training programs to welfare recipients. It is not just the problem that the poor do not possess basic, employable skills, but also that the lack of these skills hinders them in training. Many of the poor lack the literacy and computational skills necessary to benefit from training programs (Levitan 1988). It has been estimated that 70 percent of all welfare recipients would need remedial education before qualifying for even the most menial and poorest paying jobs (Gideonse and Meyers 1989: 35).

A second cost that has been gaining much attention is the provision of childcare facilities for recipients of the JOBS program under the Family Support Act of 1988. This issue has grown due to the feminization of poverty. Although individuals in female-headed households constitute only 15 percent of the U.S. population, they account for nearly half of the poverty population (Levitan 1988: 7). Female-headed families are more likely to experience poverty and for longer periods than male-headed or two-parent families (Rushefsky 1990: 132). These single mothers have become dependent upon welfare, partly because of their parental responsibilities at home. If they were provided with childcare facilities, these single mothers might be inclined to enter the labor market (Harrington 1987).

The result of the Family Support Act will likely be the same as previous employment and training programs. It is doubtful that these training and employment programs established by JOBS would be truly effective because of the limited resources being applied to the program. The Family Support Act will likely continue to promote the work ethic and maintain a vast amount of low wage workers. While many of the non-working poor may enter the labor force, most of them are likely to remain poor (Gideonse and Meyers 1989: 29; Levitan 1988; Hylton 1989)). Without the funding necessary to take full advantage of training and employment programs, the unemployed will be unable to truly escape poverty (Karger 1989).

RECOMMENDATIONS

To propose an effective reform instrument for welfare policy that attacks both the results and causes of poverty, policies must be set forth addressing the present economic structure of the United States. First, a new breed of workers that possess modern technical skills and a higher education to effectively and competently apply new technologies are desired by the private sector. Second, the past welfare strategies have not been able to control the surge in the poverty rate.

To address these problems, a multi-generational program that is both curative and remedial in nature needs to be implemented to provide training and opportunity to the working poor, the non-working poor, and their families. Although this policy recommends that money is appropriated for remedial education and training, it advocates the devotion of resources to curative strategies in attacking the causes of poverty at an early stage. By adhering to this strategy, the need for remedial education and training will be reduced in the years ahead as those who will someday be entering the labor market will be already be well equipped to find quality employment.

The guidelines of this curative and remedial strategy are as follows:

1.   **Continuation of employment programs for the non-working poor accompanies by increased funding.**

The labor market will not likely employ all able-bodied adults and pay them a living wage as some proponents of employment programs claim. This is due in part to the fact that at the heart of business lies the competing concepts of costs and revenue. Employers are very aware of the additional costs of training new employees and anyone who would require excess training or supervision would be a costly burden (Gideonse and Meyers 1989: 34). Further, the welfare stigma that is attached to participants often labels them as potential employees who would require much training and supervision. Thus, the welfare stigma has handicapped the poor in the labor market (Gideonse and Meyers 1989: 34).

The poor are not equally able to compete for jobs with non-welfare recipients and are therefore less likely to secure gainful employment (Wilson 1987). To aid welfare recipients in this problem, the JOBS program that provides for state employment programs should be continued. The adherence by states to this provision would assist the poor in securing employment and thereby gaining income that would assist them in surpassing the poverty level.

2.   **Remedial Job Skill Training and Education programs to provide skills to the working and non-working poor and to induce the poor to enter the labor market.**

A program is needed that would not only address the issue of controlling poverty rates for future generations, but also and more urgently dealing with the issue of 32.3 million adults currently impoverished (Levitan 1988: 6). To reduce the poverty rate among workers, remedial training programs can provide a means for welfare recipients to acquire the skills and education demanded by the market place. In particular, literacy programs and basic skill training represent two remedial programs that would alleviate those presently impoverished.

While providing these types of programs to recipients, government is promoting a means of self-sufficiency. If these recipients gain adequate employment and apply their trained skills, work incentives in the form of income above the poverty level, as well as above welfare assistance levels, will keep the recipient in the labor market and less dependent upon welfare. The benefit of moving welfare recipients into the labor force would mark an important step toward lowering the poverty rates for the present generation.

Upon completion of remedial training, welfare recipients will be in need of assistance in finding work. Job skill training is futile unless work can be found following graduation from the program. To assist the poor in finding work, employment programs should be used as a supplement to Job Skill Training programs. In doing so, a link between training and employment is established which can potentially get millions of the non-working poor into the labor market.

3.   **Continuation of cash support programs as a means to keep millions of individuals out of poverty.**

As was documented previously, an estimated 23.1 million persons were kept out of poverty in 1982 by cash support programs alone. As was also noted, nearly 50 percent of the 7.6 million family heads who were above the poverty level in 1983 worked. For these workers, wages alone were not enough to set them above the poverty level.

Because cash support programs have been considered controversial, especially as they are perceived as limiting the authority of government and taxpayers, legislation could be enacted that would require employable recipients to enroll in and make an reasonable effort towards completion of employment and/or job skill training programs in order to get cash assistance. For this to be feasible, day care provisions should be made for the children of welfare recipients. This would enable parents in either single or two-parent households to participate in employment or job skill training programs. This would also provide a work incentive in cash support programs, provide government more authority in seeing that employable adults do participate in employment and/or job skill training programs, and provide accommodations for children of those who do partake in these programs.

4.   **Curative programs aimed at high-risk children at all educational levels that are in need of additional educational support.**

Research has shown that the correlation between graduating high school and attaining an income above the poverty level is very strong and positive (Levitan 1988; Anderson, M. 1978; Anderson, J. et al. 1989). This strong correlation provides rationale for investing in educational institutions and programs as to prevent poverty from growing in future years. By providing resources to increase high school graduation rates, society is benefiting those that will soon be entering the labor force.

One of the goals of welfare policy is of controlling poverty rates. Programs used to address rising poverty rates include curative strategies of attacking the causes of poverty at an early age; policies designed around our present and future generations allow this goal to be attained. Failure to graduate from high school, however, is not only a problem of the poor. Children of various income levels are represented in the high school dropout rate.

Currently, the Upward Bound and Head Start programs seek to aid youth from low-income families by providing additional educational and social support. In particular, Upward Bound aims to assist high school students in graduating and attending college. Two problems within this program's purpose exist. First, although students are not legally allowed to drop out until a set legal age, many children in essence drop out much earlier in their education by simply not attending school. For those early dropouts, the Upward Bound program will not help them because it concentrates solely on high school students. Second, the target population for Upward Bound focuses on low-income students whose families have income below the poverty level (Levitan 1988: 105). For students who do not qualify into that income category, but are still in need of assistance, the Upward Bound program is not available to them. For these reasons, the Upward Bound program should be expanded to include children at risk in all income and educational levels.

In particular, the Head Start program, similar to Upward Bound, provides services to those children of low-income families before they enter school. For these children, Head Start attempts to overcome the lack of social and educational stimulus that these youth experience in their home environment. The disadvantages that these children possess before entering elementary school can be lessened through the Head Start program to better prepare them to succeed in school (Turner 1990).

The Upward Bound and Head Start programs offer assistance to high school and preschool students, respectively. For those students not in these two educational levels, no assistance program is available to them. By waiting until high school before offering support for high-risk youth, many students have already lost interest in their education. For this reason, programs similar to Head Start and Upward Bound need to be implemented into all levels with the school system for high-risk youth.

These types of programs offer two advantages. First, it allows an attack on the social and educational consequences of poverty at an early age. While Head Start does assist those children of low-income families, learning deficiencies may not be detected until a later age. A program that offers educational assistance regardless of grade level would be able to provide support and services to such children.

Second, the social and educational consequences of poverty are not temporary, but long lasting. The skills children develop in Head Start may not be sufficient to carry them into high school without additional motivational and tutorial services. For those children who did not participate in Head Start, these needs may as they progress further in school. By offering a program that would provide services to children throughout their educational path, the needs of these high-risk children can be constantly monitored and addressed.

These policies are not to be mutually exclusive, but rather integrated and mutually re-enforcing. Welfare recipients who are employable are to use employment programs as a means of securing employment. Those individuals, who are unemployable due to a lack of job skills, are to enroll and participate in job skill training programs in which upon completion shall enter employment programs. For those recipients enrolled in employment programs or job skill training programs, cash assistance can be made available to them as they move towards employment.

The fourth recommendation recognizes that an escape from future poverty begins at an early age. This analysis recommends the inclusion of high risk children of all income levels and educational levels in the Upward Bound program as a means of attacking poverty at an early stage is necessarily linked to reducing poverty rates economy wide.

EVALUATING WELFARE REFORM

To assess the effectiveness of any policy change or expansion, the changes must be clearly defined and regularly evaluated. This process can be outlined in five steps. First, establish a period attached to the program for accomplishing the goals. Although this may be difficult, it is necessary that each individual program recommendation be evaluated every four years to maintain a continuous and regular justification for such an anti-poverty program. The four year time will correspond to both economic, political, and education cycles.

Second, because the goal of employment programs is to assist recipients in securing work, measurements of progress towards employment are to be recorded. These shall include the percentage of recipients attaining employment, the duration of employment, and whether wages secured in these jobs provide an income above the poverty level. Employment programs are crucial links in the success of other changes because they provide opportunity for those who have successfully completed remedial training programs. Therefore, the success of employment programs must be closely monitored for slippage or temporal problems in placing graduates of remedial training programs.

The another component, cash assistance, is linked with JOBS and employment programs, but will be less necessary for the future of the program. More specifically, cash assistance outlays should lower over time as the number of recipients in such programs lowers over time. This is because other policies, such as those including remedial and youth intervention programs, should reduce the number who will need the cash assistance. If this is not the case, cash assistance programs are not proving to be an incentive for participation in remedial or employment programs.

The final element for measuring success involves the curative programs designed for high-risk children. Individual school districts should be responsible for classifying and defining high-risk youth. This will lower the cultural and regional biases associated with standardized tests. These programs will be successful if the graduation rates for all high-risk youth reflect an increase as compared to past high risk, specially, and narrowly targeted youth educational policies.

CONCLUSION

In recent years, the poverty rate in the United States has been steadily increasing. As the labor market has had to adapt to recently established service sector, new skills and higher levels of education are being demanded of them. In the process, however, the productivity of American labor has remained stagnant as the resources of millions of workers go untapped as laborers are lacking the skills and education required by the labor market. As millions of American are currently impoverished, millions more will soon enter the ranks if anti-poverty policy is not undertaken.

Past poverty strategies have proven unsuccessful in controlling the recent stage of poverty rates. Therefore, a multi-generational program that is both curative and remedial in structure should be implemented to provide training and opportunity to high risk youth, the working poor, and the non-working poor. This policy recommendation advocates policy changes and expansions:

1. Continuation of employment programs for the non-working poor accompanied by increasing funding.

2. Remedial Job Skill Training and Education programs for the working and non-working poor and to induce the poor to enter the labor market.

3. Continuation of cash support payments to keep millions of individuals out of poverty.

4. Curative programs aimed at high-risk children at all educational levels that are in need of additional educational support.

These programs are to be integrated and mutually re-enforcing. Each recommendation is to build upon each of the others as to provide a structured and directional welfare policy. If an effective and efficient welfare reform is to be achieved, it must encompass and serve those who are currently impoverished by instituting job skill training and employment programs as well as attacking poverty at an early age for high risk youth through curative programs such as Upward Bound and Head Start. The implementation of this multi-generational program will represent welfare reform in that engages proactive and curative government activities which halt and subsequently reduce poverty rates and provide employment opportunities for present and future generations as workers compete for jobs in a predominantly service-oriented economy.

REFERENCES

Abramovitz, Mimi. "Why Welfare Reform is a Sham." *The Nation*. Sept. 26, 1988.

Anderson, James E., David W. Brady, Charles S. Bullock III, and Joseph Steward Jr. *Public Policy and Politics in America*. 2nd Edition. Brooks/Cole Publishing Co.: Pacific Grove, CA. 1984.

Anderson, Martin. *Welfare*. Hoover Institution: Stanford, CA 1978.

Galbraith, John Kenneth. *The Affluent Society*. Houghton Mifflin Company: Boston. 1957.

Gideonse, Sarah K. and William R. Meyers. "Why the Family Support Act Will Fail." *Challenge*. September-October 1989.

Gilder, George. *Wealth and Poverty*. Basic Books, Inc.: New York. 1981.

Harrington, Michael. "The New American Poverty." William H. Chafe and Harvard Sitkoff. *A History of Our Time*. Oxford University Press: Oxford. 1987.

Harrington, Michael. *The Other America*. Macmillan Company: New York. 1962.

Hughes, Jonathan. *American Economic History*. Scott, Foresman and Company: Glenview, IL 1987.

Hylton, Richard D. "The New Welfare Bill: When More Isn't Enough." *Black Enterprise*. January 1989.

Karger, Howard Jacob and David Stoesz. "Welfare Reform: Maximum Feasible Exaggeration." *Tikkun*. Vol. 4, No. 2. March-April 1989.

Katz, Michael B. *In the Shadows of the Poorhouse*. Basic Books, Inc.: New York. 1986.

Kaus, Mickey. "A Welfare Reform Mirage." *Newsweek:* August 3, 1987.

Levitan, Sar A. *Programs in Aid of the Poor*. John Hopkins Univ. Press: Baltimore. 1988.

Lewis, Anne C. "Getting On With It." *Phi Delta Kappan*. February 1989.

Moynihan, Daniel Patrick. "The Coming of Age of American Social Policy." *USA Today*. November 1989.

Murray, Charles. *Losing Ground*. Basic Books, Inc.: New York. 1984.

Rushefsky, Mark E. *Public Policy in the United States*. Brooks/Cole Publishing Co.: Pacific Grove, CA. 1990.

"Shaping AFDC-Linked Child Care that Meets Families' Needs." *Social Policy*. Fall 1989.

Statistical Abstract of the U.S. U.S. Bureau of the Census. Table 651. 1982-83.

Statistical Abstract of the U.S. U.S. Bureau of the Census. Tables 215, 216, 217, 219, 148, 250, 254. 1988.

Stone, Deborah A. *Policy Paradox and Political Reasons*. Glenview, IL: Scott, Foresman and Company. 1988.

Turner, Jason, Gina Barbaro, and Myles Schlank. "Head Start and Jobs." *Children Today*. May-June 1990.

U.S. Bureau of the Census. *Current Population Reports*. Series P-60, No. 133. "Characteristics of Population Below the Poverty Level: 1980." U.S. Government Printing Office: Washington, DC. 1982.

Walsh, Joan. "Fighting Poverty After Reagan." *The Nation*. March 13, 1989.

Weekly Cumulation of Presidential Documents. October 13, 1988. Vol. 24. Sept-Jan 1988-89.

"Welfare and Housing Assistance." *Journal of Housing*. July/August 1989.

Wilson, William Julius. Lecture at Southern Illinois University at Carbondale. February 13, 1991.

Wilson, William Julius. *The Truly Disadvantaged*. The University of Chicago Press: Chicago. 1987.

SECTION TWELVE

FORMAT AND EXAMPLES OF ASSIGNMENTS AND EXERCISES IN APPLIED POLITICAL SCIENCE

ASSIGNMENTS AND EXERCISES IN APPLIED POLITICAL SCIENCE

In the following pages there are three examples of writing assignments that require students to apply concepts, theories, and accepted wisdom in political science to real life experiences. These papers build on the student's training and knowledge in a subfield. Such assignments provide students with the opportunity to collect information, manage it, and make it useful by writing about it. These assignments build not only on the class materials, but offer students the opportunity to use their critical thinking and writing skills on topics and information in a nonacademic, unstructured environment. Such assignments test skills as well as mastery of subfield knowledge. The paper examples exhibit a variety of backgrounds and writing styles. These papers are personal reports of students' experiences in applying what they learned to what they observed. An explanation of the form for each type of paper precedes the examples.

First Paper: Event Analysis/Clipping Thesis

"Energy Policy Clipping Thesis" follows current events regarding a particular set of related topics covered by the media. The student follows the issues over a specified time, usually a semester, and then writes an analytical essay using the course material and the media reports as supporting evidence.

Second Paper: Participant Observer/Internship Report

"Internship Report: Campaign Volunteers: VIP's or Peons?" provides an introspective view of the relevance of fieldwork accomplished to theoretical constructs learned previously in the classroom. This assignment requires the student to identify where theory and practice conflict or agree. The work is performed outside the classroom setting.

Third Paper: Event Observation, Participation/Journal Essay

"Campaign '88: Against All Odds" combines the skills applied in event analysis with the goals of participant observer assignments. In this type of assignment, the student becomes a participant observer during a timely event, such as a campaign, while a writing in a journal, maintaining a clipping file, and attending class. It combines all necessary elements for synthesis and learning. In these assignments, while students are learning about theories, they are conducting a small amount of fieldwork and observing the larger context of the event examined.

EVENT ANALYSIS AND CLIPPING THESIS

Purpose

A clipping thesis is a file of clippings from various newspapers and magazines that have been collected over time concerning a particular issue or event. Students use these clippings to write an analysis of the event or issue. A clipping thesis has many of the properties of a journal.

- Like a journal, a clipping thesis or clipping file helps students keep track of information and reactions to current events related to a broad subject area.
- A clipping thesis, however, is focused on a particular topic or subject rather than on the broad array of daily experiences.

How to Construct a Clipping Thesis

1.   Choose an issue related to the course material. Check with the instructor for ideas or direction for choices.
2.   If possible, use at least two newspapers and one news weekly magazine as your sources. Some sources are online.
     - One of the newspapers should be a national paper such as *The New York Times*.
     - Read or skim various sources regularly.
3.   For paper-based articles, clip or photocopy articles, cartoons, and commentary that are related to your topic. Be sure to clip, photocopy, or print all of the item.
     - Be sure to put the source, date, and page number on each item paper-based item.
     - Be sure to put the source, date, and access date on each item from an online source.
4.   Attach the paper clipping or photocopy to a piece of 8 x 11 white bond paper with glue.
     - Cut and paste the clipping to fit the page.
     - Do not leave any part of the clipping hanging off the paper.
     - Place only one item per page.
5.   Place the clipping page into a notebook or folder.
6.   On the clipping page, summarize the information in the item and write your reaction to the item.
7.   Based on the body of clippings, write an analysis of the issue or event including:
     - An explanation of the origin.
     - A description of the development over the time period covered.
     - The degree of government intervention.
     - The current status of the issue.
     - A projection about future developments.
8.   Use additional sources for background on the issue or event if necessary. For large clipping files, include an index by topic when using a variety of background materials.
9.   Write an analytical essay using some of the clippings as references. Be sure to fully reference all materials used to construct the essay and to observe all standard format guidelines for typing and writing an analytical essay. Do not forget to number the all pages including those containing the clippings.

EXAMPLE OF AN EVENT ANALYSIS/CLIPPING THESIS

ENERGY POLICY CLIPPING FILE

By
Alan G. Schmidt
Professor Diane Schmidt
POLS 324
May 1, 1989
(Reprinted By Permission)

ENERGY POLICY A CLIPPING FILE

When President Carter addressed the nation in 1977 regarding the severity of the energy crisis, he stressed the need for quick and decisive action. He likened the effort to that involved in fighting a war. Carter stated that "our decision about energy will test the character of the American people and the ability of the President and the Congress to govern this nation Carter, p. 91)." During the Carter administration, many ideas were discussed and some progress was made toward a national energy policy. Since 1980, however, energy policy has become yet another political football used by opposing parties to further their own ends with little or no regard to effectively solving the long range needs of the nation.

It is unfortunate that Jimmy Carter's administration was not successful in solving some of its other domestic problems. His inability to deal with inflation, unemployment, and the hostage crisis may have led to a crisis of confidence, prompting his energy policies to be rejected or ignored (Anderson, et. al, Chaps. 2. 3, 4, and 12). The Reagan administration took every opportunity to criticize Carter as a doomsayer and a negative thinker, when in fact he was being realistic about the need for all citizens to give some thought to the kind of lifestyle they would be passing along to future generations. Without serious minded leadership in Washington and with the "don't worry, be happy" philosophy as the general attitude of the country, precious time has been lost in securing a long-range energy plan for the United States.

The individual citizen, however, should not wait around for the government to develop a coherent energy policy. According to a recent statistic printed in *Harper's*, the amount of energy that has leaked from American's windows in 1988 was equal to 522,000,000 barrels of oil ("*Harper's* Index", p. 13). Whether through ignorance or neglect, Americans are simply not embracing energy conservation as a lifestyle. Donella Meadows, in an editorial for the *St. Louis Post Dispatch*, paints the typical American's attitude about oil consumption and oil pipeline expansions as being irresponsible. According to her, Americans want more oil so that they can avoid the costs of energy waste and environmental neglect.

> "Do this so we can drive gas-guzzling cars, heat uninsulated houses, buy products made from oil and toss them away. Whatever you do, don't hold us to the standards of deliberation and care in our use of energy that we hold you to in your production of it. That would be an unacceptable infringement of our freedoms" (Meadows, p. 3b).

Clearly, Meadows is arguing for ecologically responsible alternative sources of energy and conservation instead of more exploration of gas and oil. To achieve this, each citizen must take on the responsibility of becoming familiar with the energy problems facing the country and to participate in solving them.

Yet, individuals are not solely to blame to for irresponsible behavior. Multinational oil companies, who showed a combined profit of 18 percent from 1986-1988, ("*Harper's* Index", p. 13) have been slow to take responsibility for and absorbing the costs of environmentally safe oil and gas exploration and transportation (Bertlelson, "Shell Denies..."; "Shell Oil Will Test..."). Disasters such as the oil spill by the ship Exxon Valdez have ruined the pristine waters and natural habitats along the Alaskan Coast for an indeterminate amount of time. One commentator dismisses irresponsible behavior by oil companies that have resulted in environmental disasters as just part of the costs and risks of doing business. Commenting on public outrage concerning the Alaskan oil spill, Scott Powell argues that people should support risky activities in energy exploration even if it means an occasional ecological disaster.

"It is time people in the environmental movement and the media face up to the fact that
a risk-free society is not only impossible, but that it is undesirable...[To] stay
competitive in the world economy, the United States can ill-afford an energy policy
that would short-change the development of low-cost oil, gas and nuclear energy
resources for the appeal of the "clean" alternatives such as wind and solar power,
which are less reliable and more costly " (Powell, p. 3b).

Unquestionably, then, Powell defends those who rank oil exploration research higher than research for
alternative uses because the potential benefits of oil exploration are worth the costs and risks associated with
it. While this may be true if the costs are measured in quantifiable terms of inputs and outputs, Morrow
disagrees with such cost accounting. She argues that the costs are not measured correctly.

"When they tell us that we can "afford" oil or nuclear power but not solar energy, we
will ask what they have included in their accounting. Did they count the costs to
neighbors, workers, fishermen, the environment, future generations? Did they count
the costs of normal, inevitable, predictable, terrible accidents" (Morrow, p. 3b)?

It is not the spills, the damage, or the danger, then, that drives the conflict between opposing sides vying for
influence over energy policy. The conflict in energy policy concerns which group's costs are recognized and
who, if not the government, will compensate those shouldering heaviest portion of the costs.

Perhaps the new administration in Washington will grasp the seriousness of the problem and be
willing to take a definitive stand regarding energy policy. The Bush administration has the opportunity to
take the politics out of energy policy and develop a nonpartisan approach that will stand no matter which way
the political winds are blowing. Although Bush has supported exploratory drilling for oil and gas by calling
for tax incentives and funding for research, more action is needed (O'Rourke, p. 9a). It might be wise to
assemble a commission of people from a cross section of society to work out a fair minded, nonpartisan
energy policy. Perhaps this "people's commission" can develop a plan to induce public cooperation for
conservation of existing resources, and to encourage development of new and alternative energy supplies.

Some ideas which might be discussed by this commission include setting efficiency standards on all
new housing that will be financed with government loans, emphasizing development of mass transit systems,
increasing the price of gasoline to the levels paid by citizens in similar industrial nations, continuing to
increase fuel efficiency standards for automobiles, and creating greater monetary incentives to citizens for
recycling ("EPA Lists Ways..."). Some of these ideas will be unpleasant to at least one or more sectors of
society, but the test of strong leadership is the ability to unite citizens for the common good. The short-range
political fallout from such bold policy decisions would be offset by the long-range reward of preserving the
lifestyle to which Americans are accustomed.

At any rate, the time has passed when groups can simply point the finger of blame and responsibility
to some other sector of society. Conservation, recycling and efficient use of energy, regardless of the source,
should be as natural as driving on the right side of the road and stopping at a red light. Americans need to
accept the idea of using resources wisely as a basic responsibility of all citizens, and to change their
perspective from "Not me!" to "Me too!"

SOURCES

Anderson, James E., David W. Brady, Charles S. Bullock III, and Joseph Steward, Jr. *Public Policy in American Politics*. Monterey, CA: Brooks/Cole Pub. Co. 1984.

Bertleson, Christine. Shell Denies Ashcroft's' Charge, *St. Louis Post Dispatch*, (March 18, 1989).

_____. Shell Oil Will Test Pipelines, *St. Louis Post Dispatch*, (January 22, 1989).

Carter, Jimmy. *Keeping Faith*. NY: Bantam Books. 1982.

EPA Lists Ways to Save Energy, Cut Pollution. *St. Louis Post Dispatch*, (March 18, 1989).

Harper's Index. *Harper's*, (February 1989).

Meadows, Donella H. We Are All Exxon. *St. Louis Post Dispatch*, (April 29, 1989).

O'Rourke, Lawrence, M. Bush Calls For Search For Oil, *St. Louis Post Dispatch*, (April 27, 1989).

Powell, Scott. Without Risk, Society Would Stagnate. *St. Louis Post Dispatch*, (April 29, 1989).

EXAMPLE OF A CLIPPING FILE

ENERGY CLIPPING FILE

By
Alan G. Schmidt

Author's note: This is an abridged clipping file. A good clipping file should reflect a balance of sources and interests. Originally, this clipping file contained over 250 clippings from three newspapers and six magazines. The clippings were obtained from mid-January until the end of April 1989 and included news stories, editorials, cartoons, and advertisements. The clippings were labeled, annotated, and organized chronologically. Each page of the clipping file was numbered and an index created to cross reference the clippings by issue. Needless to say, this was an excellent clipping file.

For the sake of parsimony and to minimize problems associated with copyrighted materials, only a representative sample of the original articles contained in the clipping file is included here for illustrative purposes.

Shell Oil Will Test Pipelines

By Christine Bertelson
Of the Post-Dispatch Staff

Shell Oil Co. will soon begin testing the strength of the welds along the entire 435-mile length of its Ozark crude oil pipeline, a Shell engineer says.

The testing program was prompted by a pipeline rupture that happened Dec. 24 and spilled 840,000 gallons of crude oil into the Gasconade River in Maries County, about 200 miles southwest of St. Louis.

The oil, which moved into the Missouri and Mississippi Rivers, was one of the largest oil pipeline spills in the nation. Shell has spent more than $1.5 million in cleaning it up.

The weld testing is voluntary, but the test will be conducted in accordance with standards set by the U.S. Department of Transportation's Office of Pipeline Safety, Tony Canino, a Shell spokesman at the company's Wood River refinery in Roxana, said last week.

In the Wake of the spill, an inquiry by the U.S. Environmental Protection Agency has led to a federal grand jury investigation. Subpoenas were filed Friday in U.S. District Court in St. Louis seeking acess to Shell's records of events that lead to the Christmas Eve oil spill.

The investigation will focus on whether Shell violated provisions of either the federal Rivers and Harbors Act or the

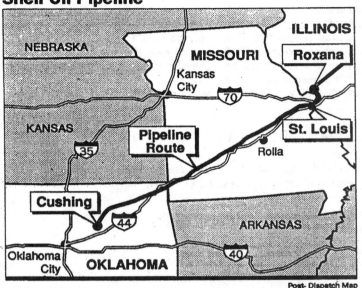

Shell Oil Pipeline

Post-Dispatch Map

Clean Water Act, sources said. Violations could result in criminal penalties and/or fines.

The weld testing is "a long and costly process" and will take at least a month to complete, said James Brown, technical superintendent for Shell Pipeline Corp.'s Mid-Continent Division.

The testing should cause "minimal" disruption in deliveries to Shell's customers, Canino said.

Water will be pumped into the pipeline at its source in Cushing, Okla., and then moved to each section of pipe to be tested.

Valves on either side of the water in a given section of pipe will be closed and the water gradually pressurized to a level 25 percent higher than the maximum the pipe was designed to withstand, Brown said.

If the welds rupture, that section of pipe will be re-placed and retested. If not, the water will be pumped ahead to the next section of pipe to be tested.

Brown said Shell was working out the details of how to get the water into the pipe and how to recapture it if a section of pipe breaks in the test. Some water may be drawn from rivers and creeks along the way, he said.

Because the water will contain some oily residue from the inside of the pipe-line, it could pose an environmental hazard if the pipe breaks, Brown said.

The Ozark pipeline is now running at about 80 percent of its normal pressure as a safety precaution, Brown said.

Welds run longitudinally along one side of the pipe, which is formed from a single sheet of rolled stell. Modern pipeline welds are routinely X-rayed to check for weak spots when the pipelines are laid, Brown said.

But X-ray technology was uncommon 41 years ago when the Ozark pipeline was installed. The welds in the Ozark pipeline were subjected only to the pressurized water tests when the line was installed and have never been X-rayed, Brown said.

The cause of the pipeline rupture remains unknown. Shell is focusing its investigation on whether a pressure surge that occured when oil was switched from one part of the pipeline to another might have generated enough force to split open the welded seam that runs the length of each section of pipe.

Shell is also investigating whether its pipeline safety monitoring equipment was working properly and whether technicians might have failed to notice signals that a rupture had occurred.

St. Louis Post Dispatch, 1/22/89

The efforts at damage control by Shell seem thorough, but wouldn't it have been better to have a routine testing system all along to prevent spills?

Shell Denies Ashcroft's Charge

By Christine Bertelson
Of the Post-Dispatch Staff

A Shell Pipe Line Corp. official has denied charges by Gov. John Ashcroft that the company buried pools of oil in the Gasconade and Missouri rivers in its cleanup of a large oil spill on Dec. 24.

But the official, R.C. McMahan, president of Shell Pipe Line Corp., agreed Friday to comply with Ashcrofts' deman that Shell pay for an outside company to oversee its cleanup of the spill.

McMahan made the remarks at a news conference Friday morning at Shell's cleanup headquarters in the town of Gasconade, about 10 miles west of Hermann.

Ashcroft accused Shell of "at best, incompetence" and "at worst, an attempted cover-up," after state investigators, led by former Shell crew workers, found pools of oil in sandbars in the Missouri River. Ashcroft has asked the state attorney general's office to force Shell to hire an outside company to oversee its cleanup of the spill.

McMahan said Shell would pay "all reasonable costs of an independent third party to assist in performing and monitoring the cleanup," if the state thinks that is necessary.

McMahan said the pools of oil that were recently found had not been hidden but were deposits of oil that had either dripped from debris floating into the Missouri from the Gasconade or deposits released after the rivers rose late last week.

A spokesman for the state Department of Natural Resources said the department viewed Shell's claim with skepticism.

"As to their claim that the oil got there naturally, I think we have to look at the evidence very closely," said William Palmer, a spokesman for the Department of Natural Resources. The state agency has been monitoring the cleanup.

"We found allegations of buried overalls, and we went out and dug them up," Palmer said. "We found allegations of more overalls on the bank, and we went out and found them. We were told about buried oil, and we went out and dug there and found the oil. The facts speak very strongly."

At the news conference, McMahan said: "We have never said the cleanup of the Missouri and Gasconade Rivers is complete, and we are continuing our cleanup efforts. We believe we have acted responsibly throughout. The environment and the welfare of the citizens of Missouri have been our foremost priorities, and we have spared no expense in pursuing the cleanup."

Shell has spen $7 million to clean up the two rivers since Christmas Eve, when a bad weld in an underground pipeline ruptured, spilling more than 840,000 gallons of crude oil.

St. Louis Post Dispatch, March 18, 1989

Why is an outside overseer necessary? What about the agencies already charged with protecting the environment? And why has the governor waited almost three months to demand an outside overseer? Couldn't the cleanup have been monitored from the start? Why does government *react* when it has the power to *act*?

Bush Calls For Search For Oil

By Lawerence M. O'Rouke
Post-Dispatch Washington Bureau

AUSTIN, Texas --- President George Bush said Wednesday that despite the Exxon oil spill in Alaska, the United States must continue to drill for oil at home to decrease dependence on foreign supplies.

The president called for a complete decontrol of natural gas and an increased use of nuclear power.

"As we all become increasingly concerned about the need for clean air, we must look more to natural gas and to nuclear power," Bush said in a speech to the Texas Legislature in Austin.

"I believe we can and must use more safe nuclear power," Bush said. "I believe that coal has a bright future. You know my confidence in natural gas." Bush's first job was as a supplier to the oil and gas industry in west Texas.

Bush traveled to Texas from California, where he had his first reunion with former President Ronald Reagan since the inauguration Jan 20.

Reagan and Bush met for more than an hour in Reagan's office in Los Angles. Afterward, Bush said he had received advice from Reagan on Europe and on other foreign policy matters.

Reagan seemed more subdued than when he was in the White House. He said that Bush was "doing just fine" as his successor.

Reagan said he didn't miss the White House. "It's in good hands," he said.

Bush is making a four-day tour of the country in an effort to lay out his policies and assert his leadership as he rounds out his first 100 days in the White House.

In his first detailed statement on energy since the Exxon oil spill March 24, Bush said, "Some are questioning the future of America's oil supply in the aftermath of the wreck of the Exxon Valdez off Alaska.

"I am as concerned as you and all Americans are by the environmental tragedy in Prince William Sound," Bush said. "We are using federal resources intelligently in the cleanup effort. We are working with industry to develop an improved plan in the event of a future spill.

"But shutting down our domestic energy production is no answer, and would merely increase our dependence on foreign oil. We must, and we will, maintain a strong domestic energy industry," Bush said.

The United States should return to "high levels of exploratory drilling" for oil and gas, Bush said.

"I propose to stimulate domestic drilling with tax credits and other incentives," he said. Research is needed, he said, to find better ways to recover oil that is left in the ground because extracting it is too costly.

St. Louis Post Dispatch, 4/27/89

It's 1989, and George Bush is making basically the same recommendations Jimmy Carter made in 1977. This shows how little our energy policy has developed over the past 12 years, which, since our demand has risen, means that we are actually in worse shape now than we were during the oil embargo of 1973!)

PARTICIPANT OBSERVATION AND INTERNSHIP REPORTS

An internship is a special course that many political science departments offer. Internships usually involve fieldwork in a governmental agency, a political party, an interest group, or some other public agency. The purpose of an internship is to give students the opportunity to combine their academic and fieldwork experiences. Usually, internship students are required to have a faculty and a fieldwork supervisor who will be responsible for co-directing the internship. In most cases, the student is responsible for producing a field report that relates a set of theoretical concepts particular to a subdiscipline of political science to what the student has observed, participated in, and experienced in the field.

Guidelines for an Internship Report.

1. Get a detailed job description of your duties and your faculty and field supervisors' expectations for your fieldwork.
   - Make sure that you are achieving the goals set for you by both your faculty and field supervisors.
   - Make sure you conduct your work in a responsible and professional manner.
2. Keep a detailed log of your day's activities.
   - Be sure that you differentiate between significant and insignificant details in your log.
   - Describe your experiences in detail and include facts and measurements.
   - Be sure to get permission from your field supervisor to record any data that might be considered classified or personal.
   - Depending on the work assigned, keep a tally or list of the number of times the same type of duty was assigned or task was repeated.
   - Put the date and time worked on each new entry.
3. Annotate each entry, writing for at least 10 minutes. If necessary, use a "stream of consciousness" writing style. Freewrite as much as possible.
   - Pose questions about why some condition exists or what purpose a particular task served.
   - Draw some conclusions about the significance of the observations and experiences.
   - How did you feel about what you observed, experienced, or participated in when it was happening?
   - How do you feel about what you observed, experienced, or participated in right now?
   - Make some connections between what you know from your academic training and what you observed, experienced, or participated in.
4. At the close of the internship, conduct a content analysis of your log.
   - To conduct a content analysis on your log, create a typology of the types of phenomena you observed, types of situations you experienced, and types of activities you participated in which are listed in your log.
     - A typology is a set of distinct categories of information.
     - In this case, one category would be observation, one category would be experiences, and one category would be activities.
   - Label each item in each category by some ranking method. Try the following but be prepared to justify the designation you give each item:

- Significant or Insignificant.
- Conforms or Does not conform to theory
♦ Identify the frequency (how many times or how often) of which each item in the typology occurred.
   - Was there any pattern in the time, place, or context in which an event occurred?
   - How many times did the same type of event occur?
5. Using your typology, prepare a report that compares theories about political phenomena or behavior with the events you observed, experienced, or participated in during your internship.
   ♦ The format for the report should be similar to an analytical essay.
      - The report should not be purely descriptive.
      - Describe the goals and expectations associated with the fieldwork.
      - Describe the context of the fieldwork.
   ♦ Assert in your thesis statement whether your observations, experiences, or activities support or cast doubt on these theories.
      - Identify a theory or parts of theories about political phenomena or behavior that are the focus of your report.
      - Suggest whether they are valid or not valid based on your fieldwork.
   ♦ Compare and contrast theory and practice.
      - Begin your comparison by briefly describing the theory or theories in question.
      - Use the events which occurred during your fieldwork as evidence to support or cast doubt on the theory or theories.
      - Clearly separate what you observed from what you experienced, and from what you actually participated in.
6. After comparing and contrasting theories with the field events, write a conclusion.
   ♦ Summarize the goals of the fieldwork.
   ♦ Review briefly the incidences where the theory was confirmed by the fieldwork.
   ♦ Review briefly any discrepancies between theory and practice.
   ♦ Suggest how the fieldwork expanded your knowledge or awareness of political phenomena or behavior. Did you benefit from this experience? How?
7. Include in an appendix of your report a copy of a letter or internship evaluation form that is signed by the field supervisor. The letter should contain an assessment of the quality of your performance related to the following:
   ♦ Dependability.
   ♦ Initiative.
   ♦ Cooperation.
   ♦ Thoroughness.
   ♦ Professional attitude.
   ♦ Assertiveness.
   ♦ Professional strengths.
   ♦ Professional weaknesses.
   ♦ Overall quality of fieldwork completed.
   ♦ Number of hours worked.

EXAMPLE OF A LETTER FOR ASSESSING A FIELD INTERN

(Be sure to ask for an evaluation of your work. It is best, even if you must use an evaluation sheet similar to the one on the following page, to ask for a letter, on the organizational stationary anyway. This letter, if you have done a good job in your internship, can be placed in your professional portfolio and sent with your career file for job interview. This example is a fictional letter.)

December 1, 1988

Dr. Redd Coetsacumin
Political Science Department
Wonifby Land College
Tue Efbyse, Virginia 17762

Dear Dr. Coetsacumin

Thank you for allowing Betsy Ross to conduct an internship with my organization. Betsy was a competent worker during our revolutionary campaign. She was courteous, dependable, and cooperative. Betsy's main strengths were her positive attitude and willingness to learn new skills. In particular, she became especially skilled in flagging discrepancies and sewing them up before the place fell apart. Her only weakness was her inexperience. She soon addressed that through hard work. Betsy completed more than her required 13 hours, and I would give her a gold star for each week she worked as a member of our staff. Given her drive and ambition, she will place her stamp on national politics someday.

Sincerely,

Imayank Quedu-Duldande
Volunteer Supervisor
Dumptha Kingsway PAC

Cc: Betsy Ross

EXAMPLE OF EVALUATION FORM FOR AN INTERNSHIP

Many internship programs have evaluation forms for assessing an intern's work in the field. In the event that your program does not, ask your faculty advisor what is necessary for evaluation. Then ask your field supervisor for a letter assessing your work and a more detailed evaluation according to the standards set by your faculty advisor. Use the one below as a guide. This evaluation, together with a letter and good fieldwork, will provide credentials for future employment.

(A Sample Cover Letter)

July 4, 1996

Imayank Quedu-Duldande
Volunteer Supervisor
Dumptha Kingsway PAC
1776 Patriots Way
Revo Loosion, MA 11776

Dear Mr. Quedu-Duldane,

Thank you for having me as an intern in your organization. I appreciate your willingness to include me among your staff. As you know, I will receive a grade based on the work I completed for your organization. Please take a moment to evaluate the work I performed. I have enclosed an evaluation form for your convenience. Please return the attached form, with your signature, to:

Dr. Redd Coetsacumin
Political Science Department
Wonifby Land College
Tue Efbyse, Virginia 17762

Again, thank you for your cooperation. I enjoyed working with you and your staff.

Sincerely,

Betsy Ross
13 Starsnstripes
Fohr Ehver, MA 11776

SAMPLE INTERN EVALUATION FORM

A.   **On the following scale, please rank your intern's performance:**

5=Excellent 4=Good 3=Average 2=Poor 1=Unacceptable

a.____Dependability
b.____Initiative
c.____Cooperation
d.____Thoroughness
e.____Professional attitude
f.____Assertiveness
g.____Professional strengths
h.____Professional weaknesses
i.____Overall quality of fieldwork completed
j.____Number of hours worked

B.   **What were the intern's major strengths?**

C.   **In what ways could the intern improve?**

D.   **What is your overall assessment of the intern's performance?**

E.   **Were the number of hours worked equivalent to the number agreed on at the beginning of the internship?**

Please sign your name to verify this assessment.

(Name)_____   (Title)_____(Date)_____

AN EXAMPLE OF A PARTICIPANT OBSERVATION/INTERNSHIP REPORT

INTERNSHIP REPORT

CAMPAIGN VOLUNTEERS: VIP'S OR PEONS

BY
CARYN M. CIEPLAK
PROFESSOR DIANE SCHIMDT
POLS 395
November 23, 1988
(Reprinted with permission)

INTERNSHIP REPORT

I have had the unique opportunity to work for a politician that has served in a vast and diverse number of elected positions. Harry "Bus" Yourell has been in public office for close to 35 years. Harry "Bus" Yourell is a very well known political figure in Cook County. His experience ranges from local trustee positions to his newly elected position of Commissioner of the Metropolitan Sanitary District-Cook County. His recent exit from his position as Cook County Recorder of Deeds was to give him the County experience needed to run for this new position. The new position will take him out of the limelight because he will be sharing it with two other people newly elected to the position. This will give him the incentive to adopt necessary changes within the scope of this office.

In his new position, Bus will be dealing with issues such as building dams, water pollution, and air pollution. My fieldwork was conducted during Bus' campaign for Commissioner. I was expected to help in the election activities. I was particularly interested in studying the role of campaign volunteers and constituency targeting election techniques. My experiences as a volunteer in Bus' campaign support the theories of incumbency advantage through constituency service, name recognition, and local party support. In particular, my experiences in working with him have inspired me to run for a local office someday.

Before my internship, my knowledge of politics was limited to what I could understand from the conversations around me and what I learned from class. Because of my inexperience, one of my main duties was to help with his election to Commissioner by being an envelope stuffer. Stuffing envelopes, though tedious, is something that every campaign headquarters must engage in and is probably one of the most effective ways to reach constituents. Through periodic mailings, constituents are given the opportunity to "get to know the candidates" by reading about their backgrounds and past records in politics. Not only does it clearly define the stances that the particular candidate takes, it provides some humor when the candidate's literature criticizes the opponent(s). Further, mailings are vital in order to effectively and efficiently reach the entire area (on a local level). Walking the precincts can be effective but it is much easier to reach people through the mail.

One interesting finding from my fieldwork relates directly to the source of the mailings. None of the mail was sent out for Bus' personal benefit. The Cook County Democratic Headquarters covered the county candidates through their mass mailings. The mail sent from Bus' office consisted mainly of literature that promoted the township candidates, the State Representative, and United States Representative. The literature, i.e. personal bibliographies, sample ballots, etc. were all signed by Bus because he is the Committeeman of Worth Township. It was apparent from this literature that Bus was closely aligned with his party.

Not only did I stuff envelopes, but I answered the telephone as well. An important part of a volunteer's job in a township office is manning the telephones when constituents call to question a candidate's position on certain issues. Again, this is not a glamorous job but it is a very important one. When constituents call to clarify a candidate's position, it is a chance to capitalize on the possibility that the person does not know enough about the candidate. If this is true, then it may be possible to convince the person to vote for your candidate.

For example, it is very common for one out of every two telephone calls to Bus' office to be from a senior citizen. They need to be dealt with very lightly and very carefully. Senior citizens are very powerful people in Worth Township and although Bus never uses his age as a way to relate to this segment, they realize that he is 69 and has been in local politics for almost 35 years. Anyone who is going to answer these types of phone calls needs to be well versed in not only the candidate's position but in what certain segments of the constituency want to hear.

Past records of the candidate play a very important role when trying to convince undecided voters to vote for a candidate. For instance, one day while I was manning the telephones, a constituent called and asked me exactly what Bus has done for them in the past that should make them vote for him in a new position. Taxes at the local level are always a major concern to taxpayers. Knowing this, I was able to tell the voter something that he did not know. Bus, as the Cook County Recorder of Deeds, was able to computerize his entire office at absolutely no cost to the taxpayer and therefore enable more efficient work output to the public. Bus also managed to increase his budget by less than one percent over the four years he was in office. Success like this can only come from years of experience. The voter on the other link of the telephone was very pleased to hear this and thanked me repeatedly for my time.

This leads me to another point that is important -- experience. When it came time for Bus to run for the Commissioner of the Metropolitan Sanitary District, it was clear that the position was something new to him. As a representative serving in the Illinois State Legislature for nine terms, Bus has dealt with local pollution topics before, whereas the other nine candidates in the running for this position had minimal exposure to this subject. His experience qualified him for this position.

Knowing of his experience, however, I was able to address many of the questions people had but not all of them. Because I was ignorant of the duties he would take over as Commissioner, I could not adequately answer some questions at first. I was uncomfortable about not knowing the answers so I read everything I could find about the Sanitary District. After researching the Commissioner's role in the Sanitary District, I felt much more confident in my discussions with constituents and candidates.

In a way, volunteering can create loyal party members and can serve as a recruiting device. For example, it is clear that as a volunteer, feeling ignorant and ineffective in helping constituents provided me with incentives to become more educated about the issues in local politics. Once I became informed, I experienced a great sense of efficacy. Researching the commissioner's role in the Sanitary District gave me more confidence in what I know about local political offices. More importantly, it has provided me with a foundation to collect information and the confidence to effectively address public problems with confidence when I run for office.

Not only do the personal contacts with volunteers help a candidate secure a loyal inner circle of trusted campaign workers, another great asset that an experienced politician can use to his advantage is the personal contacts that he has made over his years of public service. These personal contacts include both Democrats and Republicans. While in the State Legislature, Bus established some long-term relationships with members from both parties as well as with many business professionals. These relationships turn into very credible endorsements when it comes time to run for office. Further, these endorsements turn into votes when constituents are unsure of Bus' qualifications but feel strongly about one of the public figures that endorsed him.

Through working in a campaign and meeting important people, volunteers can also make important political contacts and perhaps, even establish their own network of potential supporters. By being part of Bus' campaign staff, I have had the unique opportunity to get to know several of these politicians, some more than others have. I plan to develop these relationships so that when I am ready to run for public office, I too can reap the advantages of such long-standing relationships.

I have realized several things in my tenure as an intern. First, a volunteer's job is extremely important to the success of an election. At first, when given very tedious responsibilities, I questioned my overall usefulness. But as I became more interested in politics I have come to the realization that the only way to learn is through being in the arena in some capacity. I have experienced many things, thanks to the responsibilities Bus has given me, as well as the dedication I have to Worth Township politics.

Moreover, as a volunteer, I have acquired a great deal of knowledge that I otherwise would not have learned. The knowledge I have gained about politics at the local, state, and national level is something that will forever be useful to me no matter what career I enter. I have a greater appreciation of the value of constituency service, candidate credibility, name recognition, and of volunteers in winning campaigns. In particular, I have a deeper appreciation of the value of political connections, political participation, and political education.

All this became very clear to me when I was talking to a top executive at Chrysler Corporation. He said, "Caryn, although your knowledge of the Chrysler Corporation is not near to what mine is, your knowledge of politics is far beyond that of mine. We can teach each other something." In light of this executive's comment, I feel extremely grateful for having this internship experience. Working for Bus has not only made me realize my importance as a volunteer, but also has broadened my appreciation for the knowledge I have gained both in the classroom and in the field. More importantly, it appears to have enhanced my potential for a career in politics.

AN ABRIDGED EXAMPLE OF A LOG FOR INTERNSHIP FIELD WORK

LOG OF INTERNSHIP FIELD WORK

By

Caryn M. Cieplak

October 9, 1988
2pm - 5pm
Worth Township Democratic Headquarters (WTDH)

Today was an interesting day at the office. Harry "Bus" Yourell (Bus) was his usual witty self, asking me why I was home for the weekend and not at school studying. So, I told him that I had to come home because without my help he might lose the election in November for Commissioner of the Metropolitan Sanitary District of Cook County. After our usual exchange of personal stories we (his staff consisting of Mary, Mary Ann, and Ray) and I decided to do some work. The first thing that needed to be done was telephone calls. One of the things I think I hate the most, but one of the things that clearly emerges as one of the most important parts of any campaign. This campaign's success almost totally relied upon calling constituents to make sure that they were aware of the fact that "Bus" was running for a position that would make him less visible but more powerful. Many of his supporters have been backing him for 30+ years now and helping him remain in the limelight. We needed to explain to people the importance of putting Bus on the County ticket in this position in order to be sure that all the candidates were elected.

The only exciting thing about today's work was the fact that through the use of an automatic dialing system hooked up to the phone, no one could fight over not wanting to talk to those well known citizens who will give you a three hour dissertation.

It was interesting to see how truly uneducated the voters are, and how well known Bus really is.

October 10, 1988
5pm - 7pm
Condesa DelMar

Last night was a great night, I almost didn't mind volunteering my time at Marty Russo's cocktail party. Marty is running for his 8th election into the House of Representatives of the United States and I had the opportunity to serve as an intern in his Washington D.C. office this past summer. I was given the responsibility of handing out literature on the candidates running for the local election, while watching all the big shots walk around playing important. Little did they know that there would be a private party for all Marty's past "staffers" (never use the word employee when speaking of those who work on Capitol Hill).

Anyway, after the dignitaries all got their chance to speak and everyone drank their money worth, the cocktail party ended and we (the "staffers") got to enjoy a D.J. while mingling with the local candidates and Marty's special guests which included twelve Congressmen from around the country. It was a great opportunity for me to see what these people are like outside of a public appearance. They're great.

Anyway, the night ended around 1 a.m. but not until I was invited back to Washington to interview with several different offices after graduation. I guess that doing the piddly work for awhile really does pay off. I'm actually considering interviewing with the offices that offered me the opportunity, but only because someday I plan to run for office.

November 4, 1988
10am-2pm
WTDH

With the election only four days away, it is very difficult for me to outline what I did today. The morning started out with breakfast with Bus and his staff to discuss what will be going on the next couple of days. And because I was only going to be there for two of those four days, my duties were limited to more phone calls, walking the precincts with precinct captains, as well as driving Bus to and from some political functions. The day concluded with dropping of literature and money for the judges for Tuesday's election.

November 5, 1988
12pm - 2pm
6pm - 11pm
WTDH

Saturday started out with breakfast at 8am with the staff. The usual topics of discussion were addressed, including who has to go to the rally where Jesse Jackson was going to endorse the county ticket. Naturally being the youngest member of the staff, I was chosen to stay at the office and take any last minute reservations for Bus's dinner that night. So, here I was for a couple hours bored to tears, reading the same literature over and over and getting to know the candidates like they were family.

Unfortunately, this was the most exciting part of the weekend as far as Saturday morning and early afternoon go, but then it led to something a little more exciting... I received a telephone call that Senator Lloyd Bentsen was planning to make an appearance at Bus's dinner that evening. This put the rest of the afternoon at high speed trying to find a company that could produce a sign to welcome the Senator and going to the restaurant where the dinner was to be held to meet with the Secret Service to determine whether or not it would pass security. Obviously, this put the other duties that Bus had assigned to us (by this time I had found another staffer that was working the precincts) on hold for a while but instead we were given responsibilities that we never though could happen. The afternoon proceeded when the Dukakis headquarters called with the very disappointing news that the restaurant did not pass security inspection. This shattered my entire day. We had done so much preparation in such a short time period that I thought I would never vote for the Democratic ticket in three days.

Well the dinner went on without Senator Bentsen and was a huge success nonetheless. Everyone enjoyed him or herself and were very thankful for the opportunity to interact with the local candidates. However, it wouldn't be a political function without Caryn working at some point in the night. I began the night by arriving with the rest of the staff to make sure that everything was set up: table numbers, the VIP lounge and other formalities that only staff could ever worry about. Ticket taking is probably the worst part of the night, especially when people arrive to a sit down dinner without reservations. We had 800 seats and close to 925 people wanting to eat. Needless to say, some quick action needed to be taken to find these (rude) people a place to eat. Luckily management likes the organization and were able to do some quick moving and added the extra tables that we needed. The entire night was a great success despite the misfortune of Senator Bensten not showing up and the lack of responsibility on the part of 125 people.

EVENT OBSERVATION, PARTICIPATION, AND KEEPING A JOURNAL

Purpose

Journals are useful for many reasons.

1. Journals help students organize their thoughts about current political events and social problems occurring in their community as well as in the world.
2. Journals are ways of raising students' consciousness about what they are learning and observing.
3. Journals contain information as well as personal reactions to current events and course lectures.
4. Journals can be used to keep track of thoughts or ideas in the discovery phase of a research project.
5. Journals can be used to document students' activities in an internship.
6. Journals are part personal diary, part scrapbook, and part intellectual inquiry.

What to Write in a Journal

1. **Reference**: Using a notebook, put the date and time on each entry.
2. **Observation:** Write informally about whatever you have observed that day. Describe experiences in detail and include facts and measurements.
3. **Speculations**: Write down all speculative thoughts about why something exists or occurred.
4. **Questions**: Use critical thinking skills to pose questions about why some condition exists or doubts about reasons given for a political outcome.
5. **Conclusions**: Write down any conclusions made based on observations and experiences.
6. **Connections**: Write about how experiences and observations relate to personal life and to other political phenomena.
7. **Information**: Use the journal as a scrapbook for interesting material and information. Clip and paste the information into the journal, if possible, and then write a reaction to it.
8. **Synthesis**: Use the journal to put together what has been learned in class, what has been experienced in the field, and how both relate to the larger context of politics.

Tips on Keeping a Journal

1. Use a ringbound notebook.
2. Do not use the notebook for any other purpose.
3. Always put the date and time on each page and each entry in the journal.
4. Write every day for at least 10 minutes.
5. Use a new page for each day.
6. Do not be afraid to use a 'stream of consciousness' style if stumped for something to say.

WRITING A JOURNAL ESSAY

Sometimes an instructor will require students to write an essay based on their journals. The format for the essay depends on the type of essay required and the material to be included in the journal.

1. If fieldwork was done, use the format for an internship report included in this text.

2. If an essay using some event or issues described in the log entries, collected clippings, and other materials in your journal, then use the format for a clipping thesis included in this text.

3. If the instructor requires a simple essay, use the format for an analytical essay included in this text.

4. Whatever the case, do not write your essay in a "Dear Diary" form.

5. Examine your log and materials closely.

    - Draw conclusions about patterns in behavior.

    - Find patterns that confirm (or not) those you learned about in class.

6. Decide what general statement can be made and write directly concerning that statement.

7. Avoid rambling aimlessly about feelings and events. Make a point.

8. Make an important, meaningful statement about

    - Political observation.

    - Political theory.

    - Political life.

CAMPAIGN '88:
AGAINST ALL ODDS

BY
JENNA HERHOLD
PROFESSOR SCHMIDT
POLS 318
DECEMBER 1, 1988
(Reprinted with permission)

CAMPAIGN '88: AGAINST ALL ODDS

Campaigns for congressional seats make interesting study material on American election behavior. Voting theorists disagree about what motivates voter participation in elections and what determines their vote choice. Are voters irrational, emotional, party identifiers who vote based on how candidates deliver their messages as described by the American Voter model? Or do they vote as rational actors who weigh, when possible, the candidates' positions on important issues as described by rational choice models of voting? My observations of the recent congressional election in the twenty-second district suggest that people, for the most part, are best described by the American Voter mode.

My assignment in this course was to participate in the upcoming elections in the 22nd Congressional District. So, starting from square one, I went to the College Republican's first campaign kick-off meeting, motivated by the requirements. I decided to go to the College Republican meeting simply because the Democrats' meeting time did not fit my schedule. The idea to call my parents up and ask them which party I should support crossed my mind a couple times. Nevertheless, I decided to make my own observations and then make my decisions. Reflecting back now, I think my lack of knowledge of politics and pressing issues was a blessing in disguise. I was not predisposed to support one candidate over the other. I was lucky enough to start with a clear slate and base my decisions on what was to come.

I went to the Republican meeting and listened attentively to what the panel of Republican candidates had to say. I was hardly impressed. I left the meeting still quite unsure of my political bias. I wanted to know more about the other party and what its candidates were like. What stance did they take?

The perfect opportunity came on September 14 at their first debate. The debate would clear up many my concerns and point out the differences between Poshard and Kelley. This was the first opportunity the people had to hear them speak out against one another publicly (D.E. Sept. 14:1). This was also a debut public appearance for Kelley. Unlike his opponent, Poshard's stance on the issues had already been heard by many from Poshard's past position on the Illinois State Senate for the 59th District. Kelley had his work cut out for him.

The debate touched quite a few issues, starting with the economy and the budget. Poshard came out saying he wanted to give smaller businesses chance to compete and that we hardly needed to bother spending our money to get "two of every weapon!" Naturally, Kelley addressed the defense issue by saying that there is no way we could be in negotiations with other countries unless we were the stronger forces. An issue was raised by one of the questioners on what projects they would have voted down if they had been our congressional representatives. Kelley said he would have voted down a railroad project in Southern Illinois. This comment caused quite a disturbance from the other side. I paid close attention to this type of controversy and to what induced cheers and support from each side.

From my observations, I concluded that this was very much a candidate-centered campaign. Poshard won his audience because of his enthusiasm and his ability to speak well. The other side, as a whole, did not appear educated enough about the issues to fully understand the stance Poshard was taking. Poshard, like most Democratic candidates, took the party position on many issues. But, of course, the audience was much more receptive to Poshard because he is a good, effective speaker whereas Kelley is a rather passive, reserved speaker.

This is was one of the major problems costing Kelley the election. It became very clear at this debate that what the candidate says is as important as how he says it. It all falls back to the incredible influence the IMAGE projected has on the outcome of the election. Kelley was a poor speaker. He failed to motivate the audience the way Poshard did. He did not fulfill the image that people have programmed into their ideals of what and how a candidate should act.

Even so, I supported Kelley because I liked his stance on the issues the best. In order to make a rational vote, the voter needs to first identify the issues that are of most importance to himself and then find the candidate to suit his own needs. People need to base their votes on the issues at hand and how the candidate stands on them. Unfortunately, most of the public does not know or even care enough about the issues. They too often base their decisions on what they see. The campaign strategy often becomes a game of building illusions for the candidates, whether it be through the media or by reconstructing character to meet the image ideals set in the public's mind.

Ultimately, I came out of this debate thinking that although Kelley is not the stronger of the two candidates when it comes to saying what he wants to say effectively in front of hundreds of people that mostly oppose him, what really matters is how he would vote in Congress, because that is what is going to affect me. If elections were about who is the better speaker, who can captivate a crowd, and who is better at public appearances, I would support Poshard one hundred percent of the way. Nonetheless, I made my decision finally; I chose to support Kelley because of his position on the issues that interested me the most.

After the debate, I talked to some Republican students who had decided to vote for Poshard. I cannot see any logic to their way of thinking. If they support the Republican ticket, how could they rationalize supporting Poshard? Easy, they 'like' Poshard. Simply because they 'like' a candidate better than the other, is no reason to overlook that candidate's beliefs. Such inconsistencies exemplify irrational voting behavior. The voters are no longer taking into consideration what is good for them or Southern Illinois from a political standpoint, but rather considering what appeals to their emotions.

Thus, the candidate's image remains a key to a successful campaign. That is why Poshard's campaign strategy was to stress personal issues such as his leadership qualities and his experience in Illinois politics. Furthermore, Kelley was the "defending" candidate. The twenty-second district has long since been a Democratic safe seat held by politically powerful people such as Paul Simon and Ken Grey.

In other words, Kelley, as the Republican challenger, was the candidate who had the burden of proving himself worthy. He had to counter-attack. One major point the Kelley campaign emphasized was his stance on the issues. He was consistently pushing the issues; Poshard would talk about being a strong leader and Kelley would try to get Poshard to go back to addressing the issues. He constantly attacked the issues of government waste and regional development. He tried to convince people his stance was the one to support. For example, Scott Perry reported in the Daily Egyptian, "Kelley has made an issue of Poshard's stances on such issues as abortion, gun control, and gay rights," (D.E. Oct. 6:5). Kelley's objective may have been to give people an alternative or a better choice so that people would concentrate on the issues and put aside Poshard's good leadership qualities. As he said, "leadership takes place in context," (D.E. Oct. 5:7).

Unfortunately, this was an almost impossible goal to attain because at the same time as he was trying to convince people that his positions were best, Kelley had to try to overcome Poshard's popularity and distinguish himself on the issues. In addition, Kelley had to get as much public exposure as possible. Kelley was hardly a recognizable public figure to Southern Illinoisans and he did not have a political record. To address these problems, getting out and meeting the public in one-on-one situations became a priority for Kelley.

Ultimately, Kelley's biggest obstacle and hardest to overcome was the heavy Democratic district he was competing in. He was the underdog from the start and Kelly knew he was going against the odds. (D.E. Nov. 4:3). When Kelley entered into a debate he knew the odds were that the crowd would predominantly be

Democratic and his supporters would be outnumbered. Poshard was able to go into his public appearances knowing that he was the people's choice candidate.

Even with the odds in his favor, I found it very interesting that Poshard shied away from a public appearance with Kelley on the SIU-C campus. It is known that a high percentage of the students at SIU are from Northern Illinois where there is much more of a Republican stronghold. As reported in the D.E. on October 12, 1988, "the Poshard campaign has been reluctant to meet with the Republican candidate at the University saying it gives an unfair advantage to Kelley." When Poshard stepped on his own territory he seemed to lose many of those leadership qualities, he holds when he feels confident. Poshard became nervous and reluctant.

In the end, the forum on the SIU-C campus did happen between Kelley and Poshard. This was not a debate. Nevertheless, it did give the candidates a chance to offer information to the public and show their differences. This was hardly a threat to Poshard. "I never dreamed this would happen," Poshard said when he found out he had won, late the election night," (D.E. Nov. 8:1). It was hard to believe that Poshard did not expect to win this race. Of course he did.

I am glad I got so involved in this election. I supported the candidate that I thought would best fight for my needs. Although, I must admit Poshard had good leadership qualities, I think the most important thing remains the issues. Kelley tried to convince voters that the issues should be what influences peoples' vote the most. I agree. I listened to the issues and backed Kelley for what he and the Republican Party stood for, not how he stood for it.

MATERIALS REFERENCED FOR SCRAPBOOK CLIPPINGS

Perry, Scott, "Government's Role Debated, " *Daily Egyptian* (September 14, 1988), p. 1, 5.

_____, "Kelly Criticizes Poshard's TV Ad, " *Daily Egyptian* (September 14, 1988), p. 1.

_____, "Kelly: Government Should Play Leading Role in Housing, " *Daily Egyptian* (September 14, 1988), p. 9.

_____, "Kelly, Poshard Defend VP Choice, " *Daily Egyptian* (September 14, 1988), p. 1, 5.

_____, "Kelly, Poshard Make Stances Clear, " *Daily Egyptian* (September 14, 1988), p. 1.

_____, "Kelly, Poshard Set to Debate Tonight, " *Daily Egyptian* (September 14, 1988), p. 1.

_____, "Kelly, Poshard to Debate on Campus, " *Daily Egyptian* (September 14, 1988), p. 1, 7.

_____, "Poshard, Kelly Show Differences, " *Daily Egyptian* (September 14, 1988), p. 1.

_____, "Poshard Says Constituents Get the Credit for His Victory, " *Daily Egyptian* (September 14, 1988), p. 1, 5.

EXAMPLE OF A JOURNAL SCRAPBOOK

CAMPAIGN '88

JOURNAL/SCRAPBOOK

BY
JENNA HERHOLD

(Author's Note: The following material is an abridged campaign journal and scrapbook. The assignment was to spend 10 hours working in a campaign, keep a journal, construct a clipping file/scrapbook, and write an analytical essay about the 1988 Congressional Campaign. Students were to use their journals and references to the scrapbook materials. Not all of the scrapbook or journal is reproduced here for the sake of parsimony and copyright prohibitions. The student did, however, include copies of campaign literature, buttons, stickers, and other election media in her scrapbook. Nothing is irrelevant in a journal/scrapbook. Include anything that strikes your fancy!)

CAMPAIGN JOURNAL

WEDNESDAY, SEPTEMBER 7, 1988
7:00-8:45 P
COLLEGE REPUBLICAN MEETING/SPEAKERS:

It was obvious that the College Republicans did not expect so many people at this kick-off meeting. There were hardly enough accommodations for the students. Several of the Republican campaigners from our area were at the meeting and lined up to give speeches. They too were not prepared for such a large group. I listened to what they had to say and asked questions. The speakers were thrilled to see people like myself, there to show their support.

Of the speakers, I think the one that I was impressed by most was Mike Maurizio. He was able to speak effectively and he knew the audience was young and not very educated. He addressed his issues to the audience and the audience was able to relate because of it. The other speakers were very poor speakers and I found it hard to pay attention. Even so, I showed my support and interest.

SATURDAY, SEPTEMBER 10, 1988
8:30A-12:30P
CARTERVILLE PARADE:

It was a beautiful morning for a parade! We all met at Kelley's headquarters and waited for the others to join. I helped make a few telephone calls to make sure people were able to get out of bed. Once the group had organized, we caravaned to the parade sight. "You might run across some unfriendly people 'cause Carterville is really a Democratic," one said while the others laughed. They told horror stories the whole way out there about unfriendly encounters with Democrats. I was scared. I did not know what to expect. They handed me their green campaign shirt and some literature. Kelley warned us not to put any stickers on children unless we asked them or their parents first. This is so that we did not offend anyone. The parade started and we went through the town of Carterville. I had no rude people say nasty things to me or treat me poorly. In fact, most people were very polite and receptive to all of the people helping Kelley pass out information. I enjoyed handing out the information and stickers!

WEDNESDAY, SEPTEMBER 14, 1988
6:00p-10:30P
POSHARD/KELLEY DEBATE SHAWNEE COLLEGE:

Before this, I had never been to a debate. The Shawnee gymnasium was filled with Poshard supporters. I was with the group of about ten people from Southern. It was obvious to me that Poshard was already perceived as the strongest candidate in this election. I cheered Kelley on, holding up signs and rallying for him. I was disappointed in Kelley's ability to speak. He seemed too intimidated by his opponent.

WEDNESDAY, OCTOBER 12, 1988
7:30P-9:30P
POSHARD/KELLEY FORUM:

Because I work on the Student Programming Council, I was able to help a co-chair with the set-up of the program. We had the Student Center Auditorium set aside and ordered an podium through scheduling and catering. We also ordered some refreshments for after the forum. We had to make sure that Student Center Security was aware and present at the event. Kelley was not in a good mood that night. Perhaps he was nervous about the forum, but he was certainly less than friendly. The forum started a little past the target time of 7:30 p.m. but all was going smoothly. Then, the side door leading from private back halls in the Student Center opened and two men carrying a coffin walked out on stage to everyone's surprise. The coffin was covered with 'EDUCATION' and when the two guys got on stage, one of them said, "Vince makes sense!" They hurried out of the room before anybody realized what was going on. It was an obvious slam on Kelley for his stance on education. I was shocked. After the event, I talked with people and they felt that the forum lacked any real content. I even got a chance to voice my opinions on a local television as they interviewed me. I think the forum was a good event to have but one can never be too careful with security!

MONDAY OCTOBER 24, 1988
8:00P-9:00P
COLLEGE REP. V. COLLEGE DEMOCRAT (DEBATE):

The College Republican representative took on a representative from the Democratic College organization. The debate was not structured like most debates. The audience asked the questions and the debaters took turns answering them. It simply gave them the opportunity to take a stance on the issue. There was hardly any disputing. Andy Leighton was there, but he was sitting in the audience. He was the only one that really fired up a dispute. He argued that the Republicans are ignorant to the Greenhouse Effect issues. I again, was there to support the Republican Party and help as the need arose.

FRIDAY, NOVEMBER 4, 1988
12:00NOON-1:00P
SOLICITATION TABLES

I worked the information tables on the first floor of the Student Center. I handed out information and was available to answer questions for those people with questions. Most people who stopped by were friends of the co-worker's or mine. No one came up to the table and asked serious questions.

MONDAY, NOVEMBER 7, 1988
12:00NOON-1:00P
SOLICITATION TABLES

(Same as Above.)

VERIFICATION OF CAMPAIGN WORK

1) COLLEGE REPUBLICAN MEETING: WEDNESDAY, SEPTEMBER 7, 1988 7:00P-8:45P

2) CARTERVILLE PARADE: SATURDAY, SEPTEMBER 10, 1988 8:30A-12:30P

3) POSHARD/KELLEY DEBATE: WEDNESDAY, SEPTEMBER 14, 1988 6:00-10:30P

4) POSHARD/KELLEY FORUM: WEDNESDAY, OCTOBER 12, 1988 7:30P-9:30P

5) COLLEGE PARTY'S DEBATE: MONDAY, OCTOBER 24, 1988 8:00P-9:00P

6) SOLICITATION TABLES: FRIDAY, NOVEMBER 4, 1988 12:00NOON-1:00P

7) SOLICITATION TABLES: MONDAY, NOVEMBER 7, 1988 12:00NOON-1:00P

TOTAL HOURS: 15.25

VERIFICATION: (Signed by the campaign supervisor)

Kelley, Poshard set to debate tonight

By Scott Perry
Staff Writer

Voters in the 22nd Congressional District have the opportunity tonight to see congressional candidates Patrick Kelley and Glenn Poshard discuss the issues in the first of three public debates.

Kelley and Poshard will meet face to face, taking questions from a four-member panel and the public at 7:30 p.m. at Shawnee College in Ullin.

Both candidates are seeking the seat to be vacated by Rep. Kenneth Gray (D-West Frankfort), who is retiring because of health problems. Gray has held the position from 1955 to 1975 and again from 1984 to the present.

Both have been campaigning for the congressional spot since late last year.

Republican candidate Patrick Kelley said the debate will be a good opportunity for the public to get involved and hear how each candidate stands on issues that concern the region and the na-tion, and to show the differences between the candidates.

"It's important to find the differences," Kelley said.

People haven't had the opportunity to hear both candidates speak at the same time and to see how they differ on particular issues, he said.

Kelley said he wants to present an alternative to the approach taken by those who have represented the area in the past.

"The policies of the past haven't worked," he said.

Democratic candidate Glenn Poshard said he was ready to debate but said no special preparations have been made.

"I think there is such a thing as over-preparation," Poshard said.

Poshard, who has represented the 59th District in the Illinois Senate, said his stance on the issues are clear.

"I've had the same stance on the issues for several years and I don't think it would do me a whole lot of good to go back now and try to struggle with that (changing his stance)."

Kelley, on the other hand, only has become known throughout the district since beginning his bid for Congress. His "grassroots" campaign relies heavily on getting out and meeting people.

Among the issues expected to be debated are the economy of Southern Illinois, ways of creating jobs for the region, education, taxes, defense spending, abortion, drug policies and the deficit.

The panelists for tonight's debate are: Tim Landis, Southern Illinoisian, respresenting newspaper; Bill Cromer, WEBQ, representing radio; Bonnie Wheeler, WSIL, respresenting television; and Jason Edwards, of the Shawnee College newspaper TEMPO, representing the hosting school. Barry Gowin, president of Shawnee College, will moderate the activities.

The public will be invited to ask questions of the candidates after the formal discussion is through.

Daily Egyptian, September 14, 1988.
Reprinted with permission.

Poshard, Kelly Show Differences

By Scott Perry
Staff Writer

In an atmosphere resembling a high school basketball game, congressional candidates Patrick Kelley and Glenn Poshard debated the issues Wednesday night that one of the will face in January.

About 1,000 spectators packed into the gym at Shawnee Community College, carrying the banners of their favorite candidate.

Taking questions from a four-member panel, the candidates outlined their stances on such issues as the depressed Southern Illinois economy, taxes, national defense, the war on drugs and education.

Both agreed that higher education is in trouble and that something should be done about it.

Kelley proposed a follow-up on a George Bush proposal to create a savings plan to help meet the cost of higher education.

The savings bond system is being tried in Illinois and has been very successful, according to a representative of the Illinios Bureau of the Budget.

"The needs to be a commitment to promote higher education," Kelley said.

Poshard agreed, saying "better education will mean a stronger nation."

Poshard said he is in favor of federal policies to assist anyone that wishers to go to college as long as the policies were cost savings and efficient.

Both candidates said they thought the debate was a success. Kelley said the debate was successful in bringing out the differences between the candidates, which was a pre-debate goal.

Poshard said the voters can clearly see the distinction between the candidates.

Daily Egyptian, September 15, 1988.
Reprinted with permission.

Kelley, Poshard make stances clear

By Scott Perry
Staff Writer

INA — Leadership was the "message of the day" during the second debate between Congressional candidates Patrick Kelley and Glenn Poshard.

Both men began the evening outlining the problems facing the 22nd Congressional District, giving reasons why they are best suited to take the long-held position of Rep. Ken Gray, D-West Frankfort, in the U.S. House of Representatives.

"Who can best lead this district is the question of this election," Poshard said.

Poshard, D-Carterville, made reference to his past two years as a state senator representing the 59th District.

Kelley, a faculty member of the SIU-C law school, believes his background will allow him to create common-sense solutions to the districts problems. He said his work as an educator, city con-cilman and member of an anti-drug group will aid him if elected.

Kelley, who has been condemmed for his stance on gay rights legislation, insists "the power should not be put in the hands of the government, but in the hands of the individual."

"The government should help protect the rights of those who have characteristics they can't help — sex, race — but not those that are determined by conduct," Kelley said.

Poshard agreed with Kelley despite the Democratic platform's stance on the rights of gays.

Kelley used Poshard's stance on the issue to again attack him for straying from the party's platform. He said Poshard would be obligated to vote with the Democrats in Washington.

"Sending someone to congress that will vote for (Speaker of the House) Jim Wright is like pouring gasoline on a fire," Kelley said.

Poshard said he votes based on "the best facts brought to bear and the dictates of my conscience."

On the issue of minimum wage, Kelley and Poshard took opposing stances.

Kelley said raising the minimum wage would "throw people out of work and not help those who need it."

Poshard disagreed, saying because of minmum wage people are becoming dependent on welfare.

Daily Egyptian, September 29, 1988.
Reprinted with permission.

Staff Photo by Cameron Chin

Political animals

Donald Durham of Elco shows his support for Glenn Poshard amid a field of Patrick Kelley backers at Wednesday's debate at Rend Lake College.

Daily Egyptian, September 29, 1988.
Reprinted with permission.

Kelley, Poshard defend VP choice

By Scott Perry
Staff Writer

CENTRALIA — While the vice-presidential candidates were debating the issues, the congressional candidates were debating over the vice presidential candidates.

"I think Lloyd Bensten will be a great vice president," Glenn Poshard, Democratic candidate for Congress said during a debate with Patrick Kelley Wednesday night.

The debate was the third between the candidates vying for the position being vacated by long-time seat holder Kenneth Gray, D-West Frankfort.

"I'm glad Michael Dukakis has the courage to choose someone that dosen't align with him on all the issues," Poshard said.

He used this time to defend prior allegations by Kelley that Poshard would be ineffective in Washington because of his differences with the Democratic platform.

Kelley has made several references to Poshard's views on abortion, gun control and gay rights, which stray from the Democratic platform.

Kelley continued his attack on the Democratic party saying that choosing Bensten for vice president was an attempt by Dukakis to rid himself of the liberal label the Bush campaign has placed on him.

Poshard defended Dukakis' choice by attacking Bush's choice of Dan Quayle for vice president, saying at least he didn't choose him for good looks and youth.

"What a nice way to choose a candidate," Poshard said.

Poshard also questioned Kelley's alignment with the Repubichan party.

"Do you intend to go along with our leadership? Do you?" he said.

Kelly said that he and Bush agree on all the issues and their is no reason to stary from them.

Poshard then questioned how Kelley could vote on Reagan administration issues such as acid rain legislation, social security and college grants and loans.

But the battle didn't end there.

The war on drugs also brought a heated confrontation between the candidates.

Poshard supports use of the military in ending the drug problem in America, saying it is "a national security issue."

Defending his stance, Poshard reminisced about his days in the Army. When he returned from Korea, Poshard wen to New York City to ease racial tensions.

"I was trained in the city of New York to deal with domestic affairs. This isn't a game, it's a war. It's a war on drugs."

Kelley quoted a defense official as saying, "We don't train our men to give Miranda warnings. We train them to shoot and kill."

Kelley also blamed the Democrat-controlled Congress for cutting $75,000 out of the federal budget that would aid the National Guard in efforts to control the influx of drugs into America.

Both candidates agreed that education is one of the keys to ending the drug problem.

Daily Egyptian, October 6, 1988.
Reprinted with permission.

Kelley, Poshard to debate on campus

By Scott Perry
Staff Writer

The debate that isn't a debate between Congressional candidates Patrick Kelley and Glenn Poshard will be 7:30 tonight in the Student Center auditorium.

The Congressional Candidate forum, as it is officially called, is sponsored by the Jackson County League of Women Voters with the cooperation of several local orgainizations.

Kelley and Poshard are seeking the position in the U.S. House of Representatives being vacated by long-time seat holder Kenneth Gray, D-West Frankfort.

The forum's format is similar to that of a debate in that the candidates will answer written questions from the audience. Each candidate will have four minutes to answer the question.

Each candidate also is given five minutes for their opening statements and seven minutes for their closing statements.

In a late-August interview, Jim Wilson, Poshard's campaign manager, said the Poshard campaign was being "more than generous" in organizing the three debates, which have already been held throughout the 22nd district.

The sites for the three debates were Shawnee College in Ullin, Rend Lake College in Ina and Kaskaskia College in Centralia.

Linda Helstern, president of the Jackson County League of Women Voters, said not holding a debate in Jackson County "is an insult to the community."

"There are many intelligent and informed voters in the area," Helstern said.

"SIU is the centerpoint of life in Carbondale as well as being the focal point on Southern Illinois," she said.

The Poshard campaign has been reluctant to meet with the Republican candidate at the University, saying it "gives an unfair advantage to Kelley."

Kelley is a professor at the Law School.

Wilson, using the same logic, said a gathering at John A. Logan would give the same unfair advantage to his candidate.

"Logan is in Glenn's backyard," Wilson said.

But Gail Klam, organizer of the forum, said she was able to convince Wilson there was no other site in Carbondale as suitable as the University.

The forum is open to the public, but tickerts must be obtained, Klam said.

Free Tickerts can be picked up at the Student Programming Council office on the third floor of the Student Center.

Daily Egyptian, October 12, 1988.
Reprinted with permission.

Government's role debated

By Scott Perry
Staff Writer

The foundation of America, and what needs to done to keep it strong, was the issue at hand during the Congressional Candidate Forum Wednesday night.

Glenn Poshard, Democratic candidate for the 22nd District's Congressional seat, used the analogy of his grandfather's barn to stress the importance of a strong foundation in the nation.

Poshard said his grandfather paid $150 to have the tine roof of the barn painted. At first, he said, the roof was so shiny that it could be seen for miles. But with the first hard Southern Illinois rain, the paint came off.

"And when the termites began to eat away at the foundation of the barn, he had no money with which to save it," Poshard said.

Poshard used this analogy to stage an attack on the Reagan-proposed Strategic Defense Initiative and the United States' large national debt.

Poshard said the federal government should "invest in the foundation of this country and not in a space defense system."

Republican candidate Patrick Kelley disagreed, saying the job of the national government is to provide leadership and a strong national defense.

Kelley said SDI is needed to combat the uneven balance between U.S. and Soviet nuclear weapons.

Kelley stood strong on the Republican ideal of limited government control on the affairs of the states.

Kelley said the federal government should have a limited part in the lives of Americans.

"We should encourage people to do things on their own," Kelley said. "But when people really need help, we need to be sure there will be a compassionate government and people there to

help them."

The question of legislation to ensure job security for women who take maternity leaves, led to an attack by Poshard over Kelley's summer sabbatical, which he took to write a book.

Poshard praised Kelley for writing the book but said women don't have the same security as he had when they decide to have a baby.

"And you did it with pay. We're not even talking pay for them," Poshard said.

Kelley's sabbatical was questioned since he used the time to campaign for Congress

Rennard Strickland, former dean of the Law School, defended Kelley's sabbatical saying he accomplished more on his book than he had originally planned and used only free time to work on his campaign.

Daily Egyptian, October 13, 1988
Reprinted by permission

Kelley criticizes Poshard's TV ad

By Scott Perry
Staff Writer

Congressional candidate Patrick Kelley said his opponent's "self-confessed ignorance" on defense issues should be a deciding factor in electing the next congressman to represent the 22nd district.

Speaking at his final press conference prior to the Tuesday election, was referring to a television advertisement where State Sen. Glenn Poshard, running against Kelley, says he

knows little about the complicated national defense issues, but says he does know a lot about the problems of Main Street.

Kelley said the people of Southern Illinois "deserve a congressman who knows enough about defense to keep America strong."

Poshard was unavailable for comment.

Poshard and Kelley have received much praise for a "clean" campaign, but Poshard campaign manager Jim Wilson

said he was unhappy with the recent attack on Poshard by Kelley in his advertisements.

Wilson said the Poshard camp has been running a very positive campaign with no reference to Kelley in any of their advertisements.

Kelley, however, has been using his commercials to attack Poshard, Wilson said.

In one commercial, Kelley takes issue with House Speaker Jim Wright, and Poshard's connection with him.

Kelley said as a representative

the first vote one will have to make is for speaker.

Kelley disagrees with the naming of Wright to the position of speaker because of the recent accusations that Wright has been unethical in the way does business

"Jim Wright runs the House like the dictator of a banana boat," Kelley said during his press conference.

Among the leading differences Kelley says there is between the two candidates is the way each of them hopes to bring jobs to Southern Illinois.

Kelley wants to continue with many of Reagan ideals such as low taxes, tax incentives and less government regulations.

Kelley is against the raising of the minimum wage, something Poshard is for, saying it would

throw many Americans, including Southern Illinoisans, out of work.

Kelley said he was pleased with the campaign and that he felt the momemtum was there to take him to Washington on election day.

Daily Egyptian, October 13, 1988. Reprinted with premission.

Kelley: Government should play leading role in housing homeless

By Scott Perry
Staff Writer

The role the government should play in providing housing for the homeless is one of leadership, Patrick Kelley, Republican candidate for Congress, said.

Kelley, during a press conference Wednesday, said the government should encourage and assist the private sector in meeting our housing needs. He also said the government should not bear the entire financial burden.

"I don't agree with those who assume all we need to do is spend more government money to solve our housing problem," he said.

Kelley said he disagreed with the plan proposed by Michael Dukakis that would tax developers and use union pension funds to provide for the nation's

"I don't agree with those who assume all we need to do is spend more government money to solve our housing problems."

— Patrick Kelley

housing needs.

"I'm not for a raid on private pensions," Kelley said.

Kelley said the tax would discourage development and raise the housing cost.

He said the key to creating a good housing policy was to install a policy that allows home ownership to be possible.

"The best housing policy is a sound economic policy," he said.

Kelley said strengthening the savings and loan institutions is a must if the government hopes to provide the proper environment for individual home ownership.

"We need to let people know they don't need to worry about the safety of their investment,"

he said.

Kelley used this opportunity to attack House Speaker Jim Wright.

Wright is presently being investigated for allegedly interferring with the closing of several Texas institutions.

Kelley strongly supported a voucher system which allows low-income families to live in privately owned rental propery.

Daily Egyptian, October 20, 1988
Reprinted with permission

Poshard says constituents get the credit for his victory

By Scott Perry
Staff Writer

With his wife and two children at his side, an excited Glenn Poshard raised his hand in the air, gave a big thumbs up and claimed victory in the race for the 22nd Congressional District.

"I never dreamed this would be able to happen," Poshard told a crowded room of supporters at the Marion Holiday Inn Tuesday.

"If this victory belongs to anyone, it belongs to you," Poshard said, thanking those made his dream a reality.

"No one has worked harder, no one has gone out and knocked on more doors and mailed more letters than you have. From the bottom of our hearts my family thanks all of you for this victory you have given us."

Poshard's announcement came at 10:10 p.m., three hours after the Illinois polls closed Tuesday.

In his speech, Poshard made a promise to the people of the district.

"I want to go there (Washington) and be a good congressman. I want to do what's right. I want to work hard for Southern Illinois and I want to be honest and truthful to the people. As long as we can do that we will win again, because we are going to do the best job a congressman can do. I promise you that and I thank you for it."

Poshard also used the opportunity to thank his opponent, Patrick J. Kelley, for being a "gentleman" and running "a fine campaign."

Poshard said he wished the kind of campaign run in the 22nd Congressional District could be run in every district throughout the State.

He praised Kelley, saying he has "some very deep beliefs and he's serious about those beliefs."

Poshard showed some compassion for his opponent telling the crowd he knew what it was like to lose.

Kelley called the Poshard headquarters immediately after the victory announcement was made. The two candidates spoke for about five minutes about the campaign and congratulated one another.

"I consider you my friend," Poshard told Kelley. "We'll have to get together sometime."

Kelley told Poshard, "You ran a really good campaign. I think the people of the district were pleased with the campaign."

Poshard said he planned to sleep until noon today and wake-up to a late breakfast and spend some time with his family.

After that he said he was going to get caught up on his state Senate business and prepare to go back to session next month.

Poshard said there are still a few things he would like to accomplish before heading for Washington.

Daily Egyptian, November 9, 1988.
Reprinted with permission.

President

No. of states	Candidate	votes
35	George Bush	34,980,444
8	Michael Dukakis	29,609,469
7	Unknown	

U.S. House

District	Candidate	votes
22	Patrick Kelley	46,870
	Glenn Poshard	78,631

State House

District	Candidate	votes
116	Frankie Eggemeyer	5,617
	Bruce Richmond	14,906
	Other	0
117	Jim Rea	9,842
	Other	0
118	Bob Winchester	16,981
	David Phelps	25,828
	Other	0

State Senate

District	Candidate	votes
58	L. Gene Clarke	16,048
	Ralph Dunn	26,165

State Constitution

Constitutional Convention	votes
Yes	188,613
No	613,378

Voting Age Amendment	votes
Yes	294,787
No	265,646

Delinquent Tax Scales Amendment	votes
Yes	294,787
No	215,237

State's Annorney

Candidate	votes
Michael Maurizio	8,243
W. Charles Grace	12,409
Other	0

Circuit Clerk

Candidate	votes
Bill Grob	7,774
Jennie Crawshaw	12,602
Other	0

Note: Information for table taken at 1 a.m. this moring. Story information may differ.

Daily Egyptian November 9, 1988
Reprinted with permission

SECTION THIRTEEN

ASSIGNMENTS FOR ORGANIZING AND DOCUMENTING ACHIEVEMENTS FOR RESEARCH

ORGANIZING AND DOCUMENTING ACHIEVMENTS USING PROJECT FOLDERS

This section is dedicated to helping students organizing and presenting their classwork professionally. It contains formats and examples for organizing students' research and for organizing students' work. Project folders are a set of files specifically related to a research project. Rather than leaving heaps of material all over a desk or room or keeping the material in a stack inside a notebook, a project folder contains only the materials related to the research project. The materials are summaries of information and checklists to remind students of the nature and scope of the assignment. Students should be able to write their papers directly from the sources contained in the project folder.

Constructing a Project Folder

Every research project should begin with a project file. Each item listed below should have its own section dividers:

- a copy of the professor's explicit instructions

- a writing schedule

- a draft checklist

- a copy of the standard criteria for evaluation

- an outline

- a journal/scrapbook

- notes and references

- photocopies of information

- a draft of the paper

- a backup disk of your draft and final manuscript

Professor's Explicit Instructions.

Identify the professor's instructions from the handout, syllabus, or lecture for the paper assignment and write them down.

- Check them off as you complete them.

- Recheck them as you revise your draft.

- Keep in mind the standard criteria for grading

- Keep the writing schedule handy.

WRITING SCHEDULE

Students should set a reasonable schedule to follow for their research projects. Examine your syllabus and note any explicit dates set by the professor as the assignments' due dates. Pace yourself so that you are not researching, writing, and typing a week or less before the assignment is due. Use the schedule outline below. (Adapted with permission from Corder and Ruszkiewicz, p. 703).

Date   Activity

_____ Choose a topic.

_____ Do exploratory reading for discovery of ideas.

_____ Construct working thesis sentence and scratch outline.

_____ Begin search for references, materials, and data.

_____ Complete research and note taking.

_____ Refine thesis and construct a topic outline.

_____ Write first draft.

_____ Revise draft.

_____ Type final copy; proofread and make a photocopy of it.

_____ Give the finished paper to the professor.

DRAFT CHECKLIST FOR A RESEARCH PAPER

__Page limit of the assignment ____Date due:_____
__Specific information required:

— _____

— _____

— _____

__ Title page includes the title of the paper, your name, professor's name, course number, course name, and date.

__ The paper is stapled and pages numbered.

__ You included an abstract.

__ Each paragraph is at least three sentences long.

__ You have presented evidence or examples for each point made in each paragraph and referenced each one.

__ Each paragraph in the body of the paper has at least two references, except for your original information.

__ No more than three quotes are included in the text.

     __ The quotes are absolutely necessary (delete if not).

     __ long quotes (over three lines) are indented.

__ You have used at least three articles from professional political science journals as sources.

__ Your references are parenthetical citations, footnotes, or endnotes and are in proper form according to a stylebook.

__ Tables, figures, and appendices are clearly marked, referenced in the text, and placed after the last page.

__ You have included a complete bibliography (works cited).

     __ it is in standard bibliographic form.

     __ it is typed as a hanging paragraph.

     __ it has full reference information for each entry.

     __ it is alphabetized by the last name of the authors.

__ You have checked your text carefully for typographical and spelling errors.

__ You have removed all first person references (such as I think, I believe, my opinion, I know)

__ You have removed all contractions (such as don't, it's, won't, can't)

__ You have removed all forms of linguistic bias.

     __ you have used gender neutral language.

     __ you have used culturally sensitive descriptions.

CRITERIA FOR GRADING A RESEARCH PAPER

Minimum requirements for receiving credit for the paper.

   ___Did the student do the paper as assigned?
   ___Did the student do his/her own work--no plagiarism?
   ___Did the student meet the deadline for the paper?

Point assignment for the evaluation criteria

   Excellent= 5 Good= 4 Adequate= 3 Inadequate= 2 Unacceptable= 1

   An A paper will accumulate a range of points from 100 to 90.
   A B paper will accumulate a range of points from 89 to 80.
   A C paper will accumulate a range of points from 79 to 70.
   A D paper will accumulate a range of points from 69 to 60.
   An F paper will accumulate a range of points from 59 to 20.

CRITERIA OF EVALUATION

__Format of the manuscript conforms to the instructor's criteria.
__Manuscript is well organized and well written.
__Complete and thorough description of the background or context of the research topic.
__A clear, well developed thesis statement.
__Presents a unique or interesting perspective on the topic.
__Logical development of student's argument.
__Identifies important supporting evidence, arguments, and perspectives concerning research topic.
__Identifies important evidence, arguments, and perspectives concerning research topic that does not support student's view.
__Explains all evidence, arguments, and perspectives presented concerning research topic.
__Critiques all evidence, arguments, and perspectives presented concerning research topic.
__Analysis reflects thorough understanding of the topic.
__Student addressed all issues raised in the analysis.
__No apparent factual errors.
__Very few spelling or grammatical errors.
__Evidence, arguments, and ideas are well documented. If quotes are used, they are used correctly and sparingly.
__Reference page is complete.
__References and sources used were clearly relevant.
__References and sources used were of high quality.
__References and sources used exhibit depth and breadth.
__References and sources used exhibit variety.

TIPS ON STORING NOTES AND REFERENCES

The most common way of storing notes and references is on index cards. Cards are handy but they are only useful if you can put a complete thought or summary of an argument on them. Try the following:

1.   Use 4 x 6 or 5 x 7 index cards.

- information is stored easier on them.
- both are wide enough to punch holes in so that they can be put into a ring binder.

2.   On the reference card, put the full bibliographic information on the card.

- write the last name first.
- write the library call number on the card for easy retrieval in case you must return to the source.
- annotate it with at least one sentence about the purpose of the source and one sentence about the significance of the source.
- keep the cards in alphabetical order.

3.   On the note cards put the following:

- Put the author's name and page numbers in the left-hand corner.
- put the subject in the right hand corner.
- write the summary, paraphrase, or quote on the card.
- on the bottom line of the card, write a note to yourself about where this fits into your paper.

EXAMPLE OF A REFERENCE CARD

303.380973
L767c
1987

Lipset, Seymour Martin and William Schneider. The Confidence Gap: Business, Labor, and Government in the Public Mind. Rev. Ed. MD: Johns Hopkins University Press, 1987.

These authors conduct an extensive examination of influences on public confidence in business, labor, and government. They also present evidence that news coverage shapes people's attitudes about these important political actors as well as people's perspectives on political events. They conclude that people have lost confidence in big government, big business, and big labor because of negative coverage.

EXAMPLE OF A NOTE CARD

Lipset and Schneider, pp. 403-406   Evidence/P.0.

Media is the major source of political information. Studies show direct links between political cynicism and negative news reporting. "The special impact of television is that it delivers the news to a much larger and 'inadvertent' audience than was the case before television, when only a limited segment of the population chose to follow news about politics and government. When people read newspapers and magazines, they edit the information by skipping over articles about subjects they are not interested in. Television watchers, however, are exposed to everything." p. 405

(supports the argument that media is a strong influence on public attitudes)

PHOTOCOPIES AND PRINTOUTS OF INFORMATION

Do not waste your time photocopying and printing all the sources you think you need to write the paper.

- Photocopy and print only what you believe is essential to your research.

- For Web site sources, print out the entire source—it may be gone the next time you try to access it.

- Write all bibliographic information on the photocopy or printout.

- For Web site sources, make sure that the full Web address is on the printout.

- For all sources, write the key words, search engines, index, or data based used to find the source on the copies

- Cut and paste essential data or critical information from the photocopy or printout onto an index card.

- Put material that is too large for an index card into a separate section in your folder entitled photocopies and printouts. Summarize the material on an index card.

AN OUTLINE

Keep your scratch outline, topic outline, and sentence outline handy in your notebook as you write them for easy reference as you do your research.

- Keep all revisions of your thesis sentence.

- Add to the outlines as you continue your discovery of information and ideas.

A PROJECT JOURNAL/SCRAPBOOK

In addition to your outlines, keep a journal of thoughts and ideas, tidbits of information gathered, names of good reference people, phone numbers of the library, and bits of data which do not quite fit into your project....yet!

- Be sure to date the journal entry.

- Be sure to fully identify the source of any information.

A DRAFT OF THE PAPER.

Keep a working draft in your folder at all times.

- Once you have the final copy, make a photocopy of it (or print another copy of the paper) and place it in the folder as well.

- Never destroy your draft before you have turned in the assignment and received a grade.

   ✓ Instructors are becoming increasingly vigilant in the fight against plagiarism.

   ✓ A draft can help document your efforts. See http://www.plagiarism.com.

SECTION
FOURTEEN

ASSIGNMENTS FOR
ORGANIZING
AND
DOCUMENTING
ACHIEVEMENTS FOR
CAREER DEVELOPMENT

ORGANIZING AND DOCUMENTING ACHIEVMENTS USING A PROFESSIONAL PORTFOLIO

This section is dedicated to helping students organizing and presenting themselves professionally. It contains formats and examples for organizing students' best work to use as a examples of work for the job market. Students often complain that what they do in class is not related to what they want to do for a career. This is just not true. Every activity and every skill contributes to the value of that student in the job market.

Students will eventually need to compile a set of documents to show perspective employers. Compiling a portfolio is just like putting together a project folder. In fact, a portfolio is a project folder for a job search or for advanced training. It is meant to be self-contained. All addresses and relevant professional material should be placed in this folder. The materials in a professional folder provide a template for all communication with a prospective employer or graduate school admissions committee. Students should be able to compile documents and information necessary for applications to anything from this portfolio.

PROFESSIONAL PORTFOLIO OR DOSSIER

Many colleges and universities are introducing capstone or senior professional courses into their curriculums. Sometimes the purpose of these capstone courses is to polish students' skills as well as prepare them for the job market or for graduate school. Sometimes these capstone courses are part of an educational assessment program designed to examine the enrichment of students from their major areas of study.

Whatever the case, one of the important instruments for evaluating the quality of students' work and potential is through an examination of their personal writing portfolios. Artists, designers, architects, and other professionals keep portfolios of their best work for examination by prospective employers. A comprehensive file containing prepared work for each class is equally valuable for a political science student as a job marketing strategy or to select items as evidence of the student's accomplishments to send along with graduate school applications.

Compiling a good portfolio requires students to practice almost all the techniques and skills described in this book. It requires data gathering, organization of materials to support a statement, analysis, problem-solving skills, and good writing skills for presenting or communicating to evaluators, the degree and nature of the value added to the student's professional development through education. The materials in student portfolios provide material evidence that they are worth considering for advanced training or professional position in an organization.

Students should be keeping a professional portfolio from the first day they attend classes in their college or university. In particular, they should keep a portfolio for both their major and minor areas of study. If the student uses personal computer word processing, it is best if the student stores the computer disks containing the files for each paper and for any personal reference information in the portfolio.

The portfolio should contain, at minimum the following items separated by dividers with a scratch copy and a finished copy.

- **CURRICULUM VITAE**

- **RESUME**

- **AUTOBIOGRAPHICAL ESSAY/OUTLINE**

- **COPY OF AN OFFICIAL TRANSCRIPT OF CLASSES**

- **LIST OF COURSES CATEGORIZED BY SUBFIELD**

- **REPRESENTATIVE COPIES OF WRITTEN WORK AND TESTS**

- **LIST OF PROSPECTIVE EMPLOYERS**

- **SAMPLE COVER LETTER**

- **COPIES OF LETTERS OF RECOMMENDATION OR INTRODUCTION**

COMPILING A CURRICULUM VITAE

A curriculum vitae is a professional document primarily used in academics. For the most part, the purpose of a curriculum vitae is to present, document, and communicate to an evaluator the scope, nature, and degree of the student's professional and academic training and accomplishments. It makes a first impression on an evaluator and often determines whether the student will be interviewed or accepted into a program.

The student should put as much time and thought into preparing the student's curriculum vitae as the student would put into any paper. The curriculum vitae contains information about the student's personal history, professional accomplishments, level education achieved, and professional work experience which qualifies the student for a particular job or advanced training program. It should present the student's work in its best light.

The curriculum vitae must be concise but not brief. It is similar to a resume but its focus is on academic achievements. There is no recommended length for a curriculum vitae. It must be presented in a professional and organized manner. There must no typographical errors, erasures, or any other marks on the document. If a curriculum vita is typed on a word processor, it should be printed professionally on a laser printer on good high cloth content paper. The organization's or institution's address should be typed on a mailing label to be attached to a manila envelope. Do not fold the materials. The envelope should contain enough postage to get it to the organization.

Format for Curriculum Vitae Items

Curriculum vitae should include the following items where applicable and use the headings and subheadings in the order in which they are presented here.

Personal information:

- Name
- Present address
- Present status (senior, student assistant, etc.)

Education:

List each institution attended, starting with the most recent to high school. For each entry:

- Name of university or college
- City, State, and country if not in the U.S.
- Major and minor or focus of the work
- Highest level achieved or degree granted
- Month and year degree awarded
- Beginning and ending month and year attended if no degree awarded

Publications:

This includes any of the student's work that has been published. It is rare, except for journalism students, for undergraduate students to have publications but in the event that they do, it should be on their vitae. Even editorials in the school newspaper count as publications.

- List the full reference citation of your work. List the title of the manuscript first, the name of the publication, and then the date it was published.
- List these in descending order from the most recent to the first one published.
- If you have a publication that is pending, list it first, designating it as either pending or in review.

Professional Presentations:

This includes any of the student's work that has been presented at a professional meeting. It is rare, except for students in Phi Sigma Alpha or other honors societies, for undergraduate students to have presented material professionally but in the event that they do, it should be on their vitae.

- List the title of the presentation first, your role (presenter or discussant), the name of the conference, the city, state, and country (if not in the U.S.) and then the dates of the conference.
- List these in descending order from the most recent to the first one presented.
- If you have a presentation that is upcoming, list it first, designating it as upcoming.

Professional Associations:

List any political science, social science, or other professional or honors societies to which you belong.

- List the title of the association, your role (member, president, etc.), and dates of the membership.
- List these in descending order from the most recent to the first one joined.
- If you have an official appointment to an administrative position that is upcoming, list it first, designating the appointment dates.

Private Associations:

You may, with caution, want to list private associations such as the Young Republicans, ACLU, NRA, NOW, Animal Defense League, etc. if you held official positions in them. List only those activities you feel enrich your profile. Be careful not to reveal any private activities that you do not wish to prejudice your file. Use the same format as that presented for professional associations.

Grants:

List any grants which you received during your academic career.

- List the title of the grant and your role or award, the name of the granting institution, the location of the institution (city, state, and country, if not in the U.S.) and then the dates of the grant.
- List these in descending order from the most recent to the first one received.
- If you have a grant proposal outstanding or a grant that is upcoming, list it first, designating it as upcoming or pending.

Honors and Awards:

List any scholarships, fellowships, citations of special recognition, honorable mentions in competitions, or nominations for awards.

- List the title of the honor or award, the purpose of the honor or award, your role (winner, nominee, etc.), the name of the source of the honor or award (the country, if not in the U.S.), and then the date the honor or award was given.
- List these in descending order from the most recent to the first one receive.
- If you have an honor or award that is outstanding, do not list it unless you were nominated. Then be sure to designate it as a nomination until it is resolved.

Professional Experience:

This is any work accomplished that is pertinent to political science. List all employment in political or social other organizations, research assistance provided to professors and other professionals, all volunteer work, and all consulting work.

- Specify your title first, such as student assistant or manager, the name of the organization or institution, the name of your supervisor, an brief one to two line annotation of what services your performed, and the dates of service.
- List these in order from the most recent to the first one worked.
- Be sure to use assertive words connoting activity not passivity. Use words such as aiding, advising, consulting, managing, writing, assisting, preparing, and researching.

Areas of Study:

List the subfield courses which best describe your preparation and training.

References:

List three references each from professors, employers, and/or associates from the activities listed under professional activities.

- Put the referee's name first, the referee's association or institution and official title, the referee's full institutional or association address, the referee's business telephone number.
- Be sure to ask for the referee's permission to use them as a reference. Ask them to write you a broadly framed letter of recommendation that you may keep on file at the University or College Placement Office (if there is one).
- Ask for a letter or recommendation shortly before or after you finish a course or leave a job. Do not wait until you need a recommendation. You can always request another, more specific letter later. By getting letters on file, the referees can use them to refresh their memories about the accomplishments later.
- Some people will let you keep a copy on file in your portfolio. Ask permission to have a copy for your files.
- When requesting a second letter of recommendation from someone you have not seen in a while, be sure to provide them with a copy of the old letter if have written one before.

EXAMPLE OF A CURRICULUM VITAE

CAITLIN MAGGIE SCHMIDT
100 Ezee Street
Somwherin, Illinois 62345
(393) 733-2020

EDUCATION:

1987-1991	Southern Illinois University, Carbondale, IL. B.A. Summa Cum Laude. January 1991. Major in Political Science, minor in Economics. Emphasis on policy, interest groups, and Congress.
1986-1987	Longway Community College, Frome Aniwher, IL. General Studies.
1984-1986	Podunke High School, Podunke, IL. Graduated with honors.

PUBLICATIONS:

"Students are Key to Environmental Policy Change," *Community News*, (April 1, 1990).

PAPERS:

"Student Participation in Government," Illinois Political Science Association Annual Meeting, Springfield, IL, August 1990.

PROFESSIONAL ACTIVITIES:

Reviewed *Expository Writing In Political Science* by Diane Schmidt for HarperCollins Publishers, January 1990.

PROFESSIONAL ASSOCIATION AND SOCIETY MEMBERSHIP:

Illinois Political Science Association
Phi Kappa Phi (National Honors Society)
Pi Sigma Alpha (Political Science Honors Society)

GRANTS:

Political Student Activities Grant, Undergraduate Student Activities Board, American Student Activities Association, "Mobilizing and Activating Student Participation in Government," January 1990.

HONORS AND AWARDS:

Nominated for the Best Student Paper Award for paper delivered at the 1990 Annual Meeting of the Illinois Political Science Association.

Illinois College Newspaper Award 1990
Student Activities Award 1989, 1990
Who's Who Among Women in American College and University Students. 1989.

EXPERIENCE:

Research Assistant to Ms. Boryn Phree, Clean and Healthy Agency, Carbondale, Illinois (1991-present).
Student Assistant to Dr. Gaia Green, Southern Illinois University. Survival of Humanity. (1990-91).
Student Worker for Mr. Chip Bites, Southern Illinois University, Faner Computing Lab, (1988-1990).
Sierra Club, Local Chapter Vice President, Marion, Illinois, (1990-91).

AREAS OF STUDY:

Major	*Minor*
American Government	Environmental Policy
Interest Groups	Economic Regulation
Legislative Process	Regulation/Public Administration

REFERENCES:

Gaia Green, Southern Illinois University, Political Science Department, Carbondale, Illinois 62901, (618) 628-1234. (Senior Thesis Director)

Boyrn Phree, Clean and Healthy Agency, 1289 Main St., Carbondale, Illinois, 62901, (618) 628-6781

Chip Bites, Faner Computing Lab, Southern Illinois University,(1988-1990), (618) 628-1678.

Gud D. Tooshus, Southern Illinois University, Political Science Department, Carbondale, Illinois 62901, 618-628-2340.

WHAT TO DO WITH OFFICIAL TRANSCRIPTS:

Obtain an official copy of your transcripts from each school you attended. Keep an updated copy in your files at all times. Annotate each entry.

1.   If not provided, write the names of the courses next to the course identification and the names of the instructor who taught the course.

- This will allow you to remember what courses you took and who taught them to you.

- Use this as a beginning of your professional network of associations.

2   For each course, list the skills required and reason for the grade you received.

- Be honest with yourself.

- For good grades, identify your best work and why it was good. For poor grades, identify what you did wrong or could not do well.

- List any extenuating circumstances which contributed to the poor performance such as family crisis, accident, illness, etc.

- This is the beginning of an accounting of your professional assets and liabilities.

CONSTRUCTING A LIST OF COURSEWORK

Categorize your university or college coursework by subfields and skills that adequately represent your training and preparation. Be sure to include any related courses in other disciplines and courses that provided you with technical training of any kind.

1.   List the courses that support the areas of interest specified above.

2.   List the courses that required word processing, data management, or computing skills.

3.   List the name of the courses and professors' name, and name of the institution if you attended more than one.

4.   End the page with the following statement:

(Official Transcripts Available Upon Request).

EXAMPLE OF AN ABRIDGED LIST OF COURSEWORK

CAITLIN SCHMIDT

PROFESSIONAL COURSEWORK

American Politics

Institutions - Professor Gud D. Tooshus
Pluralism and Its Critics - Mobe I. Lization
Bureaucratic Politics -Professor Ess. O. Pea

Public Policy/Political Economy

Public Policy - Dr. Menie Thengs
Politics of Environmental Policy - Professor Gaia Green
Survival of Humanity - Professor Gaia Green

Methods

Micro Computing - P.C. Mac*
Introduction to Mainframe Computing - Aski Epsidik

*All coursework completed at Southern Illinois University except where indicated.

Official Transcripts Upon Request.

PREPARING A RESUME

The purpose of a resume is to present to a potential employer, in as concise a form as possible, information about students' personal history, education, and work experience which qualifies them for a particular job. A well prepared, professional looking resume is essential for anyone seeking employment, because it makes a first impression on an employer which determines whether the will be interviewed. Students should put as much time and thought into preparing their resumes as they would any other writing assignment.

The resume must be concise. In general, the recommended length for a resume is one page. A resume is a professional document and must be presented in a professional manner. There must no typographical errors, erasures, or any other marks on the document. If resume is typed on a word processor, it should be printed professionally on a laser printer on good high cloth content paper. The organization's or institution's address should be typed on a mailing label or the envelope itself. The envelope should contain enough postage to get the materials to the organization.

RESUME ITEMS

Like any well-written document, a resume can be divided into parts. A resume should contain the items as they are listed below. All of these items can be found in your curriculum vitae, and list of courses, except the statement of your employment goals. This statement may come from your autobiographical essay.

Personal Information:

- List your full name and place it in a bold font with a 16-24 point type

- Address, and telephone number of your current and permanent address (if they are different)

- Fax, e-mail, and/or web page addresses if you have them

Employment Goals:

- This is optional

- At the beginning of your resume, state the specific position for which you are applying

- State how it relates to your career goals

Education

- List institutions you attended beginning with the most recent where you received a degree

- Include dates, institutions, cities, and degrees earned

- Include major, minors, certificates, and/or licensing

- Include your GPA if it is fairly high

- List fluency in a foreign language
- List computer or technical skills
- List relevant coursework and class projects only if they highlight important skills and training

Employment History:

- List all the positions you have held, beginning with the most recent, which qualify you for the job being offered
- List any internships or volunteer work that are related to your career field
- List your job title first, then the employer's name, city, and date
- Describe your experience, duties, and accomplishments briefly and in an assertive, active voice using words such as *conducted, planned, designed, administered, implemented, analyzed, organized, trained,* and *completed* to describe each activity

Personal Background Information:

In this section, you list any other information that you want the potential employer to know about. Be careful that you do not provide any material that may prejudice your file. Employers may not legally ask you age, gender, or race. Depending on the position and the aggressiveness of the organization in pursuing equal opportunity or affirmative action goals, you may want to list any membership in an organization that suggests your demographic characteristics or ideological perspective.

- List any honors, scholarships, or prizes you won for work you performed you have received
- List activities you engaged in such as clubs, fraternities/sororities, professional associations, etc.
- List your title first, then what you won

References:

- Do not list references on your resume
- Have a list of them with names, addresses, and telephone numbers/email/fax numbers at your interview in case someone wants to see them

EXAMPLE OF A RESUME

Caitlin Schmidt
100 Ezee Street
Somwherin, Illinois 62345
(393) 733-2020

OBJECTIVE   Research analyst for a midsize consulting firm with a special emphasis on energy and environmental policy.

EDUCATION   Southern Illinois University, Carbondale, IL.
- B.A. *Summa Cum Laude*. January 1991. GPA 3.95
- Major in Political Science, minor in Economics.
- Emphasis on policy, interest groups, and Congress.

Longway Community College, Frome Aniwher, IL. 1986-1988
- Information Management.

Computer Literacy: Microsoft Word, Excel, SPSS, Lexis-Nexus, and Internet

RELEVANT EXPERIENCE   **Research Assistant**: For Ms. Boryn Phree, Clean and Healthy Agency, Carbondale, Illinois (1991-present).   Researched sources and co-authored grants. Coordinated and trained volunteers.

Student Assistant: For Dr. Gaia Green, Southern Illinois University. Survival of Humanity. (1990-91). Assisted in developing and administering coursework. Graded and recorded course assignments.

Computing Assistant: For Mr. Chip Bites, Southern Illinois University, Faner Computing Lab, (1988-1990). Assisted in developing services for computing facilities clientele. Assisted with developing educational programs and modification of materials for clientele.

PERSONAL INFORMATION: **Vice President**, Sierra Club, Local Chapter, Marion, Illinois, 1990-1991
Nominated, Best Student Paper Award for paper delivered at the
      1990 Annual Meeting of the Illinois Political Science Association, 1990
Recipient, Illinois College Newspaper Award 1990, 1990
Recipient, Student Activities Award 1989, 1990
Recipient, Who's Who Among Women in American College
      and University Students. 1989.

References available upon request.

WRITING A COVER LETTER

In addition to the information contained on a resume page or curriculum vitae, students should include a cover letter written specifically to the potential employer.

- The cover letter may be used to reinforce the resume or curriculum information, but not to elaborate on it.

- Use the cover letter to induce support for your application by accentuating your accomplishments and skills as they relate to the position you are seeking or program you wish to enter.

- Ask for clarification when the job descriptions or program descriptions are vague or ambiguous.

- The cover letter should be brief and less formal in tone than the resume or curriculum vitae.

Format for the Cover Letter

- Write this like an executive summary.

- Use standard or block format.

- Single space your letter and double space between paragraphs.

- Keep the paragraphs at about 4-5 sentences at the most and no fewer than 3 sentences.

- Use a laser printer and bond paper.

- Tailor the letter to the position—show how your experiences and qualifications match the job duties and company goals.

- PROOFREAD!

Cover Letter Contents

Addressing the Letter

- Put your name and address first.

- Space down two lines and add the date.

- Space down two lines and put the company address, beginning with the person's name who is responsible for personnel decisions.

- Space down two lines and put the salutation in the form of Dear Mr. or Ms. If you do not know the person's name, then address it to Dear Personnel Director.

First Paragraph

- Open the paragraph with a grabber. If you know someone or were recommended by someone who works at the place you are applying or is known to the personnel director, drop the name in the first line.

- State your career objective and/or relevant training and experience.

- Mention how you know about the company, especially any research you did to find out about the company—relate that research to why you think your qualifications fit the company goals/image.

- Refer to the content of the ad you are answering and relate your skills and qualifications to each item in the ad.

- State how you can help the company achieve its goals and mission.

Next Paragraphs

- Develop your approach taken in the first paragraph.

- List the skills and qualifications you have that illustrate your strong points.

- It is your job to match the job with your skills—use active words.

- Use bullets to highlight exactly how you fulfill the requirements of the ad.

Closing Paragraph

- Encourage action—ask for the interview or say you will call for an appointment.

- Restate how well you fit the job description.

- Thank the person for their time.

Sign off

- End the letter with the word *Sincerely.*

- Space down four spaces.

- Put your name---be sure to sign the letter!

EXAMPLE OF A COVER LETTER

April 1, 1994

> Ms. Caitlin Schmidt
> 100 Ezee Street
> Somwherin, IL 62345

Ms. Cleen Itup
Personal Director
Environmental Lobbyist Inc.
1 Millyondoller Place
Washington, DC, 2001

Dear Ms. Itup,

Please accept my application for the research analyst position you advertised in the spring issue of the Sierra Club newsletter.   The position you listed sounds interesting to me because of my background in environmental politics. I have recently graduated with a bachelor degree in Political Science and am looking for a research position in a consulting firm specializing in energy and environmental problems.

Your ad states that applicants must have public relations and research skills. I am especially qualified for this position.

- I have been active for many years in local environmental movements.
- I have written several manuscripts, one of which was published, on mobilizing young people for environmental policy change.
- I have been working as a research assistant for a local environmental agency devoted to cleaning and preserving the community parks and natural areas.

If you would like to see a copy of my work on environmental policy, please feel free to contact me at (393) 733-2020. I also have letters of reference on file in the Southern Illinois University Placement Office. I look forward to hearing from you in the future.

Sincerely,

Caitlin Schmidt

AUTOBIOGRAPHICAL ESSAY/OUTLINE

Students should write a brief, one page autobiographical essay describing and highlighting their personal and professional achievements. This amounts to a "brag sheet" where students systematically describe how they developed their strengths and overcome their weaknesses. Why is this necessary? Employers and graduate school admission committees often evaluate the student based on a verbal and/or personal statement. This statement must be clear and concise; it must leave the evaluator with a positive image of the student as a potential employee or applicant. Here are a few pointers:

1. Use a personal computer word processing program to write the essay. Then revise the essay periodically. Keep the disk in your portfolio.

    - Use a topic or sentence outline to structure your essay.
    - Keep the outline and the essay.
    - Use the outline to prepare for a personal interview.
    - Use the essay as a way to prepare a cover letter or personal statement on an application where required.

2. Basically, the form for an autobiographical sketch is similar to an argument. It should focus on a concise characterization of your credentials, supported by examples that accent your positive, marketable assets and explain or minimize your academic, professional, or personal liabilities

3. The essay should have a introduction, body, and conclusion which all achieve the final goal of creating a positive image of your skills and preparation. In particular, emphasize your problem solving, writing, research, and technical skills. Accentuate but do not exaggerate or distort your achievements or liabilities.

4. Use concise examples of how you maintained and improved upon your previous accomplishments and overcome obstacles. Use whatever information available that could give a prospective employer or graduate school a reason to accept your application over others. Here are some examples:

    - you maintained a high grade point average while working two jobs.
    - how, despite your earlier problems in mathematics, you were able to master simple regression in your political methods course.

5. This essay will be central to any competitive activities you choose to address. When you must prepare a personal statement for a grant, scholarship, or fellowship applications or any other competitive activity (including job hunting), revise your outline and essay examples and statement of goals to accent where your credentials and goals converge with those outlined in each job or grant description. Your essay will be a skeleton on which you will flesh out how your credentials fit with the evaluators' goals and purposes.

EXAMPLE OF AUTOBIOGRAPHICAL ESSAY

Cleaning up the environment has been a passion for me since I was very young. My mother used to sing me to sleep with Pete Seeger's "The Garden Song" and Woody Guthrie's "This Land Is Your Land." As a youth, I worked with local scouting groups to clean up parks and natural areas. I felt a great sense of satisfaction after working and contributing to a safer, cleaner environment. As a college student, I pursued a political science degree and specialized in environmental policy because I felt that there was no substitute for a disciplined study of the problems and constraints involved in environmental protection.

The study of political science was interesting to me because of my background in environmental politics. I have been active for many years in local environmental movements and have written several manuscripts, one of which was published, on mobilizing young people for environmental policy change. In addition, I have been working as a research assistant for a local environmental agency devoted to cleaning and preserving the community parks and natural areas.

The courses I took in college have prepared me for doing research in regulatory policy and politics. I chose courses that would help me develop research and writing skills. Although my experience in my English composition course was not very rewarding, I have worked to maintain straight A's in my political science courses. Most of my political science courses required research papers and in them, I was able to improve and practice my research and writing skills. Many of the class papers I wrote received high grades.

Although I would prefer to work in the environmental policy field, I am trained to do research in a variety of areas. I believe that I can best use my problem solving, writing, and technical skills by working in a consulting firm. I have taken courses in data processing and management and would like to work with data. While my coursework in mathematics was not rewarding for me, I was intrigued with my computing courses. With some practice, I believe I could become quite good with computers.

In sum, although my life long interests have revolved around environmental politics, I am dedicated to general policy research. I have focused my university training on acquiring problem solving, writing, and technical skills. My goal is to obtain a position in a consulting firm and to pursue a career as a research analyst.

COPIES OF WRITTEN WORK

Copies of the best work students have produced during their academic training and professional activities. These copies should be kept in two forms. A graded or evaluated copy should be kept with a with a clean, unmarked copy of the work. If it was produced with word processing, the disk should be kept with the item.

1. If using a word processor, you should keep the tapes or files with the manuscripts on them with or near the work. Revise handwritten material and type them into a file as well.

2. If the paper was good but not near perfect, use the instructor's comments to correct the problems.

3. Then rank order your papers according to skill level and quality of writing.

4. Use these unmarked copies of papers as evidence of your skills and preparation.

5. Keep copies of any achievement scores from any standardized tests taken such as the LSAT, SAT, and GRE.

LIST OF PROSPECTIVE EMPLOYERS

Students should create an open-ended list of employers or graduate schools of the people they admire. These people could be school faculty, authors, or other professionals they were influenced by or impressed by their skills or credentials. The institutions or entities where these people work should be the first places they send applications.

1. Use your research skills to locate the mission statements, either implied or expressed, of institutions or entities. Intellectually, and in terms of matching your skills with the job market or graduate school, these places are the student's best opportunities for receiving a sympathetic review of your application.

2. If you know anyone of these people personally:

   • Ask for a letter of recommendation or a letter of introduction that you can keep on file. A letter of introduction need not be confidential and are often good ways of networking.
   • Ask their advice about where to apply.

A LIST OF RESOURCE MANUALS FOR CAREER MANAGEMENT AND ORGANIZATION

Asher, Donald. *The Foolproof Job Search Work Book.* Berkeley, CA: Ten Speed Press. 1995.

Career Power: A Blueprint for Getting the Job You Want. Pound Ridge, NY: Career Power Books. 1996.

Careers and the Study of Political Science: A Guide for Undergraduates. Washington, DC: American Political Science Association. 1995.

Cosman, Madeleine Pelner. *Kissing The Dragon: The Intelligent Work-Hunter's Companion.* Tenafly, NJ: Bard Hall Press. 1984.

Earning a Ph.D. in Political Science. Rev. ed. Washington, DC: American Political Science Association. 1999.

Good, C. Edward. *Does Your Resume Wear Blue Jeans? The Book on Resume Preparation.* Charlottesville, VA: 1985.

Purdue OWL Handouts: Resume Sections. 1999. <http:/owl.english.purdue.edu/files/f3.html (18 July 1999).

Reed, Jean. *Resumes That Get Jobs. Fifth Edition.* New York: Arco Publishing. 1990

Speck, Jeff. B. *Hot Tips, Sneaky Tricks, and Last-Ditch Tactics*: An Insider's Guide to Getting Your First Corporate Job. NY: John Wiley and Sons. 1989.

GLOSSARY

ABRIDGED LIST OF POLITIAL SCIENCE TERMS
FOR WRITING AND TALKING POLITICS

The following is a list of political science terms that are common to most classes. While there are plenty of terms not represented here, those that are listed represent the discourse found in political discussions from the newspaper to cocktail parties to campaign literature.

Abstract topics: are those involving values, problems, or a process.

Accountability: answering for one's actions.

Ad hominem: personalizing the issue by concentrating on the real or imagined negative characteristics of those who hold different or opposing views.

Affirmative Action: removal of artificial barriers to employment for women and minorities.

Agenda: a list of goals to achieve rank ordered by preference and importance. The presidential agenda often reflects the party platform.

Amendment: change a prior law or bill by adding to it.

Amicus curiae brief: a brief filed by a third party to inform the court.

Analysis assignments: these assignments usually ask students to examine the relationships between the parts of a political document or some political events. Typically, these assignments require the student to provide a perspective or reasoned opinion about the significance of an event or a document. Students may be required to assert and defend an opinion about what are the most important features in the constitution.

Analyze: give main divisions or elements.

Anarchism: belief that government is corrupt and should be abolished.

Antifederalists: those against the new constitution in 1780s who wanted strong states rights and weak central government.

Appeal: request to higher body for a review of lower body's decision.

Apportionment: a system that determines how legislative seats are allotted to states.

Appropriation: funding for programs and policies.

Argumentation assignments: these assignments often require the student to prove or debate a point. Typically, these assignments ask for normative assertions followed up with evidence and examples to support these assertions. For instance, instructors may ask students to provide an argument supporting (or not) automatic voter registration, random drug testing, or a constitutional amendment protecting the flag.

Aristocracy: a system of government where power to rule is held by a few people based on wealth or social factors.

Authoritarianism: rule by an individual whose power derives from the ability to coerce compliance.

Authority: power to compel others to obey.

Beliefs: These each are a state of mind related to a conviction or unconscious trust in a statement which is not fact-based or based on objective evidence. They are often associated with faith or custom. Natural rights, liberty, justice, freedom, and self-sufficiency are examples of beliefs. Like facts, they cannot be disproved and are not subject to argument.

Bicameralism: a two-chambered legislature.

Brief: a written statement by an attorney to a party in a court case summarizing the facts and issues in the case.

Bureaucracy: an administrative organization.

Calendar: legislative agenda.

Capitalism: an economic system where supply and demand determine the quantity produced and price of a good.

Caucus: a closed meeting by party officials.

Cause and effect assignments: these assignments typically require the student to speculate about the reasons some political event has occurred. For example, students may be asked why people vote, why do members of Congress worry about their images, what caused the civil war, or why some people are disillusioned with government.

Censure: method of discipline in legislatures.

Census: a method of taking an inventory of the population, done every ten years in the U.S.

Centralization: the concept of placing authority and power of government at the national level.

Checks and balances: a mechanism to grant a limited set of powers to each branch of government over the each other.

Civil rights: rights of citizenship that guarantees non-discrimination by government.

Civil servants: government employees, bureaucrats.

Classification assignments: these assignments usually ask the student to identify the pattern or system of classification such as types of voters, types of political systems, or types of committees in congress.

Classify: arrange into main divisions.

Closed primary: election to select party nominee that is open only to registered party members.

Cloture: a three-fifths vote by the Senate to end a filibuster or debate.

Coalition: a group of people or a set of groups with different interests working together for a common cause. Unions and education groups work together for more education funding from government.

Coattail effect: the effect of one candidate's popularity on other candidates of the party.

Collectivism: community centered rather than individual centered perspective.

Commerce clause: gave Congress the power to regulate commerce in Article I, Section 8.

Communism: an economic theory where the ownership of the means of production is held and shared equally by the people.

Compare: point out the likenesses.

Comparison or contrast assignments: these assignments usually ask the student to identify the differences and similarities between political roles, political systems, or political events.

Concepts: things that are felt, acknowledged such as dilemmas, processes, values, beliefs, principles, ideologies, and theories.

Conclusions: are assertions made by the author concerning the relationship between the hypothesis and the evidence.

Concurrent powers: power held by both national and state governments.

Confederacy: a system of government where states delegate power to the national government.

Conflict: a disagreement between opposing parties. Group conflict results from one set of people opposing the activities of another.

Consciousness: a feeling among people that they share something or have something in common. The war protests of the 1960s had the effect of raising people's consciousness about the undesirability of the war.

Consensus: a general agreement among a group of people. There is a consensus among citizens that voting is good.

Conservatives: in the U.S., people who prefer limited government in economic affairs but not necessarily social affairs. Outside the U.S., those who believe in a hierarchically ordered society.

Constituent: a citizen in a public official's area of authority.

Constitutionalism: the notion that government should be limited and its authority is derived through the consent of the governed, often with a written contract or constitution.

Constraint: a barrier, something that prevents some action. The fluctuations of the business cycle acts as a constraint for addressing problems of unemployment.

Contrast: point out the differences.

Criticize: give your perspective on good and bad features.

Deductive reasoning: applying generalizations or conclusions that are accepted as true to slightly different but similar situations or issues.

Definition assignments: these assignments usually ask the student to define a political concept, term, or phrases such as democracy, socialism, or capitalism. Students must provide examples of distinguishing features and differentiate the topic from others in its functional class.

Demagogue: a leader who appeals to the prejudices of others to gain popularity.

Democracy: theory of government in which the people hold power to rule.

Describe: name the features in chronological order.

Dilemmas: are undesirable situations or problems that seem to be difficult to resolve. They are often associated with unwanted and unsatisfactory conditions. They can also be related to a difficulty in achieving some preferred outcome. Political apathy, political intolerance, providing for social welfare during a recession, providing for cleaner air without devastating the coal industry, and reconciling individual liberties with the public good are examples of dilemmas.

Discuss: examine in detail.

Disincentive: an inducement not to perform some action. Policy makers place taxes on activities that are undesirable.

Divine right: the belief that power to rule is granted by a Supreme Being.

Due process: fair and equal treatment in government processes.

Efficacy: a feeling of usefulness, of purpose, of empowerment. People who vote because they believe it will change policy have a sense of political efficacy.

Electoral College: electors who meet to determine the president and vice-presidential elections.

Elite theory: a belief that power should and is controlled by a small number of people.

Equity: relating to being equal but not necessarily identical. Sometimes related to fairness and compensation. As long as the Supreme Court accepted that segregation did not deny blacks equity, it was upheld.

Evaluate: give your perspective on the value or validity.

Events: these are events that led to political outcomes or consequences or are political outcomes. The Kent State Massacre, political assassinations, campaigns, and the Nixon resignation are examples of concrete topics.

Evidence: is data. There are two kinds of data. See quantitative and qualitative evidence.

Examples: are specific references or instances of the point being made and are typically referred to as anecdotal evidence. The strength of anecdotal evidence is found in its generalizability and representativeness.

Expert opinions: are judgements made by authorities based on their experience with evidence and assessment of the facts. When facts are unavailable, expert opinions are the next strongest evidence a writer can supply to support an argument. Expert opinions and facts are the very strongest kinds of evidence a writer can use.

Explain: make clear, give reasons for.

Faction: a club, a smaller group within a group of people working for benefits for the few and not the many. The conservative faction of the Republican Party has pushed for anti-abortion legislation as part of the party platform.

Facts: are statements that can be verified. They are the strongest proof or evidence a writer can supply to support an assertion. They are also the most difficult kind of evidence to obtain.

False analogy: assuming that things that are alike in one respect are alike in other respects.

False dilemma: stating that a complex question has only two answers that are both good, both bad, or one good and one bad.

Fascism: a nationalistic, totalitarian system where power is vested in a dictator.

Federal: a system of government where power is divided between state and national governments.

Filibuster: unlimited debated in the Senate.

Fragmentation of powers: a division of powers within government to achieve the goal of limited government; implemented in the U.S. by federalism, separation of powers, and checks and balances.

Gerrymandering: redrawing district lines so that they favor a particular party, race, or ethnicity.

Grand jury: citizens selected to hear evidence to determine if charges should be issued.

Grants-in-aid: grants of money given to state and local governments to implement national goals.

Habeas corpus: a court order to inform a person in custody of the reason for detention.

Hasty generalizations: a generalization that is based on very little evidence or which overstates.

Hypothesis: is a generalization that can be tested.

Ideologies: these each has an integrated body of ideas, values, beliefs, and aspirations that constitute a socio-political program. They are associated with a desire, a need, a moral obligation, or a utopian vision. The ideas, beliefs, or values need not be socially acceptable; all that is needed is that the ideas, beliefs, and values are linked coherently. Liberalism, Conservatism, anarchism, authoritarianism, pacifism, imperialism, Marxism, fascism, Nazism, Libertarianism, nationalism are examples of ideologies.

Illustrate: give one or more examples of.

Impeachment: the first part of a process by which an official can be removed from office, in the U.S., it is done by the House of Representatives. Once impeachment is voted, the Senate then conducts a trial to remove the official from office.

Implied powers: powers of the government that are implied by other stated powers.

Incentive: an inducement to perform some action. Policy makers provide subsidize for activities that are desirable.

Incrementalist: a cautious, step by step movement toward a direction or change. The American social system is incrementalist because change occurs very slowly.

Incumbent: an official in office.

Independent: no party affiliation.

Indictment: an accusation charging a person with a crime.

Individualism: individual centered rather than community centered perspective.

Inductive reasoning: generalizing from observations or attributing a cause to a set of observed circumstances.

Inference: a conclusion based on evidence. This is based on inductive reasoning.

Inherent powers: powers not specified.

Initiative: a proposal for legislation submitted by members of the public to the public.

Institution: these are any body that engages in routinized interaction. Affiliations, association, alliances, and political organizations such as Congress, bureaucracies, political parties, interest groups, and even families are institutions.

Institutionalize: some behavior or activity that has become part of an institution, part of a pattern of behavior.

Interest group: a set of individuals with shared interests that is organized to influence policy.

Interpret: give the significance.

Iron triangle: the symbiotic relationship between bureaucracy, congressional committees, and clientele.

Justify: defend, show to be right.

Knowledge: is what we have learned from political inquiry. The true goal of all political inquiry is to contribute to a universal body of knowledge. As scholars, we are obliged to learn, to contribute to this body of knowledge.

Laissez-faire: "hands off" the economy; a belief that government should not interfere in economic affairs.

Left wing: change-oriented outlook favoring policies that help the masses.

Legitimacy: a belief that something is right, correct, and proper to do. It does not mean legal. Some laws, like the 55 mile an hour speed limit are routinely ignored because they lack legitimacy among those who like to drive fast cars; perceived right to make binding decisions.

Libel: discrediting someone's reputation in writing.

Liberals: in the U.S., people who prefer limited government in social affairs but not necessarily economic affairs. Outside the U.S., those who believe limited government in both economic and social affairs.

Libertarians: a belief in minimal government intervention in citizen's lives.

Linkage: connecting one concept or entity with another. Political parties and interest groups provide different kinds of linkages between people and government.

Lobbyists: people, usually hired, to influence public institutions for the benefit of their group or clients.

Logrolling: reciprocity, vote trading between decision-makers.

Majoritarian: of the majority, used in context with majoritarian principles. The Bill of Rights was adopted to prevent the majoritarian ideas of what is politically correct from infringing on minority rights granted in the constitution.

Majority rule: majority decisions win.

Mean: an average.

Monarchy: a political system where the power to rule is granted by divine right.

Natural Law: a concept that human behavior is governed by laws of nature.

Naturalization: a process of becoming a citizen in a land other than that of one's birth.

Nepotism: providing political favors to family members.

New Left: a liberal movement spawned in the U.S. 1960s promoting civil rights and social justice.

New Right: a conservative movement with an evangelical and intolerant perspective promoting traditional moral virtues.

Non sequitur: when two ideas are presented with no logical connection.

Norm: an expected behavior or pattern of behavior. Specialization in subject areas related to a committee assignment is a norm in Congress.

Objects: things that can be seen physically such as players, institutions, events, and policies.

Oligarchy: a political system where power is concentrated in the hands of a few, elite individuals.

Open primary: an election for a selecting a party candidate where the voters do not have to disclose their party identification or membership but may only vote in one primary.

Opinions: are judgements based on facts. A thesis sentence of an argument is an opinion. Opinions are testable and arguable because they are viewpoints arrived at through the examination of facts and evidence. Opinions are not arguments--arguments with supporting evidence are used to support opinions.

Oversimplification: stating that one event caused another when there is either no relationship or where other causes exist.

Patronage: providing a job or government benefits in return for political favors or support.

Platform: a party's agenda.

Players: these are people who have been politically important in the past or the present. Presidents, members of congress, interest group leaders, bureaucrats, judges, and are examples of political players.

Pluralism: bargaining among groups to influence political decisions. Pluralism describes group conflict in the political arena.

Plurality: the most, not but not a majority, of the votes.

Pocket veto: a way to veto a bill by not signing it within ten days following the end of a legislative session.

Police power: power to establish order.

Policies: these are or can be any decision made by any public official in any branch of government which has the force of law. Policies also include custom as well as non-decisions on problems. Congressional legislation, bureaucratic regulations, presidential orders, judicial decisions, or common law are policies.

Political action committees (PACs): a legal entity designed to legally provide money to campaigns.

Political correctness: is a term used to denote the socially accepted phrasing or perspective on an issue.

Political machine: a well connected, widely networked party organization

Political party: an organization explicitly designed to get their candidate elected to office.

Poll: survey of opinions.

Poll sample: a subset of the population.

Populism: a political philosophy promoting the interests of lower income citizens over the interests of the upper income classes.

Pork barrel legislation: a bill that promotes the interests of a particular subset of a legislator's constituency.

Post hoc fallacy: jumping to the conclusion that event A caused event B just because event A occurred earlier.

Precedent: an earlier decision used to structure a present decision. Judges use precedents to decide current cases.

Prejudices: are opinions that have been formed on insufficient or unexamined evidence. They are often thoughtless oversimplifications and typically reflect a narrow-minded view of the world. They are testable and easily refutable by the presentation of facts and evidence.

Primary election: an election within the party to determine which candidate will be the party's candidate in the general election.

Principles: these are doctrines or codes of conduct that are usually held in high esteem. Self-determination, limited government, constitutionalism, rule of law, and legitimacy are examples of principles.

Problems: are concepts or ideas that connote undesirability. They are associated with unwanted and unsatisfactory conditions. Political apathy or racism are two examples of abstract topics.

Process assignments: these assignments usually ask the student to describe how some political phenomena relate functionally to other political phenomena. For example, students may be asked to describe how media influence voting behavior or how decisions are made in committees.

Processes: refers to observable patterns of political behavior in people and groups. They are associated with procedures and mechanisms for using, acquiring and distributing political power. The methods and structure of congressional, judicial, and bureaucratic decision-making are examples of processes. Democracy, Federalism, Confederation, oligarchy, monarchy, feudalism, socialism, communism are all different processes for organizing government.

Promulgate: to make known to everyone. Laws must be promulgated so that everyone has the opportunity to know them.

Qualitative evidence: subjective or authoritative data usually from interviews, firsthand observations, inference, or expert opinions.

Quantitative evidence: objective or numerical data usually from a survey, poll, tests, or experiments.

Quorum: minimum number of members to conduct legislative business.

Ratification: a process by which states decide to accept or reject an amendment to the constitution.

Reactionary: a person who wishes to return to a previous status quo in response to progressive change.

Referendum: a procedure through which legislatures submit laws or amendments to the voters for approval.

Republic: a form of government where power resides in the people who elect agents to represent them in decision-making.

Reserved powers: powers delegated expressly to state governments.

Review: examine on a broad scale.

Right wing: a conservative, reactionary outlook favoring policies that favor the promotion of capitalism, the military and cultural conservatism.

Saliency: something that is important with connotations of being immediate, pertinent, something that is of acute interest. Media coverage of political protests heighten the saliency of the events; this often causes the right to protest to become a salient issue.

Separation of powers: dividing powers between branches of government.

Single-member district: legislators represent only one distinct set of constituents determined through apportionment of legislative seats.

Slander: a verbal disparagement against someone's character.

Socialism: in practice, system of government where the government owns the means of production and provides for the public welfare.

Sovereignty: government is supreme in power, rank, and authority and is free from external interference.

Split ticket: voting for candidates in different parties for different offices.

Spoils system: providing benefits to loyal supporters.

Statistics: are often called probabilistic evidence because they are based on probabilities of correctness and depend on strict adherence to representative sampling technique. Statistics are not facts; they are the next best things to facts when facts are unavailable. Unfortunately, statistics alone provide weak support for an argument. Together with expert opinion and examples, statistics can provide powerful support for arguments.

Statute: a law passed by a legislative body.

Straight ticket: voting for candidates only in one party for different offices.

Summarize: briefly go over the essentials.

Theocracy: a political system where the leader claims to be guided by a Supreme Being.

Theories: are sets of plausible statements or general principles offered to explain phenomena or events. Theories offer testable hypotheses or speculations about the causes of political outcomes. Theories are often modified or constrained by ideological perspectives. Democratic Theory, corporatism, the Downesian model of party competition, egalitarianism, the American Voter Model, the Domino Theory, feminism, elitism, and pluralism are all theories.

Thesis sentence: sums up the main ideas that the writer wants to make.

Totalitarianism: a political system where all aspects of social and economic life are strictly controlled by the government.

Unicameralism: a one-chambered legislature.

Unitary: a political system where power is centralized in the national government, which then, delegates power to state and/or local governments.

Utility: having use for something, used with the connotation that whatever has utility is fruitful. The many poor people have not understood the utility of voting for changing their economic or political status.

Values: these are outlooks, perspectives, and subjective or biased opinions. Values are often associated with irrational, moral, or ethical judgements. A value is a sentiment that may or may not be socially acceptable. For example, support for a political party or for racial supremacy are values which sustain vastly different levels of public support. Patriotism, individualism, collectivism, racism, and loyalty are examples of values.

Veto: a process where the president does not sign the bill but sends it back to Congress whereby each chamber must vote to pass the legislation by a two-thirds majority. If the votes do not yield a two-thirds majority, the bill is not enacted into law.

Welfare state: a governing system where the focus of policy is to maximizing the economic and social benefits to each citizen.

TEXT ACKNOWLEDGEMENTS

Student manuscripts reprinted by permission.

Allison, Annette. Building Inspection Expense Analysis: Building Inspection Department. Unpublished manuscript.

Andrews, Amy K. Education of All Handicapped Children Act of 1975. Unpublished manuscript.

Brown, Patrick. Youth Influence in Political Outcomes. Unpublished manuscript.

Cieplak, Caryn. Campaign Volunteers: VIPs or Peons? Unpublished manuscript.

Goard, Steve. Dysfunctional Behavior in the FBI. Unpublished manuscript.

Herhold, Jenna, Kelly for Congress: Campaign '88. Unpublished manuscript.

Kosenski, Christine. Chief Justice Rehnquist. Unpublished manuscript.

Linder, Lowell. Research Paper Proposal. Unpublished manuscript.

Mitchell, Thomas. A Policy Analysis for Welfare Reform. Unpublished manuscript.

_____. Outlines. Unpublished manuscript.

Pettit, Edward. The Reagan Administration Policies on Social Welfare Spending. Unpublished manuscript.

_____. Midterm Exam: Question 5. Unpublished manuscript.

_____. NEPA: America's Policy Responses to Environmental Crisis. Unpublished manuscript.

Schmidt, Alan G. Energy Policy Clipping Thesis. Unpublished manuscript.

_____. Federal Funding for NEA. Unpublished manuscript.

Schuberth, Jean M. Why Should We Worry About a Judge's Ideology if Judicial Decisions are Based on Precedent. Unpublished manuscript.

Sullivan, John T. The Kennedys and the Rockefellers: Political Dynasties' Effect on the American Electorate. Unpublished manuscript.

Walka, Christopher. A Review of the Politics of Congressional Elections. Unpublished manuscript.

BIBLIOGRAPHY

American Heritage Dictionary. Second College Edition. NY: Dell Pub., Co. 1987.

Bernstein, Theodore M. *Watch Your Language*. NY: Antheneum. 1976.

Bolles, Richard N. *The Three Boxes Of Life And How To Get Out Of Them*. Berkeley, CA: Ten Speed Press. 1981.

Bolles, Richard N. *What Color Is Your Parachute?* Annual Edition. Berkeley, CA: Ten Speed Press. 1991

Chicago Manual of Style. 14th ed. Revised and Expanded. Chicago: University of Chicago Press. 1993.

Coplin, William D. and Michael K. O'Leary. *Policy Skills Workbook*. Croton-on-Hudson, NY: Policy Studies Associates. 1988.

Corder, Jim. and John Ruszkiewicz. *Handbook of Current English,* 8th edition, IL: Scott Foresman. 1989.

Cosman, Madeleine Pelner. *Kissing The Dragon: The Intelligent Work-Hunter's Companion*. Tenafly, NJ: Bard Hall Press. 1984.

Farlow, Daniel. *Writing a Research Paper in Political Science*, IL: Scott Foresman. 1989.

Follett, Wilson. *Modern American Usage*. NY: Warner Books. 1966.

Fowler, H. Ramsey and Jane Aaron. *The Little, Brown Handbook*, 4th edition, IL: Scott Foresman. 1989.

Fulwiler, Toby. "Keeping a Journal", in Arthur Biddle and Kenneth Holland, *Writer's Guide: Political Science*, MA: D.C. Heath. 1987.

Harnack, Andrew and Eugene Kleppinger. *Online!: A Reference Guide to Using Internet Sources*. NY: St. Martin's Press. 1998.

Goehlert, Robert U. and Fenton S. Martin. Congress and Law-Making: *Researching the Legislative Process* 2nd. ed. CA: ABC-CLIO. 1989.

History of Congressional Elections. <http://clerweb.house.gov/histrecs.../elections/political/divisions.html> 10 March 1999.

Kalvelage, Carl, Albert Melone, and Morely Segal. *Bridges to Knowledge in Political Science: A Handbook for Research*, Pacific Palisades, CA: Palisades Publishers. 1984.

Kurian, George. *Datapedia of the United State, 1790-2000*. Lanham, MD: Bernian Press. 1994.

Landau, Sidney and Ronald J. Bogus. *The Doubleday Roget's Thesaurus in Dictionary Form*. NY: Doubleday and Co., Inc. 1987.

Leahy, Richard. "What the College Writing Center is--and Isn't," *College Teaching*, 38(Spring 1990), pp. 43-48.

Lester, James D. *Writing Research Papers A Complete Guide*. IL: Scott, Foresman. 1990.

Mackenzie, G. Calvin. *The Politics of Presidential Appointments*. New York: The Free Press. 1981.

Mackenzie, G.C. "The Presidential Appointment Process: Historical Development, Contemporary Operations, Current Issues," in *Obstacle Course: The Report of the Twentieth Century Fund Task Force on the Presidential Appointment Process* by G.C Mackenzie and Robert Shogan. New York: The Twentieth Century Fund Press. 1996.

Mark Twain: *Wit and Wisecracks*. Selected by Doris Bernardete. White Plains, NY: Peter Pauper Press, Inc. 1961.

Melone, Albert P. *Researching Constitutional Law*. IL: Scott, Foresman. 1990.

Pittendrigh, Adele and Jerry Calvert, "A Model for Teaching Writing in Large Introductory Political Science Classes", *Political Science Teacher*, 2 (Summer 1989), pp. 13-15.

Prentice Hall Critical Thinking Audio Study Cassette, Prentice Hall. 1989.

Reed, Jean. *Resumes That Get Jobs*. Fifth Edition. New York: Arco Publishing. 1990.

Ruggiero, Vincent Ryan. *The Art of Thinking: A Guide to Critical and Creative Thought*. 3rd. ed. NY: Harper-Collins. 1991.

Schmidt, Steffen, Mack Shelley II, and Barbara Bardes. *An Introduction to Critical Thinking in American Politics*, NY: West Publishing Co. 1989.

Shively, W. Phillips. Ed. *The Research Process in Political Science*. Itasca, IL: F.E. Peacock Publishers, Inc. 1984.

Silverberg, Robert. *Star of the Gypsies*. NY: Warner Bros. 1986.

Stanley, Harold W. and Richard G. Niemi. *Vital Statistics on American Politics*. Washington, DC: Congressional Quarterly Press. 1998.

Stokey, Edith and Richard Zeckhauser. *A Primer For Policy Analysis*. N.Y.: W.W. Norton & Co. 1978.

Strunk, William Jr. and E.B. White. *The Elements of Style*. NY: MacMillan Pub. Co. 1979.

Ward, Kathryn, et al. *Curriculum Integration Workbook*. Manuscript. S. IL. Univ. Carbondale. 1990.

Webster's *Instant Word Guide*. NY: G. and C. Merriam. 1972.

Weisberg, Herbert F., Jon A. Krosnick, and Bruce D. Bowen. *An Introduction to Survey Research and Data Analysis*. Scott, Foresman and Co. 1989.

Written Word II. Boston, MA: Houghton Mifflin. 1983.

Ziegler, David, Recognizing the Good Essay: The Learner as Teacher, *Political Science Teacher*, 2 (Summer 1989), pp. 10-12.

INDEX